America's Electric Utilities: Past, Present and Future

by

Leonard S. Hyman

Fourth Edition

Public Utilities Reports, Inc.

Arlington, Virginia

First Printing, September, 1983
Second Edition, August, 1985
Third Edition, May, 1988
Fourth Edition, May 1992

ISBN 0-910325-41-3
Library of Congress Catalog Card No. 92-060895
Printed in the United States of America

The author acknowledges the following for the use of material:

From *Tanakh, The Book of Job.* The new JPS translation
according to the Masoretic Text, copyright 1985. The Jewish
Publication Society. Used by permission.

From *Legs* by William Kennedy. Copyright 1975 by William
Kennedy. Used by permission of Viking Penguin, a division
of Penguin Books USA Inc.

To Judith, Andrew and Robert

TABLE OF CONTENTS

Part IV *(Continued)*

TABLES

TABLES

TABLES

Preface to the Fourth Edition

The electric utility industry started as the dream of a brash young inventor. Electricity, that peculiar phenomenon, ran through telegraph lines and lit the homes of a handful of tycoons. You had to be rich to use it. Today, electric utilities consume one-third of our energy. The economy stops when the electric system fails.

For eighty years, the industry moved in a straight path, always increasing its efficiency and its share of the market, always reducing prices in real terms. For the past twenty years, though, the industry ran into technical, financial and regulatory roadblocks. Finally, competition emerged in what was supposed to be a natural monopoly. True, the industry's product, electricity, is the same. The laws of physics are the same. But the industry's finances, corporate structure, management and regulation are changing, now that customers have a choice.

When I completed the first edition of this book in 1983, it was already clear that doing business as usual was a formula for disaster, and the disasters followed. While this edition follows the same format as the first edition, it is as different, in many ways, as is the industry now, and has new tables, new analyses, and discussions of current regulatory and accounting procedures.

The purpose of the book remains unchanged: to examine, in basic terms, how the industry operates, how it developed, and where it might be going. As an introductory work, it explains the required principles of accounting, engineering, economics, finance, law and physics. In order to make the sections of the book as self-contained as possible, I occasionally repeated explanations rather than forcing the reader to find the original explanation. Admittedly, specialists might find parts of the book too elementary, and even assert that something got lost in the process of simplification. They can skip over the offending section without losing track of the narrative, and go on to the sections that will help them.

The book is divided into six parts plus appendices and an index.

Part One, *Introduction: Electric Utilities in One Easy Lesson*, lays out the basic concepts and the terminology needed to understand the industry.

Part Two, *The Operation of Electric Utilities*, describes the physical laws and engineering techniques involved in the production and distribution of electricity, the fuels used, environmental issues, and how the industry plans ahead.

Part Three, *The Development and Structure of the Electric Utility Industry*, traces the history of the industry, how the present structure developed, and what forces are at work to change what worked so well for so long.

Part Four, *Regulation*, explains the legal and economic underpinnings of the present regulatory system, and examines some of the newly proposed alternatives.

Part Five, *Financial Structure*, discusses the financial and accounting procedures so important to an industry that raises and spends huge sums of money, and describes the methods used by the financial community to assess the utility industry.

Part Six, *The Future of the Electric Utility Industry*, examines where the industry might be heading in this decade.

Footnotes follow each part of the book. The three appendices provide additional information. *Appendix: Canada* describes the industry of one of the most electricity-intensive economies in the developed world. *Appendix: Selected-Bibliography* lists sources and readings. *Appendix: Chronology* covers the important events in the development of electricity from 1800 to 1990. A *Subject Index* follows the appendices.

The text of the original book was derived from a series of papers issued by Merrill Lynch Pierce, Fenner, and Smith, Inc. Colleagues at Merrill Lynch aided my efforts. Rosemary Avellis Abrams developed the statistical series on regulation. Francoise Merrien collected and arranged much of the statistical data. Meava Daniels helped to put it together in an orderly fashion. Doris Kelley, Marjorie Jones, Heidimarie West, Richard Toole, and more recently Mary Galvin and Benjamin Senter provided support and held the fort when necessary. Frances Mancusi made sure that everything in this edition ended up where it should. And, Frances Benedetto reworked all graphs and tables for this edition, a major effort.

Don Wallace of Public Service Electric and Gas, Michael Crew of Rutgers University, Ted Komosa of Merrill Lynch, and George Cohen of Cohen, Davis & Marks all read versions of the text in its early incarnations. Gordon Smith of Pacific Gas and Electric secured permission from his company for use of illustrations from PG&E's *Resource*.

At Public Utilities Reports, Inc., Randall Spencer, Nina Seebeck, Adarsh Narayan, Hugh Craig, and Maxine Minar smoothed the editorial, production and sales processes.

At home, revising this book turned into a family affair. My older son, Andrew, between graduation from Tufts and entry into Vanderbilt, did research for the project, developed statistical series and analyses, dredged up historical sources, and found simple explanations for engineering and physics questions. Younger son Robert labored at various matters, between driving lessons, but spent the most time putting together the *Chronology*. My wife Judith demonstrated that teaching computers to third graders has a commercial spinoff, as she typed away and supervised the production of the manuscript, if one can call a word-processed document that.

I am grateful for all the guidance, corrections and help, but naturally all remaining errors are mine.

Leonard S. Hyman

Part One

Introduction:
Electric Utilities in One Easy Lesson

Chapter 1

The Basics

The position that electric energy has come to occupy in our civilization is a result of its unique characteristics of ease in transportation and distribution, ease of application to the widest range of processes requiring energy, and its potential for application to almost all energy-using processes with the utmost flexibility, complete cleanliness, and safety, and with the largest and most sensitive susceptibility to control.[1]

Philip Sporn

The engineers, accountants, lawyers, economists and regulators who run the electric utility industry speak a jargon that baffles outsiders and obscures simple concepts behind a fog of specialized verbiage. Here are the basic concepts and vocabulary necessary to understand the industry, its operations, regulation, finance, ratio analysis and interaction with the capital markets.

Measurement

The industry uses a measuring system that combines Greek prefixes with units named after dead scientists.

The common prefixes are:

Kilo — thousand (1,000 or 10^3), from the Greek word for "thousand," pronounced "kill-oh" or "kee-loh," abbreviated "k".

Mega — million (1,000,000 or 10^6), from the Greek word for "large," pronounced "mehg-uh," abbreviated "M".

Giga — billion (1,000,000,000 or 10^9), from the Greek word for "giant," pronounced "jig-uh" but often mispronounced with a hard g, abbreviated "G".

Tera — trillion (1,000,000,000,000 or 10^{12}), from the Greek word for "monster," pronounced "ter-uh," abbreviated "T".

The three commonest units (and their non-technical meanings) are *volts* (electrical pressure), *watts* (size of a generating station or even a light bulb) and *kilowatt-hours* (thousands of units of output in an hour). Notice the ability to combine: a thousand volts equals one kilovolt (kV), a power station of one million watts size is rated at one megawatt (MW), and because the watt-hour is too small a unit, we commonly measure in thousands of watt-hours, or kilowatt hours (kWh). The letters and the combinations are capitalized or uncapitalized in various ways, depending on the source and the country. Do not worry. A kWh is a KWH is a kwh is a kW.h.

Operations

Utilities measure the size (capacity) of a generating station in *kilowatts* (thousand of watts), abbreviated kw, or *megawatts* (millions of watts), abbreviated mw. Those measures are equivalent to saying that a factory has 10 machines, or that a hamburger stand has 10 grills. Capacity figures tell how big a plant is, but not how much it actually produces. The unit of electrical production is the *kilowatt-hour* (kwh) — the amount of electricity produced by running a generator that is one kilowatt in size for one hour. Sales of electricity are measured in kilowatt-hours. The *revenues* of an electric company are its sales in kilowatt-hours multiplied by the price per kilowatt-hour. *Voltage* is the pressure at which electricity is pushed through power lines. Long distance *transmission* lines carry electricity at high voltages. Local *distribution* lines carry it at low voltages. The time at which demand for electricity is highest is the *peak*. A utility must have a *reserve* — spare capacity available should a power station break down during the peak period. The *reserve margin* is the reserve measured as a percentage of the peak load.

Regulation

An electric utility is supposed to be a *natural monopoly*, meaning that one producer can serve customers more efficiently than can many competing producers. In addition to avoiding the obvious inconvenience of having five or six utility companies dig up the streets, the natural monopoly provides *economies of scale* — that is, one large utility can produce and sell electricity more cheaply than could a number of small producers. Because a utility has a monopoly, a *regulatory agency* in each state assures that the utilities do not take advantage of their customers. The agencies set service standards and prices. The price (*rate*) is set to permit the utility to collect enough money to cover all operating expenses, including taxes, and to have enough *operating income* left to provide a fair *rate of return* on the money invested in the business. Investors supply the money used to build the plant and to buy the equipment that serves the customers (the *rate base*). The rate of return is determined from the utility's *cost of capital*. For example, suppose that a utility has invested $1,000 in facilities to serve its customers. The company borrowed $500 on which it is paying 10% interest ($50 a year). Holders of the utility's common stock furnished another $500. The regulators note that the loan costs 10%. After a lengthy hearing, the regulators decide that common stockholders are entitled to a return of 15% on their investment ($75 a year). Thus, the cost of capital, as calculated below, is 12.5%, the rate of return that the utility is allowed to earn.

Type of Capital	Amount of Capital		Cost of Capital		Dollar Return		
Debt	$500	x	10%	=	$50		
Stock	500	x	15%	=	75		
Total	$1,000				$125	and:	$125

$$\frac{\$125}{\$1,000} = 12.5\%$$

Regulatory agencies rarely set rates more often than annually. Certain major expenses, however, can move up or down rapidly in the course of a year. A utility might earn too little when these expenses rise, or too much when they fall. To avoid having frequent rate hearings to adjust price for these sudden shifts in expenses, most agencies allow the use of *automatic adjustment clauses* which pass on to customers changes in certain expenses. Fuel expenses, which eat up 30 to 40% of revenues, are volatile. Thus, the most common automatic adjustment is for fuel costs.

The standard regulatory framework is changing. Technological developments have encouraged competition in the generation of electricity, which requires a new look at pricing the product. In addition, regulators are seeking alternative methods of regulation that will give utilities the incentive to run more efficiently, and help customers use electricity better. The old style rate of return regulation may give way, soon, to alternatives.

Finances

Electric utility facilities are enormously expensive to build. A large power station costs a billion dollars. Rarely can electric companies set aside from the year's income enough money to pay for constructing a new plant. To pay for the plants, the companies often have to borrow money and to sell new shares of stock to outsiders (*external financing*).

Thus, the profits from new business that is served by the new plant have to be shared by an increased number of holders of the company's bonds and stock. If too many new securities are sold and if business does not grow as expected, the share of profits left for the holders of old securities might actually be less than before the expansion. *Dilution* takes place when so many new shares have to be sold to pay for expansion that earnings per share of stock are less than they would have been had no expansion and financing taken place. Dilution usually occurs when the *market value* of the stock (the price at which it sells) is less than the *book value* (the amount of money per share that common stockholders have already invested in the business plus any earnings that have been retained or saved by the company). As a result, investors and management carefully watch the ratio of *market* value to *book* value — the market price of the stock stated as a percentage of its book value. Other things being equal, a utility is better off if it can finance as much of its expansion as possible from internal sources when interest costs are high and stock prices are low.

Ratio Analysis

The financial reports of a corporation have three key parts. The *income statement* shows revenues and expenses for the year, and the net income, which is what is left over after expenses are paid. The *balance sheet* provides a statement of assets (what is owned), money owed, and money put in by shareholders. The *statement of cash flows* tells how the company raises and disposes of cash in a particular accounting period.

The balance sheet shows the sources of all money used to build the company since it was formed (the *capital*) and the percentage of capital that was borrowed and the percentage that came from shareholders (the *capitalization ratio*). If a large percentage of funds came from borrowing, the company is said to be *leveraged*. If something goes wrong, the shareholders will not be paid dividends or get back their investments until creditors (those who have lent money to the company) have been repaid. Bondholders judge the quality of their securities by whether shareholders have invested a sufficient cushion of money for bondholders to fall back on if something goes wrong and by the *pretax interest coverage ratio* ("coverage"), which measures how much income is available to pay interest charges. If $100 of income is earned and interest charges are $20, then the coverage ratio is five-to-one (5x). Financial organizations rate investment quality of bonds by letter designations. Moving from highest to lowest, designations are Aaa or AAA, Aa or AA, A, and Baa or BBB, with a plus, minus, or number added to show gradations of quality. Many investors are not allowed to own bonds rated below Baa or BBB because they are not considered to be prudent investments.

Some companies use conservative accounting procedures that tend to show the maximum expenses that can be written off in a period, and do not count income until the money is in the till, so their reported income is likely to be below that of a comparable company using liberal accounting procedures. Regulatory agencies establish accounting procedures for utilities. Some agencies are more cautious than others. Several items make a big difference in determining how solid are earnings. One is the treatment of taxes. Some companies keep income tax expenses low and show a larger profit by reporting only taxes actually paid as an expense (*flow through accounting*), a procedure becoming less prevalent. Others report not only taxes actually paid as an expense but also funds set aside for taxes that might have to be paid in the future (*normalization*). In a similar vein, a utility might defer expenses, *i.e.*, put off showing them as an expense until a future period, even though the company actually laid out the money, or it might show as current income a profit that might not be collected until some future year. Those procedures may be part of a phase-in plan whereby customers do not pay the costs associated with a new power station all at once, but spread the increased costs over a number of years, while the utility's income statement shows a profit based on the pretense that the utility is collecting all the revenues from the beginning. Certainly, the more reported income that comes from such procedures, the less conservative is the accounting.

Financial analysts also judge utilities on the basis of another item in the income statement — the *allowance for funds used during construction* (AFUDC). Companies that are building plant must raise money to finance the plant during the construction process and must pay interest and dividends on that money. Plant that has not been completed is called *construction work in progress* (CWIP). Many regulatory agencies do not allow the utilities to recover carrying charges (the cost of the money tied up in the project) on the CWIP from customers during the construction process. Accountants, however, believe that a company's current earnings should not be reduced by charges for a plant that will serve customers in future years. To offset in the income statement the charges associated with money raised to finance CWIP, the utilities add AFUDC to income. Often the AFUDC added to income is greater than interest being paid on the money for the construction project and greater than income the project will earn once it is completed. As will be explained later, the use of AFUDC is also a method of passing on to future customers the financial costs incurred during the construction period. Because AFUDC is bookkeeping income — not real dollars collected from customers — investors may be wary of companies for which AFUDC constitutes a large percentage of income. *Quality of reported earnings* is the term that describes the overall conservatism of an income statement.

Finally, to determine how profitably stockholders' money is being used, we must find out how much income is earned on every dollar invested, or the *return on equity*. If a company earns $150 for stockholders who have invested $1,000, the return on equity is 15%.

Capital Markets

Most of the money supplied to a utility from outside sources is in the form of borrowings or of equity capital (money invested by stockholders who own the business). Borrowings usually come from banks or from investors who buy commercial paper (*short term debt*), or in the form of bonds or debentures (*long term debt*). In the case of long term debt, the creditor lends money for a long period (perhaps 20 years) and receives a bond that will *mature* (be paid off) on a specified date. When owners of bonds need cash before the maturity date, they sell the bonds in the marketplace. Bondholders have no assurance that the market price will equal the price paid when the bond was issued or will equal the value of the bond at maturity (*face* or *par value*). Meanwhile, the bondholder receives a fixed interest payment (often called the *coupon*) each year. The return that the bondholder earns is called *yield*. The simplest yield is the *current yield*, the coupon as a return on the market price of the bond. If a bond sells for $100 and has a coupon of 12% ($12), the current yield is also 12%. If the same bond with the 12% coupon ($12 in interest) sells at $80, the current yield is 15%. When the bond is selling below par, $80 in this example, the investor will not only receive $12 a year in interest, but will also receive $20 more when the bond is finally redeemed (at $100 par) at maturity. In that case, the correct yield to use is the *yield to maturity*, a calculation of return that takes into account both the current return and the increase in price as the bond approaches the maturity date. In general, yield to maturity is lower for high rated (high quality) bonds. That is, when risk is lower, return is lower.

Preferred and *preference stocks* also pay fixed dividends. Many preferred and preference stocks remain outstanding for the life of the corporation, *i.e.*, they have no fixed date for repayment of investment to their owners. The shareowners must sell the shares in the market when they need to raise cash. The return is measured by the *dividend yield*, which is the annual dividend divided by price.

The *common stockholders* are the owners of the business. Their investment in it is called *equity*. In order of priority, interest is paid first, then preferred and preference dividends, then dividends on common stock, if anything is left. The same order applies if the company goes out of business. First all debts are paid in full. Then preferred and preference shareholders get their investments back. Finally, if any funds remain, the common stockholders take what is left. When something goes wrong, common stockholders' money is used to pay the holders of bonds and preferred stock. When business is good, the common stockholders collect the profits. If a company earns $1 million and has one million shares of common stock, it has *earnings per share* of $1. The company will keep some of the profits for the business (*retained earnings*) and pay the balance as *dividends*. The *payout ratio* is the dividend as a percentage of earnings. The price of a common stock is usually valued at a *multiple* of earnings, also called the price-earnings (P/E) ratio. For instance, if the stock of a company earning $1 a share sells at $7, its P/E ratio is seven-to-one, or seven times earnings (7x). Investors often pay a higher P/E for the stocks of companies whose earnings are expected to rise rapidly. The second common measure of value is the dividend yield — the dividend return on the price of the stock. The stock selling for $7 and paying a dividend of 63¢ a share annually yields 9%. Shares of companies that are expected to raise their dividends rapidly often sell at lower dividend yields. A company with a high payout ratio may not be able to raise its dividend for lack of earnings from which to pay the additional dividend. As a result, shares of that company may sell at a high dividend yield. In other words, investors will pay a higher P/E ratio and settle for a lower current dividend yield if they expect substantial improvement in the future. Investors also consider the risk level of the stock and will pay a higher P/E and accept a lower dividend yield from the investment with the lower risk.

Movements in interest rates affect bond and stock prices. When investors can earn a high return on money in the bank, for instance, they will not buy a stock or bond until its price has declined to a point at which the dividend yield or the yield to maturity is high enough to compete with returns offered elsewhere. On the other hand, when interest rates decline, investors bid up the prices of stocks and bonds until returns on them drop to levels that are close to interest rates. The market is a two-way street.

Notes

[1]Philip Sporn, *The Social Organization of Electric Power Supply in Modern Societies* (Cambridge, The MIT Press, 1971), p. 3.

Part Two

The Operation of Electric Utilities

Chapter **2**

Introduction

While the early experimenters chiefly directed their attention to the chemical effects of galvanic currents, other phenomena were not overlooked. It was soon found that, when passing through a conductor of any kind, the current evolved heat, the amount of which depended on the nature of the conductor. This thermal effect is now of great practical use in electric lighting, heating, etc.[1]

Sir William Cecil Dampier

More than a century after it began, the electric utility industry still generates most of its output in the same way: burning a fuel to heat water to turn a blade on a wheel that turns a magnet that induces an electric current into the grid. The industry transmits the electricity, in bulk, from the generating station to the place where it is used and then distributes the electricity, safely, to the individual consumers, just as before. It invests in huge fixed assets that sit idle much of the time, but must be ready to respond to customers' needs almost instantaneously.

Terminology: Watts, Volts, and Ohms

Electricity is the flow of tiny, charged atomic particles (*electrons*). Its flow through a wire is like the flow of water through a pipe. Its speed, pressure, quantity, and the resistance of obstacles to the flow all must be measured in order to properly describe the flow. The quantity of the charge (akin to gallons or liters for water) is measured by the *coulomb* (C), the charge produced by a total of 6×10^{18} (six followed by eighteen zeroes) electrons. (Charles Augustus Coulomb was a French military engineer who experimented with electrical and magnetic forces in the 1780s. He found that electric force was proportional to both charge and distance.)

The flow of water in a pipe is measured in terms of how many liters or gallons pass a point per unit of time, *e.g.,* gallons per second. An *ampere* (A) is the flow of one coulomb per second, under certain conditions of pressure and resistance. (Andre Marie Ampere, a French physicist, showed, early in the nineteenth century, that electrical forces acted on magnets and that electric currents produced forces that acted on other electric currents.)

Water may not flow through the pipe unless it is pushed, *i.e.,* under pressure, possibly from a pump. The *volt* (V) is the unit of electromotive force, or pressure.

High voltage is measured in thousands of volts, called *kilovolts* (kV). (Alessandro Volta was the Italian scientist who, in 1800, built the first electric battery.)

Clogged screens or garbage could impede (resist) the steady flow of water through the pipe. Some materials conduct electricity more easily than others. That is, they show less resistance to the flow of electrons. In addition, resistance usually rises as a metal conductor is heated. The *ohm* (Ω) is the unit of electrical resistance. It allows one volt to maintain a current of one ampere in the conductor. (Georg Simon Ohm, a German scientist, early in the nineteenth century discovered the relationship between current, voltage, and resistance, known as Ohm's Law.) Current is proportional to voltage and resistance:

$$\text{Current (in amperes)} = \frac{\text{Voltage (in volts)}}{\text{Resistance (in ohms)}}$$

In other words, if you increase the voltage while the resistance remains the same, you will push more current through. If you raise the resistance, but do not raise the voltage, less current gets through. All of which seems intuitively correct, and gets back to the water analogy.

Work and Power

Work is "the product of the force which acts on the body and the distance through which the body moves while the force is acting upon it."[2] Power is "the work done divided by the time during which the work is done"[3]. For instance, a cement block weighing ten pounds has to be dragged ten feet. The work done is 100 foot pounds. If the worker does the job in one minute, the power exerted is 100 foot pounds per minute. However, scientific, metrical, and electrical notations differ, requiring more honors for dead scientists. The *joule* (J), for all practical purposes, is the energy required to lift 98 grams (about 3.5 ounces) up one meter. (James Prescott Joule was a British scientist who, in the middle of the nineteenth century, demonstrated that heat and work were equivalent.) In our society, though, we are not impressed by the amount of work accomplished if it is done too slowly. The rate of work done is measured in joules per second, or by the *watt* (W), which is one joule per second. (The watt, of course, was named after James Watt, the Scottish inventor who developed the steam engine in the middle of the eighteenth century. For the automotive minded, one horsepower equals 746 watts.)
Thus:

$$\text{Work} = \text{Force x Distance}$$

$$\text{Power} = \frac{\text{Force x Distance}}{\text{Time}}$$

and:

$$Power = \frac{Work}{Time}$$

and:

$$Work = Power \times Time$$

Capacity vs. Output

The watt rating attached to an electrical generating station tells us that the plant can produce so many joules per second of power, but that does not tell us what the output actually was in a period, because the plant might have been running for a fraction of the time period, or not up to its fullest ability, or not at all. It is as if we said that a fast food restaurant has 12 stoves, each of which can produce one hamburger every five minutes. That does not tell us how many hamburgers were cooked in an hour, only how many could be cooked (12 per hour per stove or a total of 144). Electric utilities sell their output on the basis of thousands of watts (kilowatts) per hour. That is, if the generating station has the ability to produce at a one kilowatt rate, and does so for an hour, the plant produced one kilowatt hour (kwh), which is the standard measure of electricity output.

Capacity, Capability, and Output

Confusion exists between the output of the generating plant (measured in kilowatt-hours) and the *capacity* or *capability* of the plant, measured by the kilowatt (KW) or megawatt (MW). Capacity is the ability to produce a given output of electricity at an instant in time, and output is the amount of electricity produced in a period of time. (Technically, capacity is a rating given to the generator by the manufacturer or the utility. Capability, on the other hand, refers to the load the unit can handle without exceeding limits set to prevent operating problems.)

For an example, a pipe factory has 10 machines in it, each capable of producing one pipe an hour. If each machine works, the factory has the capacity to produce 10 pipes at once, and its output is 10 pipes an hour. Similarly, an electrical generating station that has the capability of producing 1,000 kilowatts at one time will have an output of 1,000 kilowatt-hours if it runs at maximum capacity for one hour.

In a sense, the consumer of electricity makes two different calls on the electric system, one for capacity (measured in kilowatts) and one for output (measured in kilowatt-hours). If a customer owns a machine that requires 1,000 kilowatt-hours of electricity each hour to run, the utility must set aside 1,000 kilowatts of capacity to serve that machine. The customer demands 1,000 kilowatts of capacity, and that amount is fixed. The customer, however, could run the machine any amount of time up to 24 hours a day (requiring an output of 24,000 kilowatt-hours). The output taken by the customer varies. That situation is one of the major problems of the electric utility industry, which must have the capacity available for the customer and must support that fixed plant, while realizing that the customer's need for power may vary greatly.

AC and DC

Electric currents come in two kinds: *alternating* current (AC) and *direct* current (DC). Of the two, DC is the simpler. The current flows in one direction. Batteries produce DC, which flows from one pole, through the electrical circuit, to the other pole. AC, on the other hand, changes its direction on a regular basis. Each complete trip, before reversing direction, is called a *cycle*. The frequency of the alternation is measured in cycles per second, or in *hertz* (hz). That is, 30 hertz means 30 cycles per second. (Heinrich Hertz was a German scientist who in the 1880s discovered electromagnetic waves in space, which led to the wireless, radio, and television.)

Although electric utilities started out furnishing DC, they found that it was uneconomical to transmit DC for long distances. Now, utilities generate AC for most customers, although they do transmit DC on certain routes. Since the utilities are interconnected, which means that the currents from the various systems are mixed, it is vital that they synchronize the alternations of the current, making sure that each utility reverses the current the same number of times per second in unison. Electrical appliances and equipment, moreover, have to be built for a particular number of cycles per second. In the USA, the standard is 60 hertz. In some other countries, it is 50 hertz. That lack of uniformity is why electric appliances may not work outside their native countries.

Power Factor

Electric motors work by means of an *electro-magnetic field*. The electricity that magnetizes the equipment does no work, and does not even turn the ordinary electric meter which measures the electricity that the customer takes. That component of alternating current, the *magnetizing current*, is called *reactive power*. It is measured in volts multiplied by amperes (of the reactive portion of the current) — the volt-ampere reactive, or VAR. The portion of the current that does work (and turns the meter) is *real power*, measured in watts. The total output, real and reactive, is known as *apparent power*, and is measured by the volt-ampere (VA), which is volts times amperes.

The *power factor* measures the proportion of output represented by real power, *i.e.*,

$$\text{Power factor} = \frac{\text{Real power}}{\text{Real power} + \text{reactive power}}$$

$$= \frac{\text{Real power}}{\text{Apparent power}}$$

The electrical system must produce VARs both for its customers and to maintain the operation of the system itself, components of which absorb VARs. Obviously, the utility prefers to have a high power factor, in order to get paid for services rendered. In the case of residential customers, the utility may add a fixed percentage to the bill to cover the costs. Some industrial customers must pay for VARs on a metered basis because they require so much reactive power for operation.

Summary

The key technical points to remember are that electric current operates under a pressure (voltage), and that it may be direct or alternating, and if the latter, it alternates at a standard frequency per second. The size of a generating station is measured in units of kilowatts, and the units of output by which the quantity of electric supply is measured are kilowatt-hours. That sums up the bare minimum of technical knowledge required to understand what follows.

Chapter 3

Generation, Demand and Storage

The building and equipment of the station and its distribution system required large outlays of capital, whereas the demand for light was confined to a relatively small portion of the running time. . . .[4]

Abbott Payson Usher

The electric utility industry, like Gaul, is divided into three parts. *Generation* is the production of electricity, usually at a power station. The generating operation connects to the utility system through a device called a *busbar*. (Busbar cost is the cost of generated electricity before it enters the system, and that is the traditional measure for the total cost of generating the electricity.) Right outside the generating station, there is a substation at which a step-up transformer increases the voltage of the electricity for *transmission* at high voltages to the load centers where customers are located. At the load center, the electricity has to be stepped down to the lower voltages at which it will be taken by customers. Industrial and transit users need higher voltages than commercial and residential customers, so the utility may have several different transformers which step electricity down to different voltages. The *distribution* system carries the electricity from where the transmission line ends to the customer. (See Figures 3-1 and 3-2.)

Generation

Generation is, by far, the biggest sector of the electricity business, accounting for over half of utility assets as well as of the cost of producing and delivering electricity. Most electricity is generated by burning a fossil fuel (coal, oil, or natural gas), or from the burnup of nuclear fuel, or from the force of water (hydroelectricity). The principle of production is similar for all three sources.

A magnet is surrounded by magnetic lines of force that travel from one end of the magnet (pole) to the other. The lines of force also travel from the pole of one magnet to the opposite pole of another magnet (*i.e.*, from the north pole of the first to the south pole of the second magnet). Those opposite poles attract each other. Lines of force will not travel from like pole to like pole (*i.e.*, from south pole to south pole of two different magnets). The like poles repel each other. Back in 1819, Hans Oersted, the Danish physicist, noticed that a wire carrying an electric current would

Figure 3-1
Electricity Simplified

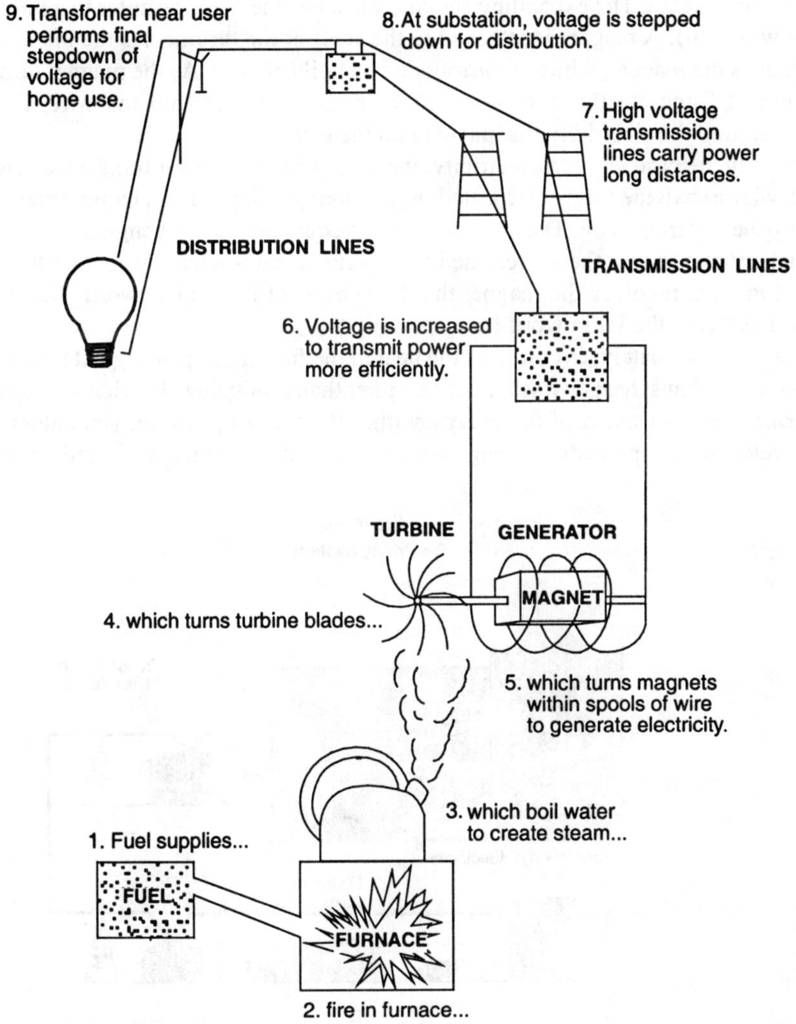

9. Transformer near user performs final stepdown of voltage for home use.

8. At substation, voltage is stepped down for distribution.

7. High voltage transmission lines carry power long distances.

DISTRIBUTION LINES

TRANSMISSION LINES

6. Voltage is increased to transmit power more efficiently.

TURBINE   **GENERATOR**

MAGNET

4. which turns turbine blades...

5. which turns magnets within spools of wire to generate electricity.

3. which boil water to create steam...

1. Fuel supplies...

FUEL

FURNACE

2. fire in furnace...

deflect a magnet. In 1831, Michael Faraday, the British experimenter, discovered that if he moved a wire through the lines of force of a magnetic field, the field created (induced) an electric current in the wire. That discovery is the basis for almost all electric generation today.

In the standard steam turbine, fuel is burned in order to heat water until it becomes steam. The expanding steam turns a turbine blade (similar to a pinwheel or windmill). A magnet is attached to the shaft of the turbine. As the blade turns, so does the magnet, which is surrounded by coils of wire. As the magnet turns, its lines of force cut the wire, and induce electric current into the wire, thereby generating the electricity that passes into the electricity network.

In the case of hydroelectricity, the force of falling water turns a waterwheel on whose shaft the magnet is located. Again, the spinning magnet induces electricity into the electric circuit. The gas turbine is the equivalent of a jet engine. Rather than make steam to turn the wheel, the burning fuel creates a hot gas jet that turns the turbine that revolves the magnet that induces electricity. (The word "turbine" is derived from the Latin word for a spinning top.)

Unfortunately, over half of the heat in the fuel ends up going out the smokestack as exhaust heat or wasted steam, rather than producing electricity. In order to make use of as much of the energy within the fuel as possible, generators have developed two procedures: *cogeneration* (called combined heat and power in

Figure 3-2
Electricity System

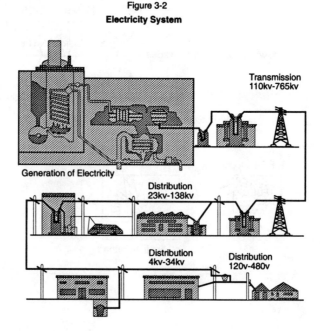

Generation of Electricity

Transmission
110kv-765kv

Distribution
23kv-138kv

Distribution
4kv-34kv

Distribution
120v-480v

Courtesy of Pacific Gas & Electric

Britain) and *combined cycle generation*. In cogeneration, the waste heat (usually steam) is sold to some nearby industrial firm which might have had to burn fuel to produce steam needed for industrial processes. Thus, cogeneration is an energy-efficient process that produces two usable products: electricity and steam. The combined cycle plant combines a gas turbine and a steam turbine. The gas turbine produces electricity, and its waste heat is passed on to the steam turbine, thereby reducing the fuel needed to heat up the water to reach the temperature of steam. The steam turbine then produces electricity in the normal fashion. A normal steam turbine might convert only 35% of the heat content of fuel to electricity (35% efficiency), but a combined cycle plant can reach 50% efficiency, producing a significant fuel saving.

Getting back to the magnet, as it moves in a circle within the generator the lines of force cut the wires, thereby inducing an electric current. But as the magnet turns, the angles of the lines of force in relation to the wire change, the number of lines of force cut increases and decreases, the current gets stronger and weaker, and it reverses direction, again and again. This fluctuation differs from the unchanging characteristics of DC (Figure 3-3). It is customary to describe the rise and fall of voltage before the current reverses direction as a cycle of 360 degrees, and the location in the cycle as the phase. Thus, in Figure 3-4, one can find a point three quarters of the way toward completion of the cycle or at 270 degrees. Early in the development of electric generation, engineers figured out that if they could put three spools of wires in the generator, the revolving magnet, as it approached each spool, would induce electricity into it. Due to the fact that each spool picks up the induced electricity slightly after the previous spool, the electric currents in the three wires do not rise and fall in voltage or reverse direction at the same time. They are out of step, or out of phase, by 120 degrees, as in Figure 3-5. The electricity is delivered in three separate lines, one from each coil. (Note the three lines, or sets of three lines, on high voltage transmission towers.) Industrial customers may use all three phases in their motors. Residential customers have appliances that require only one phase,

Figure 3-3
Direct Current

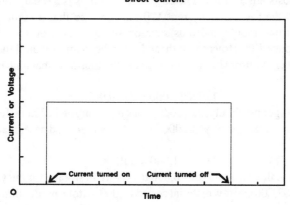

Figure 3-4
Alternating Current

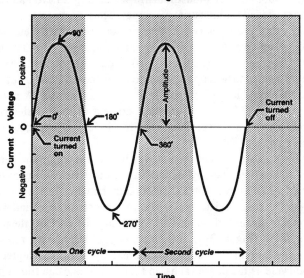

and the distribution network has to be wired to take those differences into account.

Most electric utility systems must produce power at the generator when the customer wants it. Because usually the power cannot be produced in advance and stored for the moment it is needed, the utility must have enough production facilities available to meet the maximum demand on its system whenever that occurs. Much of that generating plant will not be in use for most of the day, but only when demand is there. Perhaps an example will demonstrate the awkwardness of such a situation.

Take the case of a toy company that makes all of its sales in December. It will sell 12,000 toys in that month. Each toy machine makes 100 toys a month. The toy machine can be rented for $1,000 a year and only annual leases are available. The raw material costs are $1 a toy. The cost of storing toys is $100 a thousand toys a month. Should the toy company rent 120 machines so that it could produce all 12,000 toys in one month and thus save on storage costs, or should it rent 10 machines, produce 1,000 toys a month, and store the inventory until the December rush? The answer requires simple arithmetic. In the first case, machine rental would be:

$$120 \times \$1,000 = \$120,000$$

and with no storage costs likely, the production cost would be $120,000 for rental plus $12,000 for raw materials, or $132,000 in total. In the second case, machine rental would be:

$$10 \times \$1,000 = \$10,000$$

and if we assume that an average of 6,000 toys were in storage for the year, storage costs would be $7,200 and raw material costs $12,000, so total production costs would

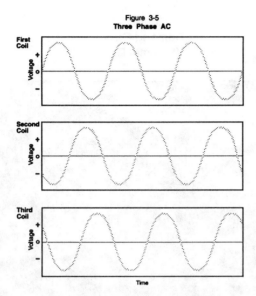

Figure 3-5
Three Phase AC

be $29,200. The answer is clearcut. There is no reason to have 120 machines on which rent is paid standing idle for 11 months of the year. It is too expensive.

The problem, however, is that the electric utility usually cannot store its production, and must have the generators ready to meet that period of maximum demand. The machines must be in place even if they are expensive to maintain and stand idle for much of the time. The utility's daily load pattern might look like that in Figure 3-6. Load also varies during the year, with heavy demand during the heating and air conditioning seasons, as can be seen in Figure 3-7.

The utility has to serve the entire load, but it does not need the same kind of power plant to do everything. For instance, in examining the daily and monthly charts, demand appears never to go below 100 megawatts. On the other hand, demand goes above 300 MW for only brief periods. The utility wishes to minimize the investment it has in plant that is likely to be idle most of the time, and wants the plant that will be in operation most of the time to be as reliable and economical as possible.

The solution is to build what are called *base load* plants to meet the minimum around-the-clock load. Because fixed costs can be spread over many hours of operation, those plants tend to be large and expensive-to-build machines that burn low cost fuels. The base load plants are built for steady running. If demand on the system becomes unstable or unpredictable (as has been the case in recent years) and dips below the expected base load, then base load generating units have to be run below their capacity or turned on and off. That kind of use puts strains on the plants and is inefficient.

At the other extreme, the utility builds and runs *peaking units* for those brief

Figure 3-6
Demand Curve
(Summer Day)

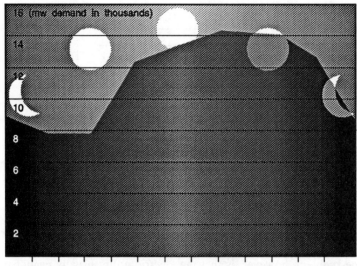

2am 4am 6am 8am 10am Noon 2pm 4pm 6pm 8pm 10pm Midnight

Courtesy Pacific Gas and Electric

Figure 3-7
Monthly Maximum Load

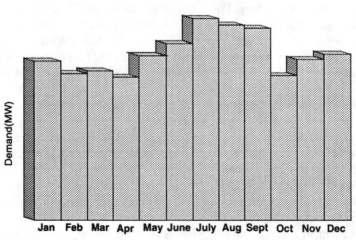

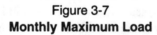

Courtesy of Pacific Gas and Electric

periods of maximum (peak) demand on the system. Those units are generally inexpensive to build (because fixed costs have to be spread over a brief period of usage), but fuel costs often are high. The industry also has an intermediate category of generators that are used less than base load and more than peaking units.

In order to be able to build larger generating units, have power available at times of emergencies, plan systems without duplicating the work of neighboring companies and increase their ability to buy low cost power from others, electric utilities join in regional *power pools*. The companies in the pool work together to assure a reliable, low cost power supply for a large area. Often power plants within the pool are owned jointly and power within the pool is dispatched from a central control point. In a sense, a number of companies run their generation and transmission operations on a joint basis.

In the production of electricity, roughly two-thirds of the caloric content of the fuel is lost up the smokestack or into waterways in the form of waste heat. In the United States, the power plants may be located far from potential customers for the waste heat. Perhaps if the power plant could be built where the user of heat is situated, then more of the heat that is contained in the fuel could be used. That is the principle of *cogeneration*, an old idea with a new name. A small power plant, placed at or near an industrial facility, produces electricity and waste heat. Some (or all) of the electricity is consumed at the industrial facility and the balance, if there is any, is sold to the electric utility. The waste heat is used in industrial processes. (Some industrial processes might produce waste heat that could be applied to help generate electricity, too, reversing the concept.) The concept behind cogeneration is to waste as little fuel as possible. Under Federal and some state laws, the price for cogeneration power to the utility is set at the utility's avoided costs (what electricity would have cost from the generating station that was displaced by the cogenerated power). Depending on the size and ownership of the cogenerator, return earned on the cogeneration investment may not be regulated.

Considering the huge sums invested in generating facilities, the utility concerns itself with the generating unit's availability, or the percentage of time that the unit is available for use, whether the unit is used or not. Clearly, availability is something within control of the management. How much the machine is actually used on average, however, might depend on the timing of the customers' demands for electricity. To get a good idea of usage, one calculates the *capacity factor*, or average load on the machine as a percentage of rated capacity.

For instance, if a 500 MW machine supplies 400 MW in the first hour, 300 MW in the second hour, 500 MW in the third hour, and 200 MW in fourth hour, the average load is 1400/4, or 350 MW. The capacity factor is:

$$\frac{350 \text{ MW}}{500 \text{ MW}} = 70\%$$

Management, too, must consider the characteristics of demand for power in the utility's system. An effective management will want demand spread so that generators will be idle as little as possible. How the load is spread out and whether there is a great difference between the average demand on the system and the demand at peak is measured by the *load factor*, which is defined as average load in a particular period as a percentage of peak load. Consider the two electrical systems with identical generating capacity (600 MW) and peak load (500 MW) shown in Figure 3-8.

Clearly, with the same investment, Company B keeps its facilities running more and sells more electricity than Company A. Load factor, however, could get too high. When that happens, the utility is using its generators so much that it does not have the time available to take the units out of service for normal maintenance, which means that the utility might need extra generating units in reserve so that

Figure 3-8
Capacity and Peak Load

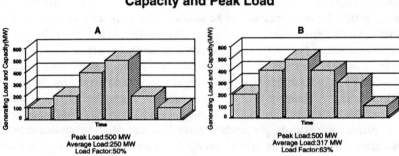

generators can be taken out of service for needed maintenance repairs.

That, in turn, leads us to the subject of the *reserve margin*. If the electric company could predict perfectly its peak demand and the times its generating units would be out of service, it could have sufficient generating capacity just to meet the peak load, without wasting money on superfluous plant. Unfortunately, utility managements must be prepared for the vagaries of demand and for unexpected breakdowns of generators. They must have additional power plants that can be put into service either immediately or after a short period of preparation. The utility may not own the power plant that is held in reserve, but it might have a contract with a neighboring utility to buy extra power when needed. In its simplest form, reserve margin is the difference between peak load and capacity as a percentage of peak load. *Capacity margin* is the difference between peak load and capacity as a percentage of capacity. In the above example, capacity is 600 MW, peak load is 500 MW, reserve margin is 20% and capacity margin is 16.7%. The actual calculations account for ability to buy from or obligation to sell to other systems on a firm basis. Assuming (at time of peak load):

$$
\begin{aligned}
C &= \text{capacity margin (\%)} \\
R &= \text{reserve margin (\%)} \\
Co &= \text{own system capability (MW)} \\
Cp &= \text{capability under firm purchase from others (MW)} \\
Cs &= \text{firm obligations to sell capability to others (MW)} \\
P &= \text{own system peak load (MW)}
\end{aligned}
$$

then:

$$
R = \left(\frac{Co + Cp - Cs - P}{P} \right) \times 100
$$

and:

$$
C = \left(\frac{Co + Cp - Cs - P}{Co + Cp - Cs} \right) \times 100
$$

The proper generating reserve margin depends on the characteristics of the system, such as types of generators, load growth, and availability of power from neighboring companies. Theoretically, a utility with a large number of small power plants can get by with a lower margin because the odds are against having several plants out of service at the same time. A utility with a few large plants might need a high reserve margin to guard against the possibility that one plant representing a large percentage of capacity might go out of service. A utility whose plants often go out of service would need a higher reserve margin than a utility with plants that operate well. If conditions of demand were erratic (perhaps because of extremely high, low, or unpredictable temperatures), the utility might need a high reserve margin to protect it against the unexpected. Finally, some utilities make large sales to interruptible customers whose service the utility can turn off at will. Such a utility need not invest in a large amount of reserve capability because it has the option to cut off customers during difficult periods. The desired reserve margin is set by a loss of load probability (LOLP) analysis designed to assure that major power outages will be limited to one day in a given number of years (usually 10).

Until recently, emphasis has been placed on ensuring that capacity is available to meet the peak load. That emphasis, however, has been extremely expensive because of the cost of building generation plants. Utilities have begun to experiment with the management of demand, known as *demand side management* (DSM), so that the peak load can be cut down to obviate the need for the generating capacity. Load can be influenced by charging more for power at certain times of the day or year, or it can be controlled directly by the electric utility (load management). In load management, the electric company connects a control device to one or more appliances on the customer's premises. During periods of high demand, the electric company turns off the appliance for a period of time, thereby making it less necessary for the utility to keep generating reserves. In a sense, the utility has created additional interruptible customers. Tests indicate that, for many systems, the cost of load management equipment per kw of demand reduced is less than that of capacity added to meet each kw of additional demand.

So far we have discussed the electric system as if power could not be stored, and as a result generating units either had to be available to meet demand or demand had to be repressed to fit available generating capacity. Actually, power can be stored, if the utility is fortunate to have the right sort of terrain nearby. The pumped storage hydro plant is such a facility. During off peak periods, such as the middle of the night, the utility uses power from its most efficient base load generating station (probably a nuclear power plant) to pump water into a reservoir on the top of a mountain. The water is stored in the reservoir until demand rises to the level at which the utility needs additional power. At that point, the water is released, descends through pipes, and turns electrical turbines. The spinning turbine generates electricity in the same manner as in an ordinary hydroelectric facility. The pumped storage plant is like a huge rechargeable battery. Other storage research is going on based on the same principles.

In Table 3-1, we can see some of the trends of the last three decades. In the 1960s, growth in both sales and peak load was high. The industry's capacity, however, rose more slowly than peak load. That was possible because the industry started with a high reserve margin that could be allowed to fall. The load factor declined a bit. In addition, the industry was able to generate an increasing amount of electricity for each kilowatt of installed capacity. (In theory, if a generator worked perfectly all year, one kilowatt of capacity could produce 8,760 kwh of power in a normal year and 8,784 kwh in a leap year.) In the 1970s, sales and peak load growth became unstable, probably because of sharply higher prices and increased sensitivity to weather conditions (because of the popularity of air conditioning and electric heating). The industry, however, was adding capacity as if nothing had happened to demand, because the plant additions had been planned years before the slowdown. Reserve margin rose, indicating that many utilities were carrying the burden of plant in excess of need. The load factor continued to drop. The worst indicator was the sharply declining amount of power generated by each kilowatt of capacity in place.

To some extent, the industry's problems became circular. It could not operate large, new base load generators as planned because demand did not materialize as projected. When the plants were operated under suboptimal conditions, they did not perform well. If plants did not perform well, higher reserve margins were required, and operating costs rose, thereby raising the price of electricity. Price was raised even more because cost of facilities had to be spread over an unexpectedly low level of kwh sales. That triggered another fall in demand and worsened the operating situation. In the 1980s, demand grew slowly, but the industry installed new generating facilities even more slowly, and did a better job of utilizing existing plant. The challenge in the 1990s will be to encourage demand side management, so that the

Table 3-1

Sales, Demand and Capacity
Total Electric Utility Industry
1960-1990

Year	% Change in KWH Sales to Ultimate Customers	% Change in Peak Load	% Change in Capacity at Peak	Reserve Margin %	Load Factor %	Ratio of KWH Generated to Average KW of Capacity (Total USA)
	(1)	(2)	(3)	(4)	(5)	(6)
1960	8.9	6.1	7.0	31.5	65.5	4688
1961	5.5	6.0	8.3	31.0	64.8	4588
1962	7.7	7.3	4.8	31.0	64.9	4649
1963	7.1	6.6	6.0	30.2	65.2	4624
1964	7.2	8.5	5.5	23.7	64.2	4619
1965	7.1	6.5	5.7	22.9	65.0	4677
1966	9.0	9.2	5.2	18.4	64.7	4793
1967	6.5	5.0	7.2	20.8	65.3	4747
1968	8.6	11.5	8.1	17.2	63.5	4800
1969	8.7	8.3	7.7	16.6	64.1	4831
1970	6.4	6.6	8.9	19.0	63.9	4733
1971	5.4	6.3	8.1	20.9	63.2	4583
1972	7.6	9.3	8.1	19.6	62.5	4601
1973	8.0	7.7	8.9	20.8	62.0	4468
1974	-0.1	1.5	7.0	27.2	61.2	4122
1975	1.9	2.2	7.9	34.3	61.4	3915
1976	6.7	4.0	4.1	34.5	62.6	3943
1977	5.5	6.9	3.5	30.2	61.4	3915
1978	3.4	3.0	5.8	33.7	62.1	3879
1979	3.3	-2.4	2.3	36.7	64.4	3816
1980	2.0	7.2	2.4	30.7	61.1	3773
1981	1.2	0.3	2.5	33.3	61.6	3676
1982	-2.4	-3.1	2.4	41.0	62.1	3488
1983	2.9	7.9	1.8	33.3	59.5	3562
1984	5.6	0.8	1.3	33.9	59.7	3687
1985	1.1	2.1	2.9	35.0	62.0	3629
1986	2.1	3.6	1.9	33.0	60.7	3562
1987	3.4	4.0	2.3	30.6	60.8	3608
1988	5.0	6.7	2.1	25.0	59.5	3751
1989	2.6	-1.1	1.8	28.6	62.2	3828
1990	1.8	4.2	1.7	25.6	60.4	3830
Averages:						
1960-1970	7.5	7.4	6.7	23.8	64.6	4704
1979-1980	4.5	4.7	5.8	28.0	62.3	4159
1980-1990	2.3	2.9	2.1	31.8	60.9	3672

Note:
Averages for 11 year periods.
Sources:
Edison Electric Institute, *Statistical Year Book of the Electric Utility Industry* (Washington, D.C.: EEI, various dates), Tables 2,7,12,38, and *1990 Financial Review*.

utilities do not have to install uneconomical generating plant, and then to put up the right generating stations, and incorporate non-utility owned generators into the system.

Transmission and Distribution

The high voltage transmission system carries the electricity from generating stations — often located far from the load center at sites that offer proximity to water and fuel — to the load centers. In the process transmission losses reduce the electricity available for customers, and those losses may make it uneconomical to transmit electricity for excessively long distances. (Ironically, new high voltage DC transmission is acting as a long distance carrier, but the lines need expensive equipment at both ends to integrate them into the AC network.)

The high voltage transmission network is not a single conduit that moves electricity from point A to point B. Nor can generating stations be attached to it anywhere. All the transmission lines within a regional grid are connected together in a network. Electricity does not necessarily flow directly, but may loop around on a circuitous route because of the way intervening lines are loaded, and that loop flow could cause disturbances in the utility system being traversed for which the disturbed utility may not be compensated. Furthermore, the flows may load some lines more than others and power stations may have to be sited so as not to exacerbate power flow problems. Kirchhoff's Law states that the total amount of current flowing into a junction must equal the total flowing out, which means that utilities cannot fill up a particular line at will, because that line's throughput will be affected by what is going through any other line originating at the same junction. As an example, in Figure 3-9, five amperes of current reach junction A, and three amperes

Figure 3-9
Kirchoff's Law

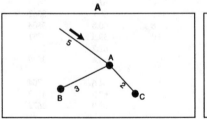 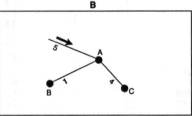

go to B and two amperes to C. If for some reason demand at C is great, pulling in four amperes, then only one ampere can get to B, even though the line can carry more. Thus, thanks to Kirchhoff's Law, it may be hard to fully utilize all lines in the network.

DC transmission lines are used for certain long distance routes that carry electricity from point to point, rather than as part of a complicated network. DC transmission is especially useful in transmitting electricity from two normally isolated regions which are unlikely to be producing their alternating current in synchrony. The DC link takes AC at one end, converts it to DC for transmission and then at the other end converts it back to AC whose alternations are in phase with those of the receiving system.

The low voltage distribution system that delivers the electricity to the customer requires many smaller wires, and numerous substations that take the higher voltage and step it down to low levels for neighborhood use. Although high voltage lines are invariably above ground, due to the immense cost of burying them and trying to dissipate the heat that would build up underground, distribution lines often are underground, especially in urban areas. At the end of the distribution line, right on the customer's premises, the meter is located, measuring how much electricity (in kwh) the customer takes. Until recently the meter was the only device on the customer's premises: prosaic, reliable and unchanged for many years. Now, with the revolution in microelectronics, utilities can read more than quantity of kwh consumed, and they can install devices that control what appliance goes on, and even send automatic meter readings to a central point.

Chapter 4

Fuels

. . .the electricity-generating sector was noted to be a prodigious and growing consumer of primary energy itself, from coal, nuclear fuel, natural gas, oil, hydropower, biomass, and a variety of other sources. More than one-third of all the primary energy used in the United States currently goes into generating electricity.[5]

Department of Energy

The electric utility industry started by burning coal. When long distance transmission became possible, the industry exploited hydropower sites, but coal has remained the dominant fuel for the entire history of the industry.

Trends

Picking a fuel is not always a question of what burns best or what is nearby. Many utilities in the 1960s switched from coal to oil to avoid the environmental problem involved in burning coal. In the early 1980s, many of the same utilities switched from oil to coal to cut down dependence on foreign oil. Natural gas is a clean, efficient fuel, but the short-lived natural gas shortage caused the Federal Government to attempt to force electric utilities off gas in order to reserve that fuel for supposedly superior uses. In the late 1980s and early 1990s, thanks to the abundance and cleanliness of natural gas and the efficiency of new gas turbines, electric utilities and non-utility generators turned to natural gas as a fuel. Use of water power depends on the availability of good hydropower dam sites. Most of the major sites have been utilized or are in park areas, so few large scale hydropower projects (excluding pumped storage) have been built recently. Higher fossil fuel costs in the future might make small hydro projects economical again. From the early 1960s, a handful of nuclear power plants produced a minuscule portion of the nation's power, but electric utilities had great hope for what appeared to be an economical and benign source of energy. Environmental opposition, changing rules for construction and safety, and skyrocketing costs have retarded the growth of nuclear power.

What else is there? Geothermal energy produces a small amount of power in California. In logging regions, burning waste wood produces some electricity. The industry is experimenting with solar energy, windmills, agricultural wastes and just about anything else. For the near term, however, conventional power sources will dominate the mixture.

As Table 4-1 illustrates, generating mixes have changed. Some of the variation is attributable to fluctuations in water conditions, to coal strikes, and to plant shutdowns, but the trend shows a clear substitution of oil for coal between 1965 and 1973. Thanks to overoptimistic expectations for nuclear energy costs, aided by fear that the USA was running out of natural gas, the industry launched a push toward nuclear power, which fizzled, thanks to miscalculations of nuclear cost as well as of demand for electricity, not to mention a loss of public confidence after the Three Mile Island nuclear accident in Pennsylvania in 1979. By 1980, coal had taken back half of the output, oil and gas were unpopular, and nuclear plants were starting to contribute to the energy supply. No nuclear plants, though, were ordered after 1973. In 1990, despite legislation regulating pollutants and worry about greenhouse gases, coal has increased its dominance over the electric fuel market, and nuclear has reached what will be its peak contribution until nuclear energy can be resurrected in a more palatable form.

Policy

In order to burn coal in a time of more stringent environmental rules, electricity generators are experimenting with methods of burning coal more cleanly, or even turning the coal into gas, removing the impurities during the gasification process, and then burning the gas. Simply burning natural gas, though, is an easier alternative. Natural gas is clean, it contributes less to greenhouse warming than coal, and gas-fired power plants are easier to build and run than coal-fired stations. Many people object to burning natural gas to generate electricity, believing that natural gas should be reserved for other uses. Coal, in turn, they say, is best suited for the generation of electricity. Therefore coal should be the fuel for electric generation, despite the fact that gas is cleaner and more economical, while gas is reserved for "superior" uses. (That command approach, in which it is assumed that a central bureaucracy knows best, has been tried before, and there is little evidence that the assumption is correct.)

Proponents of nuclear power, too, push for its revival on the grounds that it is required in order to reduce acid rain and greenhouse warming (nuclear generation does not produce smoke or carbon dioxide), or to cut down on import of foreign oil (although most oil imports go to transportation). Again, the electric companies are supposed to ignore economics and public opinion, and to plunge into nuclear power for the public good.

All of this brings up a question: should utility fuel choices be matters of public policy? The utility should try to develop a diversified fuel mix, so that it will not become vulnerable to shortages or to price swings for one fuel. That is prudent business judgment, even if it occasionally means sticking with one fuel that is more expensive than the others. Presumably, the ups and downs of the different fuel

Table 4-1

Generation by Energy Source
Total Electric Utility Industry
1960 - 1990

Year	Coal	Oil	Gas	Nuclear	Hydro and Other
	(1)	(2)	(3)	(4)	(5)
1960	53.5	6.1	21.0	0.1	19.3
1961	53.2	6.0	21.4	0.2	19.2
1962	52.9	5.5	21.7	0.2	19.7
1963	53.9	5.7	22.0	0.3	18.1
1964	53.5	5.8	22.4	0.3	18.0
1965	54.1	6.1	21.1	0.3	18.4
1966	53.6	6.9	22.0	0.5	17.0
1967	51.9	7.4	21.8	0.7	18.2
1968	51.5	7.8	22.9	1.0	16.8
1969	49.0	9.6	23.2	0.9	17.3
1970	46.1	11.9	24.4	1.4	16.2
1971	44.3	13.5	23.2	2.4	16.6
1972	44.2	15.6	21.4	3.1	15.7
1973	45.6	16.9	18.4	4.5	14.7
1974	44.4	16.0	17.1	6.1	16.3
1975	44.4	15.1	15.7	9.0	15.8
1976	46.3	15.7	14.5	9.4	14.1
1977	46.4	16.8	14.4	11.8	10.6
1978	44.2	16.5	13.9	12.5	12.9
1979	47.8	13.5	14.7	11.3	12.7
1980	50.8	10.7	15.1	11.0	12.4
1981	52.4	9.0	15.1	11.9	11.6
1982	53.2	6.6	13.6	12.6	14.0
1983	54.5	6.3	11.9	12.7	14.7
1984	55.5	5.0	12.3	13.6	13.7
1985	56.8	4.1	11.8	15.5	11.8
1986	55.7	5.5	10.0	16.6	12.2
1987	56.9	4.6	10.6	17.7	10.2
1988	57.0	5.5	9.3	19.5	8.6
1989	55.8	5.7	9.5	19.0	9.9
1990	55.5	4.2	9.4	20.6	10.3

Source

EEI *Statistical Year Book*, Tables 14, 21, and 22.

cycles will even out. But it is not prudent business judgment to simply ignore the low cost alternative, because, in an increasingly competitive marketplace, another supplier could take advantage of the low cost fuel and take away the utility's customers.

Unfortunately, what seems the lowest cost fuel to the utility and its customers may not be the lowest cost fuel to society. As an example, utilities bought cheap and dirty coal, refusing to buy cleaner coal on the ground that their customers did not want to pay the higher cost. But the consequence of that action was that people downwind of the utility paid bigger laundry and medical bills. Those costs (external costs in economic jargon) did not enter into the utility's calculations. In the same way, the USA took no steps, in the 1980s, to limit the import of cheap oil. (Doing so, free market proponents argued, would have interfered with the marketplace and burdened the economy.) But America spent billions in the 1991 Persian Gulf war to protect oil supplies. The oil users got the benefit of cheap oil, but everybody paid taxes to protect that supply. The cost of protection never affected the price of oil because the oil companies did not bear the costs. Thus, some regulators want the utility to consider not only the direct costs of fuel to the utility, but also the costs of that choice to society.

Until the 1970s, utilities chose their fuels without interference. Then the government stepped in, not only mandating fuels but even specifying what technology could be used to clean the fuels. In the 1980s, the pendulum swung back to freedom of choice, possibly as far as it could go. Perhaps, in the 1990s, regulators will curb that freedom in order to inject societal considerations into the choice.

Chapter 5

Environmental, National Defense, Social and Philosophical Considerations

Thus, what confronts us is not a series of separate crises, but a single basic defect — a fault that lies deep in the design of modern society.[6]

Barry Commoner

Modern economics does not distinguish between renewable and non-renewable materials, as its very method is to equalize and quantify everything by means of a money price . . . From a Buddhist point of view . . . this will not do. Non-renewable goods must be used only if they are indispensable.[7]

E. F. Schumacher

For years, electric utilities ran their operations unchallenged, finding and implementing engineering solutions for all operational problems. That simple life ended in the turbulent 1960s, but many utility executives and their regulators were slow to comprehend the change. They fought to maintain control, as before, and they lost.

National Policy

Utilities operate under government controls. They can pass costs on to captive customers. They cannot move their operations out of reach of the government. There are a handful of large utilities, compared to millions of businesses and households, so they are easier to supervise. For all these reasons, it has been convenient to use utilities as instruments of government policies. In wartime, of course, the utilities followed government orders involving fuel, construction, and customer priority. From the 1960s on, the Federal Government pressured the utilities to build more transmission systems (to prevent regional blackouts), to switch from oil to other fuels (reduce imports of oil that threaten national security), to reduce use of natural gas in electric generation (to free up scarce gas for residential customers), to clean up water and air pollution (often specifying how to do it), to buy electricity from cogenerators (who were more efficient because they produced electricity and usable steam), and to open up their transmission lines to others (encourage competition by providing a means of transmitting energy). Thus, the operations of the electric utility are affected by considerations of national interest, and any cost associated with those operating changes may be borne by the utility's customers or stockholders, unless the government provides a subsidy.

Environmentalism

The environmental movement — which gathered strength in the turbulent 1960s and influenced legislation in the 1970s — baffled electric utility executives. What did those people want? At first, it seemed as if environmentalists wanted to protect the scenery. Consolidated Edison, in the early 1960s, decided to site a pumped storage project on Storm King Mountain, one of the most dramatic locations on the Hudson River, an attempt that ignited local opposition. The management of Con Edison seemed to have little notion of what the problem was, and persisted in its efforts for years before throwing in the towel. The Storm King affair showed that environmental groups could block utility projects. Engineers would not have their own way unopposed.

Admittedly, power plants and transmission lines are huge, obtrusive, unsightly structures, so electric utility management began to view the problem in cosmetic terms:

Since utility facilities are so prevalent a part of the landscape, beautification and preservation of scenic values are elements which must be incorporated into the policies and programs of every utility.[8]

The term "beautility" came into fashion for a short while, referring to attempts to locate facilities esthetically or to place distribution lines underground.

Environmental Issues

The environmental opponents facing the industry often had ideological or philosophical motivations that went beyond protecting the landscape or saving an obscure but endangered species. They wanted a decentralized economy fueled by local, small-scale power facilities utilizing renewable resources. They viewed electric power as wasteful, because more than two thirds of the heat content of the fuel went up the smokestack unused. Most concluded that it would be better, environmentally, if society consumed less energy instead of building more power stations, and that society could do so without economic harm.

Grass roots groups delayed or stopped power plant and transmission projects, but it may be that environmentalists had the most lasting impact on the industry by using economic arguments. They encouraged regulators and utilities to reexamine capital spending where the utility's chosen course of building plant was more costly than alternatives such as spending money on helping customers use less electricity.

They pushed regulators to examine pricing policies that fostered uneconomic usage of electricity. Those economic reforms have prevailed. So did Federal laws that regulated discharges of hot water and pollutants, and encouraged cogeneration in order to save energy.

Power stations generally require huge amounts of water. The water is discharged at a substantially higher temperature than the surrounding water. The hot water could have untoward environmental consequences for aquatic animals and plants, so electric utilities must build cooling ponds, canals, and enormous cooling towers to lower the temperature of the water, before discharging it.

When fossil fuels are burned, particulates and harmful gases are emitted from the smokestack. One of the earliest solutions to the problem was to build tall stacks, so that pollutants would not concentrate near the power plant, but would be spread by the wind. If enough power plants had followed that procedure, of course, the country would have turned grey. The industry installed precipitators, scrubbers and filters to prevent particles from escaping. It installed scrubbers, to remove sulfur oxides, and then had to deal with the problem of removal of the waste material produced in the scrubbers. Some companies switched from coal to low sulfur content oil to avoid the scrubber problem. Others switched to low sulfur coal. Water and air pollution control equipment adds significantly to the cost of a power plant and decreases output and reliability.

High voltage transmission lines have been criticized for more than just appearance. They have been denounced for everything from bringing on headaches and nervous disorders in workers and in farmers plowing the fields under the lines to disturbing the milking habits of local cows. Studies and counterstudies provide a confusing picture. Local opposition to routing of lines has made it difficult to place transmission corridors. Transmission towers have been bombed in several places.

Transmission and distribution systems, the wiring in houses, and electric appliances emit electromagnetic fields (EMF) which may be associated with incidences of cancer and other ailments. Studies of EMF are under way. The utility industry may have to reduce the risk from EMF by widening the rights-of-way around power lines, reconfiguring those lines, making greater use of DC (which does not produce EMF) and shielding offending facilities. Manufacturers of office equipment and home appliances might have to add shielding, too. Although evidence to date is fragmentary, additional studies could force the industry to make expensive modifications in order to contain EMF.

Finally, the creation of carbon dioxide is a problem inherent in the burning of fossil fuels. A buildup of carbon dioxide and other greenhouse inducing gases in the atmosphere might create a greenhouse effect that would warm the atmosphere, change precipitation patterns, and even melt the polar ice caps enough to flood coastal areas. Research on this question is in its infancy, but the problem is made more serious by the claim that we could increase the carbon dioxide to the damaging levels before we finish the research, unless the ocean or forests could act as a sink for carbon dioxide long enough for us to come to grips with the problem.[9]

Other environmental objections are aimed at particular fuels. Even hydropower is not considered benign by some because the huge dams destroy flowing rivers, change aquatic habitats, and require long transmission lines to carry power to the load centers.

Underground coal mining may be dangerous and unhealthy. Surface (strip) mining scars the landscape if done improperly. Burning coal produces not only carbon dioxide, but also particulates, sulfur oxides, and acid rain. The waste material that comes from filtering and scrubbing at the power plant must be disposed of, too. Burning coal may be especially offensive in densely inhabited areas. Some of the difficulties, though, can be alleviated by burning coal with a low sulfur content. In addition, experimentation indicates that coal can be processed to reduce pollution.

Nuclear Power

Although many would assert that the environmental danger from coal is greater than from nuclear power, nuclear power has been a main target of environmentalists.[10] As one critic put it, in a relatively temperate statement about nuclear power:

Again, no one knows what the chance of a major accident actually is and reassurances that cite very tiny probabilities must be taken with a grain of salt. Highly improbable events have a way of happening anyway in complicated technological systems, as the 1965 Northeast power blackout, the sinking of the "unsinkable" Titanic and the failure of other "fail-safe" and "fool-proof" systems have demonstrated.[11]

Objections to nuclear power vary all over the lot:

♦ The Federal Government has subsidized nuclear power, and as a result, cost comparisons between nuclear power and alternatives are biased in favor of nuclear. This is true, but other environmental policy favorites such as solar energy and public transport have been subsidized, too.

♦ A nuclear power station can blow up like a bomb. Almost all experts deny this possibility for American reactors with their diluted fuel within a strong containment vessel.

♦ The cooling system of the reactor could malfunction, precipitating a nuclear fuel meltdown or boiler explosion that might penetrate the containment structure, loosing radioactivity into the environment. The Three Mile Island containment vessel remained intact during and after the 1979 accident there. The nuclear accident at Chernobyl in 1986 did scatter radiation widely, but that type of reactor does not have the same type of containment system as Western reactors.

♦ Nuclear material in transit could be hijacked or involved in a serious accident. This is possible, but unlikely due to security measures and types of containers in which material is transported.

♦ A nuclear accident near a major city would harm a large number of people. Obviously, that is true by definition, but nuclear plants are not located in city centers, although, ironically, one recommendation of an environmental study made in the 1960s was "that earnest examination be conducted on the feasibility of siting nuclear plants in urban areas..." [12], in order to reduce both urban air pollution and the need for high voltage transmission lines.

♦ The government and the industry have no means of disposing of nuclear wastes whose radioactivity will last for thousands of years. That is true, in the sense that utilities need to store high level wastes at the generating station because the Federal Government, which has responsibility for disposal, has not constructed a permanent disposal facility, and may not complete one for decades. The United States chose not to remove certain radioactive materials through reprocessing of the fuel, but it has not been able to certify any geological repository as suitable, either, all almost a half century after the beginning of the nuclear age.

♦ The nuclear power station, upon retirement, will have to be removed and the site cleaned up at great expense. The cost of decommissioning could exceed estimates. That, of course, remains to be seen.

Some environmental objections to nuclear power seem in the category of: anything can happen so do not take any risks. Others are based on clear failings of the nuclear effort. Nuclear power, though, does not produce acid rain or greenhouse gases, and does not depend on the whims of unstable Middle Eastern governments. Should not that make it the choice of environmentalists? Probably not. Environmentalists would argue that there are less expensive alternatives, such as more efficient use of energy (so that the nuclear plant will not be needed) or so-called "soft" or renewable technologies, such as solar power. Oddly enough, after years of fighting to go the nuclear route, many utility executives seem to have come to the same conclusions, although their reasons may be more economic and political than environmental. [13]

Other Considerations

Some of the objections to electric utility operation have been political-sociological-philosophical in nature, with origins in the various protest movements of the 1960s. Perhaps the arguments seem dated, but they had an impact, and could return to vogue in a different milieu. Sociological and philosophical objections may underlie some of the fights about health and safety. Our environmental laws address matters of health, safety, and preservation. They do not consider whether centralized generation of power is socially or economically objectionable. If one believes that central generation of power is a threat to society, what better way to stop it than to raise environmental objections? A court case to preserve an obscure flower can stop a power project better than a political campaign to replace a power station with wood stoves. If campaigning against its perceived environmental dangers is really a method to stop central station power, then no amount of measures to fix the objectionable elements of the power system will succeed in mollifying the opposition. The philosophical-sociological objections to central station power fit into two categories, thermodynamic and political.

Central station power, opponents maintain, creates a mismatch between the quality of energy and the tasks for which the energy is used. For instance, boiling water to turn a turbine to send electricity to an electric motor may be the best way to turn the electric motor. It may not be the best way to heat water to lukewarm for a bath. The bath water could be heated more efficiently by applying a flame to water in the house. In other words, why heat water to several hundred degrees in the boiler of the generator to heat water several tens of degrees in the bathtub?[14] The previous question is about second law efficiency. Aside from giving us additional insight, second law efficiency may have become fashionable because it leads to a desired answer. Low quality heat should be used to do low quality work. Solar energy is of low quality and should be used to raise temperatures to relatively low levels (*i.e.*, room, pool, and water heating needs). That analysis is correct in the sense that more energy is lost when high temperature processes are used to produce low temperatures. The problem with an analysis that only considers energy is that improvement in energy efficiency, no matter how measured, incurs costs. It may be more expensive (as measured in money) to save energy than to waste it. Perhaps that would not be the case if energy were priced properly, but there could still be instances where the cost of increasing the energy efficiency of a project exceeds the value of the energy saved.

The second argument against central station power is that it is a coercive technology that saddles us with diseconomies of scale, is unsafe militarily, puts control of our destiny in the hands of a few, and prevents the development of a benign, decentralized society based in part on soft technologies. Basically, the argument calls for the dismantling of our industrial society, which cannot last anyway because it is based on non-renewable energy resources. That attitude, unfortunately, was not taken seriously by utility managements, regulators and investors, which may explain, in part, why they did not fully comprehend some of their opponents. Ironically, as will be discussed later, proponents of a freer, less regulated utility environment also advocate less emphasis on central station power for economic rather than political reasons.

Environmental Challenges

Environmentalism is a strong force. It has reappeared with renewed vigor, after dormancy in the 1980s. The electric utility industry continues to face environmental challenges:

◆ *Acid rain* — That term, coined by British scientist Angus Smith in 1852, encompasses the deposition of acidic emissions, both wet and dry. Acid rain is an international issue.[15] The acid rain does not always fall in the country of origin. Legislation passed in 1990 will force utilities to clean up a large part of their pollution output, but the 1990 law, for the first time, attempts to utilize market forces to produce results, as opposed to the "command and control" approach of the past, in which the government told utilities what to do and how to do it. No doubt correcting the problems will cost money, but the utilities have the flexibility to try new fuels, clean up coal, and even buy and sell the right to pollute. The challenge is to achieve the desired pollution reduction at the lowest cost.

◆ *Siting* — It has become increasingly difficult to find locations for generating stations and rights of way for transmission lines. The NIMBY (not in my back yard) syndrome could throttle development of needed facilities.

◆ *Nuclear* — Finding a place to put a nuclear waste repository may be the nuclear industry's most prominent environmental challenge, but there are others, too. The poor operating and safety characteristics of reactors in the former Soviet bloc could revive antipathy toward nuclear power. Talk of revival of nuclear power usually fails to get beyond the talking stage in part because of lack of public confidence in nuclear safety. The new generation of nuclear reactors, planned for the 1990s, will have to have safety and environmental features acceptable to the public, or they will not be built.

◆ *Global warming* — Carbon dioxide (derived in part from burning carbon fuels) and other gases may be warming the atmosphere: the greenhouse effect. The global warming trend could affect precipitation patterns, food production, and the depth of the ocean. Certain fuels, such as natural gas, produce less greenhouse gas. Nuclear power produces no greenhouse gases. Thus, fuel procurement policies might have to be modified. Carbon dioxide could be scrubbed from the generation process, at great expense. Or, governments could attempt a market based solution, by taxing the output of greenhouse gases in the hope that energy-producing firms would reduce carbon dioxide output in order to avoid the tax. No doubt, many people will propose that using less energy (conservation) will be the most cost-effective method of reducing the greenhouse effect.

◆ *Electromagnetic fields* — Known collectively as EMF, these fields are produced along transmission lines, in local distribution equipment, and in home appliances such as electric blankets. EMF may be implicated in the causation of various orders, including cancer, but the evidence to date is scattered and uneven in quality[16]. Electric utilities may have to take steps to shield distribution equipment, reconfigure transmission lines and widen rights of way surrounding transmission lines. The question will be whether to take steps now or wait for irrefutable evidence of harm.

Although many in the electric utility industry will view environmental problems as another set of obstacles, those same problems create opportunities for utilities. Firms that have extreme difficulty meeting the latest environmental hurdles may turn to electric utilities for solutions. That is, the utilities may be able to do a better job of producing clean energy. Or the utilities may be willing to invest in assets that help customers reduce energy consumption. But the greatest opportunity for utilities may come about from pollution control rules aimed at the internal combustion engine, the ubiquitous polluter. Restrictions on pollution from conventional automobiles could lead to the revival of electric vehicles.

No doubt, utilities will be the targets of new environmental rules, just because they are so easy to control. But utilities also have the expertise, and resources to develop new markets created by environmental restraints.

Chapter 6

Operations, Demand and Planning

The market price ... is regulated by the proportion between the quantity which is actually brought to market, and the demand of those willing to pay the natural price of the commodity ... which must be paid to bring it thither. Such people may be called the effectual demanders, and their demand the effectual demand ... It is different from the absolute demand. A very poor man may be said ... to have a demand for a coach and six; he might like to have it; but his demand is not an effective demand, as the commodity can never be brought to market in order to satisfy it.[17]

Adam Smith

Electric utilities must begin to build many facilities well ahead of the time the facilities will be needed, simply because it takes so long to complete them. To further complicate matters, the new facilities will last for decades. The electric utility must have a good estimate of what the customer will buy over a long period of time or the plant that is built could prove to be either unnecessary or inadequate.

Choosing the Right Facility

Not only must the utility estimate the amount of electricity that it will sell, but it must also project the timing of the sales. Will the customer buy the power steadily around the clock and throughout the year, or will demand for power be bunched around peak periods? If the former is the case, the utility will put in expensive-to-build, but inexpensive-to-run, base load generators. If the latter, it will install cheap-to-build but expensive-to-run peaking units. Or, as another alternative to peaking units, it may try to control demand at the peak, through special pricing or by means of electronic devices that turn off customers for brief periods, rather than by building peaking units.

As an example, a base load generating unit costs $1,000 to build, the fixed costs and interest on borrowing the money to build it are $150 per year, and the unit burns a cheap fuel, runs efficiently, and therefore has operating costs of 5¢ per kilowatt-hour produced. A peaking unit, on the other hand, costs $300 to build, the fixed costs and interest paid for the investment is only $45 per year, but the unit burns an expensive fuel, runs inefficiently and has operating costs of 20¢ per kilowatt-hour generated. Both plants should last the same number of years. There are 8,760 hours in a 365-day year. The electric utility expects to need a new generating unit 3,000 hours per year. Which one should it choose?

For the base load plant, total cost will be:

$150 for interest

plus 3,000 hours x 5¢ per hour operating costs ($150)

or $300 per year.

For the peaking unit, total costs will be:

$45 for interest

plus 3,000 hours x 20¢ per hour operating costs ($600)

or $645 per year.

Obviously, the base load plant is cheaper. On the other hand, if the utility only needed the plant for 300 hours, during the hottest hours of the day in August, then the decision might be different. For the base load plant, total costs are:

$150 for interest

plus 300 hours x 5¢ per hour operating costs ($15)

or $165 per year.

For the peaking unit, total costs are:

$45 for interest

plus 300 hours x 20¢ per hour operating costs ($60)

or $105 per year.

The utility must also plan ahead by choosing the right fuel for the power station. (Stations that can burn several fuels are flexible but also more expensive to construct.) The choice of fuel depends on location, price, availability, national security and environmental considerations. Those factors can change radically during the period of construction and the life of the plant.

Planning For Demand

In the days when demand for electricity grew at a steady pace, power plants could be completed quickly, fuel costs were stable and environmental rules almost non-existent, planning was easy. The ruler was the best tool for projection.

Between 1960 and 1973, electricity sales rose every year, never more than 9.0% nor less than 5.4% in any year. In ten of the years, the sales increase was in the 7%-9% range. Peak load grew steadily, too, going up between 5.0% and 11.5% each year. In ten years, the numbers ranged between 6% and 9%. Load factor was equally steady, staying between 62% and 66%, with nine years in the 64%-66% range. The electric company's projection might not be on target every year, but it was not likely to be far off. The companies planned and built plant with confidence. After 1973, patterns of demand became unstable, with annual changes in sales ranging from -2.4% to 6.7% and peak load growth fluctuating wildly from -3.1% to 7.9%. Load factor deteriorated, falling between 59.5% and 64.4%. Yet, even before 1973, the Yom Kippur War and the upheaval in the oil markets, there were problems. In the early 1960s, the load factor held up and reserve margin fell. The pattern of load was relatively steady. The industry felt that it could cut down on its reserves without endangering service. In 1965, the lights went out in the Northeast.

Figure 6-1

Reserve Margins
1960-1990

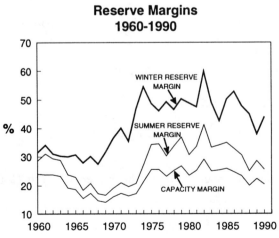

Table 6-1

Load Factor, Reserve Margins and Energy
Sales by Class of Customer
Total Electric Utility Industry
1960-1990
(%)

Year	Load Factor	Reserve Margin (Non-Coincident Winter Peak)	Reserve Margin (Non-Coincident Summer Peak)	Capacity Margin (Non-Coincident Peak for Year)	Industrial % Electric Sales (Large Light & Power)
	(1)	(2)	(3)	(4)	(5)
1960	65.5	31.5	28.6	24.0	50.5
1961	64.8	34.0	31.0	23.7	48.2
1962	64.9	31.0	29.3	23.7	48.2
1963	65.2	30.2	28.8	23.2	46.8
1964	64.2	30.0	23.7	19.2	46.0
1965	65.0	30.7	22.9	18.6	45.4
1966	64.7	27.9	18.4	15.5	44.8
1967	65.3	30.1	20.8	17.3	43.9
1968	63.5	27.4	17.2	14.7	43.1
1969	64.1	31.6	16.6	14.2	42.7
1970	63.9	36.4	19.0	16.0	41.2
1971	63.2	40.1	20.9	17.3	40.4
1972	62.5	35.4	19.6	16.4	40.5
1973	62.0	46.8	20.8	17.2	40.4
1974	61.2	54.5	27.2	21.4	40.5
1975	61.4	48.7	34.3	25.6	38.2
1976	62.6	46.1	34.5	25.6	39.2
1977	61.4	49.3	30.2	23.2	38.8
1978	62.1	46.6	33.7	25.2	38.8
1979	64.4	50.3	36.9	26.8	39.2
1980	61.0	48.8	30.7	23.5	37.3
1981	61.0	47.5	33.6	25.2	38.1
1982	62.0	59.9	41.3	29.2	36.7
1983	59.5	49.1	33.3	25.0	36.3
1984	59.7	42.6	34.0	25.3	36.6
1985	62.0	50.2	35.0	25.9	35.6
1986	60.7	52.9	32.8	24.7	34.8
1987	60.8	47.9	30.6	23.4	34.6
1988	59.5	45.1	25.0	20.0	34.5
1989	62.2	38.0	28.6	22.3	34.8
1990	60.4	44.0	25.6	20.4	34.7

Sources

Edison Electric Institute, *Statistical Year Book of the Electric Utility Industry* (Washington, D.C.:, EEI, various dates), tables 7,38,40, and *1990 Financial Review* (Washington, D.C.: EEI, 1991).

Managements had to rethink procedures and need for facilities, but power plants take a while to build, and reserve margin fell more. Then, in the 1970s, as the new capacity went into service, load patterns deteriorated and so did growth in demand, probably because economic growth slowed below expectations, service industries (which are less energy intensive than heavy industry) began to dominate the economy, and because the price of electricity rose in relation to other prices. A consumer would be sensible to cut use throughout the year, but still take the usual load at peak (during periods of discomfort) if the tariff did not discourage peak use. When this explanation is coupled with increased electric heating penetration (because of the natural gas shortage) and greater air conditioning saturation, the decline in the load factor is understandable. In the 1980s, with the real price of electricity declining (due to falling fuel prices), usage picked up, but at an uneven pace. The industry, though, avoided putting in new facilities, so that reserve margins fell. The load factor hovered around 60%. Table 6-1 documents the trends in reserves, load factor and lessening importance of large industrial users of power. As shown in Figure 6-1, the imbalance between summer and winter reserve margins increased, despite the growth of electric heating. Clearly, making use of facilities on a year-round basis became a problem for the industry.

On a simplified basis, demand for electricity is determined by five variables:

♦ Economic activity — Prosperity means more electricity used by business and more appliances owned by consumers.
♦ The price of electricity in relation to other prices — If electricity becomes cheaper than other goods, especially competing types of energy, people will use more electricity.
♦ Weather — Air conditioning and electric heating sales are affected by weather conditions.
♦ The structure of the economy — Shift of emphasis to or from energy intensive industries, or even the movement of industry to or from this country, will affect the demand for power.
♦ Technology — A stream of inventions and technological improvements will produce processes that require more electricity than old ones, or make it possible to operate with less power.

An analyst trying to determine the trend of electricity consumption in a utility's service area might also focus on demographics, the strength of the utility's conservation and insulation programs, the availability of alternative sources of energy, new businesses entering the service area and the pricing structure of the utility's electricity. To further complicate matters, nowadays large utility customers could choose to generate their own electricity or buy from outside sources other than the utility. Therefore the utility could predict correctly the demand for electricity in its territory, but not necessarily how much of that electricity will be demanded from it.

In the 1950s and 1960s, sales of electricity steadily increased. Planning ahead seemed an easy job. Sales would continue to grow the way they had grown. Power plants could be added to the system with the assurance that they would be needed. You did not need a complicated model to predict demand for electricity. Even if sales and peak load growth could not be forecast exactly, capacity often preceded requirements, so the worst that could happen was that a few utilities on occasion had more plant than they needed for a year or two.

By the 1970s, demand for electricity reacted to destabilizing influences, such as the unavailability of other fuels, environmental rules that encouraged users to take electricity instead of burning their own fuels, and sharply higher prices for electricity that discouraged consumption. In the 1980s, with the real price of electricity falling, consumers were willing to use more, although usage grew more slowly. How can you build for the future when you do not know what the future will bring? Two basic methods are used for projections: they could be characterized as the "bottom up" and "top down" methods.

The bottom up method is conceptually simple, but complicated in practice. The analysis examines all major uses of electricity and then predicts how those uses will grow over time, taking into account technological change, structural modifications of the economy, demographic trends, availability of fuels, price of electricity and alternatives, environmental restrictions, consumer preferences, new industrial processes, conservation, economic conditions and other factors. All the uses of electricity are then added up to derive total consumption of electrical energy. Hence the bottom up name. The approach has the advantage of focusing attention on the individual uses of electricity, but the disadvantage of forcing the analyst to predict structural and technological changes. The bottom up analyses — if not carefully prepared — may contain engineering or ideological biases, assumptions that users will take certain steps to increase or decrease demand, when in reality it may not be economical to do so. (Two examples come to mind. A metals manufacturer might be shown to increase demand because a new, efficient process uses more electricity. In reality, though, the manufacturer might choose to move manufacturing to a less developed country where energy costs are lower rather than improve processes in the United States. A residential consumer, according to the analysis, will reduce consumption of electricity by putting in a more efficient heating system. Unfortunately, in the real world, the price of electricity may be set below its real value, so perhaps the residential customer will not put in the initially more expensive heating unit, because the long term savings are not evident to him. In either case, the analysis could go wrong.)

The bottom up method usually begins with extremely detailed breakdowns of current usage for each sector of the economy. Unfortunately, the estimates of end use are often based on surveys whose results vary from one another, so the bases for the projections are rough. In the residential and commercial sectors, which account for over 60% of all electricity sales, the usage could be broken down into many segments, but not so for the industrial sector:

Approximate 1990 Electricity Consumption by Sector

Residential		*Commercial*		*Industrial*	
Heating	10%	Heating	20%	Motor drives	65%
Cooling	15	Cooling	25	Other	35
Water heating	10	Lighting	40		100%
Refrigerator	20	Other	15		
Freezer	10		100%		
Other	35				
	100%				

The analysts estimate growth in number of households, the saturation level of each appliance (what percentage of households have the appliance), whether new appliances will be larger or smaller or more energy efficient, the availability and price of competing fuels, the number of residents in each household, changes in the living space per household and insulation techniques. They attempt to gauge the impact of new uses for electricity and for substitutes for electricity (such as solar heating) and even the impact of shifting patterns of consumption (such as from watching television to playing computer games).

For the commercial sector the analysis focuses on the growth of floor space, new buildings, heating, cooling and insulation techniques, trends in usage per square foot or per employee, and the overall direction of the economy.

Analysis of the industrial sector is more complex. Some industries, prodigious consumers of electricity, are likely to react to a change in its price or availability by redesigning manufacturing processes or even moving the facility elsewhere. Obviously, making motors more efficient would have a major impact on industrial sales. Certain industries, such as aluminum, iron and steel and industrial chemicals, not only are among the biggest consumers; electricity also accounts for a significant percentage of their expenses. Analysts look into that part of the manufacturing process that uses the most electricity and determine how new techniques will affect consumption of electricity. They examine the price and availability of electricity relative to other fuels. They look into whether foreign countries can offer better conditions for those industries. Then these engineering and industrial analyses will be joined to an examination of how the industry will fare given certain rates of growth for the economy as a whole.

Then the analysts add in their estimates for economic growth, the pricing and availability of competitive fuels, whether new energy-saving or energy-using technologies develop, constraints due to environmental and political reasons, and whatever else is in their bag of tricks. The effort is elaborate, allows one to test different assumptions, but is only as good as the myriad estimates that go into it.

In order to avoid the complications of the bottom up approach, one can, instead, start with a measure of economic activity, such as the gross national product, and observe the past relationship between energy consumption, GNP, and the price of electricity and its substitutes. Then, one can determine demand for electricity in the future based on projections of growth in GNP and change in prices of electricity and its substitutes. In other words, start with the biggest variable and then work downward to the amount of electricity that will be demanded as a result of a given level of economic activity. That is the top down approach. It, too, has hazards. Can we be certain that past relationships between economic activity and electricity usage will hold in the future? Can we make good projections for GNP and energy prices? Unfortunately, the record of our econometric seers is not perfect.

Perhaps one should use both methods and understand the uncertainties involved. Coming to grips with the uncertainties, though, may mean that what was a rational capital investment policy when demand seemed more certain is no longer as rational today. Perhaps utilities will no longer seek the supposed economies of scale derived from the operation of large power stations because they will be uncertain whether demand for power will require the large station, or whether the large station could be completed when it will be required. They might, instead, build smaller generating units that could be built more quickly if needed, and if not needed, less money will be at risk and less plant will stand idle.

Elasticity of Demand

Econometric analyses can provide us with guidance, although the results from study to study are not that consistent, which should not be surprising because the studies rarely deal with the exact same questions or time periods. Table 6-2 shows the results for 25 studies of the reaction of electricity users to changes in price of electricity (price elasticity of demand) and reaction to changes in economic conditions (income elasticity). Because there is often a delay between the time the price of electricity changes (or economic conditions improve or decline) and the time that the consumer reacts to the change, we must consider the immediate reaction of the consumer of electricity (short run) and the delayed reaction (long run). As an example, if the price of electricity goes up sharply, consumers will immediately turn off lights or reduce the thermostat (short run) but will not replace lighting fixtures or put in a more efficient furnace (long run) until the fixtures or furnace wear out.

Numerous studies made since the sample shown in Table 6-2 explored elasticity in different periods and in various countries. They examined not only how much demand for electricity varied with price and with income, but also how easily electricity could be substituted for other factors of production, such as capital and labor. As usual, the results varied greatly. Table 6-3 gives some of the conclusions. Interestingly, those studies show that electricity and other factors of production are substitutable for each other, although the elasticity of substitution varies from period to period. Furthermore, the studies show that price elasticity of demand became more significant after the energy crisis of the early 1970s. That conclusion may be due to the imperfections of the statistical techniques, or it may

Table 6-2

Range of Values for Elasticity of Demand of Electricity to Price and Income (or Economic) Variables[a]

| | Price | | | | | | Income or Economic Activity | | | | | |
| | Short Run | | | Long Run | | | Short Run | | | Long Run | | |
	High	Low	Mean	High	Low	Mean	High	Low	Mean	High	Low	Mean
Residential	-0.80	-0.54	-0.23	-4.54[b]	-0.46	-1.17[b]	2.00	0.10	0.44	1.08	0.22	0.61
Commercial	-0.66	-0.25	-0.40	-1.54	-0.56	-1.08	—	—	—	1.38	1.15	1.27
Industrial	-0.20	-0.10	-0.15	-1.24	-0.74	-0.94	0.87	0.07	0.47	0.70	0.68	0.69

Notes

a   25 studies published after 1975.

b   Excluding -4.54 outlier, high is -2.1, mean is -0.98.

Source.

Resources for the Future, *Price Elasticities of Demand for Energy - Evaluating the Estimates* (Palo Alto: Electric Power Research Institute, September 1982), pp. 3-68 to 3-72, 3-88, 3-99.

be valid, in the sense that people do not react until the price increases are severe. Or, it may be that manufacturers do not provide more energy-efficient alternative products until the price increases for electricity seem both large and permanent. Whatever the reason, the studies do indicate that elasticities are not fixed, and users of the studies had better be cautious in application to practical policymaking.

Table 6-3

Elasticity Studies Published After 1982

	1960-72	1973-80
Nine European Countries (Hesse & Tarkka)(a)		
Industrial Price Elasticity	-0.1	-0.3

	1962-80	
Canadian Industry (Andrikopoulos and Brox)(b)		
Short run price elasticity	-0.8	
Long run price elasticity	-0.5	

	1979
Pacific Northwest Households (Henson)(c)	
Price elasticity (change in rate structure)	-0.2

	1973 - 1983
USA (Thomas, Carlson and Plummer)(d)	
Price elasticity:	
Short run residential	-0.4
Short run industrial	-0.3
Long run residential	-0.7
Long run industrial	-1.0

	1950 - 1987
USA (Studness)(e)	
GNP elasticity (1st year)	0.3
GNP elasticity (total)	1.4
Price elasticity (1st year)	-0.1
Price elasticity (total)	-0.4

	1964 - 1973	1977 - 1985
USA (EIA)(f)		
Price elasticity	-0.73	-0.25

Sources:
(a) Dieter M. Hesse and Helena Tarkka, "The Demand for Capital, Labor and Energy in European Manufacturing Industry before and after the Oil Price Shocks," *Scand. J. of Economics* 88 (3), 529-546, 1986.
(b) Andreas A. Andrikopoulos and James A. Brox, "Demand Systems for Energy Consumption by the Manufacturing Sector", *Journal of Economics and Business*,1986; 38: 141-153.
(c) Steven E. Henson, "Electricity Demand Estimates under Increasing - Block Rates," *Southern Economic Journal*, July 1984, pp. 147-156.
(d) Thomas C. Thomas, Richard C. Carlson and James L. Plummer, "A New Ball Game in Industrial Electric Rates," *Public Utilities Fortnightly*, Aug. 21, 1986, pp. 15-19.
(e) Charles M. Studness, "The Price of Electric Demand and Utility Forecasts", *Public Utilities Fortnightly*, Sept. 29, 1988, pp. 36-37.
(f) Department of Energy, Energy Information Administration, *Short-Term Energy Outlook Methodology* (Washington, D.C.: EIA, July 1985), pp. 66, 75.

Weighing the values in Table 6-2 by electric sales, and assuming that commercial customers are sensitive to economic activity (in the short run) in a manner similar to residential customers, the elasticities for electricity demand as a whole would be about:

-0.2 for short run price elasticity

-1.1 for long run price elasticity

0.5 for short run economic or income elasticity

0.8 for long run economic or income elasticity

A negative number indicates (as would be expected) that energy sales move in the opposite direction from price. That is, a 10% increase in the price of electricity would produce a 2% (0.2 times 10%) decline in demand for power. Over the long term, though, a 10% increase in price could lead to an 11% (1.1 times 10%) drop in electricity sales. However, if economic activity (or income) rises 10%, this has a positive effect on demand for electricity, pushing up sales by 5% (0.5 times 10%). In the long run, perhaps after new equipment and appliances are purchased, that 10% rise in income will help push up sales of electricity by 8% (0.8 times 10%).

In reality, just as with the engineering-oriented bottom up analysis, the top down econometric studies are complex, and the investigator must often settle for out-of-date or inadequate data.

1960-1990 Results

Having introduced all the caveats, it is worth examining trends over time, in order to see some of the factors that influence the demand for electricity. The examples that follow are designed to give the reader an idea of some of the analyses and problems involved in studying the variables. They are not a substitute for a thorough and rigorous statistical analysis.

We begin with the most difficult question: how to predict peak load. Utilities must have enough capacity to meet demand at the peak period, or they will have to cut off customers. Looking only at the summer peak, we surmise that demand varies with economic activity, weather conditions, and the price of electricity. Different companies, though, do not reach peaks in demand simultaneously because heat waves do not hit the entire country at once, and because economic activity is not equally strong everywhere at the same time. The nationwide peak demand shown for the summer is actually based on the non-coincident peak loads of all the reporting companies. So, the peak load figure for the United States is an approximation of reality, possibly a fiction, and we are not sure when it takes place. For this analysis, we will assume that the peak takes place during July when kilowatt-hour sales tend to be high. Obviously, the individual utility can do a more precise analysis for its own peak period.

Table 6-4

Peak Load, Price, Economic Activity
and Weather
1960-1990
(% Changes)

Year	Summer Peak	Real GNP (3rd Quarter)	Cooling Degree Days (July)	Real Price of Electricity (3rd Quarter)	Real Price of Electricity Four Preceding Years (3rd Quarter)
	(1)	(2)	(3)	(4)	(5)
1960	6.0	2.4	-7.8	-0.6	-1.6
1961	6.2	3.0	2.0	-0.7	-0.6
1962	5.7	6.0	-10.0	-1.3	-0.2
1963	7.0	4.3	12.2	-1.9	-1.0
1964	9.7	5.0	6.6	-2.6	-1.1
1965	6.5	5.9	-14.8	-2.6	-1.5
1966	9.2	5.7	27.5	-3.4	-2.1
1967	5.0	2.9	-23.0	-2.2	-2.6
1968	11.5	4.8	12.2	-1.9	-2.7
1969	8.3	2.0	7.2	-3.7	-2.5
1970	6.6	-0.1	-2.1	-1.3	-2.8
1971	6.4	2.7	-11.6	3.5	-2.3
1972	9.3	6.0	4.3	0.3	-0.9
1973	7.8	4.9	7.1	1.0	-0.3
1974	1.6	-1.6	0.0	14.6	0.9
1975	2.2	0.3	-5.4	3.9	4.7
1976	4.0	5.2	-6.4	2.3	4.8
1977	6.9	6.0	24.7	3.8	5.3
1978	3.0	3.9	-12.6	-0.9	6.0
1979	-2.4	1.8	-4.6	0.7	2.3
1980	7.2	2.2	27.9	8.2	1.5
1981	0.3	4.2	-11.6	4.9	2.9
1982	-3.1	-3.0	-4.3	2.3	3.2
1983	7.9	4.9	12.1	-0.7	4.0
1984	0.8	6.5	-19.0	4.4	3.6
1985	2.1	2.9	8.4	-1.4	2.7
1986	3.6	2.6	9.4	0.0	1.1
1987	4.0	3.8	-0.6	-3.3	0.5
1988	6.7	4.5	8.0	-3.0	-0.1
1989	-1.1	2.4	-13.8	-1.1	-1.9
1990	4.2	1.0	0.6	-2.6	-1.9

Notes Column 1:   % change non-coincident summer peak from previous year.

Column 2:   % change in real GNP, third quarter to third quarter.

Column 3:   % change in cooling degree days for July in current year from July in previous year.

Column 4:   % change in real price of electricity third quarter to third quarter. Price changes determined for industrial users from Producers price Index and for all non-industrial users from Consumers Price Index. Quarter price is unweighted mean for three months. All price changes deflated by GNP deflator for quarter. Price change for peak determined by weighting industrial and non-industrial price changes by percentage of total sales accounted for by each group in year.

Column 5:   Above procedure repeated for four years preceding immediate past year. Compound annual rate of growth for four year period.

Sources: Column 1:   Edison Electric Institute, *Statistical Year Book* (various issues), and *1990 Financial Review.*

Column 2:   U.S. Department of Commerce.

Column 3:   U.S. Department of Commerce. National Oceanic and Atmospheric Administration. *State, Regional, and National Monthly and Seasonal Cooling Degree Days. Weighted by Population (1980 Census).* (Asheville, N.C.: U.S. Dept. of Commerce, Sept. 1981, May 1985, June 1987 and June 1991).

Column 4:   Bureau of Labor Statistics. *Monthly Labor Review* (various issues).

Column 5:   Bureau of Labor Statistics. *Monthly Labor Review* (various issues).

Our measure of economic activity will be the GNP in the quarter of peak summer sales, almost invariably in the third quarter of the year. Weather affects demand for electricity, but what measure represents weather conditions at the peak when peak load throughout the country is non-coincident? The proxy for weather selected was cooling degree days in the month of the peak. (A cooling degree day is the number of degrees by which the average temperature on the day exceeds 65 degrees Fahrenheit.) This is an imperfect measure for many reasons, but especially because peak demand is affected by number of days of heat buildup, whether the hottest days come on the weekend or during the work week, or when factories are on vacation, not to mention such factors as humidity, time of day, wind, rain, etc.

Price of electricity affects demand, but its price in isolation is not helpful. After all, if the price of electricity goes up 5% when all other prices rise 10%, the real price of electricity in relation to other goods will fall. An analysis can tackle the question by comparing the price of electricity to alternatives such as oil or gas, on the assumption that customers switch fuels depending on price. Or, we can assume that electricity is just one more commodity competing for the consumer's dollar and look at its price action relative to that of all prices. For the sake of simplicity we will take the latter course, showing the change in price of electricity relative to the change in price of all goods and services as measured by the GNP deflator, (*i.e.*, if electricity prices rise 5% when all other prices rise 3%, then the real price of electricity moves up 2%.)

Reaction to today's price change might also be delayed until an appliance wears out and can be replaced by a more efficient one. That is, the relationship between price and usage might be a lagged one. Table 6-4 includes the change in price from last year's peak quarter to this year's, and the compound annual change in price during the four years preceding the immediate past year. (That is, for 1970, we show the percentage change in price that took place in 1970, and then another price change that has the effect of averaging the price change that took place in 1966, 1967, 1968, and 1969.)

Figure 6-2

**Percent Changes in Economic
Activity,Pricing,Peak Load
and Sales 1960-1990**

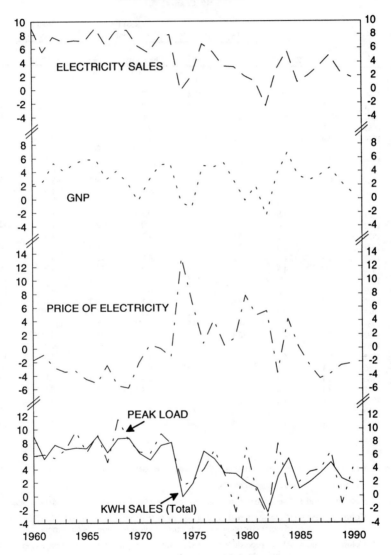

Table 6-5

Sale of Electricity, Economic Activity,
Weather and Price,
1960 - 1990
(% Change)

Year	Kwh Sales	Real GNP	Degree Days		Real Price Current Year		Real Price Four Preceding Years	
			Heating	Cooling	Electricity	Gas	Electricity	Gas
	(1)	(2)	(3)	(4)	(5)	(6)	(7)	(8)
1960	9.0	2.2	7.0	-11.4	-1.7	1.6	-2.5	0.0
1961	5.5	2.6	-3.8	-2.8	-0.9	2.6	-1.7	0.7
1962	7.7	5.3	3.3	1.0	-2.8	-1.0	-1.5	1.7
1963	7.0	4.1	0.9	1.8	-3.4	-3.0	-2.2	0.6
1964	7.2	5.3	-5.0	-1.2	-3.3	-1.6	-2.3	0.0
1965	7.1	5.8	1.0	-2.5	-4.5	-2.7	-2.7	-0.9
1966	9.0	5.8	3.5	-0.7	-5.1	-4.9	-3.5	-2.3
1967	6.5	2.9	-1.9	-6.9	-2.5	-2.3	-4.0	-2.9
1968	8.6	4.1	1.3	6.7	-5.5	-4.7	-3.7	-3.0
1969	8.7	2.4	1.3	4.1	-5.8	-3.7	-4.5	-4.6
1970	6.4	-0.3	-1.5	5.2	-2.1	-2.6	-4.7	-3.7
1971	5.4	2.8	-2.7	-3.6	0.5	0.7	-4.0	-3.3
1972	7.6	5.0	3.9	-5.0	0.0	2.6	-3.2	-2.5
1973	8.0	5.2	-8.8	9.3	-1.3	1.9	-1.9	-0.7
1974	-0.1	-0.5	2.5	-11.0	13.3	10.0	-0.7	0.6
1975	1.9	-1.3	1.2	5.6	6.8	23.9	3.0	3.8
1976	6.7	4.9	6.1	-12.3	0.7	16.5	4.5	9.3
1977	5.5	4.7	-2.7	25.1	4.1	15.4	4.7	12.8
1978	3.4	5.3	7.9	-5.1	0.4	3.1	6.1	16.3
1979	3.3	2.5	-3.6	-9.4	1.5	6.3	3.0	14.4
1980	2.0	-0.2	-1.4	19.2	7.8	13.7	1.7	10.2
1981	1.2	1.9	-4.2	-8.9	4.8	6.3	3.4	9.5
1982	-2.4	-2.5	2.1	-6.1	5.5	14.9	3.6	7.3
1983	2.9	3.6	0.1	12.4	-3.6	10.5	4.9	10.3
1984	5.6	6.8	-2.3	-4.8	4.3	-3.5	3.5	11.3
1985	1.1	3.4	2.7	-1.6	0.2	-4.8	2.7	6.9
1986	2.1	2.7	-7.2	4.7	-2.4	-10.8	1.5	3.9
1987	3.4	3.4	0.5	2.3	-4.4	-8.9	-0.4	-2.5
1988	5.0	4.5	7.7	1.5	-3.7	-3.5	-0.7	-7.0
1989	2.6	2.5	-0.4	-7.7	-2.5	0.3	-2.5	-7.0
1990	1.8	1.0	-15.4	8.2	-2.2	-3.7	-3.3	-6.0

Notes   Column 1:   % change in total KWH sales to ultimate customers.

Column 2:   % change in real GNP.

Columns 3 and 4: % change in sum of heating degree days and cooling degree days in year.

Columns 5 and 6: % change in real price of electricity (natural gas), deflated by GNP deflator. Price of electricity (gas) is average price in year for ultimate customers.

Columns 7 and 8: Above procedure repeated for four years preceding current one. Compound annual rate for four year period.

Sources: Column 1:   Edison Electric Institute. *Statistical Year Book* (various issues).

Column 2:   U.S. Department of Commerce.

Columns 3 and 4: U.S. Department of Commerce. National Oceanic and Atmospheric Administration. *State, Regional, and National Monthly and Seasonal Cooling Degree Days. (Heating Degree Days). Weighted by Population (1980 Census).* (Asheville, N.C.: U.S. Dept. of Commerce, Sept. 1981, May 1985, Nov. 1985, June 1987 and June 1991).

Columns 5 to 8:   Edison Electric Institute, American Gas Association, EIA.

The raw data tell us little. There are too many variables influencing demand for electricity at the peak period. Various statistical techniques can help us sort out which variables seem to be associated more with the changes in peak load. One such technique, known as multiple regression, attempts to derive a formula that accounts for the movement of one series of numbers (the dependent variable) by the influences of various factors (the independent variables) on the dependent variable. As an example, we would use this technique to determine whether the sale of peanut butter (dependent variable) is influenced by television commercials, the price of peanut butter, and the number of five-year-olds in the population (independent variables). In reality, this analysis does not tell us for sure that one variable causes movement in another. It just shows that there could be an influence and how much confidence we can place in that influence.

The variables used in the first analysis are:

PK   =   % change in peak load (dependent variable)
GNP3   =   % change in GNP, third quarter to third quarter
CDD   =   % change in cooling degree days in July.
Pp1   =   % change in relative price of electricity from third quarter last year to third quarter this year.
Pp4   =   % compound rate of change in relative price in third quarter in four years preceding the immediate past year. (Period begins five years before current year.)

The analysis produces a formula (or regression equation) with the results in percent. The coefficients (the numbers by which each variable is multiplied in the equation) are like the elasticities given in Tables 6-2 and 6-3. The numbers in parentheses shown under the coefficients are T statistics, which indicate the statistical significance (how much we can rely on the coefficient) of each coefficient. The higher the absolute number (ignore the plus or minus sign) of the T statistic, the more confident we can be. The first number is a constant, an add-on that does not change, although the other independent variables do change from year to year.

$$Pk = 2.81 + 0.719(GNP3) + 0.128(CDD) + 0.011(Pp1) - 0.643(Pp4)$$
$$(3.87) \qquad (4.15) \qquad (0.09) \qquad (-3.92)$$

It looks as if Pp1 does not explain much of what happens to peak load, and, in fact, seems to indicate that when price goes up, so does peak usage. Obviously, people do not use more electricity because its price rises. The equation explains 69%

(0.69) of the movement in peak load. (The coefficient of determination, measured by r^2, is a quick test of the value of the equation. The perfect score is 100% (1.00). Other tests, though, should be performed before accepting the analysis.) Since Pp1 does not contribute to the analysis, we can omit it, and the results are:

$$Pk = 2.83 + 0.712(GNP3) + 0.128(CDD) - 0.636(Pp4)$$
$$(4.23) \qquad\qquad (4.23) \qquad\qquad (-4.44)$$

The r^2 is 0.69. Obviously, by using data for the entire country, as if peak always takes place simultaneously in July, and as if the average price of electricity in the quarter is what people pay at peak, and as if overall July cooling degrees approximate the weather at peak, we are making heroic assumptions, and should not get upset if the statistical analysis only shows that we are on the right track. No doubt, an analysis that focuses on the right price, weather and economic variables for the local territory served by the utility would produce better results.

The equation, though, shows that peak load growth is subject to big swings even with small changes in the factors that influence peak load. For instance, using the second formula, let us assume that economic activity, weather, and lagged price all increase 3%. What happens to peak load?

	Coefficient	x Change in Variable	=	Formula (Rounded)
Constant	2.83	—		2.83%
GNP3	0.712	3%		2.14
CDD	0.128	3%		0.38
Pp4	-0.636	3%		-1.91
		Change in Peak Load (Pk)		3.44%

But if economic growth slows down to 1%, weather is 1% cooler, and the four year price increase is 4%, then:

	Coefficient	x Change in Variable	=	Formula (Rounded)
Constant	2.83	—		2.83
GNP3	0.712	1%		0.73
CDD	0.128	-1%		-0.13
Pp4	-0.636	4%		-2.54
		Change in Peak Load (Pk)		0.87%

Utilities must design systems that cope with highly variable swings in peak load, caused by unpredictable factors such as weather and economic activity. It may be more efficient to attempt to control these swings through demand side management (which means controlling customers' use at peak periods or pricing the electricity in such a way that customers cut back at certain times) rather than to have the generating capacity available to meet uncontrolled peak demand.

Looking at trends in kwh sales is a more satisfactory process. Again, we assume that consumption of electricity is affected by economic conditions, weather, price increases in the current year, and price increases during the preceding four years. We also add to the analysis the price action of natural gas, a competitor for electricity's market. All data appear on Table 6-5.

The weather proxies consist of the total cooling degree days and the total heating degree days in the year. (A heating degree day is the deviation of the mean temperature of the day below 65 degrees Fahrenheit). This should capture both air conditioning and heating sales. Economic activity is represented by change in real GNP. The change in the real price of electricity and of natural gas is shown for the current year, and on a compound basis for the four preceding years. Natural gas is a competing fuel. If its price rises too much, its users might turn to electricity, and vice versa.

Where:

KWH = % change in KWH sales
HDD = % change in heating degree days in year
CDD = % change in cooling degree days in year
GNP = % change in real GNP
P1 = % change in average real price of electricity in year
P4 = % annual change in real price of electricity in four preceding years
G1 = % change in average real price of natural gas in year
G4 = % annual change in real price of natural gas in four preceding years.

The equation is:
KWH = 1.25 + 0.755(GNP) + 0.110(HDD) + 0.030(CDD)–0.205(P1)–1.06(P4) +
$\qquad$ (5.88) $\qquad$ (2.14) $\qquad$ (1.07) $\qquad$ (–2.54) $\qquad$ (–6.74)

$\qquad$ 0.150(G1) + 0.267(G4)
$\qquad$ (3.47) $\qquad$ (3.36)

The r^2 equals 0.88, which does explain most of the year-by-year change in kilowatt-hour sales. We might want to simplify the analysis, though, because the weather variables seem to add little to the analysis. (That conclusion, of course, is counter-intuitive. We know that customers use more electricity when the weather is hot to cool buildings and more when the weather is cold to heat buildings. But our calculations, based on annual, nationwide data, may smooth over the swings in weather in a way that distorts the results.) Thus, we can calculate a formula for percentage change in kilowatt-hour sales with fewer variables:

$$KWH = 1.06 + 0.806(GNP) - 0.236(P1) - 1.01(P4) + 0.179(G1) + 0.245(G4)$$
$$(6.10) \qquad (-2.88) \quad (-6.17) \quad (4.16) \qquad (2.97)$$

The r^2 is 0.85, but we have simplified the analysis. The regression analysis shows that kwh sales rise when the economy (GNP) improves, decline when the short run real price of electricity (P1) rises, decline when the long term real price trend for electricity is up (P4), all of which makes sense, and kwh sales rise when the short run (G1) real gas price and the long-term trend in real gas prices (G4) are up, which also makes sense in that higher gas prices reduce the competitiveness of natural gas versus electricity. To simplify the results, let us assume that the GNP goes up 3% in the year, the real price of electricity in the year rises 2%, the average real price escalation for electricity has been 4% over the past four years, this year's real gas price fell 1% and the four year real price trend for natural gas has been down 2% per year. Substituting those values in the formula, we get (in %):

$$KWH = (1.06) + 0.806(3) - 0.236(2) - 1.01(4) + 0.179(-1) + 0.245(-2) =$$
$$-1.70\%$$

This sort of statistical analysis must be carried much further, though, before accepting its results. Some of the variables might interrelate with each other, to some extent, so that they are not all working independently. Also, while the equation gives the general picture, it may not work well in all years studied. As an example, it may explain well the early years of the period studied but not the later years, so it might not prove to be a reliable guide to making predictions. At least, though, the coefficients are not far from those indicated in Table 6-2, so we may be moving in the right direction. But we still do not know whether past relationships, as shown in the equations, will hold in the future. Further study might show that the relationships are changing, in which case sophisticated techniques might be used to forecast those structural shifts.

As crude as this analysis is, it shows that sale of electricity is sensitive to weather, economic conditions, and price. The analysis also shows that a rising price for a competitive fuel (natural gas) aids the sale of electricity. Even the price analysis leaves much to be desired, because we are not examining price at the margin, *i.e.*, what the last kwh taken costs the customer. Furthermore, if the impact of price is lagged, then today's price hike may dampen sales for years to come. This is an uncomfortable conclusion for utilities that have to hike prices sharply to pay for large, new power stations. The vague notions that consumption of electricity fell off due to "conservation" must be replaced by a hardheaded analysis of the factors that affect demand if utilities and regulators are to engage in realistic planning. Electricity sales might be controlled by price even if economic activity does take off. Both regulators and utility managements have been reluctant to use price to clear the market, but doing so could be an alternative to meeting unfettered demand by building huge power stations.

What is the moral of the story? Forecasting is an imperfect process, but good statistical techniques, combined with reasonable assumptions and common sense should provide guidance to managements and help to prevent multi-million dollar mistakes. Furthermore, simply going through the process of deciding on the assumptions to use, and then the statistical analysis, helps to clarify the range of uncertainty in the forecast, which, in itself, is valuable. Some of the industry's problems in the past came about because of bad forecasts. The answer, though, is to improve the forecasts and understand the forecasting process better, not to eschew the technique altogether.

Planning Requirements in the New Environment

It is difficult to predict what customers will want, given all the factors that influence demand for electricity. Putting up large power stations is a risky investment under conditions of uncertainty. The new stations, moreover, have been expensive, raising overall costs per kwh of output. That has led many utilities to invest in demand side management (DSM), on the theory that it is cheaper to help customers use less electricity (thereby allowing the utility to serve more customers with existing plant) than to build new facilities. As an added advantage, DSM investments are numerous and small, thereby reducing the risk of putting all one's eggs in one basket (the new power station).

Regulators and utilities then take the concept of seeking alternatives another step forward. When the utility believes that it has to secure additional sources of power, it must examine all practicable methods, which might encompass building its own power station, contracting to buy from another firm's power station (if the other firm can do the job for less), or adopt demand side management programs that reduce the consumption of existing customers in order to free up output for new demand. DSM measures could include installing energy-efficient light bulbs for customers, encouraging more insulation in houses, or equipping air conditioners with radio-controlled switches that allow the utility to turn down the units during peak periods.

In the old days, a utility or group of utilities handled all aspects of planning and production. Many were self-sufficient organizations. Now, the utility must integrate into its operations independent suppliers of electricity with varying operating characteristics and levels of dependability. It will plan major, long-term purchases of power from distant utilities, and arrange transmission over long distances. It will have to accommodate numerous demands on its own transmission network from independent power producers, and from other utilities with connecting transmission systems. It has to explain to regulators why the chosen path is the least cost path. Planning and operating the utility no longer are nobody's business but the utility's.

Planning and operating are more complicated now that demand projections are less certain, and the utility has to weigh the alternatives before acting. At the same time, the new decision-making procedures may reduce risk and cost for the utility and its customers.

Chapter 7

Summary

Electricity seems destined to play an important part in the arts and indus-tries. The question of its economical application to some purposes is still unsettled, but experiment has already proved that it will propel a street car better than a gas jet and give more light than a horse.[18]

Ambrose Bierce

Electric utilities had one rule for decades: bigger meant more efficient. By the 1970s, the rule seemed less and less true. For years, costs declined, prices could be reduced, and demand was strong and growing steadily. In the 1970s, growth of demand flattened as the price of power shot up. The industry used to enjoy praise for its activities. In the late 1960s, environmentalists attacked the "living better electrically" concept, sales promotion, smokestacks, and decried a supposed nuclear peril. Industry leaders were now on the defensive. The world had truly been turned upside down for utility employees and security holders. Change had to take place. In the 1980s, utility managers regrouped, revised procedures, and attempted to stabilize their organizations during a period of moderate growth.

If predicting the path of operations were simply a matter of forecasting technological change or fuel availability, the job would be hard enough. But that is only a small part of the job. Utilities will choose technologies because of economic and financial limitations, too. The Federal Government will force changes for reasons of national security. Some choices will be made because they represent the path of least resistance to environmental, regulatory or economic pressures. The only certainty is that the electric utility industry will continue to be buffeted by what the Edison Electric Institute referred to euphemistically as the "transitional storm."[19] The transition, to the EEI, was the period between the fossil age of yore and the era of inexhaustible fuels in the future. Unfortunately, the age of inexhaustible fuels has receded into the distant future, which means that the electric industry must deal with the same fossil fuels that contribute to air pollution and atmospheric warming.

In the 1990s, the utilities and non-utility generators will go into the building business, to erect needed facilities. Most new plants will burn coal or natural gas. For the moment, no nuclear plants are on the drawing boards. Small scale sources, such as geothermal, hydro, cogeneration, the fuel cell, solar and wind should play an increasingly important role, especially if they are constructed for deregulated (hence more profitable) operations, as seems to be the thrust of present policy.

Whether the flowering of small scale, decentralized generation leads to the demise of central station power is another question. One could argue that a breakthrough in photovoltaic energy could reduce or eliminate the need for central station power, and that possibility alone ought to encourage electric utilities to reduce their exposure to such risk by cutting down commitment to expensive central generating facilities. At the same time, when comparing the cost of a new technology (such as solar photovoltaics) to that of the existing central station power (which is not fully utilizing its capacity), the comparison should be between the fully allocated costs of the new technology and the incremental costs of central station power. If that is understood, it will be a while before a new technology takes hold. (The implication for the profitability of the utility would not be healthy, but letting the market go to competitors might be even more unhealthy.)

The nuclear plants of the future, fusion reactors that could use sea water as a fuel, are decades away from use. A revival of nuclear power would be more likely if the industry standardizes its design around smaller, uniform, safer designs for conventional reactors, several of which are under development, but which are not likely to produce electricity before the turn of the century, if they are built.

The utility industry seems to have ended its love affair with mammoth size. A large power plant that works poorly can put a strain on an electrical system. Putting huge sums into one machine increases the risk of doing business. Putting in a massive plant could leave the utility with a large amount of unused capacity until demand grows into the capacity, which could take years. Perhaps, when money costs were low, the carrying costs on the temporarily excess capacity were more than offset by the economies of scale inherent in larger units. Whether that is the case now is another question. Large plants have still another problem: they are built for the base load, not for on-and-off use. Unfortunately, load has been more unstable than expected in some systems, so the large unit has to be operated under less than optimal conditions. Finally, the biggest question of all is whether size has reached a point at which economies of scale are no longer meaningful.

Many utilities could reduce the risk of their present mode of operations by putting more emphasis on small power units, cogeneration, conservation measures, and load management techniques. Those measures, however, may not work everywhere. Much will depend on the characteristics of the service area. Diversity of energy source will be an important consideration in order to maintain reliability.

The electric utility industry has not been known for its quick response or imaginative actions (in part because of the nature of the construction and regulatory processes). However, under pressure now from regulators and investors and facing high capital costs and greater risks, the industry is responding faster than before.

Notes

[1]Sir William Cecil Dampier, *A History of Science and Its Relations with Philosophy and Religion* (Cambridge: University Press, 1948), p. 217.

[2]Henry Semat, *The Fundamentals of Physics* (New York: Rinehart, 1957), p. 104.

[3]Semat, *op. cit.*, p. 110.

[4]Abbott Payson Usher, *A History of Mechanical Invention* (Boston: Beacon Press, 1959), p. 403.

[5]U.S. Department of Energy, *Interim Report National Energy Strategy* (Washington, D.C.: U.S. Department of Energy, April 1990), p.111.

[6]Barry Commoner, *The Poverty of Power: Energy and the Economic Crisis* (New York: Alfred A. Knopf, 1976), p. 3.

[7]E. F. Schumacher, *Small Is Beautiful: Economics As If People Mattered* (New York: Harper & Row Perennial Library, 1975), p. 60.

[8]Electric Utility Task Force on the Environment, *The Electric Utility Industry and the Environment, Report to the Citizens Advisory Committee on Recreation and Natural Beauty by the Electric Utility Industry Task Force on the Environment* (no place or date of publication. Library of Congress Card No. 68-57661), p. 11.

[9]For discussion see: W. B. Broecker, T. Takahashi, H. J. Simpson, T. H. Peng, "Fate of Fossil Fuel Carbon Dioxide and the Global Carbon Budget," *Science*, Vol. 206, 26 October 1979, p. 409; Ronald A. Madden and V. Ramanathan, "Detecting Climate Change Due to Increasing Carbon Dioxide," *Science*, Vol. 209, 15 August 1980, p. 763; Michael Shephard, "The Politics of Climate," *EPRI Journal*, Vol. 13, No. 4, June 1988, p. 4.; Richard Warrick and Philip D. Jones, "The Greenhouse Effect: Impacts and Policies," *Forum*, Vol. 3, No. 3, Fall 1988, p. 48; Environmental Issues Section, *Forum*, Vol. 4, No. 4, Winter 1989, pp. 5-46.

[10]For a discussion of studies of relative risk, see John H. Herbert, Christina Swanson, and Patrick Reddy, "A Risky Business," *Environment*, July/August 1979, p. 28.

[11]John Holdren and Philip Herrera, *Energy: A Crisis in Power* (San Francisco: Sierra Club, 2nd printing, 1973), p. 77.

[12]Electric Utility Task Force, *op. cit.*, p.13.

[13]Leonard S. Hyman, "Reviving Nuclear Requires Broad Technology Fix," *Forum for Applied Research and Public Policy*, Vol. 6, No. 4, Winter 1991, p.67.

[14]This argument about efficiency depends on the laws of thermodynamics. This first law (conservation of energy) states that work done by a machine equals the value of the heat applied to the system less the heat given up. In an engine it is not possible to transform into work all the heat applied, so efficiency is measured as the work done by the machine as a percentage of heat applied. This is first law efficiency, and it is generally 30%-to-40% for a power station. The second law of thermodynamics (entropy) states that energy becomes less and less available. Thus, although energy is never lost (first law), it becomes less available to do work. Measurement of second law efficiency focuses on the end use of the work. Going back to the original example, if two-thirds of the energy content of the fuel is lost in the generation process, and then the electric coils in the water heater at home push up the temperature of the water to a level that is so hot that the hot water must be diluted with cold, a lot of energy has been wasted to produce lukewarm water. Perhaps a more efficient method would be to heat some cold water with a flame in the house. Second law efficiency often is as low as one-tenth of first law efficiency. The argument basically concludes that since the universe will eventually run out of energy that can be converted to work, we should stop wasting energy now.

[15]D. W. Schindler, "Effects of Acid Rain on Freshwater Ecosystems," *Science*, 8 January 1988, Vol. 239, p. 149.

[16]Taylor Moore, "Pursuing the Science of EMF," *EPRI Journal*, Vol. 15, No. 1, Feb 1990, p. 4.

[17]Adam Smith, *An Inquiry into the Nature and Causes of the Wealth of Nations* (New York: The Modern Library, 1937), p. 56.

[18]Ambrose Bierce, *The Devil's Dictionary* (New York: Dover Publications, 1958) p. 35.

[19]Edison Electric Institute, *31 Answers to 32 Questions About the Electric Utility Industry* (New York: Edison Electric Institute, 1976), unnumbered.

Part Three

The Development and Structure

of the Electric Utility Industry

Chapter 8

Introduction

... the dynamo became a symbol of infinity ... he began to feel the forty-foot dynamo as a moral force, much as the early Christians felt the Cross ... Before the end, one began to pray to it; inherited instinct taught the natural expression of man before silent and infinite force ... Between the dynamo ... and the engine house ... the break of continuity amounted to abysmal fracture ... No more relation could he discover between the steam and the electric current than between the Cross and the cathedral.[1]

Henry Adams

The Victorian naturalists believed that *"natura non facit saltum,"* nature does not leap. By that they meant that evolution or progress was a gradual affair. Unfortunately, the fossil record did not show such a gradual sequence, but seemed to be discontinuous, indicating sudden change or cataclysmic events rather than gradualism. The Victorians, however, persisted in their theory, asserting that the apparent discontinuity meant the connecting fossil links had not yet been discovered. Who can beat that argument? Fossil hunters still have not found some of those links, and some modern scientists theorize that perhaps nature does make leaps.

The development of electric power was one of those enormous events that changed our history, affected our engines, transportation, homes, lifestyles, communications, science, distribution of population and industry, and it tied us to a central source of energy. Although many of the components existed before Edison, it was he who discovered how to put together and make workable the components to create the electric power industry.

The present structure of the electric utility industry may be the result of historical, political, accidental as well as economic causes, rather than the inevitable result of natural peculiarities of the industry. The concept of the regulated natural monopoly, if not already obsolete, may soon be. The dinosaur, a highly successful beast for a long time, disappeared relatively quickly, some say, apparently unable to cope with a massive change in the environment. For a while many wondered whether the electric utility industry would go the way of the dinosaur, unable to adapt to a new, more uncertain, more competitive environment that followed the disasters of the 1970s and 1980s. But, after several bankruptcies, many billions of dollars of losses, and numerous management changes, it looks as if the industry will still be around, in a leaner, more competitive, more flexible form.

9

Edison

I saw for the first time everything in practical operation. I saw that what had been done had never been made practically useful.[2]

Thomas A. Edison

Electric utilization technology is important since it is sometimes overlooked that electric energy cannot be produced and stored; electric energy can only be developed and used if the utilization equipment and technology for its use have first come into being.[3]

Philip Sporn

Neither electricity nor electric lighting began with Edison. The English led the way in the early years of the nineteenth century. In 1808, Sir Humphrey Davy sent a battery powered electric current through the space between two carbon rods and produced a blue-white arc of light. In 1831, Michael Faraday invented the dynamo, which, when turned by a steam engine, supplied a cheap electric current by means of electromagnetic induction.

America spawned a host of electricians, inventors, and tinkers. The telegraph, invented in 1844, depended on batteries and the wits of an army of itinerant, hard living telegraphers who learned about electricity first hand, improved the product, and took their knowledge elsewhere. Thomas Edison started as a telegrapher, improved the instrument, worked on the phonograph, and made viable that instrument of doubtful paternity, the telephone, before he went on to create the incandescent light and the electric utility industry.[4]

Davy's arc light caught on, despite drawbacks: the carbon burned up, the fumes were disagreeable and dangerous, the battery power was expensive, the light glared, and the lamps were wired in series. The arc lamp was used in a production of the Paris Opera in 1844, in English lighthouses in the 1860s, was exhibited in the Philadelphia Exposition of 1876, and lit the streets of Paris in 1877. The arc lamp, however, clearly was unsatisfactory for ordinary illumination. The gas light industry's monopoly seemed safe.

Beginning in 1820, a string of Frenchmen, Russians, British, and Americans tried to build an incandescent lamp. The electricity would light up a filament enclosed in a glass bulb that contained a vacuum or an inert gas. Because of a combination of imperfect vacuums and poorly chosen filaments, the experimenters could not create durable, workable lights. Perhaps the development of the high vacuum Crookes tube served to respark the interest that produced incandescent lamps from Joseph Swan in England and from Edison in the United States.

The Edison System

In 1878, Edison was looking for a new project for his Menlo Park laboratory, but decided against the intense arc light. With a characteristic insight that distinguished him from his competitors, Edison worked not only on the light but on the entire system of delivery. He described to reporters a system of central station power, with small household lights attached to meters. He decided that a slum district should be the first served because of the potential electric motor load. Edison said, "The same wire that brings the light will also bring power and heat — with the power you can run an elevator, a sewing machine, or any mechanical contrivance, and by means of the heat you may cook your food."[5] Scientists and rival inventors predicted failure, but Edison had a long string of successes behind him. Gas light stocks fell.

Grosvenor Lowrey, Western Union's lawyer, put together Edison's financial backing, a Morgan-Vanderbilt syndicate, after telling them that "Edison has discovered the means of giving us an electric light suitable for every day use, at vastly reduced cost as compared with gas."[6] The claims were grossly exaggerated. Nevertheless, on October 15, 1878, preliminary papers were drawn for the Edison Electric Light Co. Edison assigned to it all the electric light devices that he would invent in the next five years. The articles signed on November 15, 1878 said the company's "objects . . . are to own, manufacture, operate and license the use of various apparatus used in producing light, heat and power from electricity."[7]

In the year that followed, Edison worked on the vacuum, the filament, and a dynamo that maintained a constant pressure. By October 1879, Edison had a working incandescent lamp. Months later, he patented an electric distribution system. In 1880, Edison continued to improve his product and spent a great deal of time on the entire electric system while competitors stole his lighting ideas. He also made his first big sale, to Henry Villard of the Northern Pacific. Villard became an investor in the electric utilities and a founder of one of the great holding companies. Villard bought for the ship *S.S. Columbia* the first isolated lighting system sold.

Edison soon discovered that his backers wanted to collect patent royalties, not to invest new money in manufacturing facilities. (His backers also discovered that Edison was difficult to deal with, prone to making promises, did not keep to a schedule, and made no attempt to control expenditures.) Consequently, Edison had to set up on his own the Edison Lamp Co. to manufacture lamps, and the Edison Machine Works to manufacture dynamos. Both companies paid royalties to the Light Company.

The next question was: who would buy the lights and equipment? Edison conceived of the large central power station that would distribute through lines to the customers. That meant large capital expenditures, negotiations with city councils to get use of the streets, bribes, and delays in sales until the system was completed. Edison's backers instead favored sale of isolated power stations (for factories, hotels, yachts, and the residences of the rich). The Light Company organized the Edison Co. for Isolated Lighting and the Edison Electric Illuminating Co., the latter being its first electric utility. In the beginning, the electric utility industry had plenty of competition, despite the uniqueness of the product. Edison's lamp had to compete with gas light in the cities and with other forms of illumination elsewhere. And his utility had to compete with his isolated power plants.

Edison carefully planned the New York utility system. He picked an area in downtown New York because it had 1,500 gas light customers and the potential for 750 electric motors, so power could be sold both day and night. He wanted to serve the financial district for the prestige involved in doing so.

In characteristic Edisonian fashion, the great man's plans were overambitious, schedules fell by the wayside, the project came in at a cost several times over the estimate, and meters were not ready, all of which resulted in no bills for months. Investors were discouraged. September 4, 1882, however, the day on which the Pearl Street Station went into business to serve 85 customers with 400 lamps, marked the beginning of the electric utility industry.

By the end of 1883, only two cities had central station power. The banks would not lend money to finance the projects. Electricity was too expensive for the average customer, and remained so into the early 1900s. The isolated power plant (especially in small towns that did not have gas light) was the big seller (334 by the spring of 1883). Because some of the purchasers of equipment did not have enough cash to pay for all equipment or royalties, the Light Company or its affiliates had to take for payment the securities of many local lighting companies. To develop the electric utility industry would require a great deal of cash, and Edison's financiers were not eager to put up cash. Edison described the Light Company as "the leaden collar."[8] He took control of the company in 1884.

AC vs. DC

While Edison was seizing control of the Light Company, he was losing control of the technology of the industry. Thompson-Houston, a company that infringed on his patents, overtook Edison in building central stations. From a technological standpoint though, George Westinghouse, inventor of the air brake, saw the opportunity to break into the electrical industry in a way that quickly put Edison on the defensive. As Thomas P. Hughes pointed out, "The Edison system had a major technical flaw — the extreme expense of distributing electricity at low voltage."[9] Edison designed his lamp for 100V operation. At that low voltage, Edison's system suffered high transmission losses. Edison could not raise the voltage for transmission and then lower it for distribution because the device that raises or lowers voltage, the transformer, does not work with direct current.

With Edison's DC system, it was too expensive to distribute electricity more than one mile from the power station. In Europe the English firm of Gaulard and Gibbs and the Hungarian firm of Ganz and Company, in 1883-1885, developed alternating current transformers. In 1886, George Westinghouse formed the Westinghouse Electric Company, purchased the Gaulard and Gibbs rights, and started selling AC electric systems. Then in 1888, Nicola Tesla, a Croatian immigrant fired by Edison, announced his polyphase AC system. That same year Westinghouse bought the rights to Tesla's system. Westinghouse saw the potential for locating a central station at the source of water power or coal, shipping the power for great distances at high voltages, and then stepping down the power for distribution. Edison, with his investment in DC, opposed the new system, saying it was dangerous, which he decided to prove. Edison always had a good public relations sense. In 1888, he opened up his laboratory to Harold P. Brown, who developed the AC electric chair, as proof that AC was dangerous. Names were suggested for the process: electromort, dynamort, electrocide and Westinghoused (this last from Edison himself).

But inventing a practical AC system did not in itself solve all the problems. It just created others. Systems that were AC or DC could not be linked. Customers could not move their electrical equipment from one system to another. Charles S. Bradley, another former Edison worker, in 1888 invented the rotary converter, which converted DC to AC. Westinghouse bought him out. Then the Westinghouse engineers tackled another problem. The electric systems served different types of customers from different generators with different types of currents, often requiring their own circuits. For instance, low frequencies seemed better for motors and high frequencies for light bulbs, so one electrical system served motors and another lighting. Each had a small generator, because neither system was large enough to require a big one, so the system could not gain economy of scale in generation. (That is, the larger generator was more efficient than the smaller one.) Not to mention, of course, the added expense of having two sets of wires to carry the electricity. An electric company of the time might need different circuits for motors, streetcars, AC lamps, DC lamps, electric furnaces, and arc lighting.

The Westinghouse engineers developed a universal system in which the polyphase AC generator at the central station produced electricity that went to a local substation where it was transformed to the form required by the user. The system had many winning characteristics. One was a realization of economies of scale in generation. The second was the need for only one wiring grid. The third was that one generating station could serve a wider area. The fourth was that the new system could benefit from load diversity. The lighting load came at certain hours of the day, and the generator serving only that load would be idle the rest of the day. The streetcars took most of their electricity during the rush hours, and generators serving them might have little demand at other times. Factory motors took their electricity during the period between the rush hours. One generator connected to all three loads, running most of the time, might serve in the place of three generators each working part of the day. In 1893, the backers of a revolutionary plan to move electric power from Niagara Falls to Buffalo chose AC power. George Forbes, a British engineer involved in the project, commented: "The greatest step . . . in the distribution of electricity since . . . 1878 was the use of alternating currents . . . which was simply achieved . . . against the opinions of everybody who seemed to be capable of giving an opinion."[10] The universal system, in concrete form, became the Niagara Central Station Plan or Niagara Plan, the blueprint for future development in the USA. But it developed after fierce resistance from founding father Edison, in the war of the systems: AC vs. DC. In some cities, as will be noted later, there were utilities that supplied AC power and others that supplied DC. Edison backed the wrong horse and stubbornly clung to his notions, possibly because he could not accept the ideas of others.

Exit Edison

Edison also developed the first electric railroad, but he never pursued the concept because he was too busy setting up the Pearl Street Station. Draper, Van De Poele, and Sprague took up the idea and in 1886 the first electric street railway went into service. By 1889, there were 154 street railways in the United States. The street railway load soon exceeded that of electric lighting. Edison had always understood the importance of a power load to the success of his central station system. Ironically, that load came from a product whose development he dropped. Some of those railways produced their own power. The street railway company had the potential to serve other electric customers. The utility, on the other hand, could get the street railway's business if its price was sufficiently low. One could argue that the electric utility had to compete against the street railway's ability to produce power. Perhaps the load diversity of the universal system gave the utility the edge in terms of producing at lower costs.

In a little more than a decade, Edison put more than a half century of research into practical application, conceived and invented an entire industry, and then became a reactionary who hampered the industry's progress and threatened to fossilize it at a primitive stage of development. Edison's role in the industry ended bitterly. Henry Villard returned from Europe with the backing of powerful German firms and, in 1889, combined all the Edison ventures into the Edison General Electric Co. Villard wanted to create an international electric trust. The new holding company was to manufacture and sell central stations and to form new central station companies in which it owned 80% of the stock. The problems compounded themselves.

The new central stations would not show returns for several years. Edison did not develop new electrical products and fought AC systems. Thompson-Houston and Westinghouse grabbed away business until Edison General Electric only had about 40% of the industry's volume. The company needed cash and it needed an AC system. Villard discussed merger terms with Westinghouse, then with Thompson-Houston. At that point, in 1892, J.P. Morgan stepped back into the picture. He not only forced a merger with Thompson-Houston, but he put Thompson-Houston's management in charge. Villard was out. He devoted his time thereafter to running what became one of the huge utility holding companies, The North American Co. Another dispossessed Edison associate, Samuel Insull, took over the presidency of a small Chicago utility. Edison General Electric became General Electric. In 1896, General Electric and Westinghouse exchanged patents, a move typical of the age of trusts, so even General Electric used Westinghouse's concepts. The age of Edison had ended.

Chapter **10**

The Industry Organizes

We will make electric light so cheap that only the rich will be able to burn candles.[11]

Thomas A. Edison

The early years were confused ones. Franchises in a city often were non-exclusive and sometimes competitive. Each manufacturer would give a particular franchisee the exclusive right to use that manufacturer's equipment in a given territory. Some companies operating in the same city provided AC while others provided DC. Areas served varied from a city block "each way"[12] to the entire city. Companies had different purposes: arc lighting for streets, lighting for houses, power for industrial uses. In the same city, voltage and frequencies differed. In Chicago between 1882 and 1905, 29 franchises had been granted, three of which were citywide.

In Chicago, the city council was notoriously corrupt and the franchise negotiation centered around payoffs. At one point, a citywide franchise was granted to a group for no other purpose than to have the franchise bought out by a competitor. Such confusion and fragmentation made it difficult to develop standardized products, limited the mobility of large users of power, and — it later became evident — prevented the electric utility from achieving the benefits of load diversity and economies of scale. In a perverse way, however, the confusion and fragmentation created a healthy competition that prevented the technology of the electric industry from ossifying in its first decade and that caused the entrepreneurs who ran the utilities to experiment in the way they did business.

The Insull Analysis

By 1892, Samuel Insull and other leaders of the Association of Edison Illuminating Companies had formulated an understanding of the economics of the electric utility business that has remained basic to the industry to this day. Those leaders realized that the industry had high fixed costs because of the investment needed to meet peak load and to distribute power. At the same time, the cost of operating the plants was fairly low. The question became how to translate that into profits, especially in an industry in which managements had already concluded that they were selling a luxury item. (The Welsbach mantle had been introduced for gas lighting and gas was substantially less expensive than electricity.)

Insull of Chicago Edison was a leader. He began a sales campaign, cut prices below published schedules when necessary to get customers, and wrote long term contracts for large customers. Yet, did he know his costs? On a trip to England, Insull discovered the answer in Brighton, where Arthur Wright of the municipal power company had invented a demand meter. He set the price of electricity to cover two costs: fixed and operating. The price of the initial block of electricity would cover the fixed costs involved in meeting the maximum demand. The charge thereafter would largely cover operating costs. That meant that the price for the first block of usage would be high but that it would decline thereafter as quantity sold increased.

As Insull continued the analysis, he concluded that profit was determined not by load but by the percentage of time that the power plant was in use. The idea was to keep that plant running as much as possible and to find electric customers who would need power when other customers did not. As an example, the buildup in the traction load occurred during the rush hours, and the lighting load occurred at night after the traction load had fallen off.

The load for engines, motors, elevators, and other modes of business demand was sandwiched between the twin peaks of the traction load. The same power plant could serve all three loads because they did not occur simultaneously. The traction company, however, had its own power plant, the industrial user could have had its own isolated power plant, and the lighting customer depended on the utility. Three power plants could be replaced by one, thereby producing substantial savings in overhead costs. Diversity of load created savings. An additional saving could result from the use of large power plants, which seemed to be more economical than smaller ones. The utility could not only gain the savings from diversity of load, but it could also produce the power more cheaply (with its large generating unit built to serve many customers) than could the isolated customer with its small generating unit. The utility could benefit from diversity of load and from economies of scale.

Building the Business

The utilities supposedly produced 42% of all electricity in 1902 (and probably less than that due to the omission of reporting from the multitude of isolated power plants in hotels and other commercial and institutional establishments). How did the utility get customers to connect to it, to drop the gas company as a supplier, to use electric motors, to buy from the utility instead of self-generating? One answer was to run more efficiently, put in larger, better generators that required less fuel per kwh produced. Another was to build transmission lines that brought cheap hydroelectric power from dams to the load centers. The Niagara line was one of the first. As another example, in 1901, the Oakland Transit Company, a street railway operator, needed cheap power. The Bay Counties Power Company was formed to do the job, and built the longest transmission line in the world, 140 miles, from a hydroelectric

Table 10-1

Energy and the Economy on a Per Capita Basis
1882 - 1912
(1902 = 100)

| | Kwh Production | | | Energy | Real Prices of | | |
	From Utilities	All Sources	Real GNP	Usage (BTU)	Electricity	Oil	Coal
	(1)	(2)	(3)	(4)	(5)	(6)	(7)
1882	--	--	65E	49E	132	84	--
1892	16	--	89	74E	143	69	83
1902	100	100	100	100	100	100	100
1907	216	217	103	147	58	81	93
1912	378	342	97	154	46	76	84

Notes

Column 3:	NBER - Kendrick Series for GNP and GNP deflator (for all columns).
Column 5-7:	Residential (lighting) cost per kwh, oil revenue per barrel, bituminous coal per ton.

Sources

Columns 1-2, 4, 6-7:	U.S. Department of Commerce Bureau of the Census, *Historical Statistics of the United States 1789-1945* (Washington, D.C.: U.S. Government Printing Office, 1949), pp. 142-159.
Column 3:	U.S. Department of Commerce, Social and Economics Statistics Administration, *Long Term Economic Growth 1860-1970* (Washington, D.C.: U.S. Government Printing Office, 1973), pp. 182-183, 222-223.
Column 5	Edison Electric Institute, *EEI Pocketbook of Electric Utility Industry Statistics* (New York: EEI, 1977), p. 33.

site to Oakland, then tied three dams together over its transmission system and soon became a power wholesaler for the region. But customers had to find new uses for electricity, and they did, in a plethora of home appliances, and manufacturers had to appreciate that electricity required operating methods that were different. In the old factories, all machines were tied by belt to a revolving drive shaft turned by the central source of power. Originally, manufacturers thought of electricity as another means of turning the central shaft. Then they realized that machinery need not be physically tied to a central shaft at all. It could be operated independently, each machine with its own electric motor. That change allowed manufacturers to redesign the factories and the production processes. Consumption of electricity shot up, at a pace far greater than that of the economy or of other energy sources, while price fell, in real terms.

Generating capacity and sales rose astronomically, and in the early 1900s, the proportion of output self-generated by industry began to decline. The electric industry remained largely investor owned, with a steady fuel mix, but little else was steady. Utilities built larger plants, ran them more, and dramatically reduced fuel consumption per kwh.

The industry started with the lighting load, and its plant sat idle when the lights were out, as they were for much of the day. Persuading manufacturers to buy electricity from the local utility added the power sales component to the revenue mix. Then the electric railways not only grew in volume, but they switched more of their load to the local utility as opposed to generating all of their own needs. That new-found balance, diversity, added to revenues (Table 10-2).

Although electric utilities did an impressive job of building sales, and cutting costs, the financial results were unimpressive even thirty years after the pioneering era. Given the accounting standards of the day, it is difficult to draw conclusions with certainty, but it appears that the industry was depreciating its plant as if the facilities would last for more than 100 years. If depreciation expense were adjusted upward, to reflect writedown of plant over 30 to 40 years, then reported earnings for common stockholders would be halved, and with realistic accounting the electric utility shareholder actually earned a return no greater than what would have been available by buying a corporate bond. That is scarcely an indicator that the managements knew their costs, priced their product properly, or exercised their monopoly power to extract unconscionable profits. (More details are available in Chapter 11.)

One fact was certain: the United States led the world in the field of electrification. Comparing the activities in Chicago, Berlin and London shows the results of smart marketing and efficient operations (Table 10-3). Insull in Chicago sold more electricity per capita, ran larger power stations, kept the plants running longer during the day, did the job with less of a generating reserve, convinced the normally independent streetcars companies to take power from the utility, and charged customers less. Whether the American utility magnates of the early days were doing their shareholders any good or not, they were an enterprising, aggressive lot who

Table 10-2

Electric Utility Generation and Distribution
1887-1912

	Losses	Lighting	Power	Railway	Total
	(1)	(2)	(3)	(4)	(5)
%					
1887	25	69	6	0	100
1892	25	63	10	2	100
1897	31	61	6	2	100
1902	28	42	26	4	100
1907	23	32	25	20	100
1912	22	24	28	26	100
Kwh-millions					
1887	44	120	11	0	175
1892	75	190	30	5	300
1897	250	485	50	15	800
1902	650	985	602	100	2,337
1907	1,331	1,870	1,500	1,160	5,862
1912	2,546	2,752	3,254	3,017	11,569

Notes

  Losses (Col.1) includes utility use. Lighting (2) equivalent to residential and commercial. Power (3) is largely industrial. Railway (4) includes local traction and interurban.

Source

  Electrical World, Vol. 80, No. 11, p.546

worked with zeal to overcome obstacles and who sold their product with religious fervor.

Industry Structure

Why did the industry evolve as it did in the image of the gas industry? Edison controlled only one central station company, which was not a financial success for years, so one cannot attribute the industry's structure to him, although he did conceive the setup. Could the traction company have expanded its generation to non-rush hours and sold the load over the electric utility's lines? Could the isolated industrial plant have done the same? Could the generation and transmission company, as exemplified by Bay Counties Power Company, have developed into an independent component of the industry? Was there an inherent advantage to one company having a monopoly over all aspects of electric power production,

Table 10-3

Chicago, Berlin, London
1910-1912

	Chicago	Berlin	London
Sales/capita (kwh)	291	83	49
Average size of power station (kw 1000s)	37	23	5
Load Factor (%)	41	33	25
Reserve Margin (%)	12	44	60
Sales Mix (%)			
Lighting	19	24	61
Power	12	45	27
Traction	69	31	12
	100	100	100
Price/Kwh (¢)	2.2	3.9	4.8

Source

Thomas H. Hughes, *Networks of Power*
(Baltimore: Johns Hopkins, 1983), p.258)

transmission, and distribution? Several possible answers exist:

♦ An inherent advantage existed in load diversity, economies of scale in generation, and economies of scale in serving many customers (such as in billing and maintenance).
♦ The technology of the time did not allow for a system with power derived from various sources.
♦ Potential competitors had so many problems with their principal businesses that they could not worry about ancillary activities.
♦ The electric utility business was insufficiently profitable to warrant the attention of potential competitors.
♦ The electric utility pursued a low price policy — either because it did not know its true costs or because it was sufficiently farsighted to give up current profits for future gains — that forced out the competition.

Despite its acceptance in industry folklore, the first and easiest explanation is not completely convincing as the sole explanation. It is hard to see, for instance, what major additional economies of operation occur as a result of owning businesses as different as local distribution, long distance transmission, and power generation. Competition between generators of energy (in sales through a common distribution grid) might have been a problem, given the many kinds of equipment in existence in the early days, but not after the spread of AC and standardization of frequencies and voltages. The traction companies were shaky financially, heavily in debt on a short-term basis, and the panic of 1896 sent a number of them into bankruptcy. The traction magnates may have had their hands full with their own ventures. Electric utilities were not extraordinarily profitable, borrowed heavily to produce a decent return on equity, and did not have what would now be considered sound accounting practices. In addition, some of the electric utility managements were determined as well as farsighted, and pushed their service at every opportunity. Finally, that was the age of the trust. The Sherman Act, passed in 1890, was rendered toothless by unenthusiastic enforcement and later by a Supreme Court ruling that reasonable trusts were legal. For a businessman to attempt to drive out or to buy out his competitors was not unusual. Those who did so did not need to develop a natural monopoly rationale. Furthermore, financial and manufacturing interests made large sums by consolidating and controlling numerous firms in an industry, regardless of whether the newly joined businesses were more or less profitable or efficient than before. Traction and lighting companies often fell under common ownership, and that either destroyed the possibility of competition or helped those companies to realize the benefits of natural monopoly, depending on one's outlook. Clearly, the industry's structure developed for a variety of reasons.

Perhaps the triumph of the electric utility over the isolated supplier occurred because the utility was willing to settle for (or consistently ended up with) a lower return than the isolated supplier. Under those circumstances, there would be little point in competing with the utility.

Financing and Regulation

Financing patterns for the industry evolved during that period. Originally, the industry sold 20-year sinking fund mortgage bonds, with the mortgage on a particular property. (A sinking fund requires payment of part of the debt each year.) That was not ideal for an industry constantly in need of cash. Insull innovated by developing an open-ended mortgage not linked to a particular property, with no limit on amount outstanding, without sinking fund, and with a 45-year maturity. The debt outstanding could reach 75% of the completed plant. Insull also had peculiar notions of depreciation: "The Insull theory was that there was no such thing as depreciation until definite action was taken to retire facilities as obsolete or inadequate. Then the retirement was spread out over future years."[13]

To pull off that kind of financing, one had to be able to convince the investor that the utility would be around for a long time. Unfortunately, the franchise handed out by the city council was often for a shorter period than the life of the utility plant. The city councils of that day were notoriously corrupt. Franchises were granted on receipt of payoffs and franchises were not renewed when the franchisee fell out of political favor. Perhaps if the granting of the franchise and the regulation (what little there was) of the utility were in the hands of a non-partisan state agency instead of a partisan city council, financing would have been easier and cheaper.

That raised the question: would it be easier to sell all those securities, which depended on the unchanging character of the industry and the permanence of the utility, if the utility had no competition? With no sinking funds, no depreciation to speak of, and no funds set aside to pay debt, the industry could only pay off debt by selling new debt. The investor had to have confidence in the long term future of the utility to make such an investment.

In 1897, Charles Tyson Yerkes, the streetcar magnate of Chicago, got fed up with paying off the city council. His allies introduced in the state legislature a reform bill to extend the streetcar franchise for 50 years and to put streetcar companies under the jurisdiction of a non-partisan state agency. Unfortunately, a reporter got wind of a fund Yerkes had set up to buy votes, and the legislation was killed. That may have been the first serious attempt to bring about state regulation.

In 1898, in his presidential address before the National Electric Light Association (NELA), Insull proposed that electric utilities be regulated by state agencies that would fix rates and set service standards. If a community did not like the service it was getting, it could buy the utility at the depreciated value of the plant. The idea did not go over well, and NELA set up a committee to discuss the matter.

The idea became increasingly appealing as a movement grew to make the electric utility business municipally owned. Between 1896 and 1906, the number of municipal systems more than tripled. If the public favored the municipally owned system as opposed to the unregulated investor owned utility, perhaps the public would relent if the investor owned utility were regulated so that it could not take advantage of consumers. In 1907, both NELA and the National Civic Federation came out in favor of state regulation of electric companies. In that year also, three states established regulatory agencies. By 1916, 33 states had such agencies.

The electric industry was regulated, partly because of economies of scale and partly because of political needs. In fact, Douglas Anderson, in a study of the origins of regulation, concluded that:

> the concept of state regulation was both compatible with the ideas and political needs of progressives and expedient for safeguarding the material interests of the utilities. From 1907 to 1913, philosophical compatibility and commercial expediency combined to produce a political necessity.[14]

Was the electric utility industry regulated because it was a monopoly, or did it become a monopoly because it was regulated? The standard texts always assume the former and never ask the question. Perhaps the answer is not as self-evident if the question is asked.

Competition in the electric utility industry had all the hazards expected in an industry with high fixed and low variable costs. The competitors could cut prices until only variable costs were covered. "Cutthroat competition" it was called. If a utility had overexpanded, it would have every reason to cut prices to induce as much demand as possible to cover at least part of its fixed costs, possibly thereby ruining a competitor. As Eli Clemens put it:

> Before the passage of the public utility laws competition was looked upon with favor and the resulting rate wars were seen as the only means of escaping from outrageous monopoly prices. Any advantages were purely of short duration. . . .[15]

Why? Because the price war ended with the destruction of one competitor, or with a merger of the competitors. The war ended and the winner jacked up prices to recoup losses. At another point, Clemens notes:

> Some industries may seek regulation and public utility status to escape the rigors of a competitive life. Other industries may prefer the profits of the open market and may be more or less forcibly placed in the public utility category. . ..[16]

The business cycle must also have had some effect on the utility executives. Perhaps prices could be adjusted upward by regulation during the slack periods to protect profitability. That would only work, however, if the regulators prevented would-be competitors from undercutting the utility's higher price. That is, a monopoly would help to preserve profitability. As J.M. Clark wrote:

> It soon became evident that railroads were not the only industry using large fixed capital and subject to the "peculiarities" of constant and variable costs. It became evident that economic law did not insure prices that would yield "normal" returns on invested capital, because the capital could not get out if it wanted to, and so had to take whatever it could get.[17]

In other words, the utility management may have sought regulation to maintain profitability. The origin of regulation, thus, may not simply be the inevitable result of a natural monopoly situation.

Structure in Place

By the early 1900s, the industry's structure had evolved into the integrated (distribution, transmission, and generation) utility company operating under state or local regulation that reinforced the exclusive nature of the local franchise. The utilities realized economies of scale in generation. They took advantage of savings derived from diversity to bring in more customers. The next step involved geographic expansion and regional integration.

Chapter 11

Expansion and Holding Companies

Corporations have always been susceptible to control by concentration of voting power . . . But it is elemental . . . that, the larger the number of shareholders, the more easily may a small concentrated block of minority shares exercise sway over all the rest . . . But the more important point to note is that, the wider the diffusion of ownership, the more readily does effective control run to the intermediaries. Financially, the matter is dangerous, for it tends to transform a contingent outstanding charge upon earnings into virtually fixed charges thereon. The cessation of dividends, either to employee holders or to consumers, is bound to be so productive of discontent and unrest that every nerve will be strained to the utmost, even overlong, to prevent their cessation.[18]

William Z. Ripley

The industry expanded in every way. Managements pushed for increasingly large and efficient equipment. New transmission lines made it possible to expand service from the central cities into rural areas. Sales promotion efforts pushed the use of electricity for more than lighting. Rationalization of franchises, diversity of load, the economies of scale that occurred with larger units, improved transmission facilities, and attempts by utility managements to forestall potential competition by buying up competitors all reduced the number of electric power systems. The price for electricity fell, both absolutely and relatively. Manufacturers developed new uses for electricity. Demand skyrocketed.

Electrifying the Economy

The electric utility industry put in facilities that lowered the costs of production: replacing the old reciprocating engine of Edison's day with the steam turbines invented in England by Charles Parsons in 1884, installing larger and more efficient generators, bringing in cheap hydropower from distant sites. At the same time, between 1900 and World War I, enterprising inventors developed new electrical appliances, such as the vacuum cleaner, radiant heating, the washing machine, the refrigerator and the lumbago belt. By 1911, thanks to the development of the ductile metal filament lamp, electric lighting had ceased to be a luxury compared to gas lighting. After the war inventors produced the electric razor, the dishwasher and the

Table 11-1

Electricity Output and Pricing
(1902 - 100)

	Electricity Production		Total		Real Price of		
	Total	Utility Only	Energy Consumption	Real GNP	Electricity	Coal	Oil
	(1)	(2)	(3)	(4)	(5)	(6)	(7)
1902	100	100	100	100	100	100	100
1907	237	234	161	126	78	91	81
1912	415	461	185	142	62	84	76
1917	728	1,015	235	157	42	114	110
1922	1,025	1,740	207	176	36	138	103
1927	1,699	3,008	276	226	35	90	82
1932	1,665	3,166	201	176	46	74	69

Notes

Column 4:   NBER - Kendrick Series (1958 $).

Column 5-7:   Average utility revenue per kwh (5), average realization per ton of bituminous coal (6), average realization per barrel of oil (7), all deflated by GNP deflator (NBER - Kendrick to 1927, BEA in 1932).

Sources

Columns 2-3, 5-7: *Historical Statistics (1789 - 1945)*, pp. 142, 146, 155-159.

Column 4:   *Long-Term Economic Growth 1860 - 1970*, pp. 182-183

electric mouse trap, too. With electricity prices falling compared to other energy sources, thanks to greater economy of operations, not only did electricity production rise faster than overall consumption of energy and economic activity, but production by electric utilities rose even faster than electricity production as a whole. (See Tables 11-1 and 11-2.) Electricity lighted more homes over time, but remained out of reach for the bulk of the population until the late 1920s. Electric power, though, made faster inroads in the industrial sector. (See Table 11-3.) Furthermore, outside the commercial and industrial sector, the industry convinced the electric traction companies to buy electricity from it instead of relying wholly on self generation. (See Table 11-4.)

Operating Better

Originally, the electric utility industry was urban-oriented. DC power could

Table 11-2

Electricity Capacity and Output
1902-1932

| | Generating Capacity (a) (c) | | | Utility % of Total Capacity | Generation (b) (c) | | | Utility % of Total Generation | Investor-owned Utilities % of Utility | |
	Utility	Industrial	Total	Capacity	Utility	Industrial	Total	Generation	Capacity	Generation
	(1)	(2)	(3)	(4)	(5)	(6)	(7)	(8)	(9)	(10)
1902	1.2	1.8	3.0	40	2.5	3.5	6.0	42	91	92
1907	2.7	4.1	6.8	40	5.9	8.2	14.1	42	92	95
1912	5.2	5.8	11.0	47	11.6	13.2	24.8	47	92	95
1917	9.0	6.5	15.5	58	25.4	18.0	43.4	59	94	96
1922	14.2	6.3	20.5	69	43.6	17.6	61.2	71	95	95
1927	25.1	9.5	34.6	73	75.4	26.0	101.4	74	93	94
1932	34.3	8.5	42.8	80	79.4	20.0	99.4	80	93	94

Notes

(a)   Millions of KW.

(b)   Millions of Kwh.

(c)   Traction included in industrial category.

Sources

EEI Pocketbook (1979) and *Historical Statistics (1789-1945)*.

Table 11-3

Electrification of the Economy
1899 - 1932

| | % of Population in Electrically Lighted Dwellings | Power in American Industry (Horsepower) | |
| | | Mechanical (%) | Electrical (%) |
	(1)	(2)	(3)
1899	—	95	5
1902	2E	—	—
1904	—	88	12
1907	8E	—	—
1909	—	74	26
1912	16	—	—
1914	—	61	39
1917	24	—	—
1919	—	45	55
1922	39	—	—
1925	—	27	73
1927	63	—	—
1932	70	—	—

Sources

Column 1:   *Electrical World*, various issues.

Column 2-3:   *Electrical World*, Vol.91, No.1, p 34.

not be distributed far from the central station. Isolated generating stations served the small towns even after the systems within a city had been tied together. Yet there were clear advantages to tying together the urban and rural loads, as Samuel Insull discovered. He noted that Chicago had a winter peak and the farm towns a summer peak. Although transmission costs were high between towns, large scale central station generation was cheaper than having numerous isolated power plants.

Other companies also consolidated various local systems, to tie together efficient power plants with small local distribution systems. Even that was not enough, as power plants grew larger. In Pennsylvania, where Gifford Pinchot was governor, the state developed the Giant Power scheme, under the guidance of engineer Morris Cooke. That proposal, made in 1925, called for giant mine-mouth power stations connected by high voltage transmission lines to local distribution

Table 11-4

Electric Utility
Sales to Ultimate Customers
1902-1932

Kwh-millions	Residential	Commercial and Industrial	Other	Total
	(1)	(2)	(3)	(4)
1902	0.1E	2.0E	0.1E	2.2
1907	0.3E	3.9E	1.0E	5.2
1912	0.9	6.3	2.6	9.8
1917	1.7	15.4	4.4	21.5
1922	3.9	26.3	5.7	35.9
1927	7.7	45.3	8.3	61.3
1932	11.9	43.1	8.7	63.7
%				
1902	5E	90E	5E	100
1907	6E	75E	19E	100
1912	9	64	27	100
1917	8	72	20	100
1922	11	73	16	100
1927	13	73	14	100
1932	19	67	14	100

Notes

Other (Column 3) largely traction railway sales.

Sources

Historical Statistics (1789-1945), p. 159.

utilities. Cooke's Giant Power Survey Board upset existing utilities by advocating the licensing of new companies that could enter the generating and transmission businesses. The industry opposed the legislation, with one detractor raising the specter of communism, and the proposal died. But, in 1926, Philadelphia Electric got a license to develop the Conowingo hydroelectric project, which was of such a size that the electricity had to be sold throughout the region. Three companies, Philadelphia Electric, Pennsylvania Power and Light, and New Jersey's Public Service Electric and Gas, decided to set up a regional transmission network to allow them to share Conowingo's output, and that of other power stations, and to benefit from load diversity throughout the region. The 1927 agreement by the three companies created the PNJ Interchange, the first integrated, centrally dispatched power pool in the nation. The PNJ interchange allowed the three utilities benefits from load diversity, because the greatest demands on the three systems did not come at the same times, and to save money by only operating the most efficient facilities in the

Table 11-5

Electric Utility
Operating Statistics
1902-1932

	Production per KW of Generating Capacity (Kwh)	Average Size of Utility Plant Prime Mover (KW)	Coal Equivalent burned per Kwh Generated (lbs.)	Hydroelectric % of Generation (%)	Hydroelectric % of Capacity (%)
	(1)	(2)	(3)	(4)	(5)
1902	2,068	539	6.5	—	24
1907	2,164	847	5.5	—	33
1912	2,240	1,467	4.0	39	33
1917	2,838	2,061	3.5	40	31
1922	3,074	3,813	2.5	39	29
1927	3,007	6,765	1.8	38	27
1932	2,309	8,539	1.5	41	27

Sources

Historical Statistics (1789 - 1945) for all columns.

Electrical World (various issues) for column 3.

three systems.

Overall, though, the utilities squeezed greater output per kilowatt of capacity out of their facilities, put in service larger and larger plants to take advantage of economies of scale, burned less and less fuel to produce a kwh, and derived a large proportion of output from low-cost hydroelectric projects. (See Table 11-5.)

During much of this era of sales growth and technological progress, electric utilities managed to earn unspectacular profits (probably even more unimpressive than they appear if the books properly accounted for depreciation expenses). The stock market performance of utility shares seems to verify that conclusion. (See Table 11-6.)

Holding Companies Form

Taking control of a number of smaller systems and putting them together could be profitable and would help to consolidate the overly fragmented industry. Centralized ownership, moreover, could facilitate raising money and engineering

Table 11-6

Financial Ratios and Market Indicators
Investor Owned Electric Utilities

| | Return on Average | | Debt Ratio | Depreciation Reserve as % of Plant | Dividend Payout Ratio | Average Bond Yields | Average Stock Price Index | |
| | Capitalization | Common Equity | | | | | Utilities | Industrials |
	(1)	(2)	(3)	(4)	(5)	(6)	(7)	(8)
1902	—	—	—	—	—	3.3	117	38
1907	—	—	—	—	—	3.8	72	37
1912	5.2	7.1	47	3.1	43	3.9	86	50
1917	5.7	7.8	49	5.6	54	4.1	74	63
1922	7.5	10.3	53	8.1	60	4.9	71	65
1927	7.4	11.2	54	6.6	89	4.3	116	119
1932	6.3	7.9	53	7.9	95	4.7	79	47

Notes
Columns 1-6:   in %
Column 6:   20 year corporate bonds
Columns 7-8:   Cowles indices

Sources
Columns 1-5:   EEI Pocketbook
Columns 6-8:   Historical Statistics (1789-1945), pp. 279-281.

the best systems. The electric utility holding company, which could be traced to Edison's original plans and similar efforts of United Gas Improvement, blossomed. The original electric utility holding companies were established for a variety of reasons. The North American Company was the creation of Henry Villard, who enthusiastically invested in utility operating companies and who attempted to turn Edison General Electric into a worldwide trust. The North American Company, established in 1890, was reorganized from Villard's old Oregon and Transcontinental Co. (Its steamship Columbia had the first isolated power plant in 1880.) Villard wanted to take over all the electric utilities in a thickly populated area and to gain profits from the economies associated with unitary control. He started with Milwaukee, bought traction lines in St. Louis, and purchased a minority interest in Detroit Edison. In the same year, Thompson-Houston set up United Electric Securities to own the holdings of companies that had paid for equipment with securities.

American Light and Traction was founded in 1900 to buy local utilities. From that point, the holding company was on its way. Electric Bond & Share, which held securities paid to General Electric for equipment, was established in 1905. The original reasons to set up a holding company were as different as the companies themselves:

♦ Engineering firms received stock in utilities for services rendered. (If the utility failed, the engineers might end up with the whole utility.)
♦ Investment holding firms might be forced to take over companies that they promoted which had performed poorly.
♦ Equipment manufacturers took securities instead of cash.
♦ Operating gains could be derived from consolidation or common ownership.

The profits to the holding company also were derived in diverse ways:

♦ The obvious way: efficient operation increased the value of the securities owned.
♦ The holding company provided engineering services to subsidiaries at an inflated cost.
♦ The holding company collected big fees for arranging financing for the subsidiaries.

The states regulated the operating subsidiaries that sold electricity. Their expenses were passed on to customers. Nobody regulated the holding companies. In 1927, the U.S. Supreme Court made it more difficult for states to control the activities of a local operating utility.[19] The case involved the sale by a Rhode Island utility of electricity to a Massachusetts utility at a price that the Rhode Island regulators thought was too low. The court said that the sale involved interstate commerce, which was not the business of state regulators. Obviously, a holding company could arrange interstate transactions between subsidiaries, and not care what local regulators thought, as long as it could convince Federal regulators (the Federal Power Commission) that all was well. Nobody could stop it from over-charging the subsidiaries. There was a definite advantage to controlling large congeries of subsidiaries because the bigger and more numerous the subsidiaries, the more money that could be milked from them for the benefit of the parent holding company. Naturally it was good business to control the greatest possible assets with as little capital as possible. The best way to do so was to engage in pyramiding (a small amount of capital at the top of the pyramid controls huge assets under it) and to see to it that outside shareholders had as few rights as possible. Some holding companies were solid operations run for no other purpose than to coordinate and make efficient the operations of the subsidiary companies. But the holding company movement became a craze because of the promotional profits to be made. The holding companies were condemned and fell because of the excesses committed. The present structure of the electric utility industry is the direct result of legislation designed to destroy the holding company that did not have an operating rationale for its existence.

As promoters saw the huge profits to be gained from the holding company business, they began to bid against each other to buy operating properties to put into the holding companies. Sometimes the promoters had to resort to odd measures to make things look good. One could, for instance, combine electric and ice properties, hiding the fact that most of the earnings were coming from the competitive, unsafe, and dwindling ice business. A good promoter could put together a combination of companies, sell preferred stock and bonds to the public to pay for the properties, take 10% or more as a commission, and keep the bulk (or all) of the voting common stock of the holding company, thereby remaining in control without having paid a cent into the business.

Between 1922 and 1927, the number of holding companies rose from 102 to 180, while the number of operating companies fell from 6,355 to 4,409. The mania for acquisition finally led, in 1928, to an investigation by the Federal Trade Commission. In 1932, the eight largest holding companies controlled 73% of the investor owned electric business.

The structure of Insull's empire gives an idea of how things worked. The Insull interests controlled 69% of the stock of Corporation Securities and 64% of the stock of Insull Utility Investments. Those two companies together owned 28% of the voting stock of Middle West Utilities. Middle West Utilities owned eight holding companies, five investment companies, two service companies, two secu-rities companies, and 14 operating companies. It also owned 99% of the voting stock of National Electric Power. National in turn owned one holding company, one service company, one paper mill, and two operating companies. It also owned 93% of the voting stock of National Public Service. National Public Service owned three building companies, three miscellaneous firms, and four operating utilities. It also owned 100% of the voting stock of Seaboard Public Service. Seaboard

Public Service owned the voting stock of five utility operating companies and one ice company. The utilities, in turn, owned eighteen subsidiaries.

The Insull empire operated in 32 states, and owned electric companies, textile mills, ice houses, a paper mill, and a hotel. With a capital investment of about $27 million, Insull controlled at least half a billion dollars of assets in 1930. What made that job so easy was that voting stock constituted a small portion of the capitalization of the constituent corporations within the empire. One could argue, in fact, that Insull controlled the lowest level operating companies by means of an investment equivalent to less than 0.01% of the securities issued by those subsidiaries. Figure 11-1 shows the structure of the empire.

Leverage Explained

The leveraged structure served to magnify the fluctuations in income shown at the subsidiary level. Even worse, however, was that investors might forget their standing in the structure. The common stockholders of a subsidiary operating company might be safer than the debt holder of the top tier holding company. We can illustrate that with a simple example. (See Figure 11-2.)

All the voting stock of the top holding company, Universal Electric Holding Co., is owned by the promoters who set up the deal. With a $50 investment, they control, through the Eastern States Securities subholding company, two electric operating companies and one ice company (Down East Electric, White Mountain Power, and Hudson River Ice) with $12,000 of assets. Those companies have to sell (altogether) $400 a year of securities, which is arranged (for a fee) by the holding company and sold through the promoter (for a commission). The fee and commission amount to $40 a year. The two operating companies also pay an inflated service charge to Universal for engineering advice and services. Furthermore, Universal's promoters have just bought another electric company for $3,000 and they intend to sell it to Eastern States Securities for $4,000 (the extra $1,000 being a finder's fee). On top of all those benefits, there were opportunities to misrepresent the financial picture of the system by creating fictitious profits from the sale (at inflated prices) of one company to another within the system.

If we exclude all the extras and look at the leverage inherent in the business, the cardinal principles of holding company finance would be as follows:

♦ The senior securities of the top holding company are junior to the junior securities of the operating company.
♦ Everything that happens at the operating company level is magnified by the time it reaches the holding company level.

We can trace the flow of income from the three operating companies to the parent holding company, starting with a good year. (See Figure 11-3.)

Figure 11-1
The Insull Organization

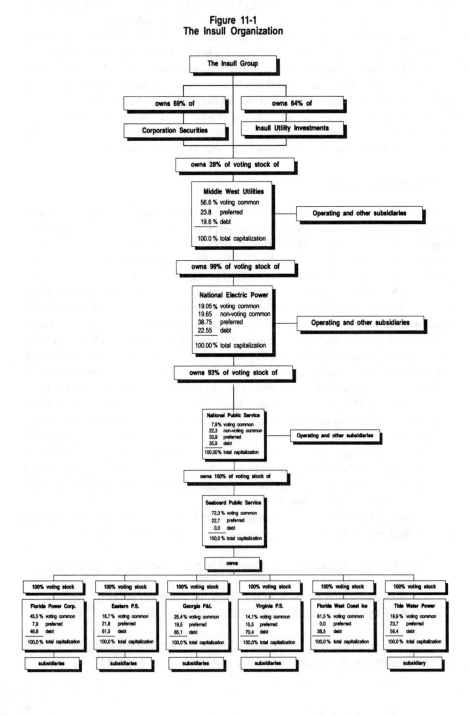

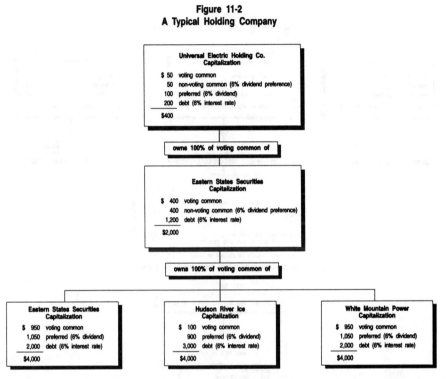

Figure 11-2
A Typical Holding Company

Then earnings decline because the economy slows down and the ice business suffers from a cool summer and from the inroads of the electric refrigerator. The consequences are catastrophic. In tracing the flow of income, keep in mind that the non-voting common stock has a preference for dividends over the voting common, so that it might be paid a cash dividend while the voting common gets nothing. (See Figure 11-4.)

Thus, a 25% decrease in operating income at the operating subsidiary level wipes out the ability of the top holding company, Universal, to pay its preferred and common dividends as well as its interest obligations. Note that owners of preferred stock and non-voting common of Eastern States were paid but not the preferred stockholders or debt holders of Universal. Junior security holders of subsidiaries are ahead of senior security holders of the parent.

Failure

Promotion of securities from within the holding company group became big business. Not only did the investment bankers sell securities to the general public, but the companies also sold securities to employees, and the meter readers peddled securities to unsuspecting customers of the utility. Many of the purchasers did not

Figure 11-3
The Flow of Income in Good Times

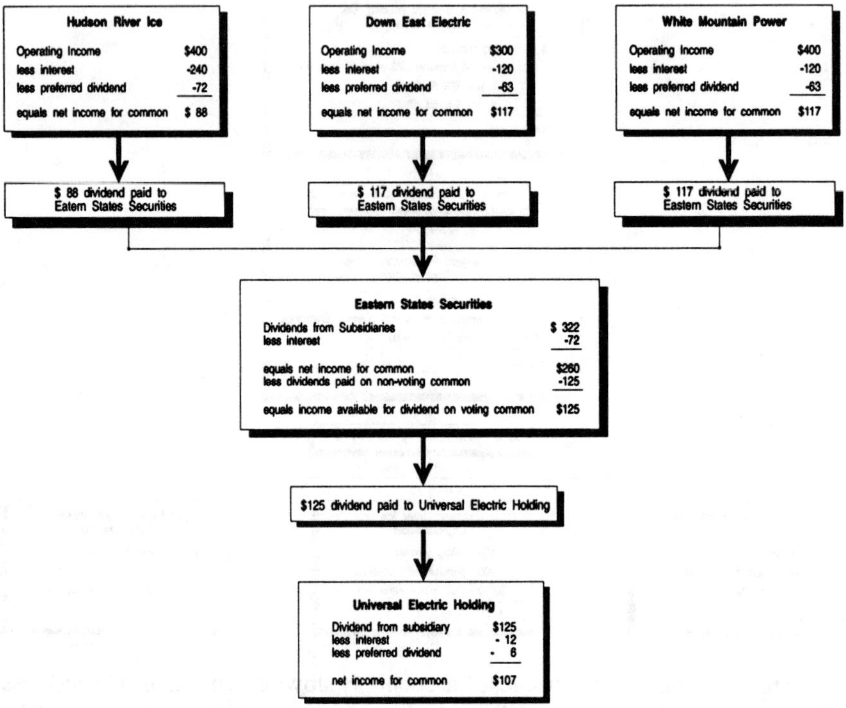

Hudson River Ice	
Operating Income	$400
less interest	-240
less preferred dividend	-72
equals net income for common	$ 88

Down East Electric	
Operating Income	$300
less interest	-120
less preferred dividend	-63
equals net income for common	$117

White Mountain Power	
Operating Income	$400
less interest	-120
less preferred dividend	-63
equals net income for common	$117

$ 88 dividend paid to Eastern States Securities

$ 117 dividend paid to Eastern States Securities

$ 117 dividend paid to Eastern States Securities

Eastern States Securities	
Dividends from Subsidiaries	$ 322
less interest	-72
equals net income for common	$260
less dividends paid on non-voting common	-125
equals income available for dividend on voting common	$125

$125 dividend paid to Universal Electric Holding

Universal Electric Holding	
Dividend from subsidiary	$125
less interest	- 12
less preferred dividend	- 6
net income for common	$107

understand what they were buying, thereby increasing their bitterness when the securities proved to be poor investments.

Why did the holding companies fail?

♦ Financial leverage magnified the effect of the economic downturn on the successive layers within the holding company system.

♦ Continued expansion of facilities into the Depression created liabilities that became a strain to the system when new demand for service did not materialize to produce a return on the new facilities.

♦ Overpayment for operating properties created obligations that could not be met when the income from the properties did not rise at the expected rate.

♦ Banks called loans that already had been invested in fixed assets, so no cash was available to pay off the loans.

♦ Excursions into non-electric businesses were often unsuccessful and proved disastrous when the Depression came.

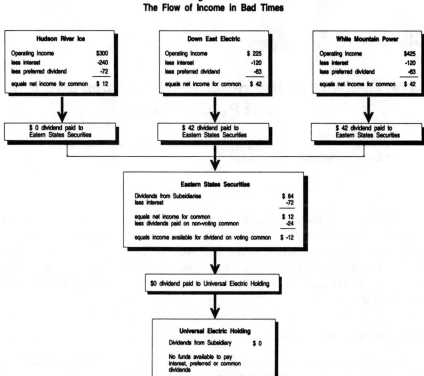

Figure 11-4
The Flow of Income in Bad Times

♦ Some money raised by the holding company used securities of the subsidiaries as collateral. When the market declined in 1929, the value of the collateral fell below the level required by the collateral agreement, thereby triggering demand for payment. The holding companies lacked ready cash, so they defaulted on the loans.

♦ The questionable transactions of some managements reduced investor confidence and encouraged punitive action from the government.

Many of the holding companies might have survived the Depression and continued in business to this day if left alone. The mood of the times was against them, however, and legislation shattered those giant combines into hundreds of component parts.

Chapter 12

The Breakup of the Holding Companies and the Rise of Public Power

A Holding Company is a thing where you hand an accomplice the goods while the policeman searches you.[20]

Will Rogers

The New Deal encompassed the Great Depression and World War II. During the Depression, sales sagged, but the local operating utilities remained solvent. During the war, they expanded again. That was not the only story, though. The New Deal turned the industry upside down, breaking up the holding companies, building up governmentally owned power agencies, and spreading electrification to rural America.

Government Ownership

The idea of Government ownership of utilities did not spring forth Athenalike, fully developed from the collective heads of Franklin D. Roosevelt's Brain Trust. At the turn of the century, there were numerous municipally owned electric utility systems. In fact, in terms of numbers, municipally owned systems outnumbered privately owned ones through the mid-1920s.

Until 1905, Congress let utilities build and operate dams "for ever and for nothing," to quote Gifford Pinchot, Theodore Roosevelt's Chief Forester.[21] Under Roosevelt, the Federal Government began to charge fees for the erection of dams on navigable rivers and it limited the period of use through licenses. In 1920, the Federal Power Commission was set up to regulate the rates, financing, and services of its hydropower licensees.

The Federal Government took a small role in the generation of electric power, even under Herbert Hoover, who sponsored the Boulder Dam, but who argued that the Government-generated power should be sold to investor owned utilities. The Federal Government also owned a dam at Muscle Shoals in Alabama, a dam built to supply power to a World War I nitrate works. Republicans hoped to sell the dam to private interests, but Senator Norris of Nebraska led the opposition that kept Muscle Shoals in Federal hands.

George Norris typified the opposition to private power. He fought for public ownership of power facilities in Nebraska, and he saw "the dawn of the electric age," but he did not want to see it develop by means of private ownership. "The power trust is the greatest monopolistic corporation that has been organized for private greed," he declared, and then went on to accuse it of buying legislatures, clergymen and even the Boy Scouts.[22] Al Smith wanted New York State to own and operate hydropower facilities. Franklin Roosevelt, the next Governor of New York, planned to have the state build a hydro plant on the St. Lawrence River. John Dewey and Felix Frankfurter saw electric power in terms of a great social issue.

To what did those leaders object? The electric utility industry — despite a jerry-built financial structure and the exploitation of subsidiaries — had a good record of lowering prices and extending service, although only about two-thirds of the population and 10% of farms had electricity. Perhaps the feeling was that electric power was an extraordinary force the development of which had to be pushed beyond the limits set by the need to make a profit. Perhaps the anti-utility sentiment was opposition to the excesses of the holding company craze. Perhaps it was nothing more than a continuation of populism. Whatever the reason, private power was a political issue, as was Government exploitation of hydroelectric sites. (It may be a simplification, but some might have argued that the rivers belonged to the people and so should the power.)

New Deal Activism

On September 21, 1932, in Portland, Oregon, Democratic candidate Franklin D. Roosevelt delivered a speech in which he presented his power policies. Roosevelt denounced the "Insull monstrosity" and implied that other public utilities operated at the same level. He then proposed that the Federal Government establish four hydropower projects: the St. Lawrence, Muscle Shoals, Boulder Dam, and the Columbia. "Each of these in each of the four quarters of the United States will be forever a national yardstick to prevent extortion against the public and to encourage the wider use of that servant of the people — electric power."[23]

Within a year, the Roosevelt Administration began to implement the promises. The huge projects, which furnished work to the unemployed, combined power generation, flood control, navigation, and area development. Boulder Dam, begun in 1928, was finished in 1936. The Tennessee Valley Authority and Bonneville Power Administration built dams on the Tennessee and Columbia River systems. Ironically, Roosevelt could do little in his home state because the Senate would not confirm a treaty with Canada to develop the St. Lawrence.

The Federal agencies sold their power first to publicly owned distribution systems. The lure of cheap Federal power convinced many municipalities to take over the local power distributor. In addition, the Rural Electrification Administration poured money into farmer owned cooperatives formed to bring electricity to the hinterlands. For years thereafter, investor owned utilities lived in fear that they would lose customers to Federally supplied distribution systems.

Was Roosevelt's yardstick a fair one by which to judge the performance of investor owned utilities? Not really, because the Government agencies could be financed entirely by low cost Government debt and because the apportionment of costs among navigation, flood control, and power production could be adjusted to change the bookkeeping cost of power. Whatever the validity of Roosevelt's rationale, his push for public power created jobs, remade the physical, social, and economic faces of two river valleys, and set investor owned utilities on notice that they no longer had the markets to themselves and could lose business if they could not put up a good show against what was probably unfair competition.

Holding Company Act

Public power was the first part of the New Deal's campaign against the investor owned utilities. The second part was the Public Utility Holding Company Act of 1935. For years, regulators, scholars, and financiers noted that the operating electric companies were supervised by local regulatory agencies, but that nobody supervised the holding companies that controlled (and often exploited) the operating companies. The collapse of several holding company systems added to the worry about those farflung creations.

In 1928, the Federal Trade Commission (FTC) began a long investigation of the holding companies that led to the Act of 1935. The FTC criticized all the abuses: control of an entire system by means of a small investment at the top of a pyramid of companies, sale of services to subsidiaries at excessive prices, buying and selling properties within the system at unreasonable prices, intra-system loans at unfair terms, and the wild bidding war to buy operating companies. These abuses tended to raise the cost of electricity to the consumers. When the operating company was overcharged for services, it attempted to pass on the overcharge in the form of higher rates. When the holding company (or its subsidiaries) paid an inflated price for a property, that property had to earn a higher income than otherwise would have been the case in order for the purchaser to meet the interest and dividend charges associated with the overpriced purchase. (Although the holding company organization should have been a means to reduce costs, introduce efficiencies, and add to the investment the safety derived from diversity, it often added to both costs and risk.)

The FTC noted that within 18 holding company systems, there were 42 subholding companies and 91 utility operating companies. Of the $8.6 billion of assets held by that sample, $1.5 billion represented purchase prices above the original cost of the assets. If we assume that the cost of capital on the excess purchase price was the same as on previously existing assets, we could argue that the total utility system's return had to be 22% higher than would have been the case for the component parts.

The Holding Company Act accomplished the following:

♦ Interstate holding companies had to register with the Securities and Exchange Commission (SEC). By definition, a company that owned

10% or more of the voting securities of a gas or electric utility was a holding company. The holding company fell under the jurisdiction of the SEC and had to conform to certain rules.

♦ The "death sentence" clause of the Act broke up holding company systems that were not contiguous and eliminated the intermediate holding companies from the financial structure.

Some holding company systems had broken up anyway, but the SEC dismembered others. Between 1935 and 1950, 759 companies were separated from the holding company systems. Between 1938 and 1958, the number of registered holding companies declined from 216 to 18. Since the passage of the Act, only one holding company has been formed.

Setting the Stage

Even during depression and wartime days of the New Deal, the electric utility industry continued to expand and to cut costs. (See Table 12-1.) Government supported entities, such as the Rural Electrification Administration, brought electricity to the farms. (In 1930, only 10% of farms had electricity, but by 1945, the number was close to 45%.) The industry fared less well, financially, as it struggled with reorganization and lost territory to governmentally-owned (public power) utilities. Perhaps, though, the most significant change in the industry was the devolution of operating control from holding companies to locally operated utilities that would concentrate on service more than on fancy financial framework.

Table 12-1

From Depression through War
1932-1945

	1932	1945	% Change
Real GNP (1958 $billions)	154	437	184%
Energy Consumption (Btu trillions)	18,022	36,030	100
Electricity Production (kwh millions)	99,359	271,255	173
Real prices (1958 $)			
Electricity (¢ / kwh)	7.08	2.89	-59
Oil ($/bbl)	2.16	2.04	-6
Coal ($/ton)	3.25	5.12	58
% Electricity Produced by			
Privately owned utilities	75.0	66.7	—
Publicly (government) owned utilities	4.9	15.3	—
Industry and transport	20.1	18.0	—
Average size utility plant (mw)	8,539	12,895	51
Production per kw of capacity (hrs)	2,309	4,440	92
Coal equivalent per kwh produced (lbs)	1.5	1.3	-3
Return earned on average capital (%)	6.3	6.6	5
Return earned on average equity (%)	7.9	8.2	4
Bond yields (%)	4.7	2.6	-45
Utility stock index (S&P electric)	16.64	14.94	-10
Industrial stock index (S&P 400)	5.37	14.72	174

Sources

    See Tables 11-1 to 11-6.

Chapter **13**

The Good Old Days: 1945 — 1965

Public utility . . . stocks are susceptible . . . of valuation . . . within precise limits. . . . This results from the high degree of stability of utility earnings, the reasonable predictability of growth trends, and the general improbability of any sudden or unexpected developments . . . continued and substantial long-term growth can be looked forward to with a high degree of confidence.[24]

Graham, Dodd and Cottle, with Tatham

After World War II, it looked as if the electric utilities would continue, inevitably, on the road to lower costs and greater sales, and they did through the mid 1960s, when the process ground to a halt with the most disastrous electrical failure in American history.

Economic Trends

Energy consumption grew with the economy in 1945-1965, but electricity sales rose at a far faster pace. No doubt what helped most was the dramatic and continuing drop in the real price of electricity, compared to the price of other fuels. Throughout the period, industrial generators of electricity continued to generate more, but they contributed a declining percentage of total electrical output. Public power agencies added to their market share for much of the period, and disputes between public-power and investor-owned utility interests made the headlines. But the fervor of the New Deal days and the rapid addition of new customers seems to have been replaced by a more business-like approach. (See Tables 13-1 and 13-2.) Electric utilities managed to keep up with rapid postwar demand and increase operating efficiencies, despite the confusion caused by the breakup of the holding companies, most of which were finally liquidated in the early postwar days.

Generation

Much of the success in reducing costs was due to continuing improvements in the generating process. The industry pressed for larger generating stations, in order to realize greater economies of scale. In the late 1940s, most steam plants were under 100,000 kw in size, and a plant in the 200,000 - 500,000 kw range was huge.

Table 13-1

Energy and the Economy
1945 - 1965
(1945 = 100)

Year	Energy Consumption in USA	Real GNP	Electricity Used	Real Price of			
				Electricity	Natural Gas	Fuel Oil	Bituminous Coal
	(1)	(2)	(3)	(4)	(5)	(6)	(7)
1945	100	100	100	100	100	100	100
1950	108	103	144	69	69	96	102
1955	127	128	230	56	68	101	88
1960	143	143	309	50	69	91	90
1965	173	179	421	43	66	89	81

Notes

Columns 1 and 2: 1945-1950 data may contain discrepancies due to changes in series.

Columns 4-6:   Average prices of electricity and gas for all uses. Number 6 fuel oil - residential.
                Coal from Producer Price Index. Deflated by GNP deflator.

Sources

Column 1:   Energy Information Administration, Resources for the Future.
              Historical Statistics (various issues)

Column 2:   Bureau of Economic Affairs

Column 3:   Bureau of the Census

Columns 4-6: EEI, American Gas Association, US Dept. of Commerce

Table 13 - 2

Electricity Production
1945 - 1965

Year	Total	Kwh millions		Public Power	% of Generation		Public Power
		Industrial	Utility	Investor-Owned Utilities	Industry	Investor-Owned Utility	
	(1)	(2)	(3)	(4)	(5)	(6)	(7)	(8)
1945	271.3	48.8	222.5	180.9	41.6	18.0	66.7	15.3
1950	388.7	59.5	329.1	266.9	62.2	15.3	68.7	16.0
1955	629.0	82.0	547.0	420.9	126.1	13.0	66.9	20.0
1960	844.2	88.8	755.4	580.3	175.1	10.5	68.7	20.7
1965	1,157.6	102.3	1,055.3	809.5	245.8	8.8	69.9	21.2

Sources

U.S. Department of Commerce, Bureau of the Census, *Historical Statistics of the United States Colonial Times to 1970 (Part Two)*. (Washington, D.C.: U.S. Government Printing Office, 1975), p. 821.

Table 13-3

Generation
Total Electric Utility Industry
1945-1965

Year	Average Size Utility Prime Mover (Kw)	Heat Rate (Btu)	Production per KW of Capacity (Hrs)	Coal Equivalent per Kwh Produced (lbs)
	(1)	(2)	(3)	(4)
1945	13,002	15,800	4,487	1.3
1950	17,822	14,030	4,987	1.2
1955	31,913	11,699	5,037	1.1
1960	48,203	10,701	4,635	0.9
1965	71,771	10,384	4,469	0.9

Sources

Columns 1, 3: *Historical Statistics to 1970 (Part Two)*,
pp. 822, 824, 826,
Column 4: *EEI Pocketbook*

By the early 1950s, the industry was installing plants in the 500,000 - 1,000,000 kw range, and by the late 1950s stations of over 1,000,000 kw. The average size of a power station rose five fold between 1945 and 1965, but by the late 1950s, the dramatic improvements in efficiency seemed to have ended. (See Table 13-3.) The larger units were more complicated, harder to maintain, and operated at high temperatures and pressures that did not produce the anticipated operating savings. The investor owned electric utilities ran larger stations than the industry as a whole. It reduced capital investment per kilowatt installed, despite inflation. It gained from lower real fuel costs. But, by the late 1950s, operating efficiencies were getting harder to come by. (See Table 13-4.)

Transmission and Distribution

For transmission, the cost picture is not as clear. Construction costs increased on a cost per mile basis, but because the industry raised the voltage of the lines, it did get more capacity per mile. Nevertheless, in the early years after the war, the cost of transmission, either on a per mile or per volt-mile basis, seemed to rise, at least until late in the 1950s. Transmission expense per kilowatt-hour sold rose through the Korean War and then declined. A certain percentage of electric production is not recorded as sold because it is lost over transmission lines, stolen, or just unaccounted for. If we assume that the bulk of the loss was in transmission, then transmission became increasingly efficient — after a brief postwar move in the wrong direction — as losses declined. (See Table 13-5.)

Table 13-4

Generation
Investor Owned Electric Utilities
1945-1965

Year	Av. Size of Generating Plants (1,000 KW)	Total Industry Heat Rate (Million BTUs/kwh)	Cost of Fuel per Ton of Coal Equivalent	Fuel Cost per KWH	Av. Cost of Generating Plant ($/KW)	Cost of Incremental Gen. Plant ($/KW)	Consumer Price Index	Handy & Whitman Electric Constr. Index (North Atlantic)
	(1)	(2)	(3)	(4)	(5)	(6)	(7)	(8)
1945	19.6	15,800	$ 4.45	0.29¢	–	–	62.7	65
1946	19.6	15,700	4.89	0.32	–	–	68.0	76
1947	20.3	15,600	5.60	0.37	–	–	77.8	88
1948	21.2	15,738	6.49	0.42	116	–	83.8	94
1949	23.6	15,033	6.21	0.38	120	151	83.0	100
1950	25.9	14,030	5.95	0.35	124	173	83.8	104`
1951	28.8	13,641	6.05	0.34	128	163	90.5	116
1952	31.6	13,361	6.21	0.34	130	170	92.5	119
1953	35.0	12,889	6.32	0.33	133	161	93.2	125
1954	39.6	12,180	6.26	0.31	135	153	93.6	128
1955	44.3	11,699	6.27	0.30	138	165	93.3	132
1956	47.0	11,456	6.51	0.31	140	181	94.7	143
1957	50.5	11,365	6.94	0.32	139	130	98.0	152
1958	59.0	11,090	6.76	0.31	135	109	100.7	156
1959	65.1	10,879	6.58	0.29	137	152	101.5	159
1960	70.6	10,701	6.62	0.29	137	149	103.1	158
1961	76.5	10,552	6.45	0.28	138	139	104.2	155
1962	83.1	10,493	6.58	0.28	137	126	105.4	157
1963	88.2	10,438	6.41	0.27	136	115	106.7	157
1964	95.4	10,407	6.30	0.27	134	103	108.1	162
1965	102.9	10,384	6.23	0.27	132	101	109.9	167
% Change 1945-1965	+425	-37	+40	-7	+14 (a)	-37 (b)	+75	+157

Notes
- (a)   1948-1965
- (b)   1949-1965

Sources:
For columns 1,4,5,6: Federal Power Commission, *Statistics of Privately Owned Electric Utilities in the United States* (Washington, D.C.: U.S. Government Printing Office, various years).
For columns 2, 3, 7, 8: Edison Electric Institution, *Statistical Yearbook of the Electric Utility Industry* (Washington, D.C.: EEI, various years).

Table 13-5

Transmission
Investor Owned Electric Utilities
1945-1965a

Year	Transmission Plant/Circuit Mile of Transmission	Incremental Transmission Plant/Incremental Mile	Transmission Expense per KWH Sold (mills)	KWH Losses as % of Generation, Purchase and Interchange
	(1)	(2)	(3)	(4)
1945	–	–	0.24	9.6%
1946	–	–	0.27	10.4
1947	–	–	0.26	10.3
1948	$11,109	–	0.26	10.2
1949	11,902	$32,228	0.28	10.1
1950	12,526	25,198	0.26	10.0
1951	13,226	28,712	0.26	9.7
1952	14,284	42,101	0.28	9.8
1953	15,456	45,958	0.28	9.4
1954	16,986	65,701	0.28	9.3
1955	17,949	47,692	0.26	8.7
1956	18,816	57,916	0.24	8.9
1957	20,072	68,412	0.25	8.7
1958	21,685	72,192	0.26	8.8
1959	22,880	69,384	0.26	8.6
1960	23,906	61,831	0.25	8.4
1961	24,584	46,851	0.24	8.2
1962	25,822	73,334	0.24	8.0
1963	27,020	76,083	0.22	8.0
1964	28,007	78,422	0.22	7.8
1965	29,513	111,833	0.21	7.7
% Change 1945-65	+166%	+247%	-12%	-20%

Year	Average Trans. Plant per Circuit Volt Mile(b)	Period	Incr. Trans. Plant per Incr. Circuit Volt Mile(b)	Year	Percent of Transmission Circuit Miles by Voltage(c)		
					22-50KV	51-131 KV	132-800KV
1948	$0.16	–	–	1948	45.0	42.1	12.9
1950	0.18	1948-1950	$0.31	1950	42.9	42.5	14.6
1955	0.23	1951-1955	0.40	1955	38.0	43.0	19.0
1960	0.29	1956-1960	0.56	1960	34.8	43.4	21.8
1965	0.33	1961-1965	0.50	1965	31.8	42.6	25.6

a   22KV and over.
b   Circuit volt-miles defined as miles of transmission x voltage of transmission line. Assumes same mix of voltage for investor owned industry as for total industry.
c   Total industry.
d   1948-1965
e   1949-1965

Sources: Federal Power Commission Statistics (columns 1,2,3,4), Edison Electric Institute *Year Book* (columns 1,2).

Table 13-6

Distribution
Investor Owned Electric Utilities
1945 - 1965

Year	Average Cost of Distribution Plant/Customer	Cost of Incremental Distribution/Incr. Customer	Distribution Expense per Customer(a)
	(1)	(2)	(3)
1945	--	--	$8.33
1946	--	--	9.37
1947	--	--	10.47
1948	$187	--	11.30
1949	199	$444	11.60
1950	208	425	12.04
1951	217	444	12.46
1952	228	552	13.05
1953	241	616	13.66
1954	255	761	14.23
1955	272	797	14.18
1956	288	799	14.64
1957	306	890	14.97
1958	322	1,051	15.27
1959	336	876	15.65
1960	355	1,204	16.19
1961	370	1,294	15.62
1962	386	1,252	16.00
1963	403	1,362	16.36
1964	420	1,645	17.18
1965	437	1,303	17.48
% Change 1945-1965	+134%b	+193%c	+110%

Year	Average Distribution Plant per KW of Capacity(c)	Period	Incremental Distribution Plant per Incremental KW of Capacity
1948	$134		--
1950	133	1948-1950	$130
1955	129	1951-1955	123
1960	125	1956-1960	117
1965	126	1961-1965	130

Notes
(a) $ per year.
(b) 1948-1965
(c) 1949-1965

Sources
Federal Power Commission *Statistics*.

Capital expenditures associated with the distribution of power showed a rising trend, on a per customer basis, but remained fairly unchanged on a per kilowatt of capacity basis. Distribution expense per customer increased, but at a minimal rate after the Korean War. (See Table 13-6.)

The Business Picture

Electric utility sales, measured in kilowatt-hours, grew rapidly each year through 1965, with the exception of 1945-46. Although sales were influenced by economic fluctuations, they showed strength even in recession years, as did growth in demand for electricity at peak periods. The industry could take advantage of all the economies offered to it by the declining costs associated with new equipment and with increasing economies of scale. It could build new plants confident that the customer would use the new facilities. Furthermore, with the exception of a few tight years in the 1940s, the industry had sufficient reserve capacity to encourage new demand without fear of being unable to meet the needs of the customer. From the end of the Korean War to 1960, the industry increased its reserve margin, which then was allowed to decline to a low point in 1969. Also during that period, the industry was taking a larger share of the electric market, as evidenced by the decline in percentage of generation from non-utility sources. (See Table 13-7.)

From an operational standpoint, everything was going well. The electric industry was providing increasingly cheap power. The industry's costs were under control and actually declined in some instances, although prices within the economy were rising. Prices for power fell despite a moderate amount of rate relief through 1961 that averaged less than 1% a year. From 1962 on, rate reductions exceeded rate increases. (See Table 13-8.)

A good operating record, however, could conceal serious financial problems, especially if actions were forced on the industry by regulatory agencies that stressed short term customer benefit over long term corporate solvency. Some indicators of financial well-being tell the story.

In 1945-65, dollar investment in utility plant rose at a good rate, but not one out of line with the gains in sales. Capital spending rose rapidly after World War II but reserve margins did not rise to satisfactory levels until after the Korean War. Late in the 1950s and early in the 1960s, spending tapered off as a result of the large amount of plant that had been put into service, apparently in anticipation of future demand. Academic economists of the time asserted that utility managements had an incentive to raise the rate base to increase the earnings potential of the company. That is the Averch-Johnson effect, first discussed in a 1962 paper.[25]

For a period of time, raising capital to pay for the expansion must have been the full-time occupation of financial executives within the industry, because a large part of the capital expenditures had to be paid for with new offerings of securities. As spending tapered off and returns on investment rose, however, the need for outside financing declined. (See Table 13-9.)

Table 13-7

Electricity and the Economy
1945-1965

Year	% Change KWH Sales	% Change Peak Load	% Change Real GNP	% Total US Elec. Gen. by non-Utility Sources	Supplied by All Utilities	Supplied by Investor-owned Utilities
	(1)	(2)	(3)	(4)	(5)	(6)
1945	-2.3	-2.7	-2.8	18.0	81.3	66.1
1946	-2.4	13.6	-12.4	17.2	82.1	66.6
1947	14.0	10.2	-0.2	16.8	82.7	67.2
1948	10.7	8.5	3.9	16.1	83.6	67.5
1949	3.2	5.0	0.1	15.6	84.0	67.2
1950	12.9	13.8	8.5	15.3	84.3	68.3
1951	13.4	10.6	8.1	14.5	85.1	69.3
1952	7.7	7.0	3.7	13.8	85.8	69.2
1953	12.2	9.0	4.6	13.9	85.8	68.6
1954	6.9	14.4	-2.0	13.4	86.2	67.8
1955	17.1	4.5	8.0	13.0	86.4	66.5
1956	10.3	9.5	2.1	12.3	87.1	66.6
1957	5.3	6.2	1.8	11.8	87.8	66.8
1958	1.9	7.3	-0.2	11.0	88.6	67.3
1959	10.1	6.0	6.0	10.7	88.9	68.1
1960	9.0	6.1	2.3	10.5	89.0	68.4
1961	5.5	6.0	2.5	9.9	89.9	68.7
1962	7.8	7.3	5.8	9.7	90.3	69.0
1963	7.1	6.6	3.9	9.4	90.6	69.3
1964	7.4	8.5	5.3	9.2	90.6	69.6
1965	7.0	6.5	5.9	8.8	91.2	69.9

Sources: U.S. Dept. of Commerce (column 3). Edison Institute *Year Book* (columns 1,2,4,5,6).

Table 13-8

Price and Usage
Total Electric Utility Industry
1945 - 1965

Year	Price of Residential Electricity (¢/KWH)	Price of All Electricity (¢/KWH)	Consumer Price Index	GNP Deflator	Net Rate Increases (Decreases) as % of Electric Revenue (a)	Electric Usage per Residential Customer (KWH)	Electric Usage per Customer (KWH)
	(1)	(2)	(3)	(4)	(5)	(6)	(7)
1945	3.41¢	1.73¢	62.7	59.1	NA	1,229	5,762
1946	3.22	1.81	68.0	66.6	NA	1,329	5,422
1947	3.09	1.77	77.8	74.2	NA	1,438	5,828
1948	3.01	1.79	83.8	79.1	1.0	1,563`	6,073
1949	2.95	1.86	83.0	78.6	0.8	1,684	5,937
1950	2.88	1.81	83.8	79.9	0.3	1,830	6,377
1951	2.81	1.78	90.5	85.4	0.6	2,004	6,922
1952	2.77	1.79	92.5	86.9	1.4	2,169	7,183
1953	2.74	1.77	93.2	87.5	0.3	2,346	7,815
1954	2.69	1.77	93.6	88.7	0.8	2,549	8,127
1955	2.64	1.67	93.3	90.0	0.4	2,751	9,265
1956	2.60	1.64	94.7	92.9	0.1	2,969	9,944
1957	2.56	1.67	98.0	96.4	0.7	3,174	10,214
1958	2.53	1.71	100.7	98.4	0.9	3,389	10,227
1959	2.50	1.69	101.5	100.0	0.6	3,618	11,020
1960	2.47	1.69	103.1	101.8	0.4	3,854	11,704
1961	2.45	1.69	104.2	102.6	0.1	4,019	12,099
1962	2.41	1.68	105.4	104.5	-0.1	4,259	12,763
1963	2.37	1.65	106.7	106.1	-0.3	4,442	13,366
1964	2.31	1.62	108.1	107.7	-0.8	4,703	14,015
1965	2.25	1.59	109.9	112.3	-0.9	4,933	14,694
% Change 1945-1965	-34	-9	+75	+90	--	+301	+155

Notes

  (a) Investor owned electric utilities. Annual aggregate amounts granted as % of year's electric revenue.

Sources

  Edison Electric Institute *Year Book* (all columns), *Electrical World* (all columns).

Table 13-9

Capital Spending and Reserve Margins
Investor Owned Electric Utilities
1945-1965

Year	% Increase in Gross Electric Utility Plant	Capital Spending ($ Millions)	New Permanent Capital Raised as % of Capital Spending (a)	Reserve Margin % (b)
	(1)	(2)	(3)	(4)
1945	-1.8	350	15	26.5
1946	3.2	650	29	11.4
1947	7.0	1,235	49	6.1
1948	10.8	1,830	73	6.6
1949	10.1	2,190	64	14.2
1950	9.3	2,050	61	10.3
1951	9.3	2,134	70	11.8
1952	10.1	2,599	67	11.9
1953	11.3	2,876	82	17.8
1954	9.1	2,835	60	20.4
1955	7.8	2,719	50	18.6
1956	8.1	2,910	50	19.7
1957	9.7	3,679	67	22.2
1958	8.8	3,764	60	27.1
1959	7.7	3,383	57	30.2
1960	7.4	3,331	54	31.5
1961	5.8	3,000	52	31.0(c)
1962	5.5	3,037	48	31.0
1963	5.6	3,240	35	30.2
1964	5.4	3,558	43	23.7(c)
1965	6.1	4,055	36	22.9(c)

Notes

(a) Investor owned public utility long term financing as percentage of reported capital expenditure series. May understate percentage of capital raised externally to the extent that non-electric utility expenditures are excluded from column 2 or to the extent that short term debt becomes an increasing percentage of external financing.

(b) Total industry.

(c) Summer non-coincident peak reserve margin. All others winter.

Sources

Federal Power commision *Statistics* (column 1). Edison Electric Institute *Year Book* (columns 2,3,4).

Table 13-10

Financial Ratios
Investor Owned Electric Utilities
1945 - 1965

Year	Return on Aver. Common Equity (%)	Interest Cost Newly Issued Bonds (%)	Interest Coverage Ratio (Long Term Debt) (x)	IDC % Net Income (a)	Average Stock Price(b)	Average Book Value (b)	Market/Book Ratio (b)
	(1)	(2)	(3)	(4)	(5)	(6)	(7)
1945	8.2	2.87	4.2	0.6%	26.29	26.65	99
1946	10.5	2.74	4.6	0.9	34.05	27.16	125
1947	10.3	2.79	4.6	2.4	29.53	27.68	107
1948	9.9	3.07	4.2	4.3	27.34	28.08	97
1949	10.6	3.06	4.2	5.0	28.37	28.38	100
1950	10.6	2.86	4.2	4.6	31.23	29.09	107
1951	9.5	3.25	4.0	4.4	32.55	30.27	108
1952	10.2	3.36	4.1	5.2	35.48	31.00	114
1953	10.2	3.75	3.8	7.0	37.80	31.33	121
1954	10.5	3.11	3.8	6.2	44.30	31.85	139
1955	11.0	3.30	3.9	4.4	49.24	32.71	151
1956	11.1	3.86	3.9	3.6	49.62	33.90	146
1957	11.0	4.80	3.7	5.9	49.42	35.43	139
1958	11.0	4.18	3.4	8.0	57.96	36.77	158
1959	11.2	4.92	3.4	6.2	66.35	38.00	175
1960	11.3	4.72	3.4	5.5	69.82	39.52	177
1961	11.2	4.72	3.4	4.5	90.55	41.22	220
1962	11.7	4.40	3.5	4.3	91.50	43.29	211
1963	11.8	4.40	3.6	3.6	102.79	45.36	227
1964	12.3	4.55	3.6	3.6	108.76	47.67	228
1965	12.6	4.61	3.7	3.6	117.08	49.85	235
% Change 1945-1965	+54	+61	-12	+500	+345	+87	+137

Notes

(a) Interest during construction credit, later allowance for funds used during construction.
(b) Moody's Electric Utility Average.

Sources

Federal Power Commission *Statistics* (collumns 1,3,4). Edison Electric Institute *Year Book* (columns 2,5,6,7). Moody's (columns 2,5,6,7).

Return on the book equity of common stockholders rose moderately, in line with the returns offered by investment in new utility bonds. The utility's return on equity was well below that earned in industrial investments at the time, but the stock market performance of utility stocks was not out of line with that of industrial shares. As a result, investors probably were satisfied with the utility returns, given the presumed risk differential between utility and industrial investments.

The bondholder did not fare as well, in the sense that income available to meet long term debt interest expense declined moderately as a multiple of that expense. Because a large proportion of the industry had high bond ratings by 1965, investors apparently were willing to accept slightly lower quantitative protection because of the high quality they saw in the industry. (Table 13-10.)

Finally, the industry's method of accounting for some of the costs of financing construction can disguise the real pattern of operations. The practice capitalizes the financing charges associated with construction of new facilities by creating a credit in the income statement called interest during construction (IDC) for the period being discussed. The accounting concept makes sense. When the credit is large in relation to reported earnings, though, the investor or regulator may be misled into believing that things are better than they appear to be because IDC brings no cash from sale of power, but rather is an expectation of future earnings. Investors who prefer cash to bookkeeping credits would discount the earnings of utilities that have a high percentage of income derived from IDC. Because in the 1945-65 period IDC accounted for a minimal proportion of earnings, the quality of reported earnings held up during the period, another indicator that the overall situation was solid.

For electric utilities, the postwar period was one of reorganization out of the holding companies, mergers for some smaller utilities, minimal need for rate relief, declining costs and prices, motivation to add to the rate base, satisfied investors, and acceptable (although unspectacular) returns for owners. Although the development of the Averch-Johnson analysis questioned whether the situation was ideal, one could still argue that results were good. That environment of few operating problems and little need to question prevailing regulatory methods left few people prepared to react quickly to or understand well the problems that followed.

Chapter 14

The Decline of the Industry: After 1965

He has barred my way; I cannot pass;
He has laid darkness upon my path.
He has stripped me of my glory,
Removed the crown from my head.
He tears down every part of me; I perish;
He uproots my hope like a tree.[26]

The Book of Job, XIX, 8-10

For the next fifteen years, essentially no progress occurred.[27]

Richard F. Hirsch

As the period after 1965 unfolded, electric utility investors and managers must have felt like the puzzled Job. After so much success, what did they do to deserve such a series of misfortunes?

Background

Before examining the problems of the industry, consider the industry in relation to the economy. In 1945-1965, America's energy consumption moved in line with its economic activity. Demand for electricity, though, grew at roughly twice the rate of the economy. Some might attribute that fast pace to the development of electrical appliances, to the discovery of the convenience and cleanliness of electricity, and to smart marketing by electric utilities. Those factors helped to create demand, which in turn allowed utilities to reach for greater economies of scale and operation, which in turn sufficiently lowered the price of power to encourage the development and marketing of new electrical devices. Whether the development of new markets occurred because of the drop in the price for electricity or vice versa is a chicken or egg debate. The reality is that the price for electricity declined not only on an absolute basis but also in relation to prices as a whole and to the price for competing fuels. Electricity usage grew far faster than energy usage as a whole.

In 1965-1970, the trend toward increased use of electricity continued. The price for electricity remained flat despite a sharp upturn both in the overall cost of

Table 14-1

Energy and the Economy
1965 - 1980
(1945 = 100)

Year	Energy Consumption in USA	Real GNP	Electricity Use	Real Price of			
				Electricity	Natural Gas	Fuel Oil	Bituminous Coal
	(1)	(2)	(3)	(4)	(5)	(6)	(7)
1965	100	100	100	100	100	100	100
1970	126	116	145	81	83	94	129
1975	134	129	181	57	119	140	409
1980	144	153	217	61	279	279	341

Notes and Sources

See Table 13-1.

living and in the price for coal (the most important fuel for generating electricity). Other energy sources showed greater increases in price. In part, the continuing push toward electricity occurred because electricity prices declined in relation to other prices (*i.e.*, the real price of electricity fell). In part, it occurred because of fears that the supply of natural gas was inadequate, and because increasing environmental awareness caused some users of energy to push their environmental problems onto the electric utility by switching to central station power.

In a way, the inability (or unwillingness) of the electric utility industry to raise prices when costs of operation and capital began to rise (possibly because neither managements nor regulators realized that a fundamental change in costs was taking place) triggered the deterioration in the industry. The process of deterioration, moreover, was accelerated because the uneconomically low price for power induced increased demand, which became increasingly difficult to meet profitably at then current rates. To make matters worse, electricity was priced on a declining block basis. Each additional increment of demand was sold at a lower price than the previous increment. The declining block tariff had been designed to take advantage of economies of scale and to encourage consumption. As a result, the industry faced a new situation. Cost of production had started to rise, but electricity was priced as if costs were still declining. Sale of that incremental kilowatt-hour was becoming increasingly less profitable.

From 1970 on, the electric industry began to raise prices in nominal — but not

Table 14 - 2

Electricity Production
1965 - 1980

| | | Kwh millions | | | | % of Generation | | |
Year	Total (1)	Industrial (2)	Utility (3)	Investor Owned Utility (4)	Public Power (5)	Industry (6)	Investor Owned Utility (7)	Public Power (8)
1965	1,157.6	102.3	1,055.3	809.5	245.8	8.8	69.9	21.3
1970	1,639.8	108.2	1,531.6	1,183.2	348.4	6.6	72.2	21.2
1975	2,003.0	85.4	1,917.6	1,486.8	430.8	4.3	74.2	21.5
1980	2,354.3	67.9	2,286.4	1,782.9	503.5	2.9	75.7	21.4

Sources: EEI

Table 14-3

Generation
Total Electric Utility Industry
1965-1980

Year	Average Size Utility Prime Mover (Kw)	Heat Rate (Btu)	Production per KW of Capacity (Hrs)	Coal Equivalent per Kwh Produced (lbs)
	(1)	(2)	(3)	(4)
1965	71,771	10,384	4,469	0.9
1970	96,928	10,508	4,490	0.9
1975	143,279	10,383	3,772	1.0
1980	200,059	10,489	3,726	1.0

Sources

Columns 1-3:	*Historical Statistics. . . to 1970*
	FPC and EIA
Column 4:	*EEI Pocketbook*

real — terms. The prices of competing fuels, however, rose astronomically, making electricity look like a better bargain than ever. In that period, energy consumption grew at a slower rate than GNP as a whole, while use of electricity continued to grow faster than GNP, although the relative rate of growth between electricity and GNP was less than in any other postwar period. (See Table 14-1 for data.)

As can be seen in Table 14-2, the utility industry after 1965 supplied an increasing percentage of the electricity generated in the United States. Why did industrial generators produce a decreasing percentage of the total, despite the rising cost of central station power? Two possible reasons were that utility power did not reflect the true cost of production and therefore was a bargain, and that industrial producers were not interested in becoming regulated utilities or dealing with the environmental roadblocks to the production of electricity. In addition, the investor owned utilities continued to gain market share.

To make matters worse, the industry was building bigger and more expensive power stations that did not work as well as their predecessors. They needed more fuel to produce a kwh and they stayed in operation less time during the year. (See Table 14-3 for operating data and Table 14-4 for year-by-year data on electricity output and economic conditions.)

Table 14-4

Energy and the Economy
1965 - 1980

Year	% Change KWH Sales	% Change Peak Load	% Change Real GNP	% Total US Elec. Gen. by non-Utility Sources	% of Elec. Made Available in US Gen. by Domestic Elec. Utilities	
					Supplied by All Utilities	Supplied by Investor-Owned Utilities
	(1)	(2)	(3)	(4)	(5)	(6)
1965	7.0	6.5	5.8	8.8	91.2	69.9
1966	8.9	9.2	5.8	8.4	91.5	70.4
1967	6.6	5.0	2.9	7.8	92.2	71.0
1968	8.6	11.5	4.1	7.5	92.6	71.0
1969	8.7	8.3	2.4	7.1	92.8	70.9
1970	6.4	6.6	-0.3	6.6	93.3	72.0
1971	5.3	6.4	2.8	6.0	93.8	73.2
1972	7.5	9.3	5.0	5.6	94.0	73.0
1973	7.9	7.8	5.2	5.2	94.1	73.4
1974	-0.1	1.6	-0.5	5.2	94.2	72.8
1975	1.9	2.2	-1.3	4.3	95.5	74.0
1976	6.6	4.0	4.9	4.1	95.5	74.2
1977	5.5	6.9	4.7	4.0	95.3	75.5
1978	3.4	3.0	5.3	3.5	95.7	74.7
1979	3.3	-2.4	2.5	3.1	95.7	74.8
1980	2.0	7.2	-0.2	2.9	96.0	75.1

Notes

Column 2:   Summer peak.

Sources

Columns 1, 2, 4-6: EEI.
Column 3:   BEA.

Capital Spending and Finances

Nineteen sixty-five was a watershed year for the electric utility industry. In that year, electric utility stock prices peaked, rate reductions were at their greatest levels, interest coverage ratios reached a historic height, the Vietnam War began in earnest, and the Northeast Blackout showed that all was not well in the electric utility industry. In the period that followed, conditions turned against the industry, which made mistakes that compounded the difficulties.

Capital spending soon became a problem. In November 1965, an equipment failure at Ontario Hydro caused the collapse of the interconnected power pools throughout the Northeast, plunging that region into darkness. The Northeast Blackout forced soul-searching within the industry. Perhaps the individual electric companies had insufficient generating capacity in reserve to meet emergencies. Reserve margins had been falling for several years. Perhaps the system of high voltage interconnections between utilities or regions was inadequate to meet emergencies. Although money had to be spent to improve reliability of service, doing so would mean investment that would not necessarily lower costs nor be automatically associated with increased revenues — as would be the case if the money were spent to meet new demand for service.

Capital expenditures rose for other reasons as well. As the environmental movement gained popularity, utilities beautified plants, converted generating units to less polluting fuels, and put on line equipment that brought them into compliance with new environmental regulations. None of those moves, however, made plants more efficient or helped the utilities to meet the needs of new customers. Further-more, environmental opposition to utility activities caused delays and revisions in construction programs, thereby adding to costs. Those who ran the companies probably found it difficult to understand and to adjust to the new constraints, with the result that conflicts were frequent. Many in the industry saw the situation in superficial terms. They thought that meeting environmental demands meant beautifying substations, putting power lines underground, and designing esthetic, sky blue towers to carry the transmission lines.[28]

Furthermore, not only did the cost of electric plants rise because of inflation, but also because the industry was building a more expensive (more capital intensive, that is) kind of power plant. The difficulty in securing gas supplies discouraged utilities from building low cost gas burning plants. Instead, they turned to fuels that required more elaborate generating units. Environmental protection devices added to the cost of equipment. Construction delays and labor productivity problems surfaced during the overheated Vietnam War economy. In addition, the industry had plunged into the nuclear age. Nuclear generating plants cost more to build per kilowatt of capacity, although the higher capital costs were supposed to be offset by lower fuel costs. The industry, however, was dealing with an unfamiliar technology, and one that was feared and opposed by a vocal segment of the population. As a result of technological and political roadblocks, nuclear generating units took longer to build and were more costly than expected, and in many instances proved to be disappointing performers. (See Table 14-5.)

Consequently, capital spending accelerated, the rate base (using utility plant as a proxy) rose considerably faster than sales (and the income derived from sales), and a large percentage of the needed funds had to be raised by selling new capital. Unfortunately, the sale of securities occurred as interest rates were rising. Paying out increasingly high interest rates on an increasing amount of debt when income was not rising proportionately caused the decline of the pretax interest coverage ratio. That meant that the industry's debt was declining in quality, and that, in turn, necessitated payment of even higher interest rates. In short, not only were interest rates as a whole on a secular uptrend, but interest costs of utilities rose even more because utility bonds were becoming increasingly risky.

Table 14-5

Capital Spending and Reserve Margins
Investor Owned Electric Utilities
1965-1980

Year	% Increase in Gross Electric Utility Plant	Capital Spending ($ Million)	New Permanent Capital Raised as % of Capital Spending	Reserve Margin %
	(1)	(2)	(3)	(4)
1965	6.1	$4,055	36	22.9
1966	7.4	4,941	55	18.4
1967	8.6	6,204	53	20.8
1968	9.2	7,118	53	17.2
1969	10.1	8,357	58	16.6
1970	11.5	10,264	77	19.0
1971	11.8	12,218	73	20.9
1972	13.7	13,728	63	19.6
1973	8.7	15,291	59	20.8
1974	13.3	17,192	67	27.2
1975	10.1	16,191	74	34.3
1976	10.5	18,158	64	34.5
1977	10.8	21,297	61	30.2
1978	10.8	24,030	49	33.7
1979	11.2	26,819	48	36.9
1980	10.2	28,335	49	30.7

Sources

Column 1:   Federal Power Commission, EIA.
Columns 2-4:   EEI.

The way to stop the squeeze on margins was to raise the price for electricity or to reduce costs. The industry's costs previously had fallen sufficiently fast to maintain profitability levels even after reducing (or only minimally raising) the price for power. Productivity was on a downtrend, however, and could not be relied on as in the past.

> Improvements in labor productivity have been . . . dramatic . . . . In the subperiod for 1947-53, the average growth rate was 7.2 percent; it slipped to 7.0 percent for 1953-66 and then declined to only 4.8 percent . . . for 1966-72. . . .

> Since there has been a shift in the direction of capital-intensive nuclear power and a rapid increase in the expenditure for cooling towers and air pollution control equipment, it seems likely that capital productivity in the electric power industry has been negative in recent years. These trends combined with a phasing out or rapid conversion of gas- and oil-fired generating plants to coal burning plants will probably insure that aggregate capital productivity will continue to be negative in the years ahead. . . .The peak in the efficiency of new fossil-fired electric generating units was apparently reached around 1967.[29]

Neither regulators nor management seem to have caught the trend, and critics of the industry showed as little prescience. Metcalf and Reinemer italicized their view of the world:

> *With few exceptions . . . the price of electricity should be decreasing steadily. Electric power is a classic example of an industry in which mass production and distribution are decreasing the cost per unit.*[30]

Positive rate relief did not materialize for several years. In the interim, both the pretax interest coverage for debt and the return on stockholder investment dropped. Subsequent rate relief was insufficient to raise the ratios to previous levels. Because bond ratings also fell, the utilities had to pay higher interest charges than they would have otherwise, and during crisis periods in the bond markets, some of the poorly rated utilities had difficulty raising money at all.[31]

The common stockholder, the owner of the business, also fared poorly. Return on equity investment tapered off. In reality, however, the drop in return was greater than the numbers indicated because an increasing proportion of that declining return was derived from a non-cash credit in the income statement — the allowance for funds used during construction (AFUDC), also known as interest during construction (IDC). To make matters worse, numerous companies adopted increasingly liberal accounting procedures in other respects to maintain a pattern of gains in reported earnings. One could argue, therefore, that the overall quality of reported earnings also had fallen and that the decline in return on stockholders' equity was much greater than was apparent from the bare numbers.

Common stockholders faced two problems, sensitivity of the stock price to the movement of interest rates, and the inability of the companies to raise return earned while the return on competitive investments rose. Prices for utility stocks tend to move with changes in interest rates. A stockholder usually buys a utility stock because it furnishes a combination of a reasonable current dividend and moderate but steady growth in dividends and earnings. The total return on the investment (current dividends plus increase in the price for the stock) should be higher than the interest received on a bond, because the common stockholder assumes a greater risk than the bondholder. Investors, however, also consider utility stocks to be safe investments and substitutes for the purchase of bonds so long as the stock provides something extra to compensate for risk. Therefore, when the expected total return from the stocks becomes too low in relation to the return available from bonds, the investors sell the stocks (thereby depressing stock prices and raising the return on the stock investment) and buy bonds. The process is reversed when the bond yield is too low in relation to the return on the stocks. If we consider the market situation after 1965, the return on bonds continued to rise, but the return earned on the stockholders' investment in the electric utility continued to fall. Investors sold the stocks, thereby causing prices to decline until the return on the stocks was commensurate with returns offered elsewhere.

To use representative numbers, in 1965, the stockholders' investment in Average Electric Company was $49.85, on which the company earned 12.6% or $6.28. If we assume that the investor considered these earnings as his total return, and the investor paid $117.08 in the marketplace for that stock, then the investor was willing to settle for a 5.4% total return ($6.28/$117.08) at a time when he could have gotten 4.6% by buying bonds. (These numbers are not correct conceptually but will be used to illustrate the dilemma faced by utility investors.) In 1970, the Average Electric Company earned 11.8% on $62.32 of stockholders' investment, or $7.35. Bonds returned 8.8%. The buyers of utility shares demanded a return higher than that available on bonds, so they would only pay $79.06 for the share. At $79.06, the shares offered a return of 9.3% ($7.35/$79.06), which was more than the bond return. In both instances, the stockholders took a return less than one percentage point greater than the bond yield. By the early 1970s, investors began to worry that utility stocks might be a lot riskier in relation to bonds than previously thought. Therefore, the stocks had to offer a higher return differential than before. In 1975, Average Electric Company earned 11.2% on stockholders' investment of $74.52, or $8.35, while bonds paid 9.97%. Purchasers paid only $51.25 for the stock, for a return of 16.3% ($8.35/$51.25). In 1980, the company earned 11.5% on its investment per share of $82.72, or $9.51, while bonds yielded 13.46%. The stock sold at $54.80, for an earnings yield of 17.4%.

Table 14-6

Price and Usage
Total Electric Utility Industry
1965 - 1980

Year	Price of Residential Electricity (¢/KWH)	Price of All Electricity (¢/KWH)	Consumer Price Index	GNP Deflator	Net Rate Increases (Decreases) as % of Electric Revenue (a)	Electric Usage per Residential Customer (KWH)	Electric Usage per Customer (KWH)
	(1)	(2)	(3)	(4)	(5)	(6)	(7)
1965	2.25¢	1.59¢	31.5	33.8	-0.9	4,933	14,694
1966	2.20	1.56	32.4	35.0	-0.2	5,265	15,678
1967	2.17	1.56	33.3	35.9	-0.2	5,577	16,384
1968	2.12	1.55	34.3	37.7	0.0	6,057	17,445
1969	2.09	1.54	35.7	39.8	0.8	6,571	18,563
1970	2.10	1.59	37.5	42.0	2.2	7,066	19,380
1971	2.19	1.69	39.5	44.4	3.6	7,380	19,956
1972	2.29	1.77	39.9	46.5	3.3	7,691	20,964
1973	2.38	1.86	41.2	49.5	4.0	8,079	21,955
1974	2.83	2.30	45.8	54.0	6.3	7,907	21,488
1975	3.21	2.70	50.1	59.3	8.6	8,176	21,417
1976	3.45	2.89	55.1	63.1	5.5	8,360	22,361
1977	3.78	3.21	59.0	67.3	4.8	8,693	23,052
1978	4.03	3.46	61.7	72.2	3.9	8,849	23,315
1979	4.43	3.82	70.5	78.6	4.2	8,843	23,481
1980	5.12	4.49	83.1	85.7	7.4	9,025	23,167
% Change 1965-1980	+128	+182	+164	+172	--	+83	+58

Notes

(a) Investor-owned utilities

Sources

EEI, *Electrical World*, EIA, BEA.

The result of that combination of lower return on stockholders' equity and higher interest rates was to cause stock prices to drop until they were well below book value. Utility companies had to raise money by selling common stock below book value (true of almost all electric companies by the mid 1970s), thereby diluting the interests of their shareholders, and those companies probably invested the funds for a return unfairly low according to regulatory theory. Bonbright, for instance, held that the "current cost of common-stock capital," which is the rate of return that should be allowed by the regulators, should permit the utility "to issue more . . . stock . . . at prices . . . not less than the per-share book value of the old stock. In this way it can . . . [issue] new common stock at prices high enough to avoid 'impairing the integrity' of the investment of the old stockholders."[32]

Returns being earned were insufficient to meet Bonbright's standard of profitability. Investors were discouraged by the level of profitability in the industry. Electric utility shares declined on an absolute basis (halving between 1965 and 1975), did worse than the average industrial share, and fell to prices at which new financing was dilutionary and probably damaging to existing shareowners. (See Table 14-6 for data on pricing of electricity and 14-7 for financial ratios.)

Operating Costs

The industry ran into problems on all fronts when, after 1965, it continued to do what had served so well before: it added increasingly large generating plants. Heat rate did not improve, however, and the cost of incremental generating capacity rose far faster than either the cost of living or the utility construction index. New plant was more expensive but not more efficient than old plant. (The variability in cost of new facilities after 1978 is due to scheduling problems and wide diversity of costs of nuclear plants after the Three Mile Island accident.) Fuel prices rose sharply, especially after the 1973-74 oil embargo. The inability to utilize fuel efficiently, or to offset the effect of the dwindling importance of hydropower with the addition of nuclear power, also led to a sharp rise in the cost of fuel per kilowatt-hour. (See Table 14-8.)

The distribution sector offered little solace. The cost of incremental distribution plant per customer rose more than the cost of living, while distribution expense per customer and incremental distribution plant per kilowatt of capacity moved with inflation. (See Table 14-9.) Despite all the attention paid to transmission, results were a mixed bag in that area as well. Power losses declined, which was good news. Transmission expenses per kilowatt-hour rose about as much as the cost of living. Investment in plant per unit of transmission capacity moved at the same pace. (See Table 14-10.)

The overall trends indicated a rising cost of capital, inadequate rate relief, inability to raise productivity, a declining financial situation, and a general inability on the part of regulators and managements to cope with the economic and societal problems at hand, at least until the early 1980s.

Table 14-7

Financial Ratios
Investor Owned Electric Utilities
1965 - 1980

Year	Return on Common Equity (%)	Interest Cost Newly Issued Bonds (Moody's) (%)	Interest Coverage Ratio (Long Term Debt) (FERC) (X)	AFUDC % Net Income (a)	Average Stock Price (Moody's)(b) ($)	Average Book Value (Moody's) ($)	Market/ Book Ratio (Moody's) (%)
	(1)	(2)	(3)	(4)	(5)	(6)	(7)
1965	12.6	4.61	3.7	3.6	117.08	49.85	235
1966	12.8	5.53	3.6	4.6	102.90	51.47	200
1967	12.8	6.07	3.4	6.4	101.87	53.55	190
1968	12.3	6.80	3.1	9.2	98.37	56.41	174
1969	12.2	7.98	3.0	12.6	94.55	59.24	160
1970	11.8	8.79	2.7	17.3	79.06	62.32	127
1971	11.7	7.72	2.6	21.1	84.16	65.23	129
1972	11.8	7.50	2.6	24.2	80.20	68.39	117
1973	11.5	7.91	2.6	24.8	71.21	71.04	100
1974	10.7	9.59	2.4	28.9	48.26	72.45	67
1975	11.2	9.97	2.4	26.5	51.25	74.52	69
1976	11.5	8.92	2.4	25.8	60.10	76.37	79
1977	11.5	8.43	2.4	28.2	67.55	77.88	87
1978	11.3	9.30	2.4	31.5	63.54	79.47	80
1979	11.2	10.85	2.4	38.0	60.28	80.87	75
1980	11.5	13.46	2.3	41.2	54.80	82.72	66
% Change 1965-1980	-9	+192	-38	+1,044	-53	+66	-72

Notes

(a) Allowance for funds used during construction (FPC, FERC).
(b) Moody's Electric Utility Average.

Sources

FPC, EIA *Statistics* (columns 1,3,4). Edison Institute *Year Book* (columns 2,5,6,7).
Moody's *Public Utilities Manual*, 1987 (columns 2,5,6,7).

Table 14 - 8

Power Generation
Investor Owned Electric Utililties
1965 - 1980

Year	Av. Size of Generating Plants (1,000 KW) (1)	Heat Rate (Million BTUs/KWH) (2)	Cost of Fuel per Ton of Coal Equivalent (3)	Fuel Cost per KWH (4)	Av. Cost of Generation Plant ($/KW) (5)	Cost of Incremental Generation ($/KW) (6)	Consumer Price Index (7)	Handy & Whitman Electric Constr. Index (July, North Atlantic) (8)
1965	102.9	10,384	$ 6.23	0.27¢	$ 132	$ 101	31.5	167
1966	108.0	10,399	6.22	0.27	130	94	32.4	172
1967	113.6	10,396	6.29	0.27	128	103	33.3	179
1968	121.1	10,371	6.40	0.28	125	94	34.3	184
1969	127.4	10,457	6.58	0.29	126	132	35.7	195
1970	135.0	10,508	7.38	0.34	127	147	37.5	212
1971	147.9	10,536	8.64	0.40	125	107	39.5	229
1972	157.3	10,479	9.31	0.42	130	192	39.9	245
1973	169.0	10,429	10.65	0.49	134	166	41.2	262
1974	184.9	10,481	18.49	0.87	142	247	45.8	313
1975	199.6	10,383	21.60	1.03	152	332	50.1	362
1976	202.9	10,369	22.58	1.07	159	309	55.1	379
1977	210.6	10,449	25.50	1.24	172	425	59.0	403
1978	224.6	10,495	27.34	1.35	187	678	61.7	421
1979	231.0	10,470	31.85	1.56	196	647	70.5	466
1980	241.3	10,489	37.60	1.85	211	553	83.1	505
% Change 1965-1980	+134	+1	+504	+585	+60	+448	+164	+202

Notes
  EIA or FPC capacity data. Column 2 total electric industry. Column 3 excludes hydro.
Sources:
  FPC, EIA, EEI, *Electrical World.*

Table 14-9

Distribution
Investor Owned Electric Utilities
1965 - 1980

Year	Average Cost of Distribution Plant/Customer	Cost of Incremental Distribution/Incr. Customer	Distribution Expense per Customer(a)
	(1)	(2)	(3)
1965	$ 437	$1,303	$17.48
1966	454	1,226	17.84
1967	477	1,799	18.67
1968	501	1,672	19.31
1969	526	1,913	20.56
1970	554	1,828	22.14
1971	582	1,910	22.82
1972	645(b)	2,296(b)	24.13
1973	610(b)	-600(b)	25.51
1974	670	3,228	26.46
1975	702	2,683	27.63
1976	730	2,381	29.51
1977	760	2,198	31.76
1978	794	2,504	34.81
1979	825	1,921	37.68
1980	861	2,516	41.90
% Change 1965-1980	+97	+93	+140

Year	Average Distribution Plant per KW of Capacity(c)	Period	Incremental Distribution Plant per Incremental KW of Capacity
1965	$ 126	1961-1965	$ 130
1970	121	1965-1970	109
1975	113	1971-1975	98
1980	128	1976-1980	200

Notes
(a) $ per year.
(b) Revised series.
(c) FPC and EIA data for capacity.

Sources
FPC, EIA.

Traumatic Events

The utilities faced even more than constant erosion as four major events shook the foundations of the industry.

The Northeast Blackout of 1965 — On November 2, 1965, a broken backup relay on the Ontario Hydro system set loose a series of power disconnections and surges:

> It took twelve minutes from the time the operational interruption knocked out the relay in a little box at the Sir Adam Beck facility to produce the worst power failure in the age of electricity, engulfing 30 million people over an area of 80,000 square miles in one form or another of dark reality.[33]

After that event, the Federal Power Commission launched an investigation and instituted new reporting procedures to keep track of power outages. In its report, the FPC commented that "the initial reaction of the Northeast failure was one of general disbelief that such an incident could happen."[34] Further investigation showed that minor outages had not been uncommon in the past, and that in the years that followed the blackout, there were several noteworthy power failures. Obviously, all was not well. New power pooling procedures, an increased number of transmission lines, and more generation equipment all were needed to bring service up to standards. Moreover, the Northeast blackout shook managements and regulators out of their complacency, an attitude caused by years of fairly smooth operations and good press. The money required to improve operations was the beginning of an expenditure program that had to be independent of the direction of demand, for what utility people like to call "non-revenue producing" plant. (That term also is often used in reference to pollution control equipment. Of course, all plant is revenue producing in the sense that it goes into the rate base.)

The Arab Oil Embargo of 1973-74 — In the wake of the Yom Kippur War, Middle Eastern oil producers cut off shipments to the United States and the OPEC nations multiplied the price for oil several-fold. In response to that action, Americans reduced their consumption of electricity. As the price for fuel rose and was passed on to many customers by means of the fuel adjustment clause, price became a determinant in dampening the demand for electricity. In 1974, sales of electricity dropped from the year-earlier level, the first time since 1946 that a year-to-year decline occurred. Furthermore, the pattern of steady, rapid growth ceased. The industry had geared its capital spending and expense budget to automatic sales gains. When those gains did not materialize, the industry faced two severe problems. First, it was caught in a squeeze between high fixed costs and declining base rate revenues that resulted from a drop in sales. Second, the industry was uncertain about what to do with a capital spending program that was based on rapid growth in demand. For a while, managements and regulators viewed the slowdown in demand

Table 14-10

Transmission
Investor Owned Utilities
1965-1980

Year	Transmission Plant/Circuit Mile of Transmission	Incremental Transmission Plant/Incremental Miles	Transmission Expense per KWH Sold (mills)	KWH Losses as % of Generation Purchase and Interchange (%)
	(1)	(2)	(3)	(4)
1965	$29,513	$111,833	0.21	7.7
1966	31,151	86,795	0.21	7.6
1967	33,611	99,343	0.21	7.5
1968	35,985	125,137	0.21	7.4
1969	38,753	146,504	0.22	7.1
1970	41,320	106,615	0.23	7.0
1971	44,889	178,486	0.24	7.1
1972	47,342	117,577	0.25	7.2
1973	50,221	182,238	0.26	6.5
1974	53,150	150,636	0.29	6.8
1975	55,415	237,409	0.31	6.9
1976	58,855	320,172	0.33	6.8
1977	61,204	201,533	0.35	6.4
1978	64,407	285,646	0.37	6.6
1979	67,161	281,294	0.40	6.3
1980	70,494	302,927	0.43	6.6
% Change 1965-1980	+139	+171	+105	-14

Year	Average Trans. Plant per Circuit Volt Mile(b)	Period	Incr. Trans. Plant per incr. Circuit Volt Mile(b)	Year	Percent of Transmission Circuit Miles by Voltage(b,c) 22-50KV	51-131 KV	132-800KV
	(1)	(2)	(3)	(4)	(5)	(6)	(7)
1965	$0.33	1961-1965	$0.50	1965	31.8	42.6	25.6
1970	0.39	1966-1970	0.53	1970	29.7	39.0	31.3
1975	0.47	1971-1975	0.82	1975	29.7	36.3	34.0
1980	0.59	1976-1980	1.30	1980	30.7	33.4	35.9

Notes
(a) 22KV and over.
(b) Circuit volt-miles defined as miles of transmission x voltages of transmission line.
(c) Total industry.

Sources
FPC, EIA, EEI.

as an aberration. As a result, managements continued to make commitments to build. Those commitments proved to be not only erroneous but also a financial burden in the succeeding years. Finally, many utilities had inadequate fuel adjustment clauses. The rapid increase in fuel costs squeezed margins. The industry reeled from the financial consequences of increased costs and reduced sales. The era of rapid growth in sales had ended, but the industry's reaction was delayed.

Consolidated Edison Omits Its Common Stock Dividend in April 1974 — Consolidated Edison ran into a financial bind that culminated in the sale of some of its facilities to an agency of the State of New York and in the omission of its dividend. Con Edison's dividend omission hit the industry with the impact of a wrecking ball. It smashed the keystone of faith for investment in utilities: that the dividend is safe and will be paid. Wall Street firms, at the behest of panic-stricken clients, prepared lists that showed which utilities were in bad shape. In April 1974, the price for the average utility stock fell by 18%. By September, prices for utility stocks had fallen by 36%. That was not the kind of performance expected of utility stocks. The April drop was the greatest since March 1938, and the April-September collapse was the greatest in a calendar year since 1937. In 1974, utility stocks declined to well below book value, thereby making future financing dilutionary. Furthermore, because bond investors began to worry about the risk involved in investing in low quality utilities, selling low quality bonds also became difficult. The spread between Aaa and Baa rated bonds — almost always between 50 and 100 basis points (100 basis points equals 1%) in the postwar period — rose to more than 200 basis points by the end of 1974. Investors had to accept the possibility of financial risk in utility securities. Managements realized that not only could they not raise money at will, but that money might only be obtained at astronomical rates. Partly because of financial pressures, capital expenditures declined in 1975 for the first time since 1962. It was a new ball game, but some of the players, unfortunately, were still playing by the old rules.

TheNuclear Accident at Three Mile Island on March 28, 1979 — A cooling system malfunction started the country's first major, well publicized civilian nuclear accident. For days, reports of core meltdown, escape of radiation and potential explosion frightened the population of the Northeast. The reactor finally went out of service after having incurred several hundred million dollars worth of damage. The Pennsylvania event destroyed the complacency about nuclear power best typified by the comment often made before the accident: "There never has been a nuclear accident." Anti-nuclear demonstrations attracted thousands. Many investors made it clear that they did not want to own securities in nuclear-oriented electric utilities, probably less because of fear of the health and safety hazards of nuclear power than because of the financial hazards. Building a nuclear plant involved risking huge sums in a project that could be delayed or halted and that was often bitterly fought against by a determined opposition. The Three Mile Island disaster revealed another risk: if the nuclear plant went out of service, the power company might have to replace the lost nuclear power with far more expensive power purchased from others. If the regulators did not allow the utility to pass on to consumers the increased costs, the utility could suffer serious financial losses. General Public Utilities, the subsidiaries of which owned the Three Mile Island reactor, was forced to omit its dividend and was unable to place securities in the public market after the accident. The utility industry, the public, and the Government had placed their faith in nuclear power as a cheap, safe form of energy that would also reduce our reliance on foreign oil. Escalation of construction costs brought into question its cheapness. The Three Mile Island accident confirmed — in the minds of detractors of nuclear power — the doubts about safety. The Nuclear Regulatory Commission (NRC), severely criticized for its administrative maladroitness, imposed a moratorium on the licensing of nuclear reactors. In the period after the Three Mile Island accident, the electric utility industry, in a weakened financial condition and with excess generating capacity in many areas, cancelled or deferred nuclear projects. Nuclear power began with a dream of electricity sufficiently cheap that it could not be metered, and the electric utility industry embraced the new technology. Construction delays, cost overruns, environmental opposition, the constant need to modify plans to meet changing safety regulations, and uncertainty about Government policies, however, all demonstrated that nuclear power would not bring a golden age to the industry. In the case of some utilities, the strains of constructing huge nuclear plants destroyed their financial standing. For many others, nuclear power had lost its luster before the Three Mile Island accident. After the accident, even proponents of the nuclear effort seemed to be thinking more in terms of finishing what was already under construction than planning for additional facilities.

Closing Out the Decade

Clearly, a lot was wrong. Congress tried to encourage more efficient pricing of electricity, reduce the consumption of foreign oil, help energy conservation, and develop competition in the generating sector through the passage of the Public Utility Regulatory Policies Act (PURPA) of 1978. Title I of PURPA required utilities to develop information about costs and state regulators to examine the impact of rate structures on energy conservation. Title II created a new class of generators, qualifying facilities (QFs) that could sell electricity to electric companies. Those facilities, by and large, would be cogenerators, that would be more efficient than utility plants, because they would produce both electricity and usable steam, thereby saving fuel. But the electric industry attacked PURPA in the courts, and put off its implementation.

Oddly enough, about the time that the Federal Government was imposing new and unwanted requirements on utilities through PURPA, the courts reaffirmed

Federal supremacy in a way that pleased beleaguered utilities. A number of electric holding companies had found a way to get around restrictive state regulation. They set up wholesale generating subsidiaries that produced electricity which was sold to affiliated local distribution utilities. The Federal Power Commission (later Federal Energy Regulatory Commission) regulated the wholesale power contract between the generation companies and the local utilities, while the states regulated other aspects of the local utilities. Once the FPC set the price of the power sold to the local utility, the state regulators had to accept those power costs as legitimate. The generation function represented a large part of total costs. The utility had managed to remove those costs from the supervision of state regulators. The Rhode Island regulatory agency attempted to question the reasonableness of the wholesale rates set by the FPC for power purchased by Narragansett Electric. The Supreme Court of Rhode Island, in its Narragansett decision of December 1977[35], concluded that the FPC, alone, could set interstate wholesale rates, and that local regulators had to accept those rates as reasonable. In April 1978, the U.S. Supreme Court denied an appeal by state regulators of the Narragansett decision. (Interestingly enough, it took another state court to find a way around Narragansett. In 1983, the Commonwealth Court of Pennsylvania, in the Pike County decision[36], found that the state regulators had to accept Federal jurisdiction over the reasonableness of interstate wholesale rates, but the state could decide whether the utility had made a prudent decision in making that wholesale power purchase compared to available alternatives.)

By the end of the decade, many utilities had given up on the old pursuit of sales and scale (the last nuclear power station, for instance, had been ordered in 1973), but still others doggedly pursued the old path. Most, though, seemed more eager to just clean up the mess, and put the finances in order, and face a modest future.

Chapter 15

Stabilization and Competition: After 1980

As a regulator, I was always perplexed by the intensity of public outrage over most electric rate increases during the 1970s. Obviously, nobody likes rising prices, but in the past era of widespread inflation when all energy sectors were particularly hard hit, why weren't there riots at supermarkets and gas stations like those that erupted at utility rate hearings?[37]

Richard E. Schuler

The electric utilities staggered under the burden of high interest rates and incomplete projects while facing uncertain demand for electricity. The job of regulators — once the perfect position for the political hack awaiting the transition to Social Security — turned rough, as the besieged officials fought off angry consumers upset by higher prices. Investors saw their stocks at new lows. Would the industry survive?

More Shocks

There was more bad news to come: legal decisions, plant abandonments, huge writedowns of investments, bond defaults, another nuclear accident, and even bankruptcy.

The U.S. Supreme Court Upholds PURPA — On June 1, 1982, the Supreme Court upheld the legality of the Public Utility Regulatory Policies Act of 1978 (PURPA). The decision, *Federal Energy Regulatory Commission v. State of Mississippi*,[38] legalized the creation of a whole new industry of generators, qualifying facilities (QFs), firms that could set up generating units, and then sell their output to utilities at the utilities' avoided costs. The QFs, at first, seemed annoying interlopers, forced on utilities that would rather have not dealt with them. Few saw the significance of the decision at the time. What it did was to open up a closed system to new entrants, a process that began slowly but gained momentum when utility managements decided that it was better to buy from others than to risk their own capital under an uncertain regulatory regime.

Cincinnati G&E Reveals Inability to Complete Zimmer Nuclear Station As Planned — On October 5, 1983, Cincinnati G&E shocked investors by announcing that the Zimmer nuclear station, supposedly 97% complete, would require $2.8-$3.5 billion in additional investment and two to three years of work to be finished. That news was the first of many disastrous nuclear crises that followed. Utilities tottered on the brink of bankruptcy, scrambling for funds to complete troubled projects, or to salvage what they could from huge investments in projects that had to be cancelled despite the billions of dollars that had been sunk in them. Within twelve months, six utilities cut or omitted dividends, almost $6 billion of construction effort was consigned to oblivion, and the stock prices of the affected utilities fell 60-80% from their 1983 highs. The message was clear. Utilities with serious problems caused by construction failures and extreme cost overruns would not be made whole by regulatory agencies. Investors could not depend on regulators for guaranteed returns or for bailouts. The best they could hope for was a rescue effort that kept the utility afloat.

   Washington State Lets WPPSS Default — On June 15, 1983, this saga came to a crashing climax. The Washington Public Power Supply System or WPPSS (pronounced "whoops") was a municipal agency created to build power projects whose output would be sold to public power agencies. WPPSS chose to build five nuclear stations, the output of the first two contracted for sale to the Bonneville Power Administration, a Federal entity, and the rest to numerous, often small public power agencies. The cost estimates for the nuclear plants had more than tripled since their start in 1976, demand for electricity fell, WPPSS had to cancel two of the units, and halt construction of the third when it ran out of money. Investors sued the public power agencies that had backed WPPSS bonds through their power purchase agreements. The Washington Supreme Court ruled in June 1983, in the case of *Chemical Bank v. Washington Public Power Supply System*[39], that the public power agencies never had the authority to sign contracts with WPPSS. They were off the hook. Investors learned that not even bondholders in public agencies were safe when a nuclear project went down.

   The Russian Nuclear Reactor at Chernobyl Goes Out of Control — On April 26, 1986, unauthorized testing at Chernobyl produced a nuclear accident that destroyed the generating station, killed 31 people, forced evacuation of 116,000 nearby residents and loosed a radioactive cloud that floated over Europe. Non-Russian reactors are built differently, so the Chernobyl-type accident probably could not have happened elsewhere, a fact often cited by those who chose to believe that Chernobyl was irrelevant outside the Soviet bloc. Unfortunately, a serious, fatal nuclear accident moved from a statistical probability to something that happened. Chernobyl strengthened the credibility of those people who oppose nuclear power, and reemphasized the importance of emergency evacuation plans. In the words of Lord Marshall of Goring, chairman of the United Kingdom's Central Electricity Generating Board, "In some countries the shock has been so great that governments have made a formal decision to abandon nuclear power."[40] America's utilities have had to deal with the specter of Chernobyl even if it cannot happen here.

   Public Service of New Hampshire Goes Bankrupt — "Utility operating companies do not go bankrupt, did not go bankrupt even during the Depression, and will not go bankrupt, because regulators would not let it happen." That was the

Table 15 - 1

Energy and the Economy
1980 - 1990

Year	Energy Consumption in USA	Real GNP	Electricity Use	Real Price of			
				Electricity	Natural Gas	Fuel Oil	Bituminous Coal
	(1)	(2)	(3)	(4)	(5)	(6)	(7)
1980	100	100	100	100	100	100	100
1985	97	114	109	109	126	83	90
1990	107	130	126	95	94	61	73

Notes and Sources

(a) See Table 13-1.

complacent belief of investors. But it was wrong. Public Service Company of New Hampshire, a small utility, struggled for years to build a large nuclear station, was hampered by unfavorable regulatory rulings, spiralling costs, construction problems, obstructions caused by local governments, and finally, burdened by high interest costs, filed for bankruptcy on January 28, 1988. That had never happened before. Investors learned that they could be wiped out.

What happened to the old regulatory compact, in which the utilities agreed to invest their funds to serve customers, expecting a reasonable return, and no more, in return for which the regulators assured the utility of protection from risks? Apparently, the regulators either were unable or unwilling to provide the protection. The risk of investment, clearly, was great. Perhaps, the utility managers thought, they ought to minimize investment in facilities whose profitability was controlled by regulators. Let someone else build the power station. The utility would buy electricity from others. Some managers decided that the only way to produce growth at their corporations was to invest funds in non-utility ventures (diversification). They bought desert real estate, insurance companies, airplanes, eyeball identification devices, savings and loan associations, and issuers of second mortgages on used cars. They set up holding companies to control these diverse ventures. Most of them failed spectacularly. What did succeed, eventually, were ventures that concentrated on fuel transportation, coal mining, and electricity generation through unregulated affiliates. Utilities then cut their losses, hunkered down, avoided risk and began to concentrate on running the core business better, rather than on seeking extracurricular ventures.

Economic Trends

In the 1980s, the USA became more energy efficient, despite the fact that the

Table 15-2

Electricity Production
1980-1990
(Kwh millions and %)

Year	Total	Industrial and Other	Utility	Investor Owned Utilities	Public Power	% of generation		
						Industrial and Other	Investor Owned Utility	Public Power
	(1)	(2)	(3)	(4)	(5)	(6)	(7)	(8)
1980	2,345.3	67.9	2,286.4	1,782.9	503.5	2.9	75.7	21.4
1985	2,568.3	98.5	2,469.8	1,918.0	551.8	3.8	74.7	21.5
1990	3,039.9	232.8	2,807.1	2,201.0	606.1	7.7	72.4	19.9

Source: EEI

Table 15-3

Generation
Total Electric Utility Industry
1980 - 1990

Year	Average Size Utility Prime Mover (kw)	Heat Rate (Btu)	Production per Kw of Capacity (Hrs)	Coal Equivalent per Kwh Produced (lbs)
	(1)	(2)	(3)	(4)
1980	200,059	10,489	3,726	1.0
1985	227,419	10,429	3,586	1.0
1990	237,100 E	10,367	3,819	1.0

Note
Column 1: Change in series may distort results.

Sources
EEI, EIA.

real price of energy declined sharply. Electricity usage continued to grow faster than energy usage as a whole. (See Table 15-1.)

The production picture started to change, too, reversing the pattern of decades, as non-utility sources produced a rapidly rising percentage of the output. PURPA was responsible for this growth. (See Table 15-2.)

The industry's rush to larger and larger generating units seems to have slowed. The utilities, though, eked few additional economies out of the generating units. (See Table 15-3.)

At least, after the erratic 1970s, sales moved upward. (See Table 15-4.)

Capital Expenditures and Financing

During the 1970s, the industry made huge capital expenditures with the expectation of higher sales. The sales did not materialize. In the 1980s, the industry lowered its spending program, while sales grew. As a result, the utilities were able to reduce their excessive reserve margins, and cut back on the need to raise expensive new capital. (See Table 15-5.)

As the utilities cut back on their big plant additions, and revenues moved up due to greater demand, the utilities needed smaller and smaller price increases to

Table 15-4

Electricity and the Economy
1980-1990

Year	% Change KWH Sales	% Change Peak Load	% Change Real GNP	% Total US Elec. Gen. by non-Utility Sources	% of Elec. Made Available in the U.S.A. Generated by Domestic Elec. Utilities	
					Supplied by All Utilities	Supplied by Investor Owned Utilities
	(1)	(2)	(3)	(4)	(5)	(6)
1980	2.0	7.2	-0.2	2.9	96.0	75.1
1981	1.2	0.3	1.9	2.7	96.3	74.6
1982	-2.4	-3.1	-2.5	2.7	96.1	73.4
1983	2.9	7.9	3.6	2.4	96.1	73.4
1984	5.6	0.8	6.8	2.9	95.6	73.1
1985	1.1	2.1	3.4	3.8	94.8	73.6
1986	2.1	3.6	2.7	4.3	94.4	73.2
1987	3.4	4.0	3.4	5.4	93.0	73.1
1988	5.0	6.7	4.5	6.1	92.9	73.7
1989	2.6	-1.1	2.5	6.7	92.9	73.2
1990	1.8	4.2	1.0	7.7	92.9	72.4

Notes
Column 2:   Summer Peak.

Sources
Columns 1, 2, 4-6: EEI.
Column 3:   EIA

cover costs. Usage per customer moved up slightly. The industry was no longer battering its customers with big price hikes, and that encouraged greater consumption. (See Table 15-6.)

The financial results of all the improvement could be classed as peculiar. Utilities were stronger, but not extraordinarily so. The coverage of interest costs improved, but remained at a relatively low level. The non-cash allowance for funds used during construction (AFUDC), which had bloated the income statement with unreal earnings, declined to a minimal level. Yet the companies had a hard time translating that improvement into a better return on common stockholders' equity, possibly because they had to take huge losses from the writing off of assets disallowed by regulators and from disposal of unfortunate forays into diversification. At the same time, interest rates fell dramatically, which caused investors to revalue the utility stocks. In 1980, Average Electric Company earned 11.5% on a stockholder's investment of $82.72, or $9.51, while bonds yielded 13.46%. Pur-

Table 15-5

Capital Spending and Reserve Margins
Investor Owned Electric Utilities
1980-1990

Year	% Increase in Gross Electric Utility Plant (1)	Capital Spending ($ Million) (2)	New Permanent Capital Rasied as % of Capital Spending (3)	Reserve Margin (b)(c) % (4)
1980	10.2	28,355	49	30.7
1981	9.7	30,690	45	33.6
1982	10.0	35,350	44	41.3
1983	8.3	35,565	33	33.3
1984	8.4	35,285	31	34.0
1985	9.1	33,294	34	35.2
1986	5.4	31,023	38	32.8
1987	4.1	27,035	38	30.6
1988	3.4	23,630	33	25.0
1989	2.8	24,760	38	28.6
1990	4.5	24,289	27	25.6

(a) Revised.   (b) Total   (c) Summer.

Note
Column 3: Net permanent capital raised for all corporate uses as percent of electric capital
expenditures. Percentage of total capital spending raised through permanent financing may be
lower. Common stock, preferred stock and long term debt issues only, as reported by Ebasco
Business Consulting.

Sources
Federal Power Commission Statistics: Energy Information Administration, Statistics of
Privately Owned Electric Utilities in the United States (Washing, D.C.: U.S. Gov't Printing
Office, various years) column 1). Edison Electric Institute Year Book (columns 2, 3, 4).

chasers paid only $54.80 for the stock, for an earnings yield of 17.4% ($9.51/
$54.80). In 1990, the utility earned 10.4% on a stockholder's investment of $86.93,
or $9.03, while bonds yielded 10.0%. Purchasers paid $112.54 for the stock,
producing an earnings yield of 8.1% ($9.03 /$112.54). What produced such a
dramatic reversal in valuation? First, with interest rates lower, investors were also
willing to accept lower returns on stocks. Second, investors probably felt that the
industry was healthier and safer than before, and the lower earnings for shareholders
represented an unusual phenomenon that would be followed by better numbers once
the various writeoffs were out of the way. (See Table 15-7.)

Operating Costs

Probably the most discouraging aspect of the 1980s was the lack of real
improvement in the operating picture. The utilities ceased to add the big generating

Table 15-6

Price and Usage
Total Electric Utility Industry
1980-1990

Year	Price of Residential Electricity (¢/KWH)	Price of All Electricity (¢/KWH)	Consumer Price Index	GNP Deflator	Net Rate Increases (Decreases) as % of Electric Revenue	Electric Usage per Residential Customer (KWH)	Electric Usage per Customer (KWH)
	(1)	(2)	(3)	(4)	(5)	(6)	(7)
1980	5.12	4.49	82.4	85.7	7.4	9,025	23,167
1981	5.80	5.14	90.9	94.0	8.7	8,825	23,026
1982	6.44	5.79	96.5	100.0	7.4	8,743	22,197
1983	6.83	6.00	99.6	103.9	4.9	8,814	22,479
1984	7.17	6.27	103.9	107.7	6.6	8,978	23,152
1985	7.39	6.47	107.6	111.2	3.6	8,906	22,903
1986	7.43	6.47	109.6	113.8	2.0	9,090	23,071
1987	7.45	6.39	113.6	117.4	0.7	9,236	23,472
1988	7.49	6.36	118.3	121.3	0.6	9,498	24,167
1989	7.65	6.47	124.0	126.3	0.9	9,470	24,359
1990	7.82	6.58	130.7	131.5	1.3	9,472	24,463
% Change 1980-1990	+53	+47	+59	+53	--	+5	+6

Notes
Column 5: Investor-owned utilities.

Sources
EEI, Dept. of Commerce.

plants that had proved so disappointing, but they made little progress in deriving economies from the generating base. Cost of new plant rose far more rapidly than inflation. To the extent utilities were able to keep down costs, it was due to the falling price of fuel. (See Table 15-8.) The distribution sector showed similar results, with overall costs per customer rising faster than inflation. (See Table 15-9.) The difficulties of putting up transmission lines in a more environmentally sensitive era certainly shoved up the transmission expenses, which rose faster than inflation, too. (See Table 15-10.)

The electric utility industry used to display a pattern of declining costs. Even in the 1980s, when pressure had eased, utilities seemed unable to find enough new economies of scale to keep costs (other than fuel) rising at no more than the rate of inflation.

Table 15-7

Financial Ratios
Investor Owned Electric Utilities
1980-1990

Year	Return on Common Equity % (1)	Interest Cost Newly Issued Bonds (Moody's) (%) (2)	Interest Coverage Ratio (Long Term Debt) (FERC) (X) (3)	AFUDC % Net Income(a) (4)	Average Stock Price (Moody's)(b) ($) (5)	Average Book Value (Moody's) (6)	Market/Book Ratio (Moody's) (%) (7)
1980	11.5	13.46	2.3	41.2	54.80	82.72	66
1981	12.5	16.31	2.3	41.3	55.41	82.87	67
1982	13.6	14.93	2.4	43.3	63.56	82.34	77
1983	14.2	12.70	2.5	43.4	74.04	82.84	89
1984	14.5	14.25	2.5	39.9	71.16	83.99	85
1985	12.5	11.83	2.3	42.4	87.08	86.42	101
1986	13.1	9.61	2.4	31.4	111.11	89.06	125
1987	11.9	9.74	2.6	26.0	106.26	90.24	118
1988	9.7	10.03	2.5	17.9	97.67	89.08	110
1989	10.3	9.92	2.6	13.5	110.31	88.73	124
1990	10.2	9.69	2.5	11.2	112.54	86.93	130
% Change 1980-1990	-11	-28	+9	-73	+105	+5	+97

Notes

Columns 1, 3 (through 1985) and 4 are calculated by EIA. Column 3 (1986-1990) calculated from EIA data consistent with previous years.

Sources

Columns 1, 3 and 4 (EIA).
Columns 2, 5-7: Moody's.

Table 15-8

Power Generation
Investor Owned Electric Utilities
1980-1990

Year	Avg. Size of Gener. Plants (Total Industry) (1,000KW)	Est. Av. Size of Gener. Plants (1,000 KW)	Heat Rate (Millions BTUs/KWH)	Cost of Fuel per Ton of Coal Equivalent	Fuel Cost per KWH	Av. Cost of Generation Plant ($/KW)	Cost of Incremental Generation ($/KW)	Consumer Price Index	Handy & Whitman Electric Constr. Index (July) North Atlantic
	(1)	(2)	(3)	(4)	(5)	(6)	(7)	(8)	(9)
1980	200.1	241.3	10,489	37.60	1.85	211	553	82.4	193
1981	207.1	252.5	10,506	43.64	2.16	221	611	90.9	209
1982	213.8	254.7	10,517	45.44	2.25	235	1,064	96.5	222
1983	218.3	254.7	10,547	43.83	2.16	248	1,521	99.6	231
1984	223.5	258.6	10,385	43.46	2.14	269	1,406	103.9	239
1985	227.4	260.3	10,429	40.37	1.98	328	1,141	107.6	244
1986	232.9	264.8	10,423	34.30	1.68	360	1,577	109.6	249
1987	237.9	266.8	10,354	32.52	1.58	408	3,467	113.6	251
1988	239.3	266.1	10,328	30.75	1.50	431	3.023	118.3	273
1989	237.8	265.9	10,312	31.27	1.53	443	2,006	124.0	286
1990	237.1	265.6	10,367	30.86	1.51	471	3,442	130.7	296
% Change 1980-1990	+18	+10	-1	-18	-18	+123	+522	+59	+53

Notes

Columns 1 and 2: Due to changes in series, year-by-year data should be viewed as approximations.
Columns 1 and 3: Total electric utility industry.
Columns 6 and 7: Production plant (EIA).

Sources:

EIA, EEI.

Table 15-9

Distribution
Investor Owned Electric Utilities
1980-1990

Year	Average Cost of Distribution Plant/Customer	Cost of Incremental Distribution/Incr. Customer	Distribution Expense per Customer(a)
	(1)	(2)	(3)
1980	$861	$2,516	$41.90
1981	903	3,211	45.19
1982	950	4,726	50.62
1983	993	4,030	54.10
1984	1,050	5,123	57.71
1985	1,102	5,552	60.53
1986	1,148	2,773	60.96
1987	1,204	3,968	63.25
1988	1,269	5,692	64.74
1989	1,338	5,170	65.35
1990	1,409	6,238	65.95
% Change 1980-1990	+64	+148	+57

Year	Average Distribution Plant per KW of Capacity(c)	Period	Incremental Distribution Plant per Incremental KW of Capacity
1980	128	1976-1980	200
1985	157	1981-1985(c)	425
1990	207	1986-1990(c)	920

Notes

(a) $ per year.
(b) Revised Series.
(c) EIA data for capacity to 1980. EEI data 1981-1990.

Sources

FPC, EIA, EEI

Table 15-10

Transmission
Investor Owned Utilities
1980-1990

Year	Transmission Plant/Circuit Mile of Transmission	Incremental Transmission Plant/Incremental Miles	Transmission Expense per KWH Sold (mills)	KWH Losses as % of Generation Purchase and Interchange (%)
	(1)	(2)	(3)	(4)
1980	$70,494	$302,927	0.43	6.6
1981	74,189	331,228	0.48	6.2
1982	78,234	745,476	0.56	6.1
1983	81,313	511,176	0.60	6.7
1984	85,657	366,039	0.64	5.8
1985	89,164	399,441	0.69	6.1
1986	92,329	612,872	0.72	5.7
1987	94,548	437,270	0.73	6.3
1988	97,514	610,193	0.72	6.2
1989	101,246	680,586	0.74	6.2
1990	105,848	716,474	0.74	5.7
% Change 1980-1990	+50	+137	+72	-14

Year	Average Trans. Plant per Circuit Volt Mile(b)	Period	Incr. Trans. Plant per incr. Circuit Volt Mile(b)	Year	Percent of Transmission Circuit Miles By Voltage(b,c)		
					22-50KV	51-131 KV	132-800KV
	(1)	(2)	(3)	(4)	(5)	(6)	(7)
1980	0.59	1976-1980	1.30	1980	30.7	33.4	35.9
1985	0.71	1981-1985	1.86	1985	31.0	32.5	36.5
1990	0.86	1986-1990	7.14	1990	31.6	32.0	36.4

Notes

(a) 22KV and higher, overhead lines.
(b) Miles of transmission x voltages of lines.
(c) Total Industry.

Sources EIA, EEI.

Chapter 16

Summary

Monopoly in the local electric utility industry is so taken for granted that it is almost forgotten that competition ever existed.[41]

Walter J. Primeaux, Jr.

Electric utilities developed along the lines envisioned by Edison and his lieutenants. The electric utility vertically integrated from generation through transmission to distribution. Central station power moved decisively from supplying about 40% of electricity at the turn of the century to supplying roughly 60% during the World War I period and to 80% during the Great Depression. Perhaps not coincidentally, the industry's penetration of the market grew side by side with regulation. Regulation began at the behest of civic reformers and of important elements in the utility industry.

The holding companies formed early in the history of electric power, and became monsters that encompassed much of the industry by the 1920s. Financial abuse led to the collapse of many holding companies. The New Deal dismembered the spread-out holding companies as part of a reform of the industry. The New Deal also built permanent, huge Federal power agencies that now dominate the power markets of large areas in the South and Northwest. Today, hundreds of investor owned utilities supply about 75% of the nation's power, with the rest provided by several thousand government owned (Federal, state, and local) power agencies and from rural cooperatives.

For most of its history, the electric industry was able to take advantage of the economies available from new and ever larger plants and from increasingly efficient transmission and distribution procedures. As a result, the price for electricity fell steadily from 1882 to 1969, despite a generally upward trend in prices throughout the economy. During that period usage increased as steadily as prices declined.

That long idyll ended in the 1970s. (See Figure 16-1.) New technology seemed incapable of further reducing costs. The rapid rise in fuel costs, a lack of additional efficiencies in production, and rampant cost inflation pushed the price of electricity upward. Consequently, sales faltered. The utilities could not — or would not — adjust immediately to the new conditions. The regulators also had a hard time understanding that prices could no longer be decreased but had to be raised. The 1970s was a period of declining profitability, lowered bond ratings, falling stock prices, and an industry

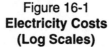
Figure 16-1
Electricity Costs
(Log Scales)

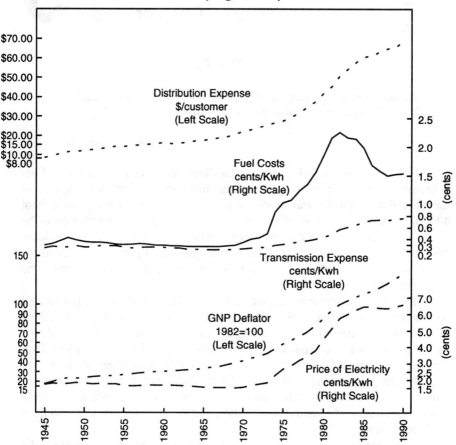

in turmoil. With the beginning of the 1980s, though, managements, legislators and regulators began to take remedial action. They cut overblown spending programs, reduced operating expenses, and rescued several utilities from collapse. They paid serious attention to efforts to help consumers use less electricity in order to put off building expensive new power stations.

What went wrong? Basically:

♦ New facilities ceased to produce the efficiencies, the economies of scale, that dramatically and without interruption reduced the cost of production for eighty years.

♦ Neither regulators nor managements acted quickly enough to reshape operations and pricing for the new era.

♦ Nuclear projects proved beyond the capability of many of the utilities attempting them. In retrospect, nuclear construction was no different than any giant project and had the same dangerous characteristics: they required thousands of workers, took years to complete, demanded skilled coordination between the many parties involved in the process, endured changes of specifications and governmental interference, strained the financial markets, and created excess capacity when completed.[42] To top off the list of insults, many nuclear plants not only worked poorly but also proved to be uneconomical.

♦ Managements did not understand price elasticity of demand until it was too late. They stubbornly clung to the notion that the diminution of sales growth was an aberration, so they shaped policies for demand that never materialized.

Utilities have changed. Managements run them as businesses, emphasize efficiency and service, and try to fend off potential competition rather than act as secure monopolists. The companies are less integrated, more likely to buy power and services from others. Regulators have discovered that they provided little incentive for efficiency or innovation, so they have begun to redesign regulation. The time of troubles may be over, but utilities are not headed back to the structure that existed in the good old days.

Notes

[1]Henry Adams, *The Education of Henry Adams* (New York: Random House Modern Library, 1931), pp. 380-381. The quotation is from the famous chapter "The Dynamo and the Virgin."

[2]Matthew Josephson, *Edison* (New York: McGraw Hill, 1959), p. 178.

[3]Philip Sporn, *Energy — Its Production, Conversion, and Use in the Service of Man* (New York: Columbia Graduate School of Business, 1963), p. 12.

[4]The questionable nature of the telephone patent is described in Robert Conot's *A Streak of Luck* (New York: Seaview Books, 1979), pp. 81-83.

[5]Conot, *op. cit.*, p. 129.

[6]Josephson, *op. cit.*, p. 185.

[7]Josephson, *op. cit.*, p. 189.

[8]Forrest McDonald, *Insull* (Chicago: The University of Chicago Press, 1962), p. 26.

[9]Thomas P. Hughes, "Technological History and Technical Problems," in Chauncey Starr and Philip C. Ritterbush, eds., *Science, Technology and the Human Prospect* (New York: Pergamon Press, 1980), p. 144.

[10]"Harnessing a Monument," *EPRI Journal*, March 1979, p. 38.

[11]McDonald, *op. cit.*, p. 20.

[12]"The Electric Century," *Electrical World*, June 1, 1974, p. 44.

[13]Harold H. Young, *Forty Years of Public Utility's Finance* (Charlottesville: The University Press of Virginia, 1965), p. 33.

[14]Douglas D. Anderson, *Regulatory Politics and Electric Utilities* (Boston: Auburn House, 1981), p. 56.

[15]Eli Winston Clemens, *Economics and Public Utilities* (New York: Appleton-Century-Crofts,

1950), p. 91.
[16]Clemens, *op. cit.*, p. 13.
[17]J. Maurice Clark, *Studies in the Economics of Overhead Costs* (Chicago: The University of Chicago Press, 1962 impression), p. 11. This point was suggested in Charles D. Stalon, "Deregulation of the Electric Generating Industry: Some Unsystematic Observations," in *Proceedings: Edison Electric Institute Sixteenth Financial Conference October 4-7, 1981* (Washington, D.C.: Edison Electric Institute, 1982). That analysis seems to question at least one assumption (free entry and exit) of the contestable market theory. See William J. Baumol, "Contestable Markets: An Uprising in the Theory of Industry Structure," *American Economic Review*, March 1982.
[18]William Z. Ripley, "From Main Street to Wall Street," 1926 essay in *The Atlantic Monthly*, reprinted in *Looking Back at Tomorrow*, Louise Desaulniers, ed. (Boston: The Atlantic Monthly, 1978), p. 125.
[19]*Public Utilities Commission of Rhode Island v. Attleboro Steam Electric Company*, 273 U.S. 83 (1927).
[20]Arthur M. Schlesinger, Jr., *The Age of Roosevelt: The Crisis of the Old Order* (Boston: Houghton Mifflin, 1957), p. 119.
[21]Schlesinger, *op. cit.*, p. 118.
[22]Schlesinger, *op. cit.*, pp. 123-124.
[23]Mary Earhart Dillon, *Wendell Willkie* (Philadelphia and New York: J.B. Lippincott, 1952), p. 42.
[24]Benjamin Graham, David L. Dodd, Sidney Cottle, with Charles Tatham, *Security Analysis* (New York: McGraw-Hill, 1962), p. 570.
[25]For a discussion of Averch-Johnson, see Alfred E. Kahn, *The Economics of Regulation* (New York: John Wiley & Sons, 1970-71), Vol. 11, p. 49.
[26]*Tanakh: A New Translation of the Holy Scriptures According to the Traditional Hebrew Text* (Philadelphia: The Jewish Publication Society, 1985), p.1365.
[27]Richard F. Hirsh, *Technology and Transformation in the American Electric Utility Industry* (Cambridge: Cambridge University Press, 1989), p. 90.
[28]*The Electric Utility Industry and the Environment, A Report to the Citizens Advisory Committee on Recreation and Natural Beauty by the Electric Utility Task Force on Environment* (Library of Congress Card Catalog Number: 68-57661) provides a view of what concerned the industry at the time.
[29]Edward F. Renshaw, "Commentary," in Walter L. Balk and Jay M. Shafritz, eds., *Public Utility Productivity: Management and Measurement* (Albany: The New York State Department of Public Service, 1975), pp. 72-73.
[30]Lee Metcalf and Vic Reinemer, *Overcharge* (New York: David McKay, 1967), p. 7.
[31]Leonard S. Hyman and Carmine J. Grigoli, "The Credit Standing of Electric Utilities," *Public Utilities Fortnightly*," Vol. 99, No. 5, March 3, 1977, pp. 24-30.
[32]James C. Bonbright, *Principles of Public Utility Rates* (New York: Columbia University Press, 1961), p. 249.
[33]William Rodgers, *Brown-out* (New York: Stein and Day, 1972), p. 11.
[34]Rodgers, *op. cit.*, p. 20.
[35]*The Narragansett Electric Company v. Edward F. Burke et al.* (119 R.I. 559; 381 A. 2d. 1 358; 23 PUR 4th 509).
[36]*Pike County Light and Power Company-Electric Division v. Pennsylvania Public Utility Commission* (77 Pa. Commw. 268; 465 A. 2d. 735).
[37]Richard E. Schuler, "The Institutional and Regulatory Structure for Providing Electric Service: A Conceptual Basis for Change," in Sidney Saltzman and Richard E. Schuler, eds., *The Future of Electrical Energy: A Regional Perspective of an Industry in Transition* (N.Y.: Praeger, 1986), p. 311.
[38]456 U.S. 472, 47 PUR 4th 1 (1982)
[39]47 PUR 4th 1 (1983)
[40]"Chernobyl and Its Legacy," *EPRI Journal*, June 1987, p. 6.
[41]Walter J. Primeaux, Jr., "A Reexamination of the Monopoly Market Structure for Electric Utilities," in A. Phillips, ed., *Promoting Competition in Regulated Markets* (Washington, D.C.: Brookings Institution, 1975), p. 175.
[42]A.J. Merrett and A. Sykes, *The Finance and Analysis of Capital Projects* (London: Longman, 1983); A. Sykes, "The Project Overview — The Key to the Successful Accomplishment of Giant Projects," in A. Sykes and A.J. Merrett, eds., *The Successful Accomplishment of Giant Projects* (London: Willis Faber, 1978).

Part Four

Regulation

Chapter 17

The Development of Public Utility Regulation

The concept of a public utility is essentially a creation of legislation, but social scientists have endeavored to rationalize legislative procedure by identifying the intrinsic common characteristics which our lawmakers have set aside for special 'public utility' treatment. . . .[1]

Joe S. Bain

We can discuss the development of public utility regulation without first defining a public utility because the historical and legal precedents for the regulation of business were established before most of the industries that are commonly called public utilities existed. Perhaps the laws came first. Then economists tried to come up with a package of common, rational industry economic characteristics that presumably made the laws necessary. Or, the laws were, possibly, a product of antibusiness thinking in the time of the Grangers, trustbusters, and muckrakers, rather than a result of a careful study of natural monopoly, declining cost curves, and all the other supposed characteristics of a public utility.

Early Regulation

Historically, governments have regulated some prices and services. Regulated businesses rarely were monopolies, but provided a service to the public or supplied a product of some importance. Early examples included ferries, bakeries, inns, and common carriers. In 1820, Congress gave the City of Washington the right to regulate the prices of bread, sweeping chimneys, and wharfage. Rhode Island, in 1839, set up a regulatory commission. Other New England states soon followed. The commissions, mainly advisory, dealt with railroads. At the behest of the gas utilities, Massachusetts, in 1885, established a regulatory board. Congress, in 1887, established the Interstate Commerce Commission, the most important regulatory body of the day. New York and Wisconsin created the first state regulatory agencies of the kind that we now know in 1907. By 1920, two-thirds of the states had utility regulatory agencies.

The agencies followed concepts established by the courts of the period. Landmark cases defined what a regulator could or should do. The first major decision in the field was *Munn v. Illinois*.[2] In 1871, the Illinois legislature passed a law to fix the rates charged by grain elevators. Several Chicago elevator owners

157

went to court, protesting that their businesses had been established before the law was enacted. The owners claimed that they had been deprived of their rights under the Fourteenth Amendment ("nor shall any State deprive any person of life, liberty, or property, without due process of law").[3]

Chief Justice Morrison Waite wrote the Supreme Court's majority opinion in the case. The Chief Justice delved into the history of price regulation and quoted Britain's Lord Chief Justice Hale (1609-1676). "Looking, then, to the common law, from whence came the right which the Constitution protects, we find that when private property is 'affected with a public interest, it ceases to be *juris privati* only'."[4] Chief Justice Waite continued:

> Property does come clothed with a public interest when used in a manner to make it of public consequence, and affect the community at large. When, therefore, one devotes his property to a use in which the public has an interest, he, in effect, grants to the public an interest in that use, and must submit to be controlled . . . He may withdraw his grant by discontinuing the use. . . .

> Common carriers exercise a sort of public office, and have duties to perform in which the public is interested. . . .

> Their business is, therefore, "affected with a public interest," within the meaning of the doctrine which Lord Hale has so forcibly stated."[5]

The Court pointed out that grain from seven or eight states had to pass through Chicago, and that the Chicago warehouses were owned by a few people who set rates together, indicating "a 'virtual' monopoly."[6] If the ferryman or innkeeper can be regulated, certainly grain elevators can:

> They stand, to use again the language of their counsel, in the very "gateway of commerce," and take toll from all who pass.

The Court then set forth what can be described as the theory of legislative ratemaking. The plaintiffs argued that the Court should set a return on their property:

> It is insisted, however, that the owner of property is entitled to a reasonable compensation for its use . . . and what is reasonable is a judicial and not a legislative question.

As has already been shown, the practice has been otherwise. In countries where the common law prevails, it has been customary. . . for the legislature to declare what shall be a reasonable compensation . . . The controlling fact is the power to regulate at all. If that exists, the right to establish the maximum charge, as one of the means of regulation, is implied. . . .

We know that this is a power which may be abused; but that is no argument against the existence. For protection against abuses by legislatures the people must resort to the polls, not to the courts.[7]

The decision in the Munn case upheld the right of the state to regulate the prices charged to the public by a business "affected with a public interest." The decision also proposed a philosophy of regulation that, if adhered to, would have made impossible the development of healthy, privately owned utilities. Price would have been set by the legislatures, with no recourse to the courts. During a period of inflation, businesses would encounter difficulties because of rigidities of price. Justice Stephen Field dissented, saying, "If this be sound law all property and all business in the state are at the mercy of a majority of its legislature."[8]

Fair Value

Fortunately, the regulation of price moved beyond the concept set forth in the Munn decision. As early as 1679, an English court held that a common carrier was entitled to a reasonable payment.[9] Determining what is reasonable can turn into more of a theological than economic or legal argument. The Supreme Court tried its hand at that question in 1898, and the result, *Smyth v. Ames*,[10] although in some ways a monument to judicial confusion about finance, revolutionized thinking about regulation[11] and put an end to the absolute right of legislatures to fix rates as they pleased.

Nebraska, in 1893, established a Board of Transportation to fix railroad rates. The railroads challenged the rates set. The issues in contention involved rate base and whether the railroads had been deprived of property without due process of law. The railroads had been built during and after the Civil War boom period. Subsequently, prices fell. The railroads wanted their assets to be valued at original cost. The State of Nebraska (represented by the silver-tongued orator of the Platte, William Jennings Bryan) wanted the properties to be valued at reproduction cost (which was lower than original cost).

The Supreme Court quickly affirmed the right of a state to set rates as long as the rates provided "just compensation."[12] The Court then defined "proper compensation":

We hold . . . that the basis of all calculations as to the reasonableness of rates . . . must be the fair value of the property . . . And, in order to ascertain that value, the original cost of construction, the amount expended in permanent improvements, the amount and market value of its bonds and stock, the present as compared with the original cost of construction, the probable earning capacity of the property under particular rates prescribed by statute, and the same required to meet operating expenses, are all matters for consideration, and are to be given such weight as may be just and right in each case. We do not say that there may not be other matters to be regarded in estimating the value of the property. What the company is entitled to ask is a fair return upon the value of that which it employs for the public convenience.

On the other hand, what the public is entitled to demand is that no more be exacted from it for the use of a public highway than the services rendered by it are reasonably worth.[13]

It is difficult for an observer, more than 80 years later, to comprehend how that confused judicial laundry list set ratemaking doctrine for more than 40 years. Consider the strange ingredients thrown into the Mrs. Murphy's chowder called "just compensation." Present costs and original costs are contradictory terms. The market value of securities depends on earning power, but earning power is what needs to be determined, and the reasoning is therefore circular. The Supreme Court concluded by saying: consider everything. For the next 20 years, regulators and utilities battled over the choice of rate base: fair value or original cost. Halfway through the period, Justice Louis Brandeis, with Justice Oliver Wendell Holmes concurring, wrote a scathing denunciation of regulatory practices. That dissenting opinion, written in the 1923 Southwestern Bell decision,[14] was ahead of its time:

The so-called rule of Smyth v. Ames is . . . legally and economically unsound. The thing devoted by the investor to the public use is not specific property, tangible and intangible, but capital embarked in the enterprise. Upon the capital so invested the federal Constitution guarantees to the utility the opportunity to earn a fair return.

The investor agrees, by embarking capital in a utility, that its charge to the public shall be reasonable. His company is the substitute for the state in the performance of the public service, thus becoming a public servant. The compensation which the Constitution guarantees an opportunity to earn is the reasonable cost of conducting the business.

Cost includes not only operating expenses, but also capital charges. Capital charges cover the allowance, by way of interest, for the use of the capital, whatever the nature of the security issues therefor; the allowance for risk incurred; and enough more to attract capital. The reasonable rate to be prescribed by a commission may allow an efficiently managed utility much more. But a rate is constitutionally compensatory, if it allows to the utility the opportunity to earn the cost of service as defined. . . .

The experience of the twenty-five years since Smyth v. Ames was decided has demonstrated that the rule there enunciated is delusive . . . .

The rule of Smyth v. Ames sets the laborious and baffling technique of finding the present value of the utility. It is impossible to find an exchange value of a utility, since utilities, unlike merchandise or land, are not commonly bought and sold in the market. Nor can the present value of the utility be determined by capitalizing its net earnings, since the earnings are determined, in large measure, by the rate which the company will be permitted to charge.

Under the rule of Smyth v. Ames . . . each step in the process of estimating the cost of reproduction involves forming an opinion. . . . It is true that the decision is usually rested largely upon the records of financial transactions, on statistics and calculations. But . . . "every figure . . . that we have set down with delusive exactness" is speculative.

The conviction is widespread that a sound conclusion as to the actual value of a utility is not to be reached by a meticulous study of conflicting estimates of the cost of reproducing new the congerie of old machinery and equipment, called the plant, and the still more fanciful estimates concerning the value of the intangible elements of an established business. Many commissions . . . have declared ... that "capital honestly and prudently invested must . . . be taken as the controlling factor in fixing . . . rates."[15]

The Brandeis dissent laid the groundwork for changes in regulation that would take place years later. It did not influence the Supreme Court of the period.

The Bluefield decision of 1923[16] set aside a decision in which a company's estimate of reproduction cost was disregarded. Then followed *McCardle v. Indianapolis Water Co.*[17], which was, to quote Wilcox, "the high-water mark of reproduction cost valuation. . . ."[18]

Bluefield is better known to regulators for another reason, a paragraph that sets forth the standards for rate of return:

> The return should be reasonably sufficient to assure confidence in the financial soundness of the utility and should be adequate, under efficient and economical management, to maintain and support its credit and enable it to raise the money necessary for the proper discharge of its public duties.[19]

Just and Reasonable

The Roosevelt era's Supreme Court backed away from an insistence on the fair value rate base. The decision in the Hope Natural Gas Co. case of 1944[20] marked the beginning of a new era of regulation. The Federal Power Commission disregarded estimates of the fair value of Hope's properties in setting a rate of return. Hope appealed the decision. Justice William O. Douglas wrote:

> . . . that "fair value" is the end product of the process of ratemaking, not the starting point. . . . The heart of the matter is that rates cannot be made to depend on "fair value" when the value of the going enterprise depends on earnings under whatever rates may be anticipated.

> We held . . . that the commission was not bound to the use of any single formula . . . in determining rates. . . . And when the commission's order is challenged in the courts, the question is whether that order "viewed in its entirety" meets the requirements of the act. Under the statutory standard of "just and reasonable" it is the result reached, not the method employed, which is controlling. It is not theory, but the impact of the rate order which counts. If the total effect of the rate order cannot be said to be unjust and unreasonable, judicial inquiry . . . is at an end. . . . Moreover, the commission's order . . . is the product of expert judgment which carries a presumption of validity. . . .

> From the investor or company point of view it is important that there be enough revenue not only for operating expenses, but also for the

capital costs of the business. These include service on the debt and dividends on the stock. By that standard the return to the equity owner should be commensurate with returns on investments in other enterprises having corresponding risks. That return, moreover, should be sufficient to assure confidence in the financial integrity of the enterprise so as to maintain its credit and to attract capital. . .[21]

Munn v. Illinois ushered in a period of legislative ratemaking. *Smyth v. Ames*, in a sense, heralded a period of judicial ratemaking (in which lawyers fought before courts over the methodology of the rate case), and *Hope* initiated the age of the regulatory commission.

Chapter 18

What Is a Public Utility?

As with other important terms . . . a definition is, at best, too general to be useful and, at worst, mere legal pedantry. To say that a public utility is a business affected with a public interest is to include piggeries and mortuary parlors. To say that a public utility supplies a service necessary to our present stage of economic life . . . is to include the United States Steel Corporation. . . . The legalistic descriptions are equivocal. . . . As a practical matter, a public utility . . . is a private enterprise over which the . . . government attempts to determine the prices received for its services rather than to allow the prices to be determined by the free play of economic forces. In the end, economic forces will dominate every situation, but temporarily and through the perspective of a short period of time, and within the myopic intelligence of the politically minded bureaucrats, they can be thwarted or measurably controlled by administrative or judicial decrees. . . . [22]

Arthur Stone Dewing

Electric, gas, telephone, and water companies are public utilities. What distinguishes those regulated industries from the insurance, milk, or stock brokerage industries, all of which are or have been regulated in various ways? The answer to that question leads us to the standard characteristics of and rationalizations for public utility designation — "rationalizations" because it is doubtful how well the standards hold true today and if they ever held true in the textbook sense. Characteristics of a public utility include:

The franchise or the designation of a service area — In the past, when a utility served only a municipality, it had to seek a franchise for its operations in the area. The franchise gave the public utility privileges such as use of the streets for its facilities. In return, the utility agreed to pay certain taxes, possibly to set rates at particular levels, and to provide a specified standard of service. The franchise usually ran for a specific period and often granted the utility a monopoly in the municipality. Eventually service areas were extended beyond municipal limits. Large service areas developed for which boundaries were set by state agencies. In general, a regulatory agency now grants a public utility a monopoly to provide a particular service to the public within a geographic area. The monopoly is a monopoly only in the legal sense. Competitors can offer alternatives to the utility's service. For example, oil, gas, solar heating, and better insulation are alternatives to electric heating. An industrial firm may choose to generate its own power, rather than buy power from the local utility.

Obligation to serve — The consumer within a service territory cannot choose between suppliers of a utility service. The utility cannot choose to serve some customers and not others, as long as the company receives a reasonable price for its services. Nor can it discriminate unduly between customers. In an unregulated industry, a customer may be turned away for reasons of poor profitability. In the utility industry, that customer would probably be served. The utility can seek rate relief to cover the additional costs caused by a new customer. The utility may not receive the rate relief requested, but the customer must still be served. Furthermore, taking on the new customer may disadvantage old customers, but they must not receive preferential treatment just as new customers cannot be discriminated against.

Necessity of the service to the public — The utility provides a service that is necessary, widely used, and for which good substitutes are not available. Those concepts, derived from Bain,[23] do not consider the question of whether an adequate substitute could be developed, if the price for the utility's service were at a sufficiently high level. (Arthur Stone Dewing, a student of history and finance who was involved in bankruptcies and reorganizations, did not have any illusions about the permanence of monopoly.) James Bonbright said, "What must justify public utility regulation . . . is the necessity of the regulation and not merely the necessity of the product."[24]

The service provided is a natural monopoly — The term "natural monopoly" has been interpreted in many ways. Some experts have argued that a utility exhibits diminishing unit costs as scale increases. If so, customers will be served at a lower cost by one large system of a monopoly than by several smaller, less efficient, competing facilities. Monopoly also prevents needless duplication of plant and equipment. The utility also may provide a not-storable service that must be supplied at peak periods by expensive plant. High overhead costs could cause competing utilities to cut prices to the level of variable costs to capture market share, and bankruptcies could result. Thus, ruinous competition could impair the industry's ability to serve the customer. Bonbright made two points about the natural monopoly. He said that natural monopoly "is due . . . to the severely localized and hence restricted markets for utility services — markets limited because of the necessarily close connection between the utility plant on the one hand and the consumers' premises on the other."[25] A manufacturing plant can have the whole country or world for its market. A utility distribution system serves a limited area. "Were it compelled to share its limited market with two or more rival plants owning duplicate distribution networks, the total cost of serving the city would be materially higher."[26] Bonbright then declared that the declining cost characteristic of utilities had been overstressed and was not a prerequisite for a natural monopoly because "even if the unit cost of supplying a given area with a given type of public utility service must increase with an enhanced rate of output, any specified required rate of output can be supplied most economically by a single plant or system."[27]

Today, the generating sector of the electric utility industry no longer seems to exhibit economies of scale, and may be ripe for control by means of competition instead of regulation. Distribution may not have shown economies of scale for years, but is any purpose served by having many companies lay their wires throughout the town? Transmission might remain a monopoly just because of the difficulty of building new lines, although a different pricing regime could produce the profit incentive that would convince firms to build more lines. What is clear is that the definitions of public utility and the rationalizations for regulation are both becoming shakier.

Chapter 19

The Purpose and Drawbacks of Regulation

Regulation was . . . a substitute for competition. Where competition was impossible, its purpose was to bring the benefits that competition would have brought.[28]

Clair Wilcox

Begin with the basic premise: the utility is a monopoly. Assume that the monopoly is permanent, despite historic evidence to the contrary. Electric light replaced gas light. The telephone reduced the value of the telegraph. Refrigerators and air conditioners put the ice house out of business. And, the automobile destroyed the trolley lines. Today, competitors challenge the monopoly status of the telephone company. Gas, electric, and oil firms fight to serve heating customers. Cogeneration facilities eat away at the market held by central station power. Soft technologists urge the government to encourage decentralized energy sources that will diminish the role of the traditional utility. The concept of the utility as a monopoly is static. It is valid only during that period when the utility dominates its market. The temporary nature of the monopoly has important implications for the rate of return and recovery of capital.

In the United States, to monopolize or attempt to monopolize is illegal under the antitrust laws. The textbooks tell us that competition breeds efficiency and innovation: competition is a force that weeds out the unfit producer and protects the consumer from exploitation. "The essence of regulation," according to Alfred Kahn, "is the explicit replacement of competition with governmental orders as the principal institutional device for assuring good performance."[29] Of course, the question remains whether we mean competition in the textbook or in the real world sense. Perhaps we should say that utilities must compete for capital and for customers in the world of imperfect competition.

Regulators try to assure that the customer receives reliable service from the utility because the customer supposedly has no choice of suppliers. Regulators must fairly apportion the costs of service so that no group of customers is charged unduly. Finally, regulators must set the overall level of revenues at a point where the utility can earn a return similar to that earned in competitive industries.

Practically, regulators do not concern themselves with quality of service unless the quality is obviously bad. The big issues in rate cases are the overall level of revenues and the apportionment of revenue sources among customers.

Regulation has been attacked from all sides. Some believe that the regulators have sold out to the utilities, while others think that the regulators are too politically oriented to treat utilities fairly. Many economists accept the concept of regulation, but quarrel with the methods used by the regulators. The complaints, too numerous to cover fully, include three fundamental objections to regulation:

The public utility's "monopoly status. . .is an illusion"[30] — An analysis based on the halcyon days of the late 1950s and early 1960s took a view that even if it had a monopoly the utility would not exploit customers because it could increase earnings by lowering rates and thereby increase sales. Therefore regulation was unnecessary, anyway. Furthermore, regulation was not only unnecessary, but actually harmful, because regulation stifled innovation. For example, a regulated company might hesitate to reduce rates on an experimental basis because the company might not be able to raise rates later if the rate reductions did not result in the expected increase in demand. Circumstances have changed, though. Studies of electrical companies cast doubt on the natural monopoly status because they indicate that economies of scale no longer prevail in some aspects of industry operation, and competition from decentralized power sources already exists. Before, the utilities would not have exploited customers because it was not in the interest of the utilities to do so. Now, critics might reason, the utility no longer has the ability to exploit the customer.

Cost of service regulation provides little incentive to be efficient — Some experts believe that under regulation, at its worst, bad management is bailed out and good management earns no reward. In addition, reducing costs might involve the utility in innovation and risk taking. If the measures taken fail, the company might even be penalized by the regulators.

Public utilities supply vital services and, therefore, should not be run on a profit basis, but should be socialized, in which case regulation would be unnecessary — Whether a government owned utility would be run differently is beyond the scope of our discussion. Nevertheless, although most of the utility industry in the United States is privately owned, social welfare considerations such as lifeline rates, rules on cutoff of service and more liberal customer deposit regulations have crept into the ratemaking and regulatory process. In that sense, industry practices, but not the industry itself, have been socialized.

Chapter **20**

Setting the Rate of Return

The regulatory commissions do not fix rates so as to guarantee that they will yield a rate of return. . . . The commission's function is simply to determine a rate which will have that result of permitting a utility to earn a fair return, if the utility's earning power and other economic circumstances . . . so . . . permit. . . .[31]

Francis X. Welch

Ratemaking in theory is a relatively simple process. To the cost of producing the service furnished is added a reasonable return to the investor. The making of public utility rates requires four basic determinations:
1. what are the enterprise's gross utility revenues under the rate structure examined;
2. what are its operating expenses, including maintenance, depreciation, and all taxes, appropriately incurred to produce those gross revenues;
3. what utility property provides the service for which rates are charged and thus represents the base (rate base) on which a return should be earned; and
4. what percentage figure (rate of return) should be applied to the rate base in order to establish the return (wages of capital) to which investors in the utility enterprise are reasonably entitled. . . .
Simple as this formula sounds, the task of the rate maker is more often than not extremely difficult.[32]

Maine Supreme Judicial Court

Regulators do not set a price for the product by considering at what price similar products sell. They do not pick a profit for the utility based on a percentage markup on sales. They go through an elaborate procedure that is based on investment made to serve the public.

Rate of Return

Revenues must be set in such a way to allow the utility to cover operating costs and to earn an acceptable level of profit. That profit is usually stated as a given return on investment in utility plant, or as a return on rate base. The system is called "cost of service ratemaking." In a sense, return on the capital invested in the business is one of the costs that must be covered. The regulator examines a utility's results for a test period to determine if the utility is earning a proper return. The regulator uses the following calculations:

	Revenue
less	Operating expenses
less	Taxes
equals	Operating income or income available to provide a return on invested capital

and

$$\frac{\text{Operating Income}}{\text{Rate Base}} = \text{Rate of Return}$$

Regulatory agencies do not necessarily accept company figures. Revenue and operating expense figures are adjusted for abnormal weather conditions and changes in the customer load. The regulators want to consider "normal" conditions. Sometimes a regulatory agency bases its decision on estimated results of a future test year on the ground that rates are being set for the future, and, therefore, should respond to projected conditions at the time that the rates will go into effect. When an estimated test year is used, the utility and its opponents may disagree in their estimates of revenue and expenses. The company and the regulators also may differ on estimates of rate base. Small differences add up, as can be seen below:

		Company Projection	Commission Projection
	Revenues	$1,000	$1,010
less	Expenses	500	495
less	Income taxes	250	255
equals	Operating income	250	260
divided by	Rate base	4,000	3,990
equals	Rate of return earned	6.25%	6.52%

With so many figures subject to adjustment, one cannot always determine if the rate order was designed to produce the allowed rate of return or if the revenues and expenses cited in the decision were adjusted to produce a return on paper that will not, in fact, be realized.

Income Taxes

An important step in rate setting is to determine the utility's tax bill, which must be subtracted before the amount of income that is available for the providers of capital can be determined. Two accounting procedures are used: "flow through" and "normalization." The methods address the problem of inter-period allocation of tax savings. Should the tax savings be used to reduce rates in the year in which the savings are received (flow through) or should the savings be spread over the life of the property which produced the saving (normalization)?

Let us consider a simplified situation. A utility uses a tax strategy that will reduce taxes by $50 in the first year, but will cause the utility to pay $50 more in the second year. Regulators have set a 13% rate of return for the utility.

Line		Year 1	Year 2
1.	Rate base	$1000	$1000
2.	Pretax income	200	200
3.	Regular income taxes	70	70
4.	Tax (reduction) or increase due to tax strategy	(50)	50
5.	Income taxes paid (3 + 4)	20	120
6.	Net income (2 – 5)	180	80
7.	Rate of return (6 ÷ 1)	18%	8%

In the first year, the utility earns more than its allowed return because of the tax savings. The regulator could require the utility to reduce its prices to bring return down to 13%. In the second year, the utility has to pay back the tax savings, so it is not earning the allowed 13% return. Regulators could raise prices to bring return up to the allowed level. If the tax saving is included in income for ratemaking purposes, as shown above, then the savings are said to have "flowed through" to customers. Other regulators do not want the price of electricity to fluctuate because of temporary tax savings. They require the utility to set aside a reserve for tax savings to be used when taxes must be paid. Because the taxes must be paid eventually, the set aside is called "deferred taxes." Using the same example as before, we have:

Line		Year 1	Year 2
1.	Rate base	$1000	$1000
2.	Pretax income	200	200
3.	Income taxes paid	20	120
4.	Taxes deferred to reserve or (withdrawn) from reserve set aside from savings	50	(50)
5.	Regular income taxes (3 + 4)	70	70
6.	Net income (2 – 5)	130	130
7.	Rate of return (6 ÷ 1)	13%	13%

Note that when tax savings are deferred (or "normalized") the effect of the swing in taxes is averaged out and the taxes shown in the income statement are as if no tax savings had been realized.

Advocates of flow through have made two arguments:

♦ Tax savings really do not diminish in the future because new investments by the utility keep generating new tax savings. Therefore, the utility will not reach the point at which the tax savings will have to be paid back, so a reserve is not necessary.

♦ If the day of reckoning does come, the utility can always ask the regulator for rate relief to cover the higher taxes. In the meantime, ratepayers could be spared the higher price that results from a set aside for "phantom taxes."

To a great extent, tax law in the 1980s has made the debate academic because many new tax benefits cannot be taken if they are flowed through. (Flow through of old tax benefits remains.) For investors, objections to flow through are more pragmatic. As will be explained later in our discussion of utility finance, flow through companies generate less cash flow per dollar of earnings and interest coverage ratios also are lower per dollar of interest expense. Both deficiencies increase the risk of the utility in the eyes of investors, thereby raising cost of capital to the company.

Justification for flow through accounting may depend on regular increases in plant and a continuation of current tax laws. Flow through accounting may guarantee that the tax benefits from a plant that will serve customers for 30 years will go to those who are customers in the early years of the plant's life, possibly at the expense of customers in later years. Present day regulators say that their successors will give the utility higher rates at the time of the crossover when taxes become greater than normal. That, however, could occur at a time when growth in demand had slackened. The utility could then face a new, highly price elastic demand curve (possibly because of the introduction of new technologies). Consequently, an increase in the price of the service to recoup higher tax charges at that time might not result in additional income. Thus, a utility that uses flow through accounting may never recoup the lost revenue and might have to pay higher taxes at a time when its financial and market position is weakening.[33]

Having determined the tax bill for regulatory purposes and subtracted that amount and the operating expenses from revenues, the remainder is available to compensate the suppliers of capital.

Calculating Return on Rate Base

Some regulators, however, consider income other than operating income when they determine how much income is available to meet capital costs, and make their determination on the basis of what is included in the rate base. For example, if regulators include in the rate base plant that has not yet been put into service (construction work in progress or CWIP), the regulators may include in income a credit intended to offset capital charges incurred before the plant is put into service (the allowance for funds used during construction).

Many methods are used to determine the rate base. We discuss seven important variants that can be combined in the rate base formula.

1) *Net original cost rate base* — The rate base is determined by the original cost of the properties, less depreciation.

2) *Fair value* — The cost of the plant is adjusted to account for at least some of the additional cost now required to duplicate the plant. Several states claim to be fair value jurisdictions, but most of the rate orders differ little from those of other jurisdictions.

3) *Average rate base* — The test year encompasses the operating results of an entire period. The rate base at one point in that period may not be representative of the investment throughout the test period. Many regulators, as a result, will determine an average of the rate base throughout the year and will use that average in the case.

4) *End of period rate base* — The rate order considers not only the experience of the past test year, but also what may occur in the future. If a utility has been adding plant at a rapid pace, the average rate base may not be representative of plant investment at the time the rate order goes into effect. Thus, the utility is unlikely to be able to earn the allowed return on the enlarged rate base. Many regulators attempt to reduce that attrition in return by using an end of period rate base.

5) *Used and useful rate base* — Should current consumers be required to pay a return on plant that is not yet in service? In a number of jurisdictions, the regulators include in rate base only plant that is actually serving customers.

6) *Construction work in progress in rate base and allowance for funds used during construction included in income* — In this approach, the regulators do not distinguish between useful and incomplete plant. Nor do they distinguish between income derived from the sale of a service and income created by a bookkeeping credit in the income statement.

7) *Construction work in progress in rate base* — In this case, the regulator agrees to have the customers bear the current burden of construction work in progress for the following reasons:

a) The plant will, in the main, serve current customers.
b) The plant will be completed in the near term. To hand down a rate order excluding the particular plant would be to regulate for the past rather than for the future. Moreover, the utility would have to file for another rate hike immediately after the new plant is placed in service.
c) The utility has a serious cash flow problem because of the size of its capital expenditure program and cannot finance the completion of the plant additions unless it can generate more cash from operations. Charging the current consumer for the capital costs of the construction program will help cash flow.

d) Making consumers pay in advance for assets that will serve them later sends a price signal about future costs to consumers, who can then begin a process of adjusting their demands to the new price level.

Let us take a simple example of some of the many returns that can be derived from the same set of numbers. In an actual case, rate base also includes some amount for working capital.

Revenues	$ 600
Operating expenses and taxes	400
Operating income (OI)	200
Allowance for funds used during construction (AFUDC)	10
Income before interest charges (IBIC)	$ 210
Beginning of year net plant in service	$2,000
End of year net plant in service (End NPIS)	2,200
Beginning of year construction work in progress	50
End of year construction work in progress (End CWIP)	100
Working capital in all periods (WC)	50

The above numbers will produce various rates of return, as shown below.

1) $\text{Rate of Return} = \dfrac{\text{OI}}{\text{Average NPIS} + \text{WC}} = \dfrac{200}{2,100 + 50} = 9.3\%$

2) $\text{Rate of Return} = \dfrac{\text{OI}}{\text{End NPIS} + \text{WC}} = \dfrac{200}{2,200 + 50} = 8.9\%$

3) Rate of return on fair value (where fair value equals 150% of the end of period net original cost of plant in service)

$= \dfrac{\text{OI}}{\text{Fair Value Rate Base} + \text{WC}} = \dfrac{200}{3,300 + 50} = 6.0\%$

4) $\text{Rate of Return} = \dfrac{\text{IBIC}}{\text{End NPIS} + \text{End CWIP} + \text{WC}} = \dfrac{210}{2,200 + 100 + 50} = 8.9\%$

5) $\text{Rate of Return} = \dfrac{\text{OI}}{\text{End NPIS} + \text{End CWIP} + \text{WC}} = \dfrac{200}{2,200 + 100 + 50} = 8.5\%$

6) Rate of Return on rate base that includes some construction work in progress without an AFUDC offset (assumes half of year end CWIP goes into rate base) and year end plant

$$= \frac{OI}{End\ NPIS + 1/2\ End\ CWIP + WC} = \frac{200}{2200 + 50 + 50} = 8.7\%$$

7) Rate of Return that includes all CWIP in denominator and only some AFUDC in numerator either by specifying a lower rate for AFUDC or including only part of AFUDC (assumes half of AFUDC)

$$= \frac{OI + 1/2\ AFUDC}{End\ NPIS + End\ CWIP + WC} = \frac{200 + 5}{2200 + 100 + 50} = 8.7\%$$

As can be seen in the above examples 1) and 2), rate of return is lower when a year end rate base is used, and the company, as a result, can justify more rate relief. As can be seen from 2) and 3), the utility may report a low return on a fair value rate base in comparison with that on an original cost rate base. Do not conclude from the examples, however, that a company using fair value can now justify a greater amount of rate relief because of the low return. Most fair value jurisdictions have tended to allow lower returns on the higher fair value rate bases. Examples 4) and 5) demonstrate that a utility might allow better returns by capitalizing credits on construction funds at a higher rate than the company can earn on plant in service, and, unfortunately, that higher return on paper may not be a good substitute for cash. Examples 6) and 7) give halfway measures that could be used by regulators that do not want to unduly encourage construction, but want to aid cash flow.

AFUDC and CWIP: A Recapitulation

To summarize, when plant is not in service and when the utility is not allowed a current return on that plant by the regulators, the company will capitalize the financing costs of the facility (allowance for funds used during construction or AFUDC) and will add those costs to the total cost of the plant. When the plant is completed, the rate base will then include both the actual expenditures on construction and the capitalized financial charges.

The utility depreciates the total cost, including the AFUDC, and earns a return on the total cost. Therefore, the consumer actually pays on the basis of total cost during the life of the plant. When the construction period is long, however, the utility has to advance large sums for financing charges, while it collects no cash from the consumer. That can create a serious cash drain for a utility with a big capital spending program. Therefore, utility investors should be concerned about the treatment of CWIP by the regulators.

The problem can be handled in several ways. (Keep in mind that there are partial solutions, too, such as adding some CWIP to the rate base.) In some jurisdictions, the plant under construction is included in the rate base, and the current consumer pays a high bill to provide a return on CWIP. In other jurisdictions, CWIP may be included in the rate base, but the rate of return is calculated to include the allowance for funds used during construction (see the following examples). In still other jurisdictions, no CWIP is permitted in the rate base, and the utility capitalizes construction costs by using allowance for funds used during construction (AFUDC). Because AFUDC is a non-cash credit, from a cash flow standpoint including CWIP in the rate base (RB) without the offsetting AFUDC is the preferred conservative method. A simplified example follows.

	Case A	Case B	Case C
	CWIP in RB AFUDC in Allowed Income	CWIP in RB and AFUDC in Allowed Income	No CWIP in RB and No AFUDC in Allowed Income
Line			
1) Operating Income	$ 80	$ 64	$ 64
2) AFUDC (8% rate)	0	16	16
3) Income Before Interest Charges	80	80	80
4) Plant in Service	800	800	800
5) CWIP	200	200	200
6) Total Plant	1,000	1,000	1,000
7) Rate Base — See Line	6	6	4
8) Allowed Income — See Line	1	3	1
9) Rate of Return Formula — See Lines	1/6	3/6	1/4
10) Rate of Return	8%	8%	8%

Note that in Case A, the utility collects $80 from operations, but in Cases B and C, it collects only $64 from operations and the balance of the income before interest charges of $80 is a $16 bookkeeping credit (AFUDC).

In addition, regulators generally include in rate base a sum for working capital. They may not allow a return on an unnecessary facility and may subtract from rate base costs of construction that they consider to be excessive. They may also reduce rate base by the amount that has been financed by cost free income tax deferrals.

Trends in Rate of Return

The final step is to set the proper return to be allowed. In the early days of regulation, when great emphasis was placed on finding the fair value of the rate base, allowed rates of return stayed in a relatively narrow range.

A phrase that was often repeated in a study of rate cases from 1915 on is, "The Commission gave no indication how the rate of return was established."[34] The Arthur Andersen compilation of rate cases from 1915 to 1960 indicates that the current method of determining cost of capital, which was pioneered by the Federal Power Commission, was first used in the Safe Harbor Water Power decision of October 25, 1946.[35] By 1949, several regulatory agencies appear to have adopted the FPC method.

The allowance for rate of return seems to have had four phases. Between 1915 and 1929, regulators granted returns in the 7 to 8% range, perhaps using level of business and interest rates as a basis. In the early years of the Depression, both interest rates and allowed returns drifted down. By the mid-1930s, returns settled in a 5.5 to 6% range and remained there until the mid-1960s. It was this thirty year period that gave many people the idea that a proper rate of return was 6%. Finally, because of strong business conditions, inflation, and sharply rising interest rates that began in the mid-1960s, rate of allowed return began a rise that peaked after interest rates began to fall in the 1980s. (See Figures 20-1 and 20-2.)

The need for substantial amounts of rate relief may have forced regulators to do more than arbitrarily choose a rate of return that was somewhat above interest rates. They paid greater attention to calculating a utility's overall cost of capital from the cost of each of the components of capital. Tables 20-2, 20-3 and 20-4 show the trends in rates of return, return on equity, and money market costs from 1915 to 1990.

In determining the cost of common equity, regulators must assess both business and financial risk. Regulators may decide that a gas company incurs a greater business risk than an electric company because of the gas company's sensitivity to unpredictable weather conditions and uncertainties about supply. Or regulators may decide that one electric company is at more risk than another because of the characteristics of its service area. Financial risk may also be measured by the size of the utility's borrowings in relation to its total capitalization. Figure 20-3 shows trends in return allowed on equity.

Calculating the Rate of Return

In theory, calculating the cost of capital or the rate of return is simple. For example, a utility borrows $500 at a cost of 8% and raises $500 of common equity.

Figure 20-1

**Rates of Return Allowed
and Interest Rates**

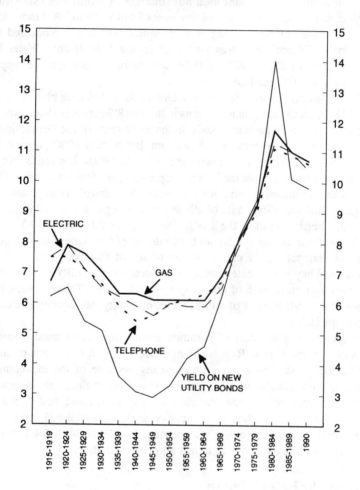

Figure 20-2

**Rates of Return Allowed
and Interest Rates
1968-1990**

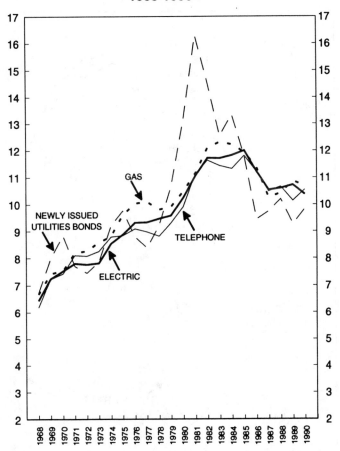

Figure 20-3

**Allowed Return on Equity
1968-1990**

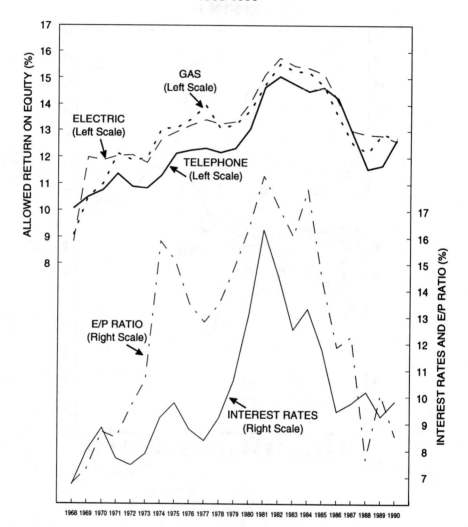

Table 20 - 1

Estimated Average Rates of Return Granted in Rate Cases
and Indicators of Costs of Capital (%)

	1915-1930	1931-1940	1941-1950	1951-1960	1961-1970	1971-1980	1981-1990
	(1)	(2)	(3)	(4)	(5)	(6)	(7)
Return Granted on Rate Base							
Electric	7.5	6.5	6.2	6.2	6.4	8.9	11.2
Gas	7.4	6.5	5.9	5.9	6.5	9.4	11.3
Telephone	7.2	5.9	5.7	6.1	6.7	8.8	11.0
Return Granted on Equity							
Electric	—	—	—	9.2	11.1	12.9	14.2
Gas	—	—	—	9.1	10.6	13.0	13.9
Telephone	—	—	—	9.6	9.6	11.9	13.7
Indicators of Cost of Capital							
Bond Yields	6.0	4.1	3.0	4.0	5.8	9.2	11.7
Earnings / Price Ratio	—	5.7	8.1	6.7	6.0	13.1	13.4

Notes

Bond yields are all for newly issued utility bonds. Earnings price ratio of Moody's Electric Utility Average.
Simple averages of annual modal values (1915-1961) for returns granted. Simple average of unweighted annual
means (1962-1990) for returns granted.

Sources

Welch. *op. cit.*, pp. 480-481.
Merrill Lynch Regulatory Data Base.
Moody's Public Utility Manual
Arthur Andersen & Co.

The regulatory agency believes that cost of equity is 13%. Thus, cost of capital
is:

Capital Component	$ Amount		Cost		Weighted $ Cost
Debt	$ 500	x	0.08	=	$ 40
Common Stock	500	x	0.13	=	65
Total	$1,000				$105

This is a 10.5% rate of return.

Table 20 - 2 (a)

Regulatory Data
1915 - 1961

Year	Modal Rate of Return (%) (Andersen)			Cases Reported (Anderson)			Long Term Interest Rates and Earnings Yield (%) (Moody's)	
	Electric	Gas	Telephone	Electric	Gas	Telephone	Newly Issued Utility Bonds	Electric Average Earnings/Price Ratio
	(1)	(2)	(3)	(4)	(5)	(6)	(7)	(8)
1915	7.0	6.0	—	6	1	0	5.80E	—
1916	8.0	7.5	8.0	3	4	2	5.70E	—
1917	7.0	8.0	8.0	3	2	1	6.00E	—
1918	7.5	6.0	6.7	6	4	2	6.65E	—
1919	8.0	6.0	7.4	5	4	2	6.60E	—
1920	8.0	8.0	7.0	6	8	5	7.40E	—
1921	7.5	8.0	8.0	7	13	6	7.31	—
1922	8.0	8.0	7.0	5	7	3	6.02	—
1923	8.0	8.0	7.5	8	9	1	5.98	—
1924	8.0	7.6	8.0	3	4	6	6.03	—
1925	7.5	8.0	8.0	2	7	6	5.61	—
1926	7.7	8.0	7.2	2	6	7	5.50	—
1927	7.0	7.5	7.0	1	3	2	5.26	—
1928	6.0	7.5	6.5	1	5	3	5.20	—
1929	7.5	7.0	7.0	3	1	7	5.21	3.80
1930	—	7.5	7.0	0	3	4	5.20	4.26
1931	7.0	8.0	7.7	3	1	1	4.71	5.43
1932	7.0	7.0	5.7	5	3	2	5.74	6.33
1933	6.0	6.0	6.5	5	7	3	4.98	4.55
1934	6.0	6.5	6.0	8	4	5	4.86	4.39

Year								
1935	6.7	7.0	6.0	8	5	3	3.84	5.65
1936	6.5	6.0	6.0	7	2	5	3.55	5.00
1937	6.0	6.0	—	4	4	0	3.55	6.21
1938	6.0	6.5	5.5	4	2	1	3.46	5.85
1939	6.0	6.2	6.0	6	2	1	3.46	6.49
1940	6.1	6.2	5.2	5	2	3	3.08	7.04
1941	5.5	6.2	5.0	1	2	1	3.07	8.77
1942	—	6.5	6.0	0	6	1	3.26	10.87
1943	6.0	6.5	5.2	3	6	3	3.26	8.20
1944	6.0	6.2	5.8	6	6	1	2.98	8.40
1945	5.5	6.5	5.5	4	5	1	2.85	6.54
1946	5.0	6.0	—	4	4	0	2.73	6.45
1947	6.0	6.0	5.5	3	5	0	2.79	7.30
1948	6.0	6.0	5.5	6	10	10	3.09	8.13
1949	5.7	6.0	6.0	9	9	20	3.07	8.33
1950	6.5	6.0	6.0	4	3	20	2.85	8.40
1951	6.0	6.0	6.0	7	6	26	3.29	7.52
1952	5.7	6.2	6.0	18	14	26	3.38	6.94
1953	6.0	6.2	6.0	13	17	21	3.77	7.35
1954	5.7	6.2	6.0	10	15	19	3.17	6.62
1955	5.8	6.0	6.0	6	17	18	3.33	6.54
1956	5.8	6.2	6.0	11	10	22	3.86	6.76
1957	6.1	6.0	6.1	10	19	23	4.74	6.90
1958	6.0	6.2	6.1	16	19	29	4.21	6.25
1959	5.8	6.2	6.5	16	16	18	4.97	5.75
1960	6.0	6.0	6.8	14	29	16	4.84	5.92
1961	5.5	6.2	6.3	6	22	5	4.70	4.78

Table 20 - 3 (a)

Regulatory Data
1935-1990

Year	Average Rates of Return (%) Welch			Average Rates of Return (%) (Merrill Lynch)			Cases Reported (Merrill Lynch)			Long Term Interest Rates and Earnings Yield (%) (Moody's)	
	Electric	Gas	Telephone	Electric	Gas	Telephone	Electric	Gas	Telephone	Newly Issued Utility Bonds	Electric Average Earnings / Price Ratio
	(9)	(10)	(11)	(12)	(13)	(14)	(15)	(16)	(17)	(18)	(19)
1935	7.0	6.7	6.0							3.84	5.65
1936	6.0	6.5	6.0							3.55	5.00
1937	6.0	6.0	5.6							3.55	6.21
1938	6.7	6.0	5.4							3.46	5.85
1939	6.2	6.0	5.3							3.46	6.49
1940	6.2	6.2	5.2							3.08	7.04
1941	6.2	5.4	5.0							3.07	8.77
1942	6.5	6.0	5.3							3.26	10.87
1943	6.5	6.0	5.3							3.26	8.20
1944	6.2	6.0	5.7							2.98	8.40
1945	6.4	5.5	5.5							2.85	6.54
1946	6.0	5.4	6.1							2.73	6.45
1947	6.0	6.0	5.6							2.79	7.30
1948	6.0	6.0	5.6							3.09	8.13
1949	6.0	5.8	6.0							3.07	8.33
1950	6.0	6.4	6.0							2.85	8.40
1951	6.0	6.0	6.0							3.29	7.52
1952	6.3	5.8	6.0							3.38	6.94
1953	6.3	6.0	6.0							3.77	7.35
1954	6.3	5.8	6.0							3.17	6.62
1955	6.0	5.8	6.0							3.33	6.54
1956	6.3	5.8	6.0							3.86	6.76
1957	6.0	6.2	6.0							4.74	6.90
1958	6.1	6.0	6.1							4.21	6.25
1959	6.2	5.8	6.1							4.97	5.75

Year											
1960	6.0	6.0	6.2								
1961	5.9	6.0	6.2								
1962	5.8	6.0	6.2								
1963	5.9	6.1	6.3								
1964	6.0	6.2	6.4								
1965	6.2	6.1	6.4	6.00	6.88	6.57	2	5	1	4.84	5.92
1966	6.5	6.6	6.7	6.43	6.50	6.38	2	1	1	4.70	4.78
1967				–	–	7.25	0	0	1	4.44	5.18
1968				6.44	6.67	6.19	4	10	10	4.39	4.85
1969				7.24	7.43	7.23	6	8	13	4.56	4.98
1970				7.53	7.54	7.44	29	31	17	8.85	8.70
1971				7.81	8.20	8.10	42	40	26	7.71	8.47
1972				7.77	8.27	8.08	84	48	59	7.46	9.62
1973				7.82	8.58	8.25	69	54	50	7.88	10.64
1974				8.55	8.82	8.80	106	58	45	9.21	15.87
1975				8.88	9.61	8.85	133	67	64	9.76	15.15
1976				9.32	10.03	9.10	112	47	55	8.80	13.51
1977				9.33	10.10	8.98	100	41	56	8.38	12.82
1978				9.47	9.81	8.82	94	67	33	9.22	13.52
1979				9.58	9.90	9.31	84	44	27	10.64	14.85
1980				10.24	10.47	9.90	114	36	53	13.09	16.38
1981				11.06	11.16	11.14	137	39	68	16.30	18.33
1982				11.73	12.10	11.63	123	80	65	14.56	17.15
1983				11.71	12.31	11.44	105	46	81	12.53	16.05
1984				11.83	12.22	11.32	79	32	42	13.33	17.80
1985				11.99	11.94	11.81	54	24	43	11.78	14.39
1986				11.22	11.37	11.21	44	18	18	9.45	11.87
1987				10.54	10.26	10.48	28	9	5	9.75	12.26
1988				10.59	10.42	10.66	19	18	6	10.19	7.70
1989				10.72	10.86	10.13	24	28	16	9.27	10.10
1990				10.37	10.69	10.55	37	30	10	9.83	8.54

Table 20 - 4

Regulatory Data
1965 - 1990

Year	Average Return on Equity (%) (Merrill Lynch)			Cases Reported (Merrill Lynch)			Long Term Interest Rates and Earnings Yield (%) (Moody's)	
	Electric (20)	Gas (21)	Telephone (22)	Electric (23)	Gas (24)	Telephone (25)	Newly Issued Utility Bonds (26)	Electric Average Earnings/Price Ratio (27)
1965	11.31%	—%	8.57%	1	0	1	4.68%	5.05%
1966	11.27	11.70	—	2	1	0	5.61	6.13
1967	—	—	9.00	0	0	1	6.01	6.54
1968	8.85	9.10	10.09	1	4	6	6.72	6.76
1969	12.00	10.51	10.52	4	4	11	7.99	7.30
1970	11.89	11.02	10.78	23	24	13	8.85	8.70
1971	12.07	12.15	11.39	33	35	20	7.71	8.47
1972	12.08	11.89	10.91	78	42	45	7.46	9.62
1973	11.80	11.96	10.85	56	48	35	7.88	10.64
1974	12.69	13.09	11.33	97	50	36	9.21	15.87
1975	12.95	13.10	12.14	128	65	56	9.76	15.15
1976	13.21	13.44	12.26	109	40	51	8.80	13.51
1977	13.41	13.96	12.34	104	44	57	8.38	12.82
1978	13.26	13.08	12.18	93	58	28	9.22	13.52
1979	13.34	13.23	12.34	92	37	25	10.64	14.85

1980	14.08	13.78	13.07	117	32	50	13.09	16.38
1981	15.13	14.74	14.65	139	37	79	16.30	18.33
1982	15.76	15.53	15.06	125	70	61	14.56	17.15
1983	15.46	15.26	14.77	106	48	87	12.53	16.05
1984	15.37	15.22	14.49	82	36	48	13.33	17.80
1985	15.16	14.70	14.64	59	32	43	11.78	14.39
1986	14.09	13.56	14.22	45	16	13	9.45	11.87
1987	12.99	12.52	12.88	29	10	4	9.75	12.26
1988	12.86	12.19	11.57	24	20	8	10.19	7.70
1989	12.83	12.89	11.70	27	32	15	9.27	10.10
1990	12.61	12.73	12.67	40	31	13	9.83	8.54

Sources for Tables 20-2, 20-3 and 20-4:

Columns 1-6:   Numbers estimated from charts in: Arthur Andersen & Co., *Return Allowed in Public Utility Rate Cases:* (1960 Edition) and *Return Allowed in Public Utility Rate Cases* (Vol. I 1915-1954 and Vol. II 1955-1961). No date or place of publication. Fair value and original cost returns are not distinguished for the series.

Column 7:   All newly issued utility bonds. Moody's *Public Utilities Manual 1990*. (New York: Moody's Investors Service, 1990). 1915-1920 estimated from high grade utility bond yields.

Column 8: $\left(\dfrac{1}{P/E\ \text{Ratio}} \right) \times 100$ for Moody's Electric Utility Average, from: Moody's *Public Utilities Manual*, 1990.

Columns 9-11:   Derived from figure on p. 481 of Welch, *op.cit.* Shows mean rates of return for cases published in *Public Utilities Reports.*

Columns 12-17:   Unweighted averages, all on original cost basis. Fair value translated to an original cost basis or omitted. Merrill Lynch Regulatory Data Base.

Columns 18:   See Column 7.

Columns 19:   See Column 8.

Columns 20-25:   Unweighted averages, all on original cost basis. Fair value translated to an original cost basis or omitted. Merrill Lynch Regulatory Data Base.

Column 26:   See Column 7.

Column 27:   See Column 8.

Usually, the commission determines the cost of each segment of the capital structure and adds the results to determine the overall cost of capital, or rate of return. Determining the cost of debt and preferred stock is fairly easy because the required interest charges and dividends are fixed. Determining the return on common equity, however, is a long and complicated process. In many states, the commission will allow a utility to earn a high return on equity if the utility has a low equity ratio, on the theory that greater financial risk requires greater compensation. In addition, many commissions consider deferred credits (usually deferred taxes) to be part of the capital structure, but they allow a zero rate of return on that segment of capital because it has no cost to the company. That is, a deferred tax is considered to be the equivalent of an interest free loan from the Government. At present, according to tax laws, however, some deferred tax credits must be allowed a rate of return.

Here are some sample calculations of allowed rates of return:

a) Cost of common equity at 12% but different costs of debt and preferred.

| | — Company X — | | | | — Company Y — | | |
		Amount	Cost			Amount	Cost
Debt	@ 5%	$50	$2.50	Debt	@ 6%	$50	$3.00
Preferred	@ 5%	10	0.50	Preferred	@ 6%	10	0.60
Common	@12%	30	3.60	Common	@12%	30	3.60
Deferred				Deferred			
credits	@ 0%	10	0.00	credits	@ 0%	10	0.00
Total		$100	$6.60	Total		$100	$7.20
		or a 6.6% return				or a 7.2% return	

b) Costs of debt and preferred are the same, but return on equity is different because of differences in equity ratios. (Actually, the cost of debt and preferred might be higher in the leveraged company.)

| | — Company X — | | | | — Company Y — | | |
		Amount	Cost			Amount	Cost
Debt	@ 5%	$40	$2.00	Debt	@ 5%	$50	$2.50
Preferred	@ 5%	10	0.50	Preferred	@ 5%	10	0.50
Common	@11%	40	4.40	Common	@12%	30	3.60
Deferred				Deferred			
credits	@ 0%	10	0.00	credits	@ 0%	10	0.00
Total		$100	$6.90	Total		$100	$6.60
		or a 6.9% return				or a 6.6% return	

c) Same assumptions as in example b) above for Company X but a 7.67% rate of return allowed on deferred credits. (The 7.67% is the weighted cost of all components of capital other than deferred credits.) Note that if the return on the deferred credits is added to the return on equity, the order, in effect, raises the return on equity, as is shown below in the recalculation on the right.

				Return on Deferred Credits Is		
				Added to Return on Common Equity		
Company X		*Amount*	*Cost*		*Amount*	*Cost*
Debt	@ 5%	$40	$2.00	Debt @ 5.0%	$40	$2.00
Preferred	@ 5%	10	0.50	Preferred @ 5.0%	10	0.50
Common	@11%	40	4.40	Common @ 12.925%	40	5.17
Deferred				Deferred		
credits	@ 7.67%	10	0.77	credits @ 0.0%	10	0.00
Total		$100	$7.67	Total	100	$7.67
		or a 7.67% return			or a 7.67% return	

The utility's cost of capital does not remain static. For instance, Company A, which maintains its capitalization ratios, has to borrow additional funds at a higher rate than the rate previously paid in order to build new plant. The regulators consider the cost of equity to be unchanged at 12%.

Utility A Expands
Capitalization and Cost of Capital
Before Expansion

	Amount		*Cost*
Debt	$ 500	@ 5%	$25
Common Equity	500	@ 12%	60
Total	$1,000		$85
			or 8.5% cost of capital

Securities Offered to Finance Expansion

	Amount			*Cost*
Debt	$ 500	@	8%	$40
Common Equity	500	@	12%	60
Total	$1,000			$100

or 10.0% cost of new capital

Capitalization and Cost of Capital After Expansion

	Amount			*Cost*
Old Debt	$ 500	@	5%	$ 25
New Debt	500	@	8%	40
Common Equity	1,000	@	12%	120
Total	$2,000			$185

or 9.25% cost of capital

In another example, utility B already has borrowed a great deal of money at a high interest rate, and the company wants to make its financial situation better by calling in some of the debt and replacing the debt with common stockholders' equity. After the recapitalization, the regulators believe that the common stockholders are not taking as much risk as before and, therefore, should be satisfied with a lower return on their equity investment.

Utility B Recapitalizes and Allowed Return Is Reduced

Capitalization and Allowed Rate of Return Before Recapitalization

	Ratio	*Amount*	*Cost*
Debt	70%	$700 @ 6%	$42
Common Equity	30%	300 @14%	42
Total	100%	$1,000	$84

or an 8.4% rate of return

**Capitalization and Allowed Rate of
Return After Recapitalization**

	Ratio	Amount	Cost
Debt	50%	$ 500 @ 6%	$ 30
Common Equity	50%	500 @10%	50
Total	100%	$1,000	$ 80

or an 8.0% rate of return

Capitalization

One would not expect the capitalization used in the rate case to be a problem. After all, the regulators need only look at the balance sheet. Life, though, is not that easy. Regulators may believe that the capitalization is not optimal and may substitute a hypothetical capitalization ratio for the real one. For example, should a company that has only common equity in a state in which regulators generally grant a 12% rate of return on equity be allowed a 12% rate of return? The company cannot be forced to sell debt, but the consumer should not have to pay the cost of the excessive conservatism. The regulators derive a rate of return by using a hypothetical capitalization ratio of 50% debt (at an 8% cost) and 50% equity (at a 12% cost). Although the rate order states that the utility is entitled to a 12% return on equity, the company can earn only 10% in actual equity because a hypothetical capitalization is used in the order.

**Rate of Return
Determined by Using Hypothetical
Capitalization**

	Ratio	Amount	Cost
Debt	50%	$500 @ 8%	$ 40
Common Equity	50	500 @12%	60
Total	100%	$1,000	$100

or a 10% rate of return

Determining the capitalization for the rate case might be a problem if the company plans to do financing after the close of hearings and requests that the regulators base their findings on a projected capitalization. The regulators might not be willing to accept the projections because the financing might not be made according to plan.

Determining capitalization (and cost of capital) when the operating utility is owned by a holding company is complicated. Many methods are used. A few of them, in a simplified form, follow.

All common stock of Operating Company (OC) is owned by Parent Company (PC). Operating Company sells its debt in the public markets. Parent Company has no other utility subsidiaries. All of its money, raised by selling debt and common stock, is invested in the equity of Operating Company. Debt of both the Operating Company and the Parent were sold at a cost of 6%.

	OC		PC		Consolidated	
	$	*Ratio*	*$*	*Ratio*	*$*	*Ratio*
Debt	$ 300	30%	$490	70%	$790	79%
Common Equity	700	70	210	30	210	21
Total	$1,000	100%	$700	100%	$1,000	100%

How can rate of return for Operating Company be calculated? The first method would be to ignore the parent-subsidiary relationship. The regulators consider OC's capitalization ratios. They might conclude that the common stockholders of OC are not exposed to much risk because of the small amount of debt outstanding. The regulators might decide upon a 10% return on equity. Rate of return is 8.8%, calculated as follows:

	Fraction of Capitalization		*Cost (%)*		*Weighted Cost of Capital (%)*
Debt	0.30	x	6.0%	=	1.80
Common Equity	0.70	x	10.0	=	7.00
Total	1.00				8.80

Some regulatory agencies use one of several variants of the double leverage method of calculation. The regulator wants to trace the subsidiary's equity capital to its source. In our example, the source is $490 of parent company debt and $210 of parent company equity. The regulator rearranges OC's capitalization as follows.

Reported Capitalization of OC	%		Double Leverage Capitalization	%
Debt	$300	30	Debt of OC $300	30
Common equity	700	70	Debt of PC used to purchase equity in OC 490	49
Total	$1,000	100	Common Equity of PC used to purchase equity in OC 210	21
			$1,000	100

Both debt components have a 6% cost. The common stockholders, however, receive a return higher than 10% because they are exposed to greater risk because of the large amount of debt that has a prior call on earnings and asset. The regulators therefore allow 19.33% on equity. Rate of return remains 8.80%.

	Fraction of Capitalization		Cost		Weighted Cost of Capital (%)
Debt of OC	0.30	x	6.00	=	1.80
Debt of PC	0.49	x	6.00	=	2.94
Common Equity	0.21	x	19.33	=	4.06
Total	1.00				8.80

Utilities oppose double leverage. The procedure assumes that cost of capital is determined by its source, not by return on alternative investments of similar risk levels. In addition, despite the wide differences in the capitalization ratio, the regulator may not be willing to adjust return allowed on equity beyond a limited range. In the previous case, the regulators might not go above a 15% return on equity, with the result that the overall rate of return drops to 7.89% and return on OC's equity drops to 8.70%.

Double Leverage Calculation

	Fraction of Capitalization		Cost		Weighted Cost of Capital (%)
Debt of OC	0.30	x	6.00	=	1.80
Debt of PC	0.49	x	6.00	=	2.94
Common equity	0.21	x	15.00	=	3.15
Total	1.00				7.89

OC Return

	Fraction of Capitalization		Cost		Weighted Cost of Capital (%)
Debt	0.30	x	6.00	=	1.80
Common Equity	0.70	x	8.70	=	6.09
Total	1.00				7.89

The third method uses consolidated figures on the theory that the holding company and its units are financed and run as a system. That method was often used in Bell Telephone rate cases, before the split-up of AT&T. The debt and preferred costs used are usually averages for the consolidated system, and cost of common is set in the usual fashion.

Return on Common Equity

The most difficult question is: how does the regulator discover the proper return on the common stock equity? No contractural relationship exists. The companies and regulators have resorted to pseudoscientific methodologies that purport to discover stockholders' needs on the basis of returns shown on other investments or from studies of capital market data. A number of methods are popular.

1) *The comparable earnings method* — In the Hope case, the Supreme Court said that "the return to the equity owner should be commensurate with returns on investments in other enterprises having corresponding risks."[36] Many rate of return experts have interpreted that as meaning that the point of reference should be the reported returns on the book equity of comparable enterprises. What is a comparable enterprise? Some practitioners have taken the terms literally — a utility should earn a return on book equity that is close to the return being earned by similar utilities. That approach solves the problem of finding comparable enterprises, but creates another one. To some extent, the return earned by the utility is a function of the return allowed in the company's last rate case. If every regulatory agency followed the policy of allowing the same return as every other regulator, the process would become circular. The criticism goes a step farther. Why should we believe that the return earned by other utilities is necessarily the return expected by investors of the utility in question? Most regulatory agencies grant higher returns than those actually earned by utilities. Rate of return allowed represents the regulatory agency's judgment about the return required by investors. Return desired by investors cannot be determined by examining return on the book equity of comparable utilities.

The difficulties of a utility-to-utility comparison are avoidable. The solution is to examine the returns earned on the book equity of industrial corporations that have characteristics similar to those of utilities. A more perplexing question then arises: how does one choose industrial corporations that are comparable to utilities? What are the characteristics of utilities? The commonly cited characteristics include the following:

a) Utilities must raise huge amounts of capital.

b) Utilities show steady sales patterns, are relatively insensitive to economic cycles, and their stock prices are relatively stable.

c) Utilities are capital intensive and often require $4 of plant to produce $1 of revenue.

d) Utilities employ small amounts of working capital.

e) Utilities hold monopolies on the provision of a particular service in a given area.

f) Utilities are capitalized to take advantage of financial leverage and borrow far more per dollar of assets than most industrial corporations.

g) Prices charged by utilities are regulated by governmental agencies.

Finding industrial companies that are comparable to utilities is difficult. Even if possible, there are additional problems.[37] For example:

♦ Industrial companies having earnings and stock price stability like that of utilities can be found mainly in monopolistic or oligopolistic industries. The returns of those companies can be attributed to monopoly power. Few would argue that a utility is entitled to a monopolistic rate of return.

♦ Accounting procedures do not allow true comparisons. An industrial corporation's balance sheet may include assets purchased at a price other than original cost. The plant may have been purchased long ago, so that the balance sheet does not accurately indicate the plant's current value, but revenues are on a current value basis. Depreciation rates of industrial firms have not been set by regulators at unrealistically low levels. Fluctuations in foreign currencies also add to the accounting complications.

One can attempt to circumvent problems of determining comparability by eliminating from the sample obviously oligopolistic firms, by avoiding companies with large foreign operations, by concentrating on industrial corporations that need to raise capital externally, and by using analyses of the risk of investing in individual securities.[38] Unfortunately, inflation has made income statements and balance sheets of firms unreliable indicators of desired returns. The reported income may be overstated — in real terms — because of the inadequacy of depreciation allowances. Depreciation on the historical cost of fixed assets will not provide enough funds to replace the fixed assets at current prices. When replacement becomes necessary, the firm must use supposed profits to make the payment. On the other hand, fixed assets might be sold for far more than book value, as a result of the revaluation caused by inflation. In the capital markets, securities — to some extent — may be priced to indicate current value of assets and an inflation-adjusted earning power.

As an extreme example, Firm X is comparable to a particular utility. Its stock sells for $10 a share, has book value per share of $100, and earns $3 a share. The plant is obsolete and inefficient. The cost of replacement is $200 per share. The company's depreciation rate is 3%. Can we say that the investor desires a 3% return, which is the return on book value? If the regulator granted a 3% return on equity to the utility, the stock price would plummet. Can we say that the correct return is 30% — the earnings return on the market value of the stock? That percentage is not really what investors expect, because they know that part of it is a return of capital resulting from inadequate depreciation rates. If the utility were to be granted a 30% return on book equity, the stock price would rise up far above book value, indicating that the allowed return is excessive.

The comparable earnings approach meets the requirement that "the return to the equity owner should be commensurate with returns on investments in other enterprises having comparable risks" (Hope Natural Gas). The comparable earnings approach is based on the audited books of large corporations rather that on attempts to read the minds of investors. The Hope decision, though, was written before the steady postwar inflation. (Wholesale prices in 1944 were no higher than they had been in 1864. Prices in 1864 were little higher than those in 1814. In 1944, there was little reason to expect the country to break out of a pattern of widely swinging price cycles about a barely rising trend line.) The distortions introduced into financial statements by inflation make comparisons difficult. The problem with the comparable earnings approach is that investors cannot always make investments that realize the returns shown on the books of the corporation. The investor seeking to place new funds must settle for the return currently available in the marketplace, or the return from the purchase of assets at current prices.

2) *The discounted cash flow technique* — For many years, regulators hesitated to use comparable earnings approach, ostensibly because of the difficulty of coming up with an acceptable sample of comparable companies. Witnesses using that approach had a tendency to be selective in their choice of comparable firms. Regulators objected that the witnesses had selected companies that would produce a desired answer. Given the adversary nature of the regulatory process, that objection was reasonable.

Rate of return experts developed alternative methods of finding a fair return on equity. Those methods "purport to give the objective judgment of the market place as to what is the cost of capital."[39] The discounted cash flow (DCF) technique is one of the most popular of those currently in use.

Discounted cash flow analysis accepts that the price of a common share equals the present value of the sum of all future income to be received from the share.[40] Assuming that the dividend payout ratio, earnings price ratio and growth rate remain constant in perpetuity, then (all numbers in decimals):

$$k = \frac{d+g}{p}$$

where:

k = expected return on investment in stock
d = dividend per share
p = price of stock
g = expected annual growth in dividend or market price of stock

To complete the analysis:
$$g = br$$

where:

b = the earnings retention rate $(1 - \text{payout ratio})$
r = expected return on book equity

The formulas are similar to those used by many investors. Unfortunately the stated assumptions present practical problems and the assumption that the stock price must remain at book value could invalidate the calculations. The basic formula also is circular. "The variable g ... is affected by r and in some cases by the expected ratio of market value to book value. The term r is the result of regulatory action and the market-to-book ratio is influenced by regulatory action. This results in independent variable g being dependent on dependent variable k of the formula which is circular."[41]

The market to book ratio affects the calculation in several ways. For example, when the market to book ratio is more than 100% and the utility must sell stock for financing, the stock's growth in earnings and dividends per share (g) will be faster than if the stock sold at or below book value. Thus, if the market to book ratio differs for two utilities the same k applied to the two stocks will produce different realized returns. To further complicate matters, the application to the book value of a return derived from the market value when book value differs from market value may be invalid.

The following examples show the effect of price on growth in earnings per share. Three utilities, with stock selling at 90%, 100%, and 110% of book value, must increase common equity by 10% to finance expansion. Each company sells stock at the market value at the end of the previous year. Each company earns 10% on equity.

Company A (90% of Book Value)	Year 1	Year 2
Common equity	$1,000.00	$1,100.00
Number of shares	100	111.1
Book value per share	$10.00	$9.90
Price per share (year-end)	9.00	—
Earnings	100.00	110.00
Earnings per share	$1.00	$0.99
% change in EPS	—	–1%

Company B (100% of Book Value)	Year 1	Year 2
Common Equity	$1,000.00	$1,100.00
Number of shares	100	110
Book value per share	$10.00	$10.00
Price per share (year-end)	10.00	10.00
Earnings	100.00	—
Earnings per share	$1.00	$1.00
% change in EPS	—	0%

Company C (110% of Book Value)	Year 1	Year 2
Common equity	$1,000.00	$1,000.00
Number of shares	100	109.1
Book value per share	$10.00	$10.00
Price per share (year end)	11.00	—
Earnings	100.00	110.00
Earnings per share	$1.00	$1.01
% change in EPS	—	+1%

The percentage change in the rate of growth caused by the market/book differential can be formulated as:

$$\frac{o}{e} \times \left[\left(\frac{m}{b} \times 100 \right) - 100 \right]$$

where:

o = dollar value of new stock offering
e = common equity before offering
m = market value of shares
b = book value of shares

Now let us attempt to determine k (expected return on investment in stock), ignoring the problem of circularity, while including and excluding the effect on growth of the market-book differential. Each of three utilities pays a 60¢ dividend. The expert witnesses have determined (based on past experience) that investors expect 4% growth from each utility.

	Company A	Company B	Company C
Dividend	$ 0.60	$ 0.60	$ 0.60
Price	9.00	10.00	11.00
D/P	6.66%	6.00%	5.45%
g	4.00	4.00	4.00
k	10.66	10.00	9.45

Does it make sense to say that investors will pay a higher price for a stock from which they expect a lower return? If the return on book equity to C were reduced to 9.45%, the stock would probably not remain at $11.00. Investors would (showing that regulators had misjudged their expectations) sell the stock until it fell to a price commensurate with the new, lower return on book equity. Investors base their expectations of return on the price of the stock, not on the underlying book value.

Growth differentials are caused by selling stock at different prices. The differentials are −1% for A, 0% for B, and +1% for C. The g and k of the formula again change, adding to the confusion:

	Company A	Company B	Company C
g	3.00%	4.00%	5.00%
k	9.66	10.00	10.45

What is the correct k to use in the rate case? The formula for k looks objective but is as subjective as the choice of comparable companies in the comparable earnings approach. Should stock price and dividend used in the formula be that of one date, or an average? If the latter, how long a period should be averaged? If the former, at what date? What selection would be representative? The answer of the expert witness is to pick the period that gives the desired result. The next step is to determine g. Should one use a past growth rate and, if so, which period should be chosen? Or should an estimate of future growth be based on investor expectations as divined by Wall Street security analysts? Some regulators have used growth in book value in a past period as a proxy for investor expectations for g.

In a 1978 decision, one commission wrote that the witness "was more pessimistic in his evaluation of investors' expectations of future dividend growth. In light of the company's poor past performance, he was of the opinion that investors anticipated a low rate of growth and were looking to the high dividend yield for the bulk of their return requirement."[42] That statement seems to say that if a company showed bad results in the past, investors expect nothing but a repetition of bad results, and deserve nothing better. And let us not forget that the witnesses in the case can pick the past period to produce the desired results. In another decision, a commission relied on the projections of "anticipated rate of growth in dividends per share" made by *Value Line*, a leading investment advisory service. The commission thought that the staff witness should have used a mean estimate for several similar companies, but said that "we believe that the DCF approach . . . provides the best estimate of a utility's cost of equity. We continued to be troubled, however, by the problem of deriving the growth term of the DCF model . . . we realize that the projections of a widely circulated investment survey such as *Value Line*, regardless of their accuracy, may provide a reliable estimate of investor expectations simply because of their influence on investor expectations. We therefore accept the anticipated growth in dividends per share projected by *Value Line* as the growth term in the DCF formula."[43] In effect, the return on equity set by the commission was really determined by the *Value Line* analyst. The commissioners showed little appreciation of the real problem of the DCF method. Investors' expectations are determined, to a great extent, by what they expect regulators to do. Regulators, in turn, make their decisions based on what investors expect. Perhaps the best way to get a generous rate order is to launch an investor relations campaign to convince stockholders that a great order is on the way. On the other hand, consumer groups could run a campaign to convince investors that a poor order is on the way.

3) *The capital asset pricing model* (CAPM)[44] — This approach to determining the proper return on equity is an offshoot of modern portfolio theory (MPT). Return on investment consists of two parts — a risk free return (such as that available from Treasury bills) and an additional return for risk. Risk is measured by comparing the volatility of return on a particular security with return in the market as a whole. That risk is measured by use of the familiar beta (B) of MPT. Thus:

$$R = Rf + B(Rm - Rf)$$

where:

R = the return expected from a security
Rf = the return on risk free securities
Rm = the market rate of return

Note that beta, as used above, does not simply show the price movements of particular stock as a multiple of the price movements of the market as a whole.

Investors have the choice of a risk free investment, and they will demand a higher return if they invest at a higher risk level. Whether beta is the proper measure of return, and whether the many assumptions underlying CAPM are realistic are matters for scholarly tomes. Is CAPM workable when applied to solving a problem: what return should be granted in a rate case? CAPM uses only past data to determine what the investor might expect in the future. Capital markets are extraordinarily unstable. A period in the recent past can be chosen to prove any predetermined hypothesis. Is there any correct past period or is the choice of period subjective? There is nothing wrong with subjectivity, but the use of a supposedly scientific CAPM formula wraps this subjectivity in specious objectivity.

Has the beta for a particular security been stable, and will it remain stable in the future? It may well be that beta has greater predictive value when applied to a portfolio than to a single security. Industries and companies have life cycles. At one time or another, electric utilities have been exciting, speculative vehicles, bankrupts, growth stocks, deteriorating income vehicles, near bankrupts, and pure income vehicles.

Does CAPM have predictive value? We are trying to determine investor expectations (the investors' predictions of their future returns). We want to know what investors expect to happen, not what already has happened. There is no reason to think that investors know in advance what will happen in a given future period. Nor can we be certain that what happened in the immediate past is what the investor expects in the immediate future. If that were the case, in fact, stocks would only go in one direction. Furthermore, there is no reason to believe that investor return is stable from period to period. In fact, the evidence is to the contrary, which provides another reason to be hesitant about applying to the future the return from a particular period in the past.

Another problem — how confident one can be about the statistical validity of the risk/return relationship at a given level of risk — may affect the results for a particular company or industry more than the results for an entire portfolio. For instance, what if the risk/return relationship in a past period looks like that of Figure 20-4? The formula risk/return relationship is shown by the straight line. But

Figure 20-4

Market Risk and Market Return by Industry Group

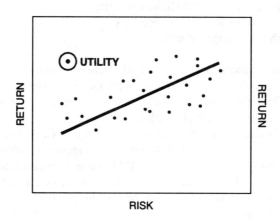

RISK

the points are not uniformly distributed about the line for its entire length.

The point representing the utility industry (circled in the figure) had a low risk level, but provided a market return substantially higher than would have been estimated from the risk/return line. In fact, note that all the low risk stocks yielded returns greater than would have been expected. Vandell and Malernee claimed that low beta stocks earn higher returns than they theoretically should.[45] If true, a CAPM formula consistently would understate the proper return for those groups.

In short, the CAPM approach attempts to determine investors' expectations of future return from the past performance of a group of stocks chosen because the stocks have risk characteristics similar to those of the security in question. Some regulators already see it as the revealed truth. CAPM, though, may be no more scientific or useful than the comparable earnings or DCF approaches.

4) *Financial integrity approaches* — Often, utilities and regulators have had

to fashion special approaches to meet specific problems, such as plummeting interest coverage ratios, the fall of stock prices to levels below book value, or financial disasters. Several approaches have been taken:

a) Set a return to produce a necessary interest coverage ratio. It may be necessary to ignore normal standards of return if a utility is to be able to obtain financing under certain conditions. Consider the following example. For simplicity, assume a zero income tax rate.

Rate base		$ 1,000
Pretax operating income		60
Operating income		60
Rate of return	$60/$1000 =	6.0%

	Capital		Return on Capital		Earnings
Debt	$500	x	8%	=	$ 40
Equity	500	x	4%	=	20
Total Capital	$1,000	x	6%	=	$ 60
Interest Coverage Ratio	$60/$40			=	1.5x

The company obviously needs rate relief because of the low return being earned on equity. The regulators have given a 10% return on equity to other companies. Can the regulators be persuaded to offer a higher return? The regulators might be told that the company must have a coverage ratio of 2.5 times total interest expenses of $40 for it to be able to sell debt in the future. If we start with an interest coverage of 2.5 times and work backward, the result would be:

Rate base		$ 1,000
Pretax operating income		100
Operating income		100
Rate of return		10%

	Capital		Return on Capital		Earnings
Debt	$500	x	8%	=	$ 40
Equity	500	x	12%	=	60
Total Capital	$1,000	x	10%	=	$100
Interest Coverage Ratio	$100/$40			=	2.5x

That approach has been used for utilities that get into tight financial positions. Regulators have not been sympathetic to its use when a utility simply desires high coverage, which would produce an extremely high return on equity.

b) Another approach is to provide equity with a return set at a fixed amount above current debt costs. In 1965-1975, interest rates doubled while return earned on utilities' equity declined. During the late 1970s and early 1980s, many utilities had to pay higher interest rates on new debt than the rates earned on common equity. In short, the protected creditor was able to make a higher return on investment than the risk-taking equity holder. In addition, for years, the return differential for higher risk of equity investment had been diminishing, despite the increasing risk of investment caused by the industry's many problems. The declining risk differential may have contributed to the poor relative performance of utility stocks in much of the 1965-1980 period. When many of the stocks sold below book value and utility investors were demoralized, the conventional methods of determining return did not work well. Some experts suggested that the proper return on equity should be set at a specific number of percentage points above long term bond yields. The differential above interest rates is a risk premium for shareholders.

c) Sometimes, due to huge writeoffs of common equity, or other assorted financial disasters, it is not possible to apply the normal rules of ratemaking. If, for instance, the utility's equity has been wiped out, setting a return on equity makes no sense because any return on a zero base is zero. A company in trouble may not be able to raise money needed for financial stabilization except through charges to customers. The regulators may fashion a financial stabilization plan that ignores the usual procedures, but sets the revenues so that they produce the necessary funds to pay off debts or to bring the utility to the point where it is again self-sufficient. Those plans usually have stated financial goals and stretch over a number of years.

d) During periods of high capital costs, heavy need for financing, or market instability, the regulator may set a return designed to keep the common stock price at or slightly above book value. According to the Hope decision, the proper rate of return must be high enough to maintain confidence in the utility's credit and to allow the company to attract capital. Despite a deterioration in credit standing, a utility may be able to attract capital (at least for a while), but possibly at a cost that would be damaging to the organization for the long term. A utility cannot be expected to maintain financial stability if each security offering is at a cost that makes the next offering more difficult. For example, a regulatory agency insists on a 6% rate of return, despite rising interest costs caused in part by falling bond quality. Each year, interest coverage declines as does the bond rating. Eventually the debt offerings cannot be sold. We assume an income tax rate of zero, and half of capital needs coming from the sale of debt.

	Years			
	1	2	3	4
Rate base (capital spending $200 per year	$1,000	$1,200	$1,400	$1,600
Operating income (6% of rate base)	60	72	84	96
Debt sold (half of capital spending)	—	100	100	100
Cost of debt sold	—	6%	8%	10%
Total debt outstanding	$ 500	$ 600	$ 700	$ 800
Interest costs (total)	$ 25	$ 31	$ 39	$ 49

$$\text{Interest coverage} = \frac{\text{Operating Income}}{\text{Interest Costs}}$$

	2.40x	2.32x	2.15x	1.96x

The regulator, through the above policy, has put investors on notice that no attempt will be made to protect the integrity of the debt. Past investors must suffer the loss of market value. Future investors must demand a current return high enough to compensate them for additional future risk. Eventually, the market dries up or the cost of financing becomes too high, and the utility can no longer attract capital at a reasonable price.

A common stockholder can act in the same manner as a bondholder. If investors consider a utility's prospects bad, or if the regulator does not realize that equity costs have risen, the investors will not buy until the price falls and provides a proper return on the market value of the shares. This raises the cost of capital to the utility. Furthermore, investors will demand a price that compensates them for any future devaluations that might result from unfavorable regulation. For example, regulators set a 10% return on equity, and the company pays out all earnings (so that return is the same as the dividend).

	Year(a)			
	1	2	3	4
Common equity	$1,000	$1,100.1	$1,200.1	$1,300.1
Number of shares	100	111.1	123.5	137.3
Book value/share (b)	$ 0.00	$ 9.90	$ 9.72	$ 9.47
Earnings on common equity (10%)	$100	$110	$120	$130
Dividends and earnings per share	$ 1.00	$ 0.99	$ 0.97	$ 0.94
Return on common demanded in marketplace (c)	10%	11%	12%	13%
Market value/share	$ 10.00	$ 9.00	$ 8.08	$ 7.23
Market/book ratio	100%	91%	83%	76%

Notes:
(a) All numbers have been rounded.
(b) Book value per share is common equity/number of shares.
(c) Return on common demanded in the marketplace is the return demanded on market value, *i.e.*, earnings per share/market value per share.

Another example shows that the market/book ratio is of vital importance to electric utilities that sell common stock. Assume that a company is allowed to earn 10% on common equity and that the company must sell $1 million of stock to meet financing needs in the year.

	Previous Year
Common equity	$10,000,000
Net income	$ 1,000,000
Shares outstanding	1,000,000
EPS	$ 1.00
Book value per share	$10.00

	This Year — After *$1 Million of* *New Common Is Sold*

A. Stock sells at 2 times book value, or $20.

Common equity	$11,000,000
Net income	$ 1,100,000
Shares outstanding	1,050,000
EPS	$ 1.05

B. Stock sells at book value, or $10.

Common equity	$11,000,000
Net income	$ 1,100,000
Shares outstanding	1,100,000
EPS	$1.00

C. Stock sells at 90% of book value, or $9.

Common equity	$11,000,000
Net income	$ 1,100,000
Shares outstanding	1,111,111
EPS	$0.99

In case A, each new share at $20 contributes $2 to earnings, *i.e.*, 10% or $20. Accordingly, earnings per share are helped by the sale. In case B, each new share at $10 earns $1 and has no effect on earnings. In case C, each new share at $9 brings in only 90¢, thereby diluting per share earnings.

Because of the dilutionary effect on current holdings of selling stock below book value, many regulators believe that earnings should be high enough to keep the stock at or slightly above book value. Because a positive correlation exists between return on equity and the market/book ratio, regulators often try to set a return on equity that will keep the stock selling near book value. Too high a market/book ratio, though, indicates to those regulators that the utility is overearning. Therefore, when the market/book ratio is low, selling new shares may be dilutive, but the regulators may have plenty of room to improve earnings if they so desire. When the market/book ratio is high, selling new shares could benefit earnings per share, but regulators could decide that the company is earning too much money. Welch wrote:

> . . . The final test that any utility enterprise has to meet, if it is to continue in business, is whether it can sell its securities on the investment market. According to the Federal Power Commission, if the return allowed cannot meet this test — if it has to sell stocks at a discount or bonds at a price giving higher yield than normally prevails in the market — that company is faced with financial difficulties. . .[46]

Bonbright discusses the sale of common stock at a price below book value in terms of "impairing the integrity"[47] of the investment made by previous stockholders. Clearly, sales at prices below book value erode the earnings potential of previously issued shares. If such sales are expected to continue for a long period, purchasers of new shares may intensify their demands for a higher return to offset the expected attrition, and thereby further increase the cost of capital.

In theory, when the return allowed on book equity is greater than the rate of return desired in the marketplace, the stock moves above book value. When return allowed on equity is below the return desired in the marketplace, the stock falls below book value.[48] Most regulators would like utility stocks to sell at a price enough above book value so that new shares could be marketed at book value. (The stock must sell above book value to provide a cushion for marketing costs.)

Some analysts have argued that a relation exists between return earned on book equity and the market/book ratio.[49] The relation varies with the level of the market, the extent of investors' willingness to pay for a higher return on equity, and even an investor's preference for current income (a high payout ratio) or growth (greater reinvestment of earnings). The following figures illustrate those differences.

In Figure 20-5 the relationships are shown at different points in the market cycle. The A line is for a period of high stock prices, the B line for the low point in the market. The utility must earn a higher return on equity (b) for its stock to sell at book value during the low point in the market cycle, than the return needed at the high point (a) of the market cycle.

Figure 20-6 shows that the slope of the regression line can change, even if the mean point for the group remains the same. In both cases, the average company earns return (a) and sells at slightly below book value. In Figure 20-6A, the

Figure 20-5

Market/Book Ratio at High and Low Points in Market Cycle

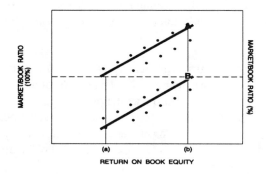

Figure 20-6

Slope of Market/Book to Return on Equity Relationship

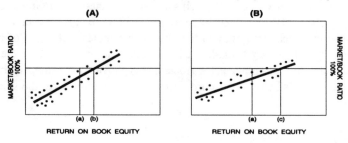

company need earn only a bit more (b) to reach book value. In Figure 20-6B, the utility must earn far more (c) to reach book value. In case A, the market highly values the additional return and is willing to pay for small increments of return. In case B, the market differentiates little between high and low returns, and a substantial rise in return is necessary to push up the market/book ratio.

Figure 20-7

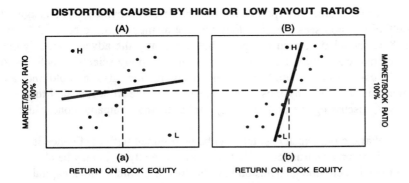

DISTORTION CAUSED BY HIGH OR LOW PAYOUT RATIOS

In Figure 20-7, the regression lines are distorted by outlying points which will pull the lines away from the trends set by most of the points. The distortion is caused by another phenomenon of the market — utility investors sometimes prefer current dividends to future growth and will pay more for a stock that has a higher divided payout ratio. Occasionally, either for reasons of policy or because earnings were higher or lower than expected, a utility's payout ratio will differ greatly from the industry norm. The stock may then sell well above or below the market/book ratio that might be expected, given the return on book equity.

The distortion of the regression line causes the same problems as in the previous set of figures. But still another, more serious problem exists. Take the two high payout companies (H). Each sells far above its expected market book ratio. From the high market/book ratio, a regulator might conclude that the company is overearning and that return on equity should be reduced. The companies (H) probably are overpaying rather than overearning. On the other hand, the two companies with low payout ratios (L) may be underpaying, rather than underearning. A number of utilities have raised dividends to push up their market/book ratios at the risk of having regulators at some future time cite the higher market/book ratios as evidence that rate relief is not needed.

In summary, the market/book ratio provides an indication of whether or not the utility is earning a satisfactory return, and whether or not the current return is fair to existing shareholders as well as to new ones. Unfortunately, the method suffers from distortions, especially when a specific utility has unusual features. Nowadays, making sense of the market/book ratio is even more complicated. First, some utilities have assets on the books that are not earning returns, and investors are more likely to pay for only that portion of book value that produces profits for them. Second, numerous companies have diversified into fields of business that command non-utility valuations in the marketplace.

Validity of Methods

Ambrose Bierce, an expert on the subject, defined a cynic as "A blackguard whose faulty vision sees things as they are, not as they ought to be. . . ."[50] Few wish to be included in such company, but apparently the adversarial, litigious nature of rate cases makes necessary a host of seemingly scientific methods to prove the case. Each method has its faults. New methods arise and old ones are declared unsatisfactory by those who have just had the truth revealed to them. Bonbright, discussing the cost of equity capital to any company, concluded:

> . . .that the only such cost that can be determined with confidence is a minimum or partial cost. That is to say, the analyst . . . may be able to reach a credible conclusion that the cost of common stock capital comes to at last some specified percent; but the extent of the probable deficiency is necessarily a matter of surmise. Hence, if the minimum estimated cost is to be used in the determination of computed "overall cost of capital," the resulting computation should be subject to a material, "judgment reached" enhancement in order to give reasonable assurance of full-cost coverage.[51]

When you add to that the point that in the past two decades, so many utilities have not even come close to earning their allowed returns, it becomes clear that the formula returns do need to be modified if they are to produce realistic results.

Chapter 21

The Rate Structure and Utility Economics

A rate system is primarily governed by practical considerations. If added use costs the consumer more than it costs the company, there is probable failure to develop services which would be worth their cost. If added use costs the consumer less than it costs the company, there is a stimulus to wasteful use.[52]

J. M. Clark

Until now, we have concerned ourselves with how the regulator determines the amount of revenue that the utility should collect to earn the allowed rate of return on the rate base. We have considered pricing in the aggregate sense. Pricing, in this case, does not necessarily serve the purpose that economists assign to pricing.

Purpose of Pricing

What purpose does utility pricing serve? For the regulator, the formula of price times volume less expenses provides the return that the utility is allowed to earn. Whether that price sends the right signals to consumers or promotes economic efficiency is a question that regulators often ignore. If prices should be higher to promote economic efficiency, the utility could earn too high a rate of return. If prices should be lower, the utility could earn a return that would be considered confiscatory, or it could go bankrupt because of failure to cover high fixed costs. Under present regulatory structure, some economists believe that the problem cannot be solved without a taxation-subsidy scheme. That is, the government would tax away excess profits when rates need to be higher to promote economic efficiency and would pay the utility a subsidy when rates need to be lower. The alternative to the taxation-subsidy arrangement would be to put the utilities under government ownership, with pricing designed to promote economic efficiency rather than profit.

Orthodox microeconomic theory holds that society will efficiently allocate economic resources when those resources are priced at the margin. Jules Joskow defined "marginal cost as the cost of society's scarce resources which must be used to produce one additional unit of some commodity or the value of resources that would be saved by producing one less unit of that commodity."[53] The consumer who purchases the product priced at the margin will do so only if the product is worthwhile enough for him to forgo the purchase of still another product priced at the margin. Through marginal cost pricing, the consumer knows how much it costs society to produce that last unit, and what costs can be avoided by not producing that unit. Bonbright refers to:

> the consumer-rationing function of public utility rates. In support of this function, rates should be made just high enough to deter potential customers from demanding services of types and in amounts for which they are unwilling to defray the costs of rendition.[54]

A few examples can illustrate how use of marginal pricing would curb some of the inefficiencies caused by our energy and utility pricing structure.

If it costs $15 to produce a new barrel of oil, and oil is priced at $10 (because some oil, found a long time ago, can be produced at $5, which reduces the average production cost to $10), oil buyers are less constrained by price. They then use more oil than they would at $15. Every barrel that they buy at $10, however, costs $15 to replace.

In another example, parallel to what happened in the telecommunications field, a utility can offer a special service because its plant is not fully utilized. The incremental cost of adding on the special service is $5 a unit. If part of the plant is allocated to the special service for regulatory purposes (despite the fact that the plant is already built and costs will not go up due to new customers), the service will not earn what the regulators consider to be a high enough return. The regulators might conclude that, because the new service is not earning a high enough return, the customers of other utility services must be subsidizing the service. For example, if another company announces that it will build a utility plant that will only provide a specialized service, then the specialized service must carry the entire cost of the plant. The company can offer the service at a cost of $15, which would include a proper rate of return. Is society better off if its assets are spent to build a new plant to provide a service for which the cost will be $15 a unit, or should the first utility be authorized to offer the service at incremental cost?

Or consider the case of a utility with 10 customers whose average cost and charge per customer is $250. Adding an eleventh customer will cost $400. The customer has an alternative to utility service: a solar cell that costs $300 for equivalent service. The utility, however, follows its previous policy of averaging costs, and now charges each of the eleven customers $264. The new customer forgoes the solar cell. Was that the right decision for the economy as a whole? Should $400 of scarce resources have been expended when $300 would have done the job?

To summarize the problem of the regulator: if a utility sets rates to cover marginal or incremental costs, consumers would be encouraged to promote economic efficiency. Depending on whether incremental costs were higher or lower than total costs, the utility might lose money, earn a return too low by legal regulatory standards, or earn too high a return. The present regulatory system may be keeping price too low for economic efficiency and may thereby be encouraging demand, or the system may be keeping price too high for economic efficiency.

Marginal or Incremental Costs

Let us briefly review the meaning of marginal and incremental costs to utilities. The short term cost curve of an ordinary business might look like that of figure 21-1:

Units of Output	Fixed Costs	Variable Costs	Total Costs
0	$1.00	$0.00	$1.00
1	1.00	0.50	1.50
2	1.00	0.90	1.90
3	1.00	1.20	2.20
4	1.00	1.60	2.60
5	1.00	2.10	3.10
6	1.00	2.80	3.80

Figure 21-1
Costs and Output

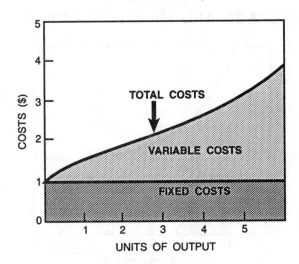

The fixed costs are those that do not change no matter how many units are being produced. Rent on factory space would be an example. Variable costs change with output. An example might be the yards of material purchased to make dresses. Variable costs do not always vary exactly with output. For instance, the dress manufacturer might be able to get a better price for material by purchasing in greater volume. Variable costs could rise faster than production output, for instance at the point when the factory is so busy that the employees are tripping each other and interfering with efficient productive processes.

Figure 21-2 shows cost curves on a per-unit basis.

Units of Output	Total Costs	Average Costs	Marginal Costs
0	$1.00	—	—
1	1.50	$1.50	$0.50
2	1.90	0.95	0.40
3	2.20	0.733	0.30
4	2.60	0.65	0.40
5	3.10	0.62	0.50
6	3.80	0.633	0.70

Figure 21-2

AVERAGE AND MARGINAL COSTS

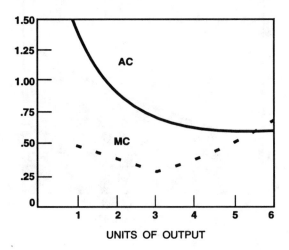

UNITS OF OUTPUT

After a certain point marginal cost (MC) rises above average cost (AC). If the product can be sold for marginal cost at a point where MC is greater than AC, the company makes a profit as can be seen in Figure 21-2.

The cost curve to a utility for which most short run costs are fixed (the utility must spend money to maintain the huge plant whether the plant is used or not) might be as shown in Figure 21-3.

Units of Output	Fixed Costs	Variable Costs	Total Costs
0	$5.00	$0.00	$5.00
1	5.00	0.40	5.40
2	5.00	0.70	5.70
3	5.00	0.90	5.90
4	5.00	1.10	6.10
5	5.00	1.30	6.30
6	5.00	1.50	6.50

Figure 21-3

UTILITY COSTS AND OUTPUT

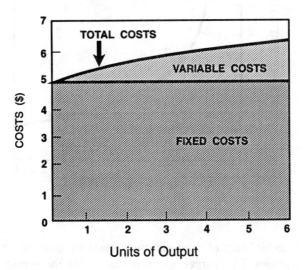

On a per unit basis, the curves would be

Units of Output	Total Costs	Average Costs	Marginal Costs
0	$5.00	—	—
1	5.40	$5.40	$0.40
2	5.70	2.85	0.30
3	5.90	1.967	0.20
4	6.10	1.525	0.20
5	6.30	1.26	0.20
6	6.50	1.083	0.20

Figure 21-4

Utility Costs per Unit and Output

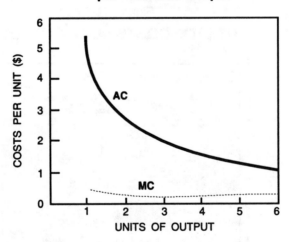

Clark, in his study of overhead costs, made the point that a utility cannot cover its expenses if it charges marginal costs when the average cost curve is declining. Figure 21-4 illustrates that problem.[55] For a strict marginalist the solution would be to charge marginal cost, and let the loss be made up indirectly by a government subsidy to the private company, or directly by means of socializing the utility. Nowadays, more people are questioning the classical analysis of utility economics. There are too many indications that, for now, anyway, the utility's average cost per unit is not declining, but may be rising. A switch to a new technology might, again, push down costs, but the current picture has led to a reexamination of old theories.

Marginalists active in the utility arena take a more practical view. Rates cannot be frequently changed. Customers cannot make long term plans (put into service new machines, air conditioners, build structures with a different design, determine work shifts, or decide on a plant site) when the only price signals they receive are short term fluctuations. Rather than worry about short run marginal costs, they say, examine long run incremental costs. How much new plant will be required to meet the growth in demand expected for the next few years? How much will it cost to produce the output of those plants? Are current rates sufficiently high to cover those new costs? If not, should rates be raised to cover those new costs, so that users understand what they will have to pay for service if they continue to increase usage? One could argue that part or all of the increase in demand is attributable to new customers. Why should old customers pay the higher costs? The answer is that the current customer does not own the utility plant and has no proprietary right to its output over the right of new customers to service.

Incremental cost analysis is being used to develop some rate structures. It has not been welcomed by some utilities, customers who would lose by its introduction, regulators, or competitors of utilities. Incremental cost analysis brings problems as well as benefits:

1) Incremental costs may be difficult to measure, especially costs for a particular class of customer. (Probably true.)

2) It may be extremely expensive to install the meters necessary to measure usage in a way that is useful for incremental costs analysis. (True, but mass production would reduce costs.)

3) Competitors may object to incremental cost pricing if the utility's long run incremental costs are below the price charged by the competitor. (Protecting a competitor should not be a reason to delay action.)

4) Certain classes of customers would be inconvenienced or disadvantaged by incremental cost pricing. (On the other hand, certain customers would benefit. Should the decision be based on which group is most vocal?)

5) Marginal pricing of one product in an imperfect economy in which many other products are not priced at the margin may not bring about efficient allocation of resources. This is the problem associated with the theory of second best. (At the same time, lack of perfection does not mean that better pricing is not superior to the present system.)

In short, marginal or incremental pricing is not problem free in the real world. If incremental costs are below average costs, even on a long term basis, who will pay the subsidy needed to keep the utility in business? If not, who should keep the extra profit if incremental is above average cost and pricing is based on incremental costs?

The Rate Structure

Service charges depend on the kind of utility, time of day, season, and kind of customer. A utility seeks to cover three different types of costs: costs that change with the number of customers, fixed charges associated with the utility plant (which must be covered whether customers are buying a lot of service or not), and variable costs that are incurred by providing a certain quantity of service. In the case of gas and electric utilities, the charge for variable costs usually includes a surcharge for changes in fuel, purchased power, and purchased gas expenses. The tariff schedule does not always spell out the three parts of the charge although the rates have been developed on a three part basis. Often the customer and fixed charge are combined.

The charge for customer costs covers the expense of billing, meter reading, and accounting, as well as the capital costs associated with investments in meters, service connections and some distribution facilities. The capacity or demand charge pays the fixed costs of the utility plant, including those operating expenses that do not vary with production of power. Customers may not always be using the utility plant, but they want that plant to be available to serve them at any time and, therefore, pay for that availability. Deciding how much plant should be allocated to a particular customer or group of customers is not simple. Generally, the key to allocation is the customer group's maximum demand on the plant at a particular time. For instance, all four of the electric company's generators are in use for the full day, two of them supplying residential customers and two supplying industrial customers. Half the capacity charges can be charged to the industrial customers and half to the residential. But what if plant is not utilized evenly all day? Perhaps the industrial customers need two of the generators only during the night, at a time when the residential customers are not taking any electricity. During the day, residential customers require all four generators. One could argue that none of the plant had to be built to meet industrial demand, and all of it had to be built to meet residential demand. Therefore, all capacity costs should be borne by the residential customers. Regulatory agencies may be reluctant to accept that kind of analysis. They might argue that the industrial customers receive benefits from the plant and should pay some of the capacity costs. Conceivably, the plant would not have been built at all if it could only serve the industrial load.

That kind of analysis is applied when constructing time-of-day, peak load, or long run incremental cost tariff schedules. Consider the case of a utility that has two classes of customers. One takes the same amount of service throughout the day. The second class takes the same amount of service for most of the day, except during peak hours when it takes a substantial amount of extra service. The utility serves the steady demand with efficient, base load plants. It serves the peak demand with another kind of plant. Both total capacity and demand at peak are 4kw, as seen in Figure 21-5. (The first part of Figure 21-5 shows a realistic breakdown of capacity and demand including intermediate load capacity. For sake of simplicity, the discussion distinguishes only between peak and base load.)

Because both classes equally share the base load plant, each class should pay the utility for that plant. Who should pay the utility for the peaking plant? The obvious answer would be the Class 2 customer, who is responsible for the peak. But is that really what should be done? If the Class 1 customer reduced usage at the peak hour, less peaking plant would be required.

Figure 21-5
A Comparison of Base, Intermediate, and Peak Periods

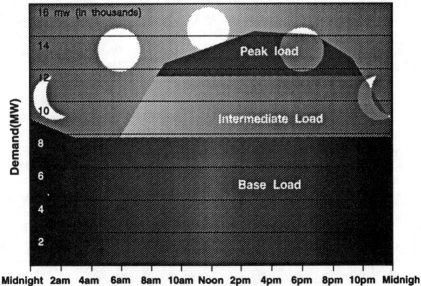

Peak Load and Capacity

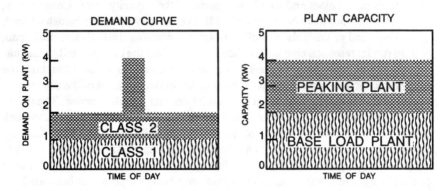

Keep in mind that a lot of confusion exists about the purpose of pricing that attempts to assign costs based on peak load responsibilities. The purpose is not necessarily to reduce demand during peak periods (although the pricing may have that effect), but to allocate costs so that those responsible for the peak demand pay the costs associated with it. With long run incremental cost pricing, incidentally, capacity charges might be set on the basis of estimates of the costs of planned capacity additions.

Some utilities have allocated capacity charges on the basis of noncoincident maximum demand. For instance, five customers (A, B, C, D, E) take 3, 1, 6, 3 and 2 units of demand at their respective maximum times of usage. The utility's capacity costs are $15. If costs are apportioned by maximum noncoincident demand, the customers would pay $3, $1, $6, $3 and $2. What if the demand pattern and capacity were as shown in Figure 21-6? Clearly, most of the plant had to be built to meet the needs of customers C and D. The others are off-peak

Figure 21-6
Noncoincidental Demand and Capacity

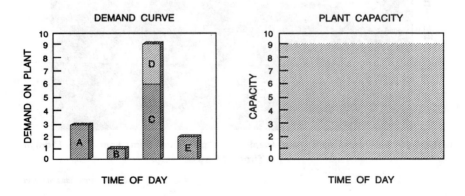

customers. The entire plant would have been built to meet the needs of C and D and those two customers should bear most (some would argue all) of the capacity costs, not just 9/15 of the costs. In short, the noncoincident maximum load method is of dubious value in allocating capacity costs.

The third method looks at average and excess demand. Part of the fixed costs are allocated by the average loads of customers. The balance of the fixed costs are allocated by how much capacity over the average is required by the customer.

Variable Costs

Variable costs associated with usage are easier to measure if the utility produces a physical output such as a kilowatt-hour of electricity or a thousand cubic feet of gas. For instance, a certain amount of fuel must be burned to produce a kilowatt-hour. After a certain number of hours of production, the generator must be taken down for maintenance and repairs. A certain number of employees are required to keep the generator running. Admittedly, every cost cannot be quantified precisely, but some vary directly with production and some do not. In addition, costs vary with the time and conditions of production. Off-peak power might be produced by the utility's low cost nuclear power station, which is kept running all the time. Power demanded at 3:00 pm on a hot summer day, when the utility's capacity is taxed to its limit, might be produced, in part, by inefficient standby generators and expensively fueled peaking units. That difference in cost should be reflected in rates. A utility may attempt to charge the customer for those differences in costs either by means of generalized rates (such as seasonal ones) or by the actual metering of the time of usage.

The fuel adjustment clause add-on also varies with use. Its purpose is to protect the utility from sudden changes in fuel costs. Because fuel prices can change quickly and drastically, the utility could suffer if it had to wait for a general rate increase to recover the higher costs. Without a fuel adjustment clause, a utility might be requesting rate changes almost monthly. Recently, some regulators have argued that the automatic nature of the fuel clause pass-on provides utility managements with little incentive to control fuel costs. The concept of the fuel adjustment clause is under scrutiny, and a few regulatory agencies have made incentive arrangements to encourage efficient operating procedures.

The Rate Schedule

A utility must add all expenses and then determine a set of rates for a customer class. The schedules specify rates by time of year, sometimes by time of day, and may include special prices for customers that qualify for conservation, volume usage, or other discounts.

A large midwestern utility has this simple schedule for its residential customers:

Facilities charge	—	$12.50 per month
Energy charge	—	9.00¢ per kwh in summer season
		8.28¢ per kwh for first 300 kwh
		in balance of year
		7.28¢ per kwh for all over 300 kwh
		in balance of year
Fuel cost adjustment		— Energy charge is adjusted for changes in fuel cost to utility

A southern utility has a more complicated residential bill:

Basic facilities charge	—	$8.30 per month
Energy charge	—	
First 350 kwh per month		7.01¢ per kwh
Next 950 kwh per month		7.96¢ per kwh
All usage over 1300		7.96¢ per kwh (July-Oct.)
kwh per month		7.49¢ per kwh (Nov.-June)

The fuel adjustment rider is included in the energy charge. Furthermore, customers with a qualifying electric water heater pay only 7.80¢ for energy in the second price block (next 950 kwh per month).

Another southern utility has these rates for residential customers:

Basic customer charge	—	$5.69 per month
Kwh charge	—	
First 900 kwh		3.84¢ per kwh
Excess over 900 kwh		2.86¢ per kwh
Fuel charge rider	—	1.59¢ per kwh

The fuel charge rider varies with the cost of fuel to the utility.

Commercial and small industrial customers may pay on a different basis.

The tariff will specify voltage, type of motors allowed and other technical matters. The tariff determines the electric bill by measuring demand in kilowatts (usually the maximum demand in the past 12 months) and consumption in kilowatt-hours. The monthly schedule for one utility is:

Basic facilities charge	—	$11.40
Demand charge	—	
First 30 kwh		No charge
Over 30 kwh		$3.65 per kw
Energy charge for first 125 kwh per kw billing demand per month	—	
First 3,000 kwh		10.00¢ per kwh
Next 87,000 kwh		5.20¢ per kwh
All consumption over 90,000 kwh		3.78¢ per kwh
Energy charge for next 275 kwh per kw billing demand per month	—	
First 6,000 kwh		5.34¢ per kwh
Next 95,000 kwh		5.22¢ per kwh
Next 39,000 kwh		5.11¢ per kwh
All consumption over 140,000 kwh		4.80¢ per kwh
Energy charge for over 400 kwh per kw billing demand per month	—	
All kwh		4.55¢ per kwh

The fuel adjustment charge is included in the energy charge. For the tariff, if demand is 1,000 kw and consumption is 100,000 kwh, the bill will be:

Facilities charge	$11.40
Demand charge	$3,540.00*
Energy charge	$5,202.00**

* (1,000 kw – 30 kw) x $3.65
** Calculated at the first schedule because customer takes less than 125 kwh per kw.

3,000 kwh at 10.00¢	$ 300.00
87,000 kwh at 5.20¢	4,524.00
10,000 kwh at 3.78¢	378.00
Total energy charge	$5,202.00

Rate schedules for industrial customers are complex. The utility must keep in service large amounts of plant to meet the needs of the industrial customer. The customer must pay the fixed charges on that plant, and that rate schedule should encourage the customers to maintain a high load factor (the relationship of average to peak demand). The schedule usually specifies the voltage at which the service is taken, too. One Midwestern utility has the following industrial tariff:

Facilities charge per month based on customer's delivery voltage —

Below 2.4 kv	$ 80.00
2.4 kv to 12.47 kv	$ 300.00
34.5 kv and 69 kv	$ 605.00
138 kv	$1,170.00

Distribution capacity charge per month based on supply line service of —

	12.47 kv *and below*	34.5 kv *and above*
For each kw	$1.00 per kw	$1.20 per kw

Demand charge per month for supply lines of —

	12.47 kv *and below*	34.5 kv *and above*
For each kw in summer	$ 13.03 per kw	$ 11.03 per kw
For each kw rest of year	$ 6.57 per kw	$ 6.07 per kw

Energy Charges per kwh for supply lines of —

Per kw of maximum demand	12.47 kv *and below*	34.5 kv *and above*
First 100 kwh	5.28¢ per kwh	5.18¢ per kwh
For next 75 kwh	4.78¢ per kwh	4.68¢ per kwh
For next 225 kwh	4.28¢ per kwh	4.18¢ per kwh
For all over 400 kwh	3.30¢ per kwh	3.20¢ per kwh

In addition, the utility's tariff has a 1.00¢ per kwh energy credit for kwh taken during designated off peak periods.

Industrial tariffs issued by another Midwestern utility are based on the voltage at delivery (four categories starting from transmission, the highest, to secondary, the lowest). Prices are in three parts: for demand (in kilovolt amperes, a measure of apparent power), energy (per kwh) and a fixed monthly service charge.

Service Voltage	Demand Charge ($/KVA)	Energy Charge (¢/kwh)	Monthly Service Charge ($)
Secondary	16.97	1.52	309.45
Primary	15.29	1.44	418.75
Subtransmission	14.04	1.42	418.75
Transmission	13.35	1.40	418.75

The bill is subject to a fuel adjustment clause, too. Off peak demand charges are disregarded within limits. And all rates are adjusted for the customer's power factor, as measured by special meters.

A Southern utility has opted for a simpler industrial tariff structure.

Basic facilities charge	$17.08 per month
Demand Charge	
First 30 kw of billing demand per month	No Charge
For over 30 kw of billing demand per month	$3.60 per kw

Energy Charge

For the first 125 kwh per kw Billing Demand per Month

For the first 3,000 kwh per month	9.88¢/kwh
For the next 87,000 kwh per month	5.37¢/kwh
For all over 90,000 kwh per month	3.76¢/kwh

For the next 275 kwh per kw Billing Demand per Month

For the first 140,000 kwh per month	4.97¢/kwh
For all over 140,000 kwh per month	4.47¢/kwh

For all over 400 kwh per kw Billing Demand per Month

For all kwh per month	4.27¢/kwh

Fuel adjustments are already included in the above schedules. Billing demand is the maximum 30 minute demand during the month. The bill is corrected when the power factor slips below a specified level. Taking the above schedule, let us calculate a sample bill. That facilities charge is $17.08. The customer's peak demand is 35 kw. The first 30kw are free but the next 5 kw cost $3.60/kw or $18.00 for the demand charge. The customer takes 2,520 kwh. That is 72 kwh per kw of demand (2,520/35 = 72). Thus the energy charge falls into the category of the first 125 kwh per kw of demand, and it is 2,520 kwh at 9.88¢ or $248.98. The total monthly bill for the customer (assuming that the power factor is in the acceptable range) is $284.06.

Price Differentials

The price of energy and other vital utility services is rising. Presumably many consumers need those services, but have difficulty paying for even a small amount of service. Some regulators have changed the rate structure so that the consumer can buy a limited (lifeline) amount of service at a low price. Once usage exceeds the lifeline amount, the price rises. That is, rates per unit go up rather than down with greater usage. When lifeline rates are applied to all customers, wealthy apartment dwellers and owners of occasionally used ski lodges as well as the poor can benefit. The loss of revenue from the low initial cost of service must be made up either by higher rates to big residential users or by higher rates to industrial customers.

As a final point about rates to different classes of customers, the key question is not how much the customer group pays per unit of output, but rather what rate of return the customer group's business provides to the utility. It may be that as a result of the time or kind of usage, industrial business brings in a 9% return when the price averages 2¢ for each unit taken, and the residential customer provides only a 6% return when his price is 4¢ a unit. Leveling the price differentials between industrial and residential customers might eliminate the supposed unfairness of a situation in which two groups pay different prices for the same product. But that attitude considers only one dimension of demand: quantity. It does not consider that what is really demanded is capacity, quantity at particular times, and even differing needs for reliability. Residential and industrial customers do not get the same service even if they take the same number of units of service (in terms of kilowatt-hours, thousands of cubic feet, or number of phone calls). Price leveling might be more discriminatory than the present system and might also bring about misallocation of economic resources.

Conclusion

Once the total revenue has been decided, a rate structure of prices to customer groups must be designed to produce the required amount of revenue. Doing so is a complicated matter and will become more complicated with the introduction of new economic and social theories.

Chapter **22**

New Regulatory Concepts

Decision theory has no solution to the problem posed by nonprobabilizable uncertainty.[56]

Ralph Turvey

Regulators have had to face the fact that their attempts to substitute themselves for the market and to protect consumers from utilities and to protect utilities from insolvencies and to hold off the march of technological progress have produced some strange results. Perhaps all those legal rulings and financial formulas have to give way to something better.

Incentives

The traditional regulatory system was designed to allow utilities to recover costs, including a fair return on capital invested. A utility that ran inefficiently recovered its high costs. One that ran efficiently recovered its low costs. The customers of the first utility suffered by paying higher prices. Those of the second enjoyed the benefits of the utility's efficiency through lower prices. The first utility paid no penalty for its poor operational results. The second collected no reward for operating well. This assumes that the poor operations were within some normal range, and not the result of an egregious error. In the latter case, the utility would be penalized. On the other hand, if the efficient utility had managed to pull off an extraordinary operational coup that lowered its costs well below the norm, there was still little likelihood of a reward for its prowess. In other words, the regulatory system had two major defects. The first was that it did not operate in a manner that simulated the competitive marketplace, because inefficient companies did not make lower profits and efficient companies did not make higher profits. The second was that the penalty and reward system that existed was asymmetrical. That is, there was a penalty for an egregious failure that could be attributed to imprudence or negligence, but no reward for exceptional achievement.

Many regulators, finally, have concluded that they cannot supervise every aspect of the utility's operations in order to encourage the utility to run better, to lower its costs, to find better ways of doing business. The answer to the problem, then, is to give the utility incentives that produce rewards for good results and penalties for poor results. Several incentive plans are in operation, and others no doubt will come along. Here are a few:

Performance Index — The regulator sets a series of operating goals, such as keeping maintenance cost increases below the rate of inflation, or getting a certain rating from a customer satisfaction survey, or running power plants at high levels of efficiency. The regulators tally the scores periodically, and then set the allowed return somewhere within a prescribed range based on the scores, with a high return when the utility scores well, and a low one when it scores badly. This type of plan may work best for a stable situation, but it has the disadvantage that the utility might find a way to neglect operations not covered in the index, or manipulate the results to improve the index rating.

Rate Moratorium — The regulators and the company agree not to change the rate structure, except for an emergency or for agreed-upon events during a specific period of time. In the moratorium period, the utility can make as much money as it can by running more efficiently, but if efficiency goes downhill, and so do profits, that is too bad for the utility. If the utility is too successful, and profits rise too much, the regulator might take rate action at the expiration of the moratorium that reduces some of the excess (by regulatory standards) profits.

Price Index or Price Cap — The British government has promoted a system in which every year's price increase is tied by a formula to the cost of living index. For instance, the formula might allow price increases equal to the change in the cost of living increase plus 1/2%, so in a year when living costs rise 3%, the allowed price increase per kwh would be 3 1/2 %. The system does not explicitly keep track of profits or rate of return. Obviously, if the utility can keep its cost increases below the allowed price changes, it can raise its profits. The system has disadvantages. For one, profits and revenue are tied to volume sold, which encourages the utility to sell more and to downplay conservation measures. The second is that the utility might try to avoid needed but unexpected expenditures because it has no way of recovering them.

Rate of Return Range — The regulator sets a range of return, such as 12% to 13%, and produces a rate order that sets prices to produce a return within the range, such as 12.5%. If the utility can bring its earnings up to the top of the range by running a tighter ship, nobody complains. On the other hand, if the utility has trouble with expenses, and earnings fall to the lower end of the range (below the 12.5% allowed return but above 12%), it cannot go back to the regulator until the earnings fall below the bottom of the range. It is a simple system, but not necessarily even-handed if the regulator sets the range in a way that makes it unlikely that the utility will get near the high end, but likely that the utility will stay at the low end.

Profit Sharing — Rather than setting limits to profitability, the regulator can give incentives that not only raise profits but also cut the price of electricity if they are successful. The regulator sets an initial allowed return or range of return. Then the regulator sets a sharing scheduling that lets the utility keep some of the profits above a certain level but uses the balance to reduce the cost of service to customers. For example, the regulator might set the allowed return at 10% to 11%. If the utility pushes earnings up to 12% through better management, the utility can keep three quarters of the excess over 11% and must give the remaining 1/4% to the customers as a price reduction. If the utility gets return over 12%, it can keep half of the excess in the 12 to 13% range and give the rest back to customers. If return gets into the 13 to 14% range, the utility keeps one quarter of the excess over 13% and gives back the rest to customers. If the return goes over 14%, the utility gives all the excess over 14% to customers. The profit sharing puts a cap on profits, but still gives the utility plenty of room to improve its operations.

So far, in the United States, regulators have favored price cap regulations for telephone companies and profit sharing for electric utilities. Also, they have combined elements of both systems in order to give incentives but not discourage needed service expenditures.

Prudence and Imprudence

Utilities used to invest in new plants on the assumption that regulators would only let them earn no more than a fair return on the investment, but earning that return was close to being assured. In the late 1970s and throughout the 1980s, spending programs ran over budget, some construction projects had to be cancelled at great loss, new plants worked poorly and often the new facility was far in excess of the needs of the utility's customers. Regulators declared that they would not grant returns on investments made imprudently. They applied hindsight to the construction process, determining what the facility should have cost if the builder had only known what was evident years later. They debated how much capacity the utility should have had if it had only known what customers were going to buy. Regulators declared that billions of dollars had been imprudently invested. Therefore, customers should not pay for those investments, which meant that the investments were worthless. That was shareholder money down the drain.

No doubt many of those projects were poorly managed or unneeded, but they were built in good faith by companies that thought they had an obligation to invest to serve the needs of the public. Too often, the regulators had ignored or even encouraged the projects during construction. The risk that investment would be disallowed from entering the rate base was new to the utilities. After experiencing those losses, utility executives have become cautious about making new investments. They want assurances, before and during the process of construction, that the expenditures will be considered prudent. Otherwise, they will not build, which might affect reliability of service, eventually. Regulators might have to institute a procedure that reassesses prudence periodically, during the construction process, and that assures recovery of investment that has been approved as prudent.

Competition, Transmission and Pricing

Parts of the industry have been opened up to competition while others have not. In some instances, regulated operations may be competing against unregulated. Unregulated generators may want to use the transmission facilities of utilities (which are regulated generators) to reach customers. Might the utility deny transmission services to the independent generator in order to favor its own generation? The transmission lines were built to serve the utility's own customers (the "native load") and have been supported by those customers. Should the utility inconvenience its own customers in order to make room for the outsider? What price should the utility charge for transmission? Those are a few of the questions prompted by the introduction of competition and the opening of access to transmission to non-utilities.

Transmission is a scarce resource, difficult to build due to environmental constraints. In a sense, it is a monopoly, and one could argue that it should be regulated in the normal fashion. Doing so, though, means pricing transmission to produce a return on the historical cost of the asset, probably far below what it could cost to build new lines. That low price encourages independent generators to use more transmission than is efficient, and discourages them from building their own transmission facilities. In fact, the low price discourages anyone from building needed lines. On the other hand, regulators would not let the utilities charge too much, or profits would shoot above allowed levels. Encouraging new generating competition might require access to transmission at low prices, possibly to the detriment of the native load. Encouraging the most efficient use of a scarce resource, transmission, might require a higher price. This issue will not go away.

Phase-In

During the 1980s, when utilities asked for and could justify the need for sharply higher prices (known as "rate shock"), regulators decided that the only way to deal with the problem was to spread the increase over several years (usually up to 10 years). This procedure is called a "phase-in." In theory, customers owe the entire rate increase from the beginning, but they only pay part of it, initially. The balance owed accrues interest, so at the end of the phase-in period, the customers have paid everything that they would have paid without the phase-in, plus interest, and are no better off. But the increase was made gradually, with the price going up every year, instead of all at once, so customers had time to adjust. The phase-in has become commonplace, and is used for what would have been considered small increases a few years ago.

Least Cost Planning (LCP)

Regulators no longer accept whatever the utility does. They want justification. They want to know that the utility picked the least cost solution to the problem, not the one that would most benefit the utility. Thus, the utility needs to decide what it is trying to do, examine the alternative methods of solving the problem, and then justify the choice to the regulator. As an example, the utility believes that it will need greater generating capacity in the future, considering present trends in the service territory. In the past, the utility would have just built a power station as a solution. Now, the utility will first determine whether the cheapest solution is to encourage present customers to use less electricity so as to free up existing supplies for new customers. If that is not the answer, the utility might see if it could inexpensively produce more electricity from existing plants. If not, should the utility build a power station or could it buy cheaper electricity from another supplier? The process may be cumbersome, but by leading the regulator through it, and getting approval, the utility might avoid painful prudence disallowances later on.

Demand Side Management (DSM)

Utilities charge prices based on regulated historic costs. That price might be lower than what it costs the utility to serve the next customer that comes along or to produce the next kwh. Customers do not get price signals that tell them what the service or kwh costs, as they would when buying products from unregulated businesses. As a result, they might take more electricity than they would if electricity were priced properly.

The utility should determine how to handle this uneconomic demand. Perhaps it would be cheaper to help the customers consume less electricity rather than build a new power station. In other words, the utility might find that insulation put into customers' attics will reduce consumption of electricity enough to avert the need for the next power station. If the insulation costs less than the power station, then the customers of the utility would be better off.

At certain times of the day, when demand is at its peak, the utility may be running its most expensive power plants. In fact, there might be times when the demand exceeds the capacity that the utility has available. Putting in a new power station just to serve a demand that lasts a few hours is an expensive proposition. Certain customers, if given a proper reward, might not take electricity during the peak period, thereby freeing up electricity for other customers who cannot or choose not to cut back during peak periods. The electric utility might attach a device to the customer that automatically cuts off usage at peak, or it might request the customer to reduce usage at peak. Many large industrial customers, in fact, take electricity on an interruptible basis, which means that they pay less for electricity with the understanding that the utility can cut off service when it deems necessary.

Utilities might take more unusual actions. One utility paid customers to junk inefficient, old refrigerators and replace them with new energy-efficient refrigerators. The utility found that it was cheaper to encourage customers to buy new refrigerators, and cut down on the customers' usage, than to put up a new power station.

All the activities designed to control demand in order to help the utility keep down costs fall into the category of demand side management. Utilities are paid by the kwh, which means that they get paid more when they sell more, but customers benefit if the utility can keep down uneconomic demand that raises costs. Regulators have wrestled with the question of how to encourage conservation activity if the utility makes nothing for the effort. Several states have come up with solutions. One is to decouple profit from sales volume, so that the utility knows that it will make a fair profit even if it succeeds in dampening sales. Another approach is to give the utility a rate of return on money invested in demand side management (sometimes a rate of return higher than the normal return). A third is to let the utility recover DSM expenditures within the year and also to collect a profit on that spending if it is successful.

Purchased Power

Many utilities buy electricity from non-utility generators as an alternative to building their own power stations. Often the state regulators require the utility to do so, but in many instances the non-utility generator has presented a lower cost alternative than the utility's own project. The non-utility generator needs to sign a long term power purchase contract with the utility in order to get financing for the project. (The lenders want to know that the generator has a paying customer for an extended period of time, so that they have confidence that they will be paid back.)

This arrangement creates new problems that do not fit into the normal regulatory framework.[57] For one, the utility takes a risk. It signs a contractual obligation for a long period of time. That obligation involves risk. Perhaps the utility will not need the electricity at some time in the future, but it still must pay for it. Perhaps the contract will turn out to be at an uncompetitively high price if future fuel prices fall, but the utility is still stuck making payments as required by the contract. Perhaps, some time in the future, the regulator will declare the contract imprudent, in which case the utility cannot pass on the costs to customers, but the utility still has to pay. Regulators set profits nowadays based on rate of return on rate base and no investment (and therefore no rate base) is involved in the contract, so the utility cannot earn a profit on the purchased power. It takes risk but earns no compensation for taking the risk. That is a peculiar business arrangement, furnishing the utility little incentive to purchase electricity from independent producers. Regulators have choices. They can force the utility to purchase from others. Or they can furnish the utility with no incentive, but hope that the utility makes the right decision. Or they can let the utility collect a markup on purchased power costs, which might reduce utility opposition to purchasing from outsiders, which is based on the fact that the utility makes no profit on purchased power, but it would have earned a return on the plant investment that was not made because the utility purchased electricity from others rather than generating the electricity itself.

Externalities

Often when producers calculate their costs, they do not include costs of production that are borne by others. For instance, a lead smelter pollutes a nearby farm, whose crops decrease. The farmer bears the cost of the pollution. The smelter does not include the cost in its calculations. For many years, electric utilities fouled the air, when they burned dirty coal without any pollution control devices. The people downwind of the smokestacks had higher laundry bills and suffered lung ailments. The utilities did not pay the higher laundry or medical bills. Then the government required pollution controls, which cost the utility money (internalized the costs) but reduced the costs borne by those downwind.

Several regulatory agencies have decided that when utilities compare costs of alternatives courses of action, they should add in the external costs. For instance, the utility has to choose between two power sources. One costs 5¢ per kwh but produces pollution and is so noisy that its operation will reduce the value of homes in the neighborhood of the plant. The second source is clean, but costs 6¢ per kwh. In theory, the company should value the costs of the pollution and noise when determining which source to choose, and it might decide that the second source is cheaper, once external costs are added in.

Calculating external costs will be difficult and the calculations will change as we learn more.

Unbundling

Electricity purchasers in America pay a price that includes the costs of generation, transmission and distribution, all bundled together. The customer cannot just buy distribution from the local utility, transmission from another company and generation from a third. It may be that the utility does not know the real costs of each of the three functions. It may be that the pricing formula is such that customers who do not take the normal mix of the three functions may not be paying properly for services rendered. In the natural gas industry, large customers can buy gas directly from the producer, pay the pipeline for transmission, and pay a transportation charge to the local gas distribution utility. In the telephone industry, customers can use or bypass the local exchange carrier when sending a message to a long distance carrier, and can choose the long distance carrier. In the United Kingdom, electricity generation, transmission and distribution are separate functions with their own price schedules.

When the utility collects all the charges, it may not care if it has properly apportioned costs between sectors. However, once customers demand one or two of the services, but not all of them, the utility had better have the right price. That issue has started to cause trouble as independent generating firms demand to use the utility's transmission lines in order to move the electricity to the purchaser. Right now, the purchaser is a utility. In the future, it could be a large industrial firm. The utility needs to spell out all the services involved in each function, and have a cost-based price for those services. Otherwise, it may encourage customers to take part of the package because those parts are priced too low, but not take other parts that are priced too high.[58]

Determining the costs of all functions is difficult to do. Not making the determination seems the recipe for commercial disaster, though, when the time comes when customers do not take the entire bundle.

Conclusion

Regulators have developed new procedures in order to deal with the lack of incentives in the normal regulatory system. They have not come to grips with the basic problem, which is that so many of the prescribed prices are wrong. Instead, they work around that issue. If the utility does not send the customer the right price signals, then it has to pay the customers (through appliance rebates or cheap insulation or free energy-efficient light bulbs) not to use electricity that they might not have used in the first place if the price were higher. When the price for transmission is too low, that encourages more use of that scarce resource, and the utilities must share the resource among all the parties that want it. They should, instead, raise the price to discourage those who could do without it. The utilities, too, abet those regulatory policies by not developing prices for all sectors of their business, possibly out of fear that customers might not take the whole package if they can pick and choose. They need not worry. The customer will pick and choose eventually, whether the utility likes it or not. But the utility might not get paid properly. More changes in the system are on the way.

Chapter **23**

Summary

Private enterprise free from the interference of the sovereign power never existed within the range of recorded history — not in ancient times, not in the medieval ages, nor in Puritan New England, nor in the California vigilante days.[59]

Arthur Stone Dewing

The concept of the regulated business preceded the formation of the industries that are currently classified as utilities. An industry does not have to be a natural monopoly to be regulated. The idea of the natural monopoly is both static and dubious. As technology changes, what may have been a monopoly at one time becomes subject to competition. If an industry that was regulated to protect the consumer continues to be rigidly regulated after the onset of competition, the regulation may end up protecting the competitor because the former monopolist is controlled by a regulatory strait jacket that prevents response to the new situation. Even without considering technological change, the consumer can find substitutes for some of the natural monopoly's services: oil and gas vs. electric heating, installation of insulation vs. purchase of more fuel, self generation vs. central station power, telephone vs. telegraph or mail. If pricing of utility services better reflected costs, more competitors might enter the field.

In theory, the regulatory process protects the consumer from the natural monopoly by simulating the results of a competitive environment. The price control system that has resulted does not seem to have achieved that goal. Usually, prices are set on the basis of average historical costs. In the late 1950s and early 1960s, regulators may have allowed returns to rise above the cost of capital. For much of the period after 1965, regulators may have been unwilling to allow companies to earn their costs of capital.

The rate case, in which costs are set, serves financial, legal, economic, and political purposes. Despite the elaborate nature of the testimony, and the length of some decisions, handing down a rate of return is not a scientific process. The investor in utilities (and the consumer) must rely on the intelligence and the good will of the regulators.

Finally, the rate structure may be designed to ration services, to bring about redistribution of wealth, to promote economic efficiency, to serve social policies, or just to assure that each customer group provides a certain rate of return. One could argue that public utility regulation, in its current form, keeps down the cost of service to certain groups of customers, prevents utilities from actually earning a fair return, encourages the wasteful use of energy, misallocates economic resources, discourages technological innovation and reduces incentives to managerial efficiency. Even regulators have noticed those infirmities, and they have launched a series of reforms that try to deal with those issues.

In short, public utility regulation has a hodgepodge of goals and some unfortunate side effects. Regulation could be better. Sometimes it is a wonder that regulation works at all.

Notes

[1]Joe S. Bain, *Industrial Organization* (New York: John Wiley & Sons, Inc., 1959), p. 589.

[2]94 US 113 (1877).

[3]Henry Steele Commager, ed. *Documents of American History* (N.Y.: Appleton-Century-Crofts, Inc., 1949), p. 147.

[4]Francis X. Welch, *Cases and Text on Public Utility Regulation*, Revised Edition (Washington, D.C.: Public Utilities Reports, Inc., 1968), p. 6.

[5]Welch, *op. cit.*, p. 7.

[6]Welch, *op. cit.*, p. 8.

[7]Welch, *op. cit.*, pp. 10-11.

[8]Welch, *op. cit.*, p. 11.

[9]*Bastard v. Bastard*, Kings Bench, 2 Shower, 82. Cited in Welch, op. cit., p. 242.

[10]169 US 466.

[11]In an 1886 decision, *Stone v. Farmers' Loan and Trust Co.* (116 US 307), the Supreme Court moved away from Munn, asserting that the courts could review rates set by a legislature. It was not until *Smyth v. Ames*, though, that the court laid out standards of reasonableness for fixing rates.

[12]Welch, *op. cit.*, p. 279.

[13]*Ibid.*

[14]*Missouri ex rel. Southwestern Bell Telephone Co. v. Missouri Public Service Commission*, 262 US 276.

[15]Welch, *op. cit.*, pp. 285-292.

[16]*Bluefield Water Works & Improv. Co. v. West Virginia Public Service Commission*, 262 US 679.

[17]272 US 400.

[18]Clair Wilcox, *Public Policies Toward Business*, Revised Edition (Homewood, Ill.: Richard D. Irwin, Inc., 1960), p. 570.

[19]262 US 679, 693.

[20]*Federal Power Commission v Hope Natural Gas Co.*, 320 US 591.

[21]Welch, *op. cit.*, pp. 301-302.

[22]Arthur Stone Dewing, *The Financial Policy of Corporations* (New York: The Ronald Press Co., 1953), pp. 309-310.

[23]Bain, *op. cit.*, p. 590.

[24]James C. Bonbright, *Principles of Public Utility Rates* (New York: Columbia University Press. 1961). p. 9.

[25]Bonbright, *op. cit.*, p. 13.

[26]*Ibid.*

[27]Bonbright, *op. cit.*, pp. 14-15.

[28]Clair Wilcox, *op. cit.*, p. 540.

[29]Alfred E. Kahn, *The Economics of Regulation: Principles and Institutions* (New York: John Wiley & Sons, Inc. 1970). Volume I, p. 20.

[30]Bonbright, *op. cit.*, p. 18.

[31]Welch, *op. cit.*, p. 478.

[32]*New England Telephone and Telegraph Company v. Maine Public Utilities Commission* (390 A 2d 8, June 28, 1978).

[33]This situation is similar to that of a company seeking a higher depreciation rate. The regulators do not want to impose unnecessarily high costs on current customers and ignore the possibility that future customers might have to pay more for service because current customers did not pay their fair share of depreciation expenses. In one case, the Federal Energy Regulatory Commission took such an approach: "For nuclear production plant, the company requested a negative 10% salvage factor.... Since the widespread growth of nuclear generating facilities is a relatively recent occurrence, there is little hard evidence on which to establish a proper salvage rate. . . . Pending further developments . . . we shall . . . base the depreciation, expense . . . on a zero salvage factor, without prejudice to a redetermination of this item when information becomes available." (Federal Energy Regulatory Commission, *Re Carolina Power & Light Co.*, Opinion No. 19, Docket No. ER 76-495, August: 2, 1978. Public Utilities Reports, 26 PUR4th — No. 1, January 5, 1979, p. 78.) Presumably, the FERC planned to wait until the plant is decommissioned, at which time there should be hard evidence. Can we believe that future customers will willingly pay the costs derived from our use of power? It is more realistic to expect unrecovered current costs to be borne by the company than by future consumers.

[34]Arthur Andersen & Co., *Return Allowed in Public Utility Rate Cases*, 1960 Edition, first page of 1929 cases, no page number.

[35]66 PUR (NS) 212.

[36]Welch, *op. cit.*, p. 301.

[37]Richard H. Adelaar and Leonard S. Hyman, "The Comparable Earnings Approach as a Useful Tool in Utility Regulation." *Public Utilities Fortnightly*, Vol. 87, No. 5, March 4, 1971.

[38]In Adelaar and Hyman, *op. cit.*, the authors eliminated from the sample regulated industries, industries with high concentration ratios, and two other small industries. The remaining sample consisted of 32 S&P industry groups comprising 191 major firms. The authors found that rate of growth in sales was an important determinant of rate of return. Because the company's demand for capital is growing faster than capital markets as a whole, the company must pay more for capital to induce portfolio managers to take the added risk of having a large percentage of their portfolios in a single security. The article also argued that to compete successfully in capital markets faster-growing utilities must be allowed higher returns than slower-growing utilities. In another article (Leonard S. Hyman, "Utility Stocks in 1967-72: A Tale of Woe," *Public Utilities Fortnightly*, Vol. 93, No. 5, Feb. 28, 1974), the author indicated that the total return on a utility stock investment might have been reduced when the utility's need for new equity capital was high.

[39]Adelaar and Hyman, *op. cit.*, p. 31.

[40]The analysis is based on Adelaar and Hyman, *op. cit.* That analysis, in turn, is derived from "Capital Equipment Analysis: The Required Rate of Profit" by Myron J. Gordon and Eli Shapiro, in Ezra Solomon (ed.), *The Management of Corporate Capital* (New York: The Free Press of Glencoe, 1959), pp. 114-145.

[41]Adelaar and Hyman, *op. cit.*, p. 33.

[42]Rhode Island Public Utilities Commission, *Re Blackstone Valley Electric Company*, Docket No. 1289, February 17, 1978. *Public Utilities Reports*, September 15, 1978, p. 318.

[43]Arkansas Public Service Commission, *In the matter of the application of Southwestern Electric Power Company* for a general rate increase, Docket No. U-2793, February 3, 1978.

[44]For two easy-to-read (and unsympathetic) analyses of CAPM, see Robert F. Vandell and James K. Malernee, "The Capital Asset Pricing Model and Utility Equity Returns," *Public Utilities Fortnightly*, July 6, 1978, and Gerald J. Glassman, "Discounted Cash Flow versus the Capital Asset Pricing Model (Is g Better Than b?)," *Public Utilities Fortnightly*, September 14, 1978.

[45]Vandell and Malernee, *op. cit.*, p. 27.

[46]Welch, *op. cit.*, p. 486.

[47]Bonbright, *op. cit.*, p. 249.

[48]Kahn, *op. cit.*, pp. 49-50, Vol. 1.

[49]Leonard S. Hyman, "Utility Stocks in 1967-72: A Tale of Woe," *Public Utilities Fortnightly*, February 28, 1974; "Market to Book Ratio: Statistical Confirmation or Aberration?," *Public Utilities Fortnightly*, December 19, 1979.

[50]Ambrose Bierce, *The Devil's Dictionary* (New York: Dover Publications, Inc., 1958), p. 27.

[51]Bonbright, *op. cit.*, p. 254.

[52]J. Maurice Clark, *Studies in the Economics of Overhead Cost*. (Chicago: University of Chicago

Press, 1923, twelfth impression, 1962), p. 324.

[53]Paul Rodgers, J. Edward Smith, Jr. and Russell J. Profozich, *Current Issues in Electric Utility Rate Setting* (Washington, D.C.: National Association of Regulatory Utility Commissioners, 1976) p. A-67.

[54]Bonbright, *op. cit.*, pp. 76-77.

[55]J. M. Clark, *op. cit.* The analysis, of course, is far more complicated than that outlined above.

[56]Ralph Turvey, *Optimal Pricing and Investment in Electrical Supply* (London: George Allan and Unwin, 1968), p.61.

[57]Lewis J. Perl and Mark D. Luftig, "Financial Implications to Utilities of Third Party Power Purchases," *Electricity Journal*, November 1990.

[58]Gordon R. Corey, "Some Observations on Bulk Power Markets in the United States," *Public Utilities Fortnightly*, September 14, 1989; "Additional Observations on Bulk Power Markets in the United States," *Public Utilities Fortnightly*, September 28,1989.

[59]Arthur Stone Dewing, *op. cit.*, p. 312, footnote e.

Part Five

Financial Structure

Chapter **24**

The Basics

Regulation of rates requires accounting information, and sound regulation requires sound accounting....[1]

Haskins & Sells

The financial structure of the electric utility industry is based on certain fundamental tenets:

◆ The electric utility industry is capital intensive.

◆ The industry is a natural monopoly.

◆ The business risk to shareholders in the competitive industry should be replaced by financial risk to shareholders in the regulated monopoly.

Capital Intensity

Everyone knows that the industry is capital intensive, that it takes three or four dollars of plant to produce one dollar of revenue. Because the customer should not be expected to pay for that much capital equipment in a short time, the cost of the plant is written off over many years. All of that is accepted as natural. Unfortunately, the naturalness is not that clear, and may be, in part, a result of the history of the industry and how people made money in it.

When the industry began, it was controlled by the manufacturing companies. The real money was made from the sale, engineering and financing of equipment, not from the sale of electricity. The industry, in its formative years, developed massive investments. Policy toward investment remained unchanged until the late 1970s.

The regulatory process also affects capital intensity. After all, we are looking at a ratio determined by dividing capital by revenue. Therefore, if revenue can be lowered, the ratio rises. Most regulators see their job as that of keeping down the revenue that the company receives. On the other hand, the utility gets paid a return on capital invested. Therefore, according to some academics[2], the management expanded the capital invested in the business, because the more capital that was invested, the higher the income of the utility. In other words, managements tried to enlarge the numerator and the regulators to decrease the denominator, thereby raising the capital intensity of the business. That argument has been dubious for close to two decades. Management had little financial incentive to invest new funds when the incremental cost of capital was greater than return earned on investment. And, after numerous disallowances of supposedly imprudent investments and the ensuing writeoffs, many managements feared to make any big investment because of the threat of losing it in the regulatory process.

The belief that the industry is capital intensive also derives from financing policies of the past, when holding companies bought operating utilities at inflated prices. Because holding companies had to earn a profitable return on those inflated investments, the amount needed to run an electric company became even higher. Just as the original builders of electric utilities made their profits from selling equipment, many of the organizers that followed made their money from the engineering fees charged to captive companies and from the sale of the utility's securities. Fees and commissions both escalated with the need to build and to raise money.

The low cost of money that prevailed for much of this century also encouraged capital intensive solutions. If the company could borrow cheaply to build a big machine, why not do so? And, it should be added, the big machine often was much more efficient than the smaller one. If money costs were low, it might be worthwhile to build a machine much larger than was actually required, because the large machine could operate so efficiently that the resulting savings offset the extra cost of borrowing more money than would have been needed to build a smaller unit. Thus, a combination of economies of scale and low cost of capital may have encouraged electric utilities to add more investment than was required.

Finally, one might argue that the industry overbuilt to produce operating economies that would prevent others from entering the business and that would drive out non-central station power.

The point of the discussion is not to deny that the industry requires a great deal of capital to produce a dollar of revenue, but to assert that the industry's capital intensity should not be accepted as completely natural.

Capital intensity results, in part, from regulation, monetary policies, economies of scale, greed of promoters, and other factors. Inertia probably carried the day for years after capital intensity ceased to be a virtue. Now that money costs are high, however, and new equipment may not be providing economies of scale, the industry is trying to reduce the need for capital in the business. Both investors and consumers may be beneficiaries.

Financial Risk

Standard theory holds that the business of the utility as a natural monopoly is not as risky as the business of a company in a competitive industry. Therefore, the utility can take greater financial risks (*i.e.*, borrow more money) than the average industrial firm.[3] Again we can ask whether that statement developed from self-evident characteristics of the industry, or as a rationalization for other practices. For example, in the early days of the industry, operating utilities were not especially profitable. They did not have cash to spare. Consequently, some promoters and vendors of equipment accepted company bonds in lieu of cash, thereby increasing the amount of debt in the capitalization. In the days of the holding companies, managements attempted to assure their control by means of ownership of a large percentage of the stock of the parent holding company. To minimize the amount of investment needed to control the holding company empire, the constituent companies financed their capital needs as much as possible by sale of debt. Another possibility is that because the utility industry tended not to be highly profitable, capital was leveraged to bring return on equity up to acceptable levels. Whatever the origins of the practice, the electric utility industry raises close to half of its capital by the sale of senior securities debt and preferred stock. Even more remarkable, those financing practices have not changed for decades, although upheavals in the capital markets have diminished the advantages of those financial policies.

Natural Monopoly

Few persons believe that electric utilities have an impregnable monopoly in the energy market anymore. After all, natural gas, oil, wind, and the sun perform some of the same functions as electricity. Furthermore, large users of electricity can produce some or all of their own power when the price of the utility's power rises excessively. Although we seldom speak of competition among utilities, competition exists in the sense that new customers for whom the cost of energy is important might locate in the service territory of a utility with favorable rates.

In discussing the financial position and the ability of a utility to increase or to reduce debt, analysts assume, for convenience, that the utility industry will remain a monopoly, that customers can always be forced to pay whatever price is necessary to provide the utility with the revenues to meet financial obligations. If a utility is not collecting sufficient revenue to set aside an adequate reserve for depreciation, future rate payers can be forced to make up the deficiency. The same comment applies to taxes whose payments are deferred. Moreover, if money is not set aside to assure the repayment of debt at maturity, the utility can sell new debt to pay off a maturing issue. The assumption is that the utility will have no difficulty borrowing to meet its needs, because a natural monopoly that provides an essential service will always be able to borrow money.

That line of argument is not necessarily correct. At some time in the future, alternatives to central station power could develop. When that happens, electric utilities will be unable to charge more than the price of the alternative energy source. The price set may be below the amount that the electric utility needs to cover depreciation charges on plant that has not been fully written off, or may be below the price needed to provide the utility with sufficient revenue to pay its debts or to pay deferred income taxes. If such a situation were to occur, the utility would no longer be a monopoly. With every rate increase, customers could be lost to alternative energy sources. The potential for competition may or may not develop in the immediate future. Regulators, however, often do not even seem to consider the possibility and, as a result, companies find themselves financing and accounting as if nothing could disturb their monopoly.

How to Evaluate the Finances of the Industry

We will examine the industry's finances by means of three financial statements: the balance sheet, the statement of income and retained earnings, and the statement of cash flows. Then, we will examine the reaction of the financial markets to the state of the industry and will consider whether past trends indicate the future.

Chapter 25

The Statement of Income and Retained Earnings

Many investors prefer companies showing a growth rate at least equal to the industry trend. However, such growth is valueless unless it can be translated into increasing investment and earnings per share.[4]

Badger, Torgerson and Guthmann

The income statement covers a specific period. It shows the amount of money that customers paid for services within that period (revenues) and the costs that were incurred by the firm to provide those services (expenses). The difference between revenue and expense is the profit or net income that is left for the owners of the business. Some of the income is paid to owners in the form of dividends. The rest is kept by the firm for use in the business (retained earnings). Although that sounds simple, how to calculate both revenues and expenses is a matter for disputes. Accounting procedures that tend to understate revenues or to overstate expenses are "conservative." Procedures that tend to overstate revenues and to understate expenses are "liberal." In addition to annual statements, most companies provide income statements on a quarterly basis, and some even publish monthly statements of income.

Simplified Statements

The following is an example of a standard income statement for an industrial concern:

Sales (revenues)	$1,000
Cost of sales (expenses directly associated with production of product)	500
Depreciation (wear and tear on machinery)	100
Interest (on borrowed money)	100
Total Expenses	700
Pretax income	300
Income taxes	100
Net income (profit)	$ 200

Income statements for utilities have been recast for regulatory purposes as follows:

Revenues	$ 1,000
Operating Expenses: Production, maintenance, etc.	500
Depreciation	100
Income taxes	100
Total operating expenses	700
Operating income	300
Interest expense	100
Net income	$ 200

The difference exists because the utility regulator is concerned with the return on capital — the interest paid to creditors of the firm and the profits available to stockholders. In our simplified statement, operating income, which is after deduction of taxes but before interest expense, represents the income available to pay the owners of the capital that has been invested in the business.

A number of utilities own non-utility subsidiaries. The accountants insist that the income statement add together the utility and non-utility businesses. The statement of income that includes all operations is "consolidated," and might be presented in one of several formats. If we take the two statements shown above, we could add them together in several ways, including:

Utility revenues	$1000	Utility revenues	$1000
Industrial sales	1000	Industrial sales	1000
Total revenues	2000	Total revenues	2000
Expenses:		Expenses:	
Cost of sales	500	Cost of sales	500
Production, maintenance, etc.	500	Production, maintenance, etc.	500
Depreciation	200	Depreciation	200
Operating expenses	1200	Operating expenses	1200
Income before interest and taxes	800	Pretax operating income	800
Interest expense	300	Income taxes	200
Pretax income	500	Operating income	600

| Income taxes | 200 | Interest expense | 300 |
| Net income | 300 | Net income | 300 |

Utility Income Statement

The actual utility income statement is more complicated, as can be seen in the following example:

Statement of Income
($ Thousands)

Line	Year Ended 1990	December 31, 1991
1. Operating Revenue	$500,000	$550,000
2. *Operating Expenses*		
3. Operation:		
4. Fuel	200,000	245,000
5. Purchased & Interchanged Power	40,000	10,000
6. Other	50,000	60,000
7. Total Operation	290,000	315,000
8. Maintenance	40,000	50,000
9. Depreciation and Amortization	35,000	40,000
10. *Income Taxes —*		
11. Current	20,000	9,000
12. Deferred	7,000	20,000
13. Other taxes	30,000	31,000
14. Total Operating Expenses	$422,000	$465,000
15. Operating Income	78,000	85,000
16. Other Income	1,000	1,000
17. Allowance for Other Funds Used During Construction	3,000	4,000
18. Income Before Interest Charges	82,000	90,000
19. *Interest Charges*		
20. Interest on Long-Term Debt	23,000	28,000
21. Other Interest	4,000	4,000
22. Allowance for Borrowed Funds Used During Construction	(5,000)	(6,000)

23. Net Interest Charges	22,000	26,000
24. Net Income	60,000	64,000
25. Preferred Dividends	8,000	8,000
26. Balance Available for Common Stock	52,000	56,000
27. Average Shares Outstanding During Year	9,000	10,000
28. Earnings Per Average Common Shares Outstanding	$5.78	$5.60
29. *Statement of Retained Earnings*		
30. Balance, Beginning of Year	138,000	158,000
Add:		
31. Net Income After Dividends on Preferred Stock	52,000	56,000
32. Total	190,000	214,000
Deduct:		
33. Cash Dividends on Common Stock	32,000	34,000
34. Balance, End of Year	$158,000	180,000

The utility sells a certain amount of electricity in the year at particular prices. Receipts from customers produce *Operating Revenue* (line 1). The costs of paying employees, suppliers, and taxes — expenses involved in producing the electricity — are called *Operating Expenses* (line 2). Expenses shown under the title *Operation* (line 3) are outlays directly related to producing and transmitting the electricity. The major item is almost always *Fuel* (line 4) that is burned in the boiler to generate the electricity. Sometimes a utility buys power from other utilities, because it does not have a generator in operation or because the power produced by the other utility is cheaper. That power is *Purchased and Interchanged Power* (line 5). The utility may sell power to other electric companies. Such interchange power receipts are shown as part of revenues, although for a time they were shown in parentheses as a deduction from expenses. *Other* expenses associated with operations (line 6) includes salaries and miscellaneous items. *Total Operation* expenses are shown on line 7.

Maintenance Expenses (small repairs and regular overhauls of equipment) are shown on line 8. Plant and equipment wears out over time or becomes obsolete and eventually must be replaced by more modern and efficient equipment. The company estimates how long the equipment is expected to last and spreads the cost of the purchase over the productive life of the asset. For example, if a machine costs $100,000 and will last for 20 years, the company will show an expense of $5,000 (one-twentieth of the purchase price) each year. That expense is called *Depreciation* (line 9). *Amortization* (also line 9) is the spreading over time of the cost of some other expenditure or loss that already took place. For instance, if a big storm did enormous damage, the regulator might tell the utility to set up a storm damage account, and then amortize the expense over five years, that is, only show one fifth of the expense in each year. Unlike other expenses, depreciation and amortization does not entail paying out money when the expense is shown on the income statement.

Income Taxes (line 10) are paid to Federal, state and local governments by the corporation. The tax figure does not always represent taxes actually paid in the year. *Current Taxes* (line 11) are those that are to be paid quickly. Often, the utility sets aside money for taxes to be paid at a future date and includes those *Deferred Taxes* (line 12) in the total of income taxes. Like depreciation, deferred taxes do not represent a cash outlay.

Other Taxes (line 13) includes taxes on real estate and on the company's revenues and are generally levied by state and local governments.

The total of all *Operating Expenses* (line 14) is subtracted from revenue, leaving *Operating Income* (line 15).

Other Income (line 16) includes the income from various affiliated companies, interest earned on investments, income tax credits and a variety of other items.

The allowance for funds used during construction (AFUDC) is split into two parts: *Allowance for Other Funds Used During Construction* (line 17) and *Allowance for Borrowed Funds Used During Construction* (line 22). Let us start by understanding the concept behind AFUDC.

A utility may have a substantial amount of money tied up for years in a facility under construction. That money had to be raised by means of borrowing or by sale of stock. The utility pays interest on borrowed money, and stockholders also expect a return on their investment even though the plant is not yet operating. How can the utility recover those costs involved in raising money to build the power plant? The answer, in many cases, is to add the cost of the money to the cost of the power plant. Once the plant is completed, the utility earns a return on the money used to pay suppliers of machinery, bricks, and construction services, plus a return on the money paid to the suppliers of capital. Furthermore, the utility will recover, by means of depreciation, all the costs of the plant, including the cost of capital.

AFUDC is a mechanism whereby the cost of money is added to the plant account on the balance sheet. The cost of money raised to build the power plant (AFUDC) is added to company income and thus increases the stockholders' equity shown on the right side of the balance sheet. Because the balance sheet must balance, under the double entry system, a similar sum is added to the plant account on the assets side of the balance sheet. Money is raised either from stockholders or from creditors (lenders). The Federal Energy Regulatory Commission (FERC) has decided that the two sources should be separated. Therefore, the utility calculates the cost of money that has been borrowed to finance the project, the *Allowance for Borrowed Funds Used During Construction* (line 22). Then, if the project is not funded entirely by means of borrowing, the utility assigns a cost to the equity money that has been raised, usually basing the cost on the return on equity that was allowed in the last rate case. The cost of equity funds is the *Allowance for Other Funds Used During Construction* (line 17).

Accordingly, AFUDC serves two purposes. It allows the utility to recover costs of plant (by means of depreciation) and to earn a return on capital costs incurred while a facility is under construction. In addition, AFUDC removes from the income statement the effects of expenses that have nothing to do with operations for the current year.

The sum of Operating Income, Other Income, and Allowance for Other Funds Used During Construction is called *Income Before Interest Charges* (line 18) and is the income available to pay the owners of capital.

Interest Charges (line 19) are divided into Interest on *Long-Term Debt* (line 20) and *Other Interest* (line 21). The latter is usually interest on bank loans and on commercial paper.

After interest charges have been subtracted, *Net Income* (line 24) remains and the money is left for the owners of the business. All owners, however, are not equal. The owners of preferred stock must be paid fixed *Preferred Dividends* (line 25) before common stockholders are paid.

The *Balance Available for Common Stock* (line 26) is a residual. To calculate the income available per share of common stock, we must know how many shares are outstanding. The number of shares outstanding changes during the year as shares are repurchased or new shares are issued. Standard practice is to use *Average Shares Outstanding During the Year* (line 27) to calculate per share data.

When income available for all common stock is divided by the average number of shares of common outstanding during the year, *Earnings Per Average Common Share Outstanding* (line 28) results.

What happens to the income left after common stockholders have been paid? That is shown in the *Statement of Retained Earnings* (line 29). The *Net Income After Dividends on Preferred Stock* (line 31) is added to the *Balance of Retained Earnings at the Beginning of the Year* (line 30). From the *Total* (shown on line 32), *Cash Dividends on Common Stock* (line 33) must be subtracted, leaving the *Balance at the End of the Year* (line 34).

Phase-In

In a number of recent rate orders, regulators decided not to implement the full amount of rate relief needed to cover the costs of a new facility, but rather to phase-in the new facility. Part of the rate increase would be deferred to a future date, thereby reducing the increase needed in the first year. In the second year, a smaller part of the necessary revenue would be deferred, and the deferral would decline year by year until the revenues reached the required level. Then rates would be increased again to cover the revenues that should have been collected in the early years of the phase-in, but which were deferred to a later date. Eventually the utility not only recovers the lost revenue but also interest on the money from the time that the revenue should have been collected until it actually was collected. Phase-in plans vary from company to company, so the accounting is not identical. Let us assume that the utility needs $75 of new rates which are phased in $25 per year for three years, then in the next three years the utility collects an extra $25 to make up for the $75 it did not collect in the first three years. Then in the seventh year, it drops the $25 that made up for the deficit in the first three years, and it collects approximately $25 interest (at 10% per year) on the revenue that was not previously collected. In the eighth year, revenue falls to what it would have been if the company simply received a $75 rate increase. Expenses are adjusted too, as part of a phase-in. If the revenue is not being shown, the expenses associated with that deferred revenue are offset by a special credit to operating expenses. That credit decreases over time as the revenues increase. Finally, the utility accrues the interest on the unpaid revenue balance in each year. The idea is to make the net income shown during a phase-in exactly the same as the net income would have been if the utility had collected the rate increase all at once. Going back to the example, let us say that expenses associated with the plant increase that required the $75 rate hike are $60. Here is how the income statement would look if the company got the $75 all at once, and if the increase were phased in:

	All at Once	Phase In First Year	Phase In Final Year
Revenue			
Old revenue	$200	$200	$200
Rate increase	75	25	75
Total revenue	$275	$225	$275
Expenses			
Old expenses	$100	$100	$100
New expenses	60	60	60
Deferred exp.	—	(40)	0
Total expenses	160	120	160
Operating Income	115	105	115
Interest on deferred revenue	—	10	0
Net income	115	115	115

Consolidation

Electric utilities might own subsidiaries that furnish services to the electric utility. Sometimes a holding company owns the electric utility and an affiliated firm that sells services or products to the electric utility. How does the group of corporations present its accounts? Not by adding up the revenues and expenses of the component companies. That would constitute double counting. One does not make money selling to oneself. The answer is to consolidate the results. Let us say that the holding company owns a utility that buys its coal from a mine owned by the holding company. The holding company has to issue its accounts. It could add up the result as follows:

	Coal Mine	Electric Company	Total
Revenues	$100	$1000	$1100
Expenses	50	600	650
Fuel Costs	——	100	100
Total Expenses	50	700	750
Profit	50	300	350

The fact of the matter is that the group only collected $1,000 in revenue, from the customers of the electric company. That is all the money that came in the door. As for expenses, the total company may show $750 including fuel, but we know that only half the cost of the coal represents expense, and the rest is profit. One has to remove the effect of selling from one affiliate to another. The means to do so is by consolidating, rather than adding:

	Coal Mine	Electric Company	Eliminate Intra-Company Transactions	Consolidated Results
Revenues	$100	$1000	($100)	$1000
Total Exp.	50	700	(50)	650
Profit	50	300	—	350

To put it simply, if the utility had owned the coal mine, there would have been no pretense that a sale had been made, and we could have ended up in the same place as the consolidated results without the complications.

Chapter 26

The Balance Sheet

Creditor, n. one of a tribe of savages dwelling beyond the Financial Straits and dreaded for their desolating incursions.[5]

Ambrose Bierce

The balance sheet shows the property and cash owned by a firm and the amounts owed to it (assets). The money that a firm owes and the source of the money used to purchase those assets (liabilities and capital) are also shown. Data are given as of the end of business on a stated day — usually the end of the year or the end of an accounting period.

The Utility Balance Sheet

The balance sheet of an electric utility is similar to that of an industrial company except that industrial companies generally put current assets and liabilities at the top of the balance sheet. Assets owned by the utility are shown on the left side (or top half) of the balance sheet.

Balance Sheet
Assets
($ Thousands)

		December 31,	
		1990	1991
Line			
1.	*Utility Plant*		
2.	In service	$1,000,000	$1,160,000
3.	Less depreciation	250,000	290,000
4.	Net plant in service	750,000	870,000
5.	Construction work in progress	100,000	120,000
6.	Net plant	850,000	990,000
7.	Other property & investments	10,000	10,000

8.	*Current Assets*		
9.	Cash & temporary investments	5,000	6,000
10.	Accounts receivable	25,000	28,000
11.	Materials & supplies	50,000	55,000
12.	Total current assets	80,000	89,000
13.	Deferred charges	20,000	20,000
14.	Total assets	$960,000	$1,109,000

Liabilities and Capital

		December 31,	
		1990	1991
15.	*Capitalization*		
16.	Common stock	$ 115,000	$ 171,000
17.	Retained earnings	158,000	180,000
18.	Preferred stock	90,000	90,000
19.	Long term debt	400,000	480,000
20.	Total capitalization	763,000	921,000
21.	*Current Liabilities*		
22.	Accounts payable	17,000	14,000
23.	Accrued expenses	10,000	4,000
24.	Bank loans & commercial paper	40,000	20,000
25.	Long term debt payable in one year	30,000	30,000
26.	Total current liabilities	97,000	68,000
27.	Deferred credits	100,000	120,000
28.	Total liabilities and capitalization	$960,000	$1,109,000

The asset side of the balance sheet shows the cost of what the company owns plus what is owed to it by others plus the value of some money that the company has already paid for future expenses.

The major items on a utility's balance sheet usually represent physical plant (machinery, buildings, and land) that is being or will be used to serve the customer. *Utility Plant* (line 1) is divided into several categories. The first is the cost of plant that has been completed and is *In Service* (line 2). That cost includes not only the money paid to the manufacturers of building products and machinery and to construction workers but also the return that was paid to those who supplied the money.

Physical plant wears out over time or machinery may lose value because it is obsolete. Every year the firm reduces the value of a piece of machinery to reflect the aging process by adding to a reserve for *Depreciation* (line 3). *Net Plant in Service* (line 4) represents the original cost of the plant less the depreciation reserve.

Most utility companies have plant under construction to meet the growing demands of their customers. Machinery, buildings, and equipment that are part of an incomplete project are called *Construction Work in Progress* or CWIP (line 5). The sum of all the money invested in plant, less depreciation, is *Net Plant* (line 6).

Many utilities have invested in other businesses. Those investments are shown under *Other Property and Investments* (line 7).

The company's plant account often is called fixed assets because the property cannot be easily moved and cannot be converted quickly into cash. *Current Assets* (line 8), on the other hand, includes cash, items that can be quickly converted into cash, and accounts that will be paid to the company within 12 months.

The utility maintains *Cash and Temporary Investments* (line 9) to pay expenses. It charges the customers for electricity used and, until the bills have been paid, the money owed to the company represents *Accounts Receivable* (line 10). The utility keeps an inventory of spare parts, office supplies, emergency materials, and a supply of fuel for its power plants, all of which are included in *Materials and Supplies* (line 11). The total of those items makes up *Total Current Assets* (line 12).

Deferred Charges (line 13) represent money that has already been paid for something that applies, at least in part, to some future period. For example, the utility paid an underwriter (investment banker) to market some bonds. The money received from the sale of the bonds will be used by the utility for a 20-year period. The expense should, therefore, be spread over the 20 years. Accordingly, the total underwriting expense becomes a deferred charge. Each year, one twentieth of the total is shown as an expense while the deferred expense item on the balance sheet is reduced by an equal amount. In another example, the company incurs some major expense because of a storm or because of the scrapping of some big project. The regulators might want that expense to be spread over several years so that consumers do not have to pay sharply higher rates in a single year to offset the total charge. The regulator tells the utility to defer the charge and to write it off (that is, to reduce the total by a specific amount) over several years. The amount of the writeoff becomes part of each year's expenses. Utilities also tend to defer fuel expenses. Most utilities have fuel adjustment clauses included in their rates whereby changes in total costs are passed on to customers. Fuel costs, however, may rise in a particular month, but be passed along to customers several months later. The utility could defer the additional fuel expense until the cost can be passed along.

The *Total Assets* (line 14) are the sum of the preceding items.

The *Liabilities and Capital* portion of the balance sheet shows the amounts that owners invested in the business and the amounts the business owes to its creditors. The utility accounts usually begin with a statement of *Capitalization* (line 15), which shows the amount that has been invested in the business for the long term. Money that cannot be taken out of the business before an appointed time (usually more than one year from the date of the balance sheet) is included in this section.

Common Stock (line 16) is the value assigned to the shares. Some common stock has a nominal or par value ($1 a share, for example), which is a holdover from the early days of corporate organization. When such shares are sold to the public, the price paid is usually well above par value. The difference between par value and the price for the stock is called paid-in surplus. For example, if stockholders purchasing 1,000 shares had invested $6,000 for a stock with a $1 a share par value, the common stock account would look like this:

Common stock ($1 par value, 1,000 shares outstanding) $1,000
Paid-in surplus   5,000

Usually, part of the year's income is paid to stockholders as dividends and part is retained for future use. The portion not distributed is *Retained Earnings* (line 17).

The sum of retained earnings, paid-in capital, and par value, or the sum of common stock and retained earnings, is common stockholders' equity. In other words, the money that common stockholders have invested in the business plus the income that could have been paid to common shareholders but was retained instead is their contribution to the capital of the enterprise.

Purchasers of *Preferred Stock* (line 18) receive a fixed dividend that must be paid before common stockholders can receive a dividend. If the company goes out of business, preferred stockholders must be paid in full before holders of the common stock are paid. In those ways, preferred stock is similar to debt. But the rights of preferred shareholders are junior to those of debt holders, and in that way, preferred stock is similar to common stock.

Long Term Debt (line 19) is money borrowed for more that one year (usually 10 to 30 years). Most long term debt is sold in the form of first mortgage bonds. Those are securities that are paid interest, generally twice a year, and that are secured by the property of the corporation.

The sum of common equity, preferred stock, and long term debt is the permanent capital or *Total Capitalization* (line 20) of the utility.

The company has obligations that must be paid within 12 months of the date of the balance sheet. Those obligations are *Current Liabilities* (line 21).

Accounts Payable (line 22) consist of bills that the company must pay within the year (usually sooner). Such bills could be for supplies and other services.

Accrued Expenses (line 23) are known expenses that the company must pay in the near term, although bills have not yet been received. For example, a utility may show money owed to employees for work already performed as an accrued expense before the paychecks are actually written. Taxes may also be treated in that way. Utilities generally raise money by selling long term securities. The utility often borrows from banks or sells short term commercial paper until it becomes convenient to repay those loans by selling long term securities. *Bank Loans and Commercial Paper* (line 24) can vary greatly from period to period, depending on when long term offerings are planned. *Long Term Debt Payable in One Year* (line 25) represents a bond issue that will be due for payment within 12 months of the date of the balance sheet.

The total of the items in *Total Current Liabilities* (line 26) should be compared with total current assets to determine whether current liabilities are covered by current assets. The difference between current assets and current liabilities is called working capital.

Deferred Credits (line 27), which could be deferred income, are similar to the deferred charges on the assets side of the balance sheet. For example, customers may pay for something in advance. The company collects the cash from the customers, but does not show the income from the transaction until the service is performed. Commonly, deferred credits are deferred income taxes, which are tax savings derived from the use of accelerated depreciation or are the investment tax credit that will be added back to income over the life of the plant the construction of which created the savings. For example, the utility installed a machine that will last for 10 years. The utility received a tax credit that represented a savings of $1,000 in taxes in the year of installation. The utility did not show the tax saving in the income statement for the year. Instead the savings were spread over the life of the machine. Therefore, the utility showed a deferred income tax expense in the income statement and created a deferred income tax credit on the balance sheet. Each year, one-tenth ($100) of the tax savings were added to income, and one-tenth of the deferred income tax credit was subtracted from that account. (The investment tax credit is no longer part of the Federal tax law, but many utilities are still accounting for investment tax credits received years ago.)

Total Liabilities and Capitalization (line 28) must, of course, equal total assets.

Phase-Ins

When a company has a phase-in plan in effect, it accumulates, as an asset, the balance that is owed to it by customers up to the time of the balance sheet date. That asset, which might have various names, may be called a *Rate Deferral*, and it appears at the bottom of the asset page, usually in the section that includes deferred charges. Why is this item an asset? Because it is like a loan made by the utility to customers which must be paid off by the customers. It is an earning asset.

Consolidation

Often, the corporation owns other corporations. In financial parlance, the parent company owns subsidiaries. The subsidiaries have assets and liabilities, and may even have their own debt outstanding. Let us say that the parent company raises $1000 by selling stock to investors, another $1000 by selling bonds to investors and invests $1000 each in the common stock of two subsidiaries. Each of the subsidiaries then sells $1000 worth of bonds to investors in order to raise more capital. Each of the subsidiaries then invests $2000 in plant and equipment.

Working out the asset side of the balance sheet, each of the subsidiaries has $2000 of plant and equipment for a total of $4000. The parent company has $2000 of assets, consisting of stock in the subsidiaries. On the liabilities side, each subsidiary has $1000 of debt and $1000 of equity (a total of $2000 debt and $2000 equity) and the parent has $1000 of debt and $1000 of equity. Should we add up the figure for the subsidiaries and the parent to get a total? The answer is no. We sense that doing so would be wrong by looking at the assets. The combined group really has $4000 worth of plant and equipment and nothing else. On the liability side, we do know that the three corporate utilities have borrowed $3000 in total, but they have only raised $1000 from shareholders, when the parent company sold stock. The accounts have to be consolidated, not added:

	Subsidiary One	Subsidiary Two	Parent	Consolidating Adjustment	Consolidated
Assets:					
Plant and Equipment	$2000	$2000	0		$4000
Common Stock Investments	0	0	$2000	($2000)	0
Total	$2000	$2000	$2000	($2000)	$4000
Liabilities:					
Debt	1000	1000	1000	0	$3000
Common equity	1000	1000	1000	($2000)	1000
Total	2000	2000	2000	($2000)	$4000

Regulators and creditors of the subsidiaries will look at the balance sheet of the subsidiaries, but common stockholders of the parent will be concerned with the consolidated statement.

Chapter 27

The Statement of Cash Flows

An extremely important characteristic of utilities is that they are "capital intensive" ... High plant investment requirements (to replace equipment. .. and meet the continued growth in the industry) impose heavy and frequent financing requirements. Accordingly, it is important that utilities be well regarded in the investment community.[6]

Haskins & Sells

The balance sheet tells what the company owns and owes at the end of a given day. The income statement helps to determine how profitable the operations of the firm were for a given period. The statement of cash flows analyzes the cash received and disbursed in a given period. There are several kinds of cash statements: the statement of change in financial position, the statement of source of funds used for construction, and the statement of cash flows.

Variations on a Theme

Let us start with simplified examples. The company collects $1,000 in cash profits from its business operations during the year. It pays a $500 dividend to stockholders. Cash in the bank at the beginning of the year is $3,000. Stock worth $3,000 is sold to raise money. The company buys a new machine costing $6,000. No money is owed on a current basis at the beginning of the period. (Current assets consisted of $3,000 cash in the bank. There are no current liabilities. Working capital is $3,000 at the beginning of the year.) Here is how the statements should appear.

Statement of Changes in Financial Position

Sources of Funds	
Profit	$1,000
Sale of stock	3,000
Total Sources of Funds	$4,000

Uses of Funds
   Purchase of machine $6,000
   Dividend   500

Uses of Funds	
Purchase of machine	$6,000
Dividend	500
Total	6,500
Increase (decrease) in working capital	(2,500)
Total Uses of Funds	$4,000

Statement of Sources of Funds Used for Construction

Sources of Funds	
Profits	$1,000
less Dividends	500
Earnings retained in the business	500
Sale of stock	3,000
Decrease in working capital	2,500
Funds Used For Construction	$6,000

Statement of Cash Flows

Cash flows from operating activities	
Profits	$1,000
Change in assets and liabilities	
Working capital	0
Net cash provided by operations	1,000
Cash flow from investing activities	
Purchase of machinery	(6,000)
Cash flow from financing activities	
Sale of stock	3,000
Dividends	(500)
Net cash from financing activities	2,500
Net change in cash and cash equivalents	(2,500)
Cash and cash equivalents at beginning of year	3,000
Cash and cash equivalents at end of year	500

Variations are possible, too, so the above statements should be viewed as skeletal examples. The *Statement of Changes in Financial Position* and the *Statement of Sources of Funds for Construction* have the advantage of simplicity in concept and terminology. Unfortunately, the accountants have opted for the third method, the *Statement of Cash Flows*, which mixes cash flows from operations with changes in working capital, calls spending on machinery a negative cash flow, and puts dividends and stock sales into one category. So that is what we have to work with until the accountants have a change of heart.

The Statement of Cash Flows

We will start with the statement of a normal utility. Keep in mind that terminology and minor items will differ from company to company.

Statements of Cash Flows (for the Year 1991)
($ Thousands)

Line		
1.	Cash flows from operating activities	
2.	Net income	$64,000
3.	Items not requiring (providing) cash	
4.	Depreciation	40,000
5.	Deferred credits	20,000
6.	Allowance for funds used during construction	(10,000)
7.	Changes in assets and liabilities	
8.	Accounts receivable	(3,000)
9.	Materials and supplies	(5,000)
10.	Accounts payable	(3,000)
11.	Accrued expenses	(6,000)
12.	Net cash provided by operating activities	97,000
13.	Cash flows from investing activities	
14.	Construction expenditures	(180,000)
15.	Allowance for funds used during construction	10,000
16.	Other investments	0
17.	Net cash used in investing activities	(170,000)

18.	Cash flows from financing activities	
19.	Dividends on preferred and common stock	(42,000)
20.	Redemptions	
21.	Bank loans and commercial paper	(20,000)
22.	Long term debt	(30,000)
23.	Issuances	
24.	Long term debt	110,000
25.	Common stock	56,000
26.	Net cash provided by financing activities	74,000
27.	Net change in cash and equivalents	1,000
28.	Cash and equivalents at beginning of year	5,000
29.	Cash and equivalents at end of year	6,000

The statement begins with a grouping entitled *Cash Flows from Operating Activities* (line 1), basically what is left over from the year's revenues after the expenses that require cash outlay (such as interest on debt, payments for fuel, or salaries) are paid. The first item (line 2) is the *Net Income*, which is reported before adjusting for any items that do not result in cash. To that we must add expenses that do not require cash outlays, or subtract reported income that does not bring in any cash. *Items Not Requiring (Providing) Cash* follow (line 3). Usually the largest such item is *Depreciation* (line 4). Any number of other expense categories could follow, but the bulk of them involve *Deferred Credits* (line 5), which usually consists of deferred taxes, that is, taxes that are shown as expenses in the income statement but which will not be paid until some time in the future. For most utilities, the biggest addition to income that involves no current cash inflow is the *Allowance for Funds Used During Construction* (line 6). Note that this is the first line in parentheses, meaning that it has to be subtracted from the cash inflows shown above it. If the utility is in the process of phasing in rates, it may show an additional subtraction to represent rate deferral, that is, income being reported but which will not be collected until some time in the future.

The accounting format just marches on, but we need to stop here for a minute. The items through line 6, the cash flows from operating activities, add up to $114 million. The income statement for 1991, shown in Chapter 25, reported $550 million of revenue. Out of those receipts, after paying expenses, the utility has generated $114 million to buy new equipment, pay debts, or declare dividends. Some of the cash produced has to be used to prepare the business for the future, or to pay off obligations incurred in the past. The utility might have to pay some suppliers that it kept waiting last year, or buy extra coal ahead of time because it looks as if there might be a coal strike next year.

Change in Assets and Liabilities (line 7) is the next grouping. When *Accounts*

Receivable (line 8) increases, it means that the customers owe more to the utility (which presumably has to take cash out of its own bank account to pay suppliers until it gets paid by the customers). In this case, accounts receivable have increased. Utilities have to keep a large stockpile of fuel and parts to ensure continuous operation. *Materials and Supplies* (line 9) have risen, requiring cash to pay for them. Suppliers have to be paid, and when *Accounts Payable* (line 10) are brought down, that too requires cash as in this example. (Of course, if the utility lets the accounts payable run up, then it would be reducing cash outflow, at least until the company had to pay its bills.) Finally come *Accrued Expenses* (line 11), which are expenses that the utility has not gotten around to paying. When accrued expenses increase, the utility has saved cash, at least until time of payment. In our example, the utility is reducing the account, paying the expenses.

The total of changes in assets and liabilities is ($17 million), that is, the total reduces cash by $17 million. Adding up the cash flows from operating activities and from changes in assets and liabilities, we come to *Net Cash Provided by Operation Activities* (line 12), a total of $97 million.

Companies do more than work with what they have on hand or what comes from the year's operations. They make investments to enlarge their productive capability, as an example, or sell off properties when they decide to get out of a business. *Cash Flows from Investing Activities* (line 13) includes such purchases and sales. For most utilities, *Construction Expenditures* (line 14) is a large figure, given the need to expand facilities to meet the demand of new customers. The construction figure, though, includes the capitalized allowance for funds, which does not represent an outflow of cash. Therefore *Allowance for Funds Used During Construction* (line 15) must be removed from the total construction figure, and the net outflow of cash for construction (not shown in the statement) really is $170 million. If the company has made *Other Investments* (line 16), that would show as an outflow of cash, and if it had sold investments, doing so would have added to cash. Altogether, lines 14 to 16 add up to *Net Cash Used in Investing Activities* (line 17), a total of $170 million.

So far, the utility has laid out $73 million more than it has taken in. Where does the money come from?

Cash Flows from Financing Activities (line 18) accounts for how the utility raises much of its cash needs. As a start, though, the utility has shareholders that expect *Dividends on Preferred and Common Stock* (line 19), which are paid out during the year and represent a drain on cash. Some of the utility's debt has to be repaid, and *Redemptions* (line 20) require cash. The utility might pay down *Bank Loans and Commercial Paper* (Line 21) or *Long Term Debt* (line 22). It might redeem preferred stock or even buy back shares of common stock. On the other hand, *Issuances* (line 23) of securities bring in cash. This utility sold *Long Term Debt* (line 24) and *Common Stock* (line 25) in order to raise funds. It could have sold a new issue of preferred stock, or taken out a bank loan, too. The *Net Cash Provided by Financing Activities* (line 26) adds up to $74 million, which is $1 million more than the shortfall we calculated previously. In other words, the financings raised more than what was spent, and the extra $1 million is the year's *Net Change in Cash and Equivalents* (line 27). If that sum is added to the *Cash and Equivalents at Beginning of Year* (line 28), we end up with *Cash and Equivalents at End of Year* (line 29).

Other Items

As usual with a diverse industry, every statement does not have the same terminology or even the same items. Many of the differences have to do with timing, that is, when the income or expense is booked as opposed to when the cash associated with the income comes in or goes out the door.

Many utilities do not adjust their prices immediately to reflect changes in fuel costs which their customers will pay through the fuel adjustment clause. They may change prices every half year. That is, in the next half year period they raise or lower prices to reflect what happened in the previous half year. In the first period, they defer the higher (or lower) fuel costs. That is, they show their expenses as if fuel prices had not changed. In the next period, they may collect the deferred charges plus interest (if customers have to pay more) or give the customers a refund (if prices fell and customers paid too much in the previous period). Deferred fuel costs often show up on the funds statement, either adding to cash flow (because the utility is collecting more from customers than is justified by fuel prices) or reducing cash flow (because the utility is collecting less from customers than it is paying out in fuel costs).

Various rate deferrals appear, too, during the early years of a phase-in. During that time, the utility is collecting less from customers than is indicated by the net income, so the portion of revenue that will be collected in the future has to be subtracted from the cash flow. At the tail end of the phase-in, the utility will be collecting the normal revenue plus revenue that had been deferred from previous years. The net income figure, then, does not reflect that extra revenue because it had already been included in income during the early years of the phase-in. But the fact is that extra cash is coming in, so the rate deferral ends up adding to cash flow in the late years of the phase-in.

Deferred taxes may switch their impact over time, also. Due to the way the tax law works in association with a utility's capital spending program, tax deferrals could last indefinitely. That is, the utility sets aside some cash for taxes that will not be paid this year, but will have to be paid some time in the future, but somehow, the utility does not reach the point where it has to pay those back taxes. As tax laws change, and as utilities cut back their own spending plans, it becomes possible that those deferred taxes might turn into a cash drain (that is, they have to be paid) some time in the future.

Finally, utilities may have to write down the value of assets because regulators believe that they cost too much or were unnecessary. Accountants say that this disallowance is a loss that has to be subtracted from the year's net income. But it does not represent a cash outlay at the time of the writeoff. Therefore, the disallowance should be added back into cash flow, given that it had been subtracted from net income.

Chapter **28**

Ratio Analysis

The objectives of security analysis are twofold. First it seeks to present the important facts in a manner most informing and useful.... Second, it seeks to reach dependable conclusions . . . as to the safety and attractiveness of a given security....[7]

Graham, Dodd and Cottle

The balance sheet, income statement and funds statement provide the raw material needed to analyze the finances of the corporation.

The Balance Sheet

The plant account is the most important section on the asset side of the balance sheet and should be examined to determine how much plant is actually in service and how much is under construction. In some jurisdictions, the regulator will not allow the company to earn a return on plant that has not been put into service, that is, a return on construction work in progress. If a large part of the utility's assets are in CWIP, and the construction program is behind schedule, the utility might be put under financial pressure while trying to finance the project.

For that matter, if the CWIP is not included in the rate base (*i.e.*, is not earning a return), the utility might need a large rate increase — possibly too large for the regulators to grant all at once — upon completion of the plant. Also, we want to compare the proposed spending program with the plant already in place. A huge spending program in relation to present facilities means that the rate base will grow rapidly, probably faster than operating income will grow unaided by rate relief. That means that rate of return on rate base will drop unless the utility gets a substantial amount of rate relief, which is difficult to obtain all at once. For a quick analysis, compare the capital spending program on utility plant (including AFUDC and expenditures for nuclear fuel) with the gross plant of the utility (the sum of plant in service, nuclear fuel and construction work in progress before depreciation and nuclear fuel amortization) at the beginning of the period.

That ratio, then, should be compared with those for other utilities. The higher the ratio of spending to plant, the more likely it is that the utility will require substantial amounts of outside financing to complete the capital expenditure effort and large rate hikes to offset the costs of the new capital. A high ratio, in short, could indicate future financial strains and regulatory problems. Here is an example:

1.	Utility plant at original cost (gross plant in service)	$1,000
2.	Less depreciation	200
3.	Net utility plant in service	800
4.	Construction work in progress	300
5.	Nuclear fuel	50
6.	Less amortization	20
7.	Net nuclear fuel	30
8.	Net utility plant	1,130

Gross plant = line 1 + line 4 + line 5 = $1,350

$$\text{CWIP as \% of net plant} = \frac{\text{line 4}}{\text{line 8}} = \frac{\$300}{\$1,350} = 26\%$$

Construction program for next three years:

9.	Capital expenditures	$400
10.	Nuclear fuel	100
11.	AFUDC	100
12.	Total	$600

Construction program as % of beginning of period gross plant =

$$\frac{\text{line 12}}{\text{line 1 + line 4 + line 5}} = \frac{\$600}{\$1,350} = 45\%$$

The capitalization also deserves attention, for both financial and regulatory reasons. When a large proportion of the capital is provided by debt, the company is said to be leveraged. The covenants or indentures that govern the company's borrowing put limits on how much debt can be sold. Many companies borrow large amounts of short term debt. Some have a permanent layer of short term debt and thus always owe money to banks or to other short term lenders. Short term debt has a different call on assets (if something goes wrong) than does long term debt, but the obligation to pay is still there.

Some companies exclude short term debt from their calculations of capitalization ratios. Doing so can be misleading. Here is an example of how inclusion or exclusion of a large amount of short term debt affects capitalization ratios.

	Amount	Capitalization Ratio or % of Total
With short term debt		
Common equity	$ 500	41.7%
Preferred stock	100	8.3
Long term debt	400	33.3
Short term debt	200	16.7
Total	$ 1,200	100.0%
Without short term debt		
Common equity	$ 500	50.0%
Preferred Stock	100	10.0
Long term debt	400	40.0
Total	$ 1,000	100.0%

Now we have a new question for credit analysts. Utilities are signing long term contracts to buy electricity from others. Those contracts are obligations of the company. Should they be viewed in the same way as debt? For the moment, they do not appear on any documents as debt, but the debt rating agencies certainly will consider them when analyzing the structure of the company.

The final question that deserves attention is: are current assets sufficient to pay current liabilities? In an emergency, selling properties could take a long time, but current liabilities would still have to be paid when due. Current assets include cash or items that can be converted quickly into cash. Therefore, the greater the ratio of current assets to current liabilities, the easier it would be for the utility to meet its obligations. Analysts of the electric utility industry have had a tendency to ignore the relation between current assets and current liabilities on the ground that a utility can easily sell securities to raise the cash necessary to pay current obligations. That was the case a number of years ago. Now, however, chaotic capital markets, the lower quality of many utility securities and the new risks within the business have made the ability to sell securities at will less certain.

The ratio of current assets to current liabilities is called the current ratio. The difference between current assets and current liabilities is working capital.

Current assets	$5,000
Current liabilities	2,000

$$\text{Current ratio} = \frac{\$5,000}{\$2,000} = 2.5, \quad \text{or 2.5 to 1}$$

Working capital = $5,000 − $2,000 = $3,000

A large amount of short term debt may create additional risk for the utility. Because short term interest rates are unstable, the company's income could be affected by the rise and fall of interest costs. A large amount of short term debt also creates financing inflexibility. To pay its debts, the utility might be forced to offer long term securities at an unfavorable time, and might not even be able to raise sufficient funds.

Capitalization plays a role in regulation. Regulators want the utility to raise money in the least expensive fashion to keep down the rates charged to customers. Regulators believe that debt financing is cheaper than equity financing, because creditors have a protected position and therefore settle for lower profits than stockholders, who take the risks. Interest charges, moreover, reduce income taxes, so part of the cost of debt can be offset through lower taxes. Here are costs of capital for two capitalizations:

Example A: Low Leverage

	Amount		% Cost		After Tax Return Calculated by Regulators	Pretax Return (35% Tax Rate) Paid by Consumers
Debt	$300	x	10%	=	$ 30.00	$ 30.00
Equity	700	x	15%	=	105.00	161.55
Total	$1,000				$135.00	$191.55

Example B: High Leverage

	Amount		% Cost		After Tax Return Calculated by Regulators	Pretax Return (35% Tax Rate) Paid by Consumers
Debt	$700	x	10%	=	$70.00	$70.00
Equity	300	x	15%	=	$45.00	69.23
Total	$1,000				$115.00	$139.23
Ratio of A to B					117%	138%

The preceding examples reveal a conflict of interest. The regulator wants the utility to finance by means of debt to keep down the cost of capital. On the other hand, the utility may want to keep down the use of debt because too much debt increases the risk and may increase interest costs enough to offset savings derived from the lower equity ratio. For example, assume that two utilities have $1,000 of capitalization, one borrowed $300 and the other $700, a storm wipes out $200 of each company's assets, and the companies must go out of business. Before stock-holders receive anything, owners of debt must be paid in full. What would be left for stockholders?

	Low Leverage	High Leverage
Original assets	$1,000	$1,000
less: Storm damage	200	200
Assets available for distribution	800	800
less: Payment of debt	300	700
Assets available for distribution to stockholders	500	100
Original stockholder investment	$ 700	$ 300
Loss of investment	200	200
Loss as % of investment	29%	67%

The Income Statement

Balance sheets change slowly, but income statements change rapidly. Those changes can tell a great deal about the utility and the direction in which it is going.

In some ways, revenue, the largest number in the income statement, is one of the least meaningful, as are the ratios developed from revenue. The reason is that revenue includes base revenue and fuel adjustment clause revenue. Let there be two companies of equal size. Company A's fuel costs are the same in the first and second year of operations. Company B's fuel costs are $50 higher in the second year and are immediately passed on to customers by means of the fuel adjustment clause.

	Company A		Company B	
	1st year	*2nd year*	*1st year*	*2nd year*
Base revenue	500	500	500	500
Fuel adj. revenue	0	0	0	50
Total	500	500	500	550

The income statement shows just the total revenue. Did Company B really have a better second year than Company A? We can carry that question a step further. Many people do ratio analysis using total revenue. Here are additional examples:

	Company A		Company B	
	1st year	2nd year	1st year	2nd year
Base revenue	500	500	500	500
Fuel clause revenue	0	0	0	50
Total revenue	500	500	500	550
Fuel expenses	300	300	300	350
Other expenses	50	50	50	50
Total expenses	350	350	350	400
Net operating income	150	150	150	150
Ratio of net income to total revenue	30%	30%	30%	27%

A standard ratio analysis would indicate that Company B was less efficient in the second year than in the first because income represented only 27% of revenue instead of 30% as in the preceding year. Actually, income was the same percentage of base revenue in both years. Thus, the standard ratio analysis of the income statement tends to be misleading and is not especially useful.

Despite the homogeneity of the industry, utilities engage in highly varied accounting practices. Although one kilowatt-hour is always one kilowatt-hour no matter where the utility is situated, $1 of earnings per share in Texas is not necessarily the same as $1 of earnings in California. Analysts refer to the differences in accounting procedures and cash flow behind the reported figures as "quality of earnings."

Whether income tax savings attributed to the investment tax credit and accelerated depreciation are deferred (normalized) or are used to reduce taxes for regulatory purposes (flowed through) can have an important effect.

Normalization refers to a method of allocating tax costs for book purposes by spreading tax savings over the life of the property. For example, assume that income tax payments have been reduced by the use of the investment tax credit. Rather than show the entire tax saving in the income statement for the current year (flow through), a deferred tax item is put into the income statement, and the tax saving is added back to earnings over the life of the property, or for some other arbitrary period. Income tax savings generated by the use of accelerated depreciation for tax purposes can be treated the same way. Rather than show the effect of the tax reduction in earnings for the duration of the period in which accelerated depreciation is greater than straight line (flow through), the utility sets up a deferred tax account and adds back the tax savings to earnings when use of accelerated depreciation has reduced the tax depreciation rate below the book rate.

Regulation requires that the utility rate structure must cover all costs of providing service, including income taxes. Yet the income tax on the tax books differs from that reported to shareholders and to commissions. For example, a utility uses accelerated depreciation for tax purposes and straight line depreciation for book purposes. In our example, accelerated depreciation results in a higher depreciation expense in early years than the straight line method. Current taxes are being reduced. At some future time, however, accelerated depreciation will be lower than straight line, and current taxes will be increased:

Accelerated Depreciation
(Tax Reporting)

	Year 1	Year 5	Year 10
Revenues	$100	$100	$100
Operating expenses	30	30	30
Depreciation	20	10	0
Pretax income	$ 50	$ 60	$ 70
Income taxes (50% tax rate)	25	30	35
Net Income	$ 25	$ 30	$ 35

Straight Line Depreciation
(Tax Reporting)

	Year 1	Year 5	Year 10
Revenues	$ 100	$ 100	$ 100
Operating expenses	30	30	30
Depreciation	10	10	10
Pretax income	$ 60	$ 60	$ 60
Income taxes (50% tax rate)	30	30	30
Net Income	$ 30	$ 30	$ 30

The utility uses accelerated depreciation for tax purposes, thereby reducing taxes, but uses straight line depreciation for book and regulatory purposes. In Year 1, the utility actually paid $25 in income taxes. In time, however, the company's taxes will rise (so long as plant subject to depreciation does not increase also). Proper accounting procedure calls for the company to report taxes on the books as if straight line depreciation had also been used for tax purposes. The difference between the $25 actually paid and the $30 that would have been paid represents deferred taxes, which will be paid some time in the future where accelerated depreciation drops below straight line depreciation.

Some utility commissions take the position that cost of service includes taxes actually paid, not taxes that might be paid in the future. Present customers are expected to pay for current costs only. Future customers can pay for future costs. Furthermore, so long as the plant account increases fast enough (thus increasing depreciation), the utility is unlikely to reach the point at which accelerated depreciation declines below straight line depreciation. If that is so, deferred taxes may never be paid. Therefore, why set aside any deferred taxes?

Let us consider the example of a growing utility that writes off $40 of original plant during a five year period, uses accelerated depreciation for tax purposes, and adds $20 to its plant account for five years. In the following statement, the depreciation on additional plant is shown separately. The example is simplified, and does not necessarily show the exact pattern of actual tax depreciation, but rather indicates how tax depreciation is higher than book depreciation in early years and lower in later years of the life of the plant.

Accelerated Depreciation
(Tax Reporting)

	Year 1	Year 2	Year 3	Year 4	Year 5
Revenues	$ 100	$ 125	$ 156	$ 196	$ 245
Operating expenses	30	38	47	59	74
Depreciation of plant in service in					
Year 1	16	10	6	4	4
Year 2	0	8	5	3	2
Year 3	0	0	8	5	3
Year 4	0	0	0	8	5
Year 5	0	0	0	0	8
Total Depreciation	16	18	19	20	22
Pretax income	54	69	90	117	149
Income taxes (50% rate)	27	34.5	45	58.5	74.5
Net income	27	34.5	45	58.5	74.5

Note that depreciation for tax purposes does not decline, because new plant is being added. The additional depreciation on the new plant offsets the fall-off of depreciation on the older plant. Using straight line depreciation, the income statement would appear as follows:

Straight Line Depreciation
(Tax Reporting)

	Year 1	*Year 2*	*Year 3*	*Year 4*	*Year 5*
Revenues	$100	$125	$156	$196	$245
Operating expenses	30	38	47	59	74
Depreciation of plant placed on service in					
Year 1	8	8	8	8	8
Year 2	0	4	4	4	4
Year 3	0	0	4	4	4
Year 4	0	0	0	4	4
Year 5	0	0	0	0	4
Total Depreciation	8	12	16	20	24
Pretax income	62	75	93	117	147
Income taxes (50% rate)	31	37.5	46.5	58.5	73.5
Net income	31	37.5	46.5	58.5	73.5

The use of flow through (vs. normalization) accounting can produce a higher reported net income with no improvement in cash flow. Note in the following example that both the flow through and normalized companies show the straight line depreciation on their books. The normalized utility, however, shows a deferred tax expense consistent with the use of straight line depreciation while the flow through company does not.

Accounts When Accelerated Exceeds Straight Line Depreciation

	Flow Through	Normalization	Tax Accounts of Both
Revenues	$100	$100	$100
Operating expenses	30	30	30
Depreciation	10	10	20
Pretax income	$ 60	$ 60	$ 50
Income taxes			
Current	25	25	25
Deferred	0	5	0
Net Income	$ 35	$ 30	$ 25
Cash flow (net income, depreciation and deferred taxes)	$ 45	$ 45	$ 45

Whether a utility uses normalization or flow through tax accounting is usually decided by the regulatory agency. Deferred taxes are legitimate expenses from a regulatory standpoint in normalized jurisdictions and must be covered by revenues. Although normalization does not increase net income, it does (as noted above) add to cash flow. Therefore, the company that normalizes has more cash flow per dollar of net income than the company that flows through and is bound to be in better financial shape, other things being equal.

Now, let us look at how flow through accounting can be used to reduce revenue requirements (that is, the rates charged customers) in the years when tax depreciation is greater than book depreciation. In the example in Table 28-1, regulators consider a 12% return on equity to be the allowed return. The company has $250 in equity. Using normalized accounting, the company earns 12%. Using flow through accounting, however, the company earns 14%, so rates must be reduced by $10 to bring return on equity to 12%. Note that by doing so, the regulatory agency reduces the cash flow and the interest coverage ratio of the company, although reported net income remains the same. (Cash flow, here, equals net income plus depreciation plus deferred taxes.)

Some items associated with the construction program are expensed for tax purposes but are capitalized for book purposes. For example, certain state and local taxes have to be paid on plant under construction. Those local taxes are legitimate deductible expenses for income tax purposes and are used by the utility to reduce its Federal income tax payments. By lowering income taxes, the reported operating income of the utility has been increased, as has the rate of return. The question remains whether that is a proper way to match expenses with revenues. The deductible state and local taxes are not shown in the income statement because they are associated with construction of plant and, therefore, are capitalized. Why should the income tax saving be included in income, for the benefit of current ratepayers who are not contributing to the upkeep of the plant under construction? The solution is to put off tax savings by means of a deferred tax expense item in the income statement.

Income tax savings are also derived from interest charges attributable to borrowing made to support construction work in progress. The logic is identical to that used in the preceding example. If ratepayers do not bear any of the burden of supporting construction work, why should they gain from the tax savings generated? The solution is to set up a deferred tax account as an operating expense to offset the tax savings. An offsetting tax credit is included in other income, because operating income had to be reduced by deferred taxes for regulatory purposes, but there was no reason to change net income. Note that in the following example, without the tax deferral, the rate of return would increase, perhaps to a level that would require a rate reduction. To reduce rates and to give current ratepayers a break may seem to be unfair, especially if those consumers are not paying any of the costs for construction because the costs are not included in the rate base. If current ratepayers are not responsible for future needs, they should not receive the benefits of construction designed to meet those needs.

The example in Table 28-2 concerns an increase in taxes because of construction. The example could just as easily be applied to higher interest costs attributable to borrowing for construction purposes.

Each new tax law changes the rules for depreciation, and the Tax Reform Act of 1986 made many changes in the definition of taxable income and also eliminated the investment tax credit. At present, tax normalization is the order of the day. Is it worth worrying about these tax accounting procedures when the tax law keeps changing and most utilities normalize? Is the discussion simply academic and dull? The answer is that the discussion certainly is dull, and may be academic at the moment. Yet regulators and tax law writers could easily resurrect concepts that have been out of favor.

The various tax laws have created formulas for depreciation. One method uses double-declining-balance or sum-of-the-years-digits for tax purposes. Another method depreciates property for tax purposes over fewer years than for regulatory purposes. For instance, a utility can depreciate a nuclear plant over a 20 year period for tax purposes, while using a 30 year period for regulatory purposes. The company can either normalize (defer) or flow through the resultant tax savings derived from using a shorter life for depreciation on the tax return than is used for rate setting. The company that normalizes has more cash flow per dollar of net income than the company that flows through the tax savings. The most recent tax laws have encouraged or required normalization accounting, so the flow through component of earnings has declined.

Table 28-1

Flow Through Used to Reduce Revenue Requirements

	Original Tax Books	Normal- ization	Flow through Before Rate Reduction	Tax Books After Rate Reduction	Flow through After Rate Reduction
Revenues	$100	$100	$100	$90	$90
Operating expenses	20	20	20	20	20
Depreciation	20	10	10	20	10
Pretax operating income	60	70	70	50	60
Interest expenses	10	10	10	10	10
Pretax net income	50	60	60	40	50
Current income taxes	25	25	25	20	20
Deferred income taxes	0	5	0	0	0
Net income	$25	$30	$35	$20	$30
Cash flow	$45	$45	$45	$40	$40
Return on equity	10%	12%	14%	8%	12%
Interest coverage ratio	6x	7x	7x	5x	6x

Table 28-2

Impact of Taxes for Construction

	Income Statement Before Construction Begins	Income Statement After Construction Begins (no deferred taxes)	Income Statement After Construction Begins (deferred taxes)
Revenues	$1,000	$1,000	$1,000
Operating expenses	500	500	500
Other taxes	100	100 (b)	100
Income taxes (deferred)	0	0	50 (d)
Income taxes (current)	100	50 (c)	50
Total expenses	$700	$650	$700
Operating income	300	350	300
Other income (inc. tax cr.)	0	0	50 (e)
Income before interest charges	$300	$350	$350
Interest charges	200	200	200
Net income	$100	$150	$150
Plant in service	4,000	4,000	4,000
Plant under construction	0	1,000	1,000
Rate of Return (a)	7.5%	8.75%	7.5%

Notes:

(a) On plant in service. Defined as operating income/plant in service.

(b) Other taxes increase to $200, but the additional $100 is capitalized for book purposes because it is a tax on plant under construction.

(c) Reduced from $100 to $50 because taxable net income has declined by $100 because of taxes on plant under construction.

(d) Deferred taxes to offset income tax savings attributable to plant under construction.

(e) Income tax credit to offset deferred taxes.

Because of the capital intensive nature of the utility business, depreciation is a major item on both the income and the cash flow statements. The composite book depreciation rate is the rate of depreciation of plant in service as shown on the books of the corporation, as opposed to the usually higher rate used for tax purposes. The book depreciation rate is a straight line rate for most utility companies. Furthermore — and this is a key point — the rate of depreciation usually must be approved by the regulatory agency that has jurisdiction over the company. Depreciation is a cost of doing business that must be offset by revenues. The higher the depreciation rate, the more the customer must pay in current utility bills. At the same time, a higher depreciation rate increases cash flow, thereby allowing the utility to finance internally more of its expansion and to have less dependence on the capital markets.

Different kinds of utility plants require different depreciation rates. A telephone company might use 7%, an electric or gas company 3% or 4%, and a water company an even lower rate. Even within an industry, the appropriate rate will vary. A hydroelectric company depreciates a dam more slowly than another company depreciates a coal burning plant. Similar utilities, however, may have different book depreciation rates. A higher rate is favorable for investors, because it creates a greater cash flow.

In the past, utilities did not *defer fuel costs* or book *unbilled revenues*. That is, they reported fuel costs as they were incurred. The customer, through the fuel adjustment clause, had to bear the cost of fuel price changes, but the fuel adjustments to rates often took place several months after the price change. The utility's earnings were reduced by the deficiency during the lag period. That lag did not matter when fuel costs were stable, but became painful during a period when fuel prices did nothing but rise. Rather than attempt to modify the fuel adjustments on a rapid basis, the regulators and companies devised a different scheme. The utility deferred the fuel expenses derived from price changes of fuel during the current period until a future period when they could be collected from customers, often with interest. In that way, the price of electricity need not be modified too often, and the utility still was protected from swings in fuel prices. Obviously, during periods when fuel costs rose, the utility's cash flow suffered because it had to wait for payment. The utility would be better off with rapid adjustments in the fuel clause so that lag was minimal. It might be better off with a fuel adjustment based on projected costs, so it would be ahead of the price change. The biggest problem with the deferral method, though, is that regulators might decide not to allow recovery of past costs. This has happened when those costs were controversial. Thus we have to be careful about utilities that have large deferred fuel costs.

In the past, utilities booked the cost of generation as incurred, but they did not show revenues until they had billed the customer. This situation produced a mismatch, because some of the production expenses were associated with electricity that had been produced but whose consumers had not been billed. That of course reduced revenues and net income. The Tax Reform Act of 1986 changed the picture.

Utilities could not ignore the potential revenues associated with the expenses. From then on, utilities showed revenues associated with sales even if the bills had not gone out. A large amount of unbilled revenue means lower cash flow per dollar of revenue.

Neither tax nor fuel accounting is as controversial a subject as the *allowance for funds used during construction* (AFUDC), which is a credit item in the income statement and is intended to be an offset to capital charges incurred before plant is placed in service. Those capitalized charges are added to the cost of the plant when it goes into service. The utility can then earn a return on the cost of the physical plant plus the capital costs incurred in building the plant. Sometimes the AFUDC rate is higher than the rate of return the utility can earn on the property once it is in service. In that situation, reported earnings are higher during construction than during operation. Unlike the sale of electricity (or of other services), AFUDC results in no cash flow. Distortion of earnings and cash flow problems are likely to be most severe for utilities that capitalize construction costs at a high rate. Several utilities use a complicated method in which a higher gross rate is used, but deferred tax offsets bring the net rate down close to the average.

In 1977, the Federal Power Commission revised the procedure for calculating AFUDC, although the results are almost the same as before. Basically, AFUDC is split into two parts: the portion resulting from raising debt money to finance the construction and the portion allocated to equity funding. Simplified versions of the old and new formats follow:

	Old	*New*
Operating Income	$400	$400
Other income		
AFUDC	50	30*
Other	10	10
Total Other Income	60	40
Income before interest charges	460	440
Interest expense	100	100
AFUDC	—	(20)**
Net interest expense	100	80
Net income	360	360

*Derived from raising equity money.
**Derived from raising debt money.

AFUDC suffers from two problems: it assumes that income spread over a period of years (the return on the AFUDC capitalized into the rate base) is as good as the return collected on CWIP in the current year, and that a bookkeeping credit is as good as cash.

Owners of debt and preferred stock examine the income statement to determine the safety of their investments. *Pretax interest coverage* — how much money is available from earnings to pay interest charges — is one of the standards used to determine the strength of a debt security. Although many persons think of a corporation's assets as protection for debtholders, what would the assets be worth if they could not generate income? Pretax income is used for the analysis because interest charges must be met before any income taxes can be paid.

For purposes of analysis, the income accounts should be restated to combine all AFUDC into the other income section and all interest into one line. The standard format and the analytical format are shown below:

	Standard	*Analytical*
Revenue	1,000	1,000
Operating expenses except income taxes	500	500
Income taxes	200	200
Operating income	300	300
Other income:		
Allowance for other funds used during construction	10	30
Income tax credits	4	4
Miscellaneous	1	1
Income before interest charges	315	335
Interest on long term debt	30	30
Other interest	20	20
Allowance for borrowed funds used during construction	(20)	—
Net interest charges	30	50
Net income	285	285

The restatement represents a reversion to the earlier method of stating AFUDC. Similar items are lumped together to prevent the possible error of calculating coverages by using net interest charges in the denominator of the coverage ratio. Unfortunately, the analytical format is better suited to equity analysis than to debt analysis and is inadequate for calculating interest coverages because it does not give figures on a pretax basis. A format for interest coverage analysis would be:

Revenue	$1,000
Operating expenses except income taxes	500
Pretax operating income	500
Interest charges	50
Pretax income (excluding other income)	450
Income taxes (net of income tax credits of $4)	196
Net income before AFUDC and miscellaneous income	254
AFUDC	30
Miscellaneous income	1
Net income	$ 285

The following example restates an income statement and the numbers are then used to calculate some standard coverage ratios for interest charges.

		Analytical (Equity)	Line by Line Formula
Line			
1.	Revenues	$1,000	
	Operating expenses		
2.	Fuel and operations*	400	
3.	Depreciation	100	
4.	Income taxes	100	
5.	Total operating expenses	600	2 + 3 + 4
6.	Operating Income	400	1 – 5
	Other income		
7.	AFUDC**	80	
8.	Income tax credits	15	
9.	Miscellaneous	5	
10.	Total other income	100	7 + 8 + 9
11.	Income before interest charges	500	6 + 10
12.	Interest charges	300	
13.	Net income	200	11 – 12
14.	Preferred dividends	50	

		Analytical (Equity)	Line by Line Formula
15.	Net available to common stock	150	13 – 14
16.	Average shares of common stock	100	
17.	Earnings per average share	$ 1.50	15 ÷ 16

*Includes rentals, the interest component of which is $10.
**Allowances for Funds Used During Construction from both sources.

		Analytical (Debt)	Line by Line Formula
1.	Revenues	$ 1,000	
	Operating expenses except income taxes		
2.	Fuel and operations*	400	
3.	Depreciation	100	
4.	Total operating expenses except income taxes	500	2 + 3
5.	Pretax operating income	500	1 – 4
6.	Total interest charges	300	
7.	Pretax income (excluding other income)	200	5 – 6
8.	Income taxes	100	
9.	Net income (before other income)	100	7 – 8
10.	AFUDC**	80	
11.	Income tax credits	15	
12.	Miscellaneous	5	
13.	Total other income	100	10 + 11 + 12
14.	Net income	200	9 + 13
15.	Preferred dividends	50	
16.	Net available to common stock	150	14 + 15

*Includes rentals, the interest component of which is $10.
**Allowance for Funds Used During Construction from both sources.

Pretax income before interest charges (income before interest charges plus income taxes) is the same as revenues less operating expenses other than income taxes.

1) The formula for *SEC coverage* (used in bond prospectuses approved by the Securities and Exchange Commission) produces the following:

$$\frac{\text{Pretax Op. Income} + \text{AFUDC} + \text{Misc. Income} + \text{Interest Comp. of Rentals}}{\text{Interest Charges} + \text{Interest Component of Rentals}} =$$

$$\frac{\$500 + \$80 + \$5 + \$10}{\$300 + \$10} = \frac{\$595}{\$310} = 1.92x$$

2) *Coverage Based on Pretax Income Before Interest Charges*: this ratio is an easily calculated substitute for the SEC coverage, especially when rentals are unavailable or are insignificant:

$$\frac{\text{Pretax Oper. Income} + \text{AFUDC} + \text{Misc. Income}}{\text{Interest Charges}} = \frac{\$500 + \$80 + \$5}{\$300} = 1.95x$$

3) *Interest Coverage Based on Pretax Operating Income*: this provides a measure of the pretax income from operations that is available to meet fixed charges. The calculation excludes the allowance for funds used during construction (a non-cash item) and other income (which may be highly variable). For our purposes, income taxes include all current and deferred income taxes shown in operating expenses. The formula for operating income coverage is:

$$\frac{\text{Pretax Operating Income}}{\text{Interest Charges}} = \frac{\$500}{\$300} = 1.67x$$

Operating income coverage should be viewed as a conservative way of measuring a utility's standing. It requires a simple calculation, too, and does not need any numbers such as interest component of rentals which may not be readily available.

4) *Cash Income Coverage*: utilities differ in how much of the revenue that can be converted into cash (before payment of taxes and interest) due to different depreciation policies and the existence of phase-in components of income that are not cash revenues. Because depreciation is one of the utility's major non-cash expense items, we include depreciation in the ratio shown below. AFUDC, which

is one of the major non-cash credits in the income statement, should be omitted from a conservative coverage ratio, which is what happens when we look at pretax operating income, which does not include AFUDC. This ratio is calculated according to the formula:

$$\frac{\text{Pretax Operating Income} + \text{Depreciation} - \text{Non-cash Phase-in Credits}}{\text{Total Interest Charges}}$$

In our example, there were no phase-in items, so the coverage would be:

$$\frac{\$500 + \$100}{\$300} = \frac{\$600}{\$300} = 2.00x$$

Even that ratio may fail to include some cash coming in, especially that derived from the amortization of nuclear fuel (which is akin to depreciation of the investment in nuclear fuel as the fuel is burned), or other amortizations. Check out the income statement and the cash flow statement to find ongoing cash items that should be included in the coverage numerator.

5) *Preferred Dividend Coverage*: Utilities often have preferred stock in their capitalizations. Much of the analysis that we are using here also is suitable for analysis of preferred stocks, except that the coverage ratio must be adjusted. Take our example, which we have recast for an easier calculation.

	Revenue	$1,000
minus	Operating Expenses	500
equals	Pretax Operating Income	500
minus	Interest Charges	300
equals	Pretax Net Income	200
minus	Income Taxes (50% rate)	100
equals	Net Income	100
	Preferred Dividends	50

In a previous illustration, we have shown pretax interest coverage to be:

$$\frac{\$500}{\$300} = 1.67x$$

Using our example, many analysts would calculate preferred dividend coverage as:

$$\frac{\$100}{\$50} = 2.00x$$

But, as Graham and Dodd pointed out long ago,[8] that would be an absurdity. How can the senior security have less coverage than the junior security? Is the preferred stock really safer than the debt? Thus, preferred coverage has to take into account the senior claims ahead of the stock. Unfortunately, that cannot be accomplished easily because the debt has a claim to earnings before taxes, while the preferred claim is junior to taxes. The solution is to put the preferred claim on a pretax basis too. We can then ask how much income before taxes has to be earned to pay the preferred dividend. Under that formulation, preferred dividend coverage becomes:

$$\frac{(\text{Income Before Interest Charges} + \text{Income Taxes})}{\text{Interest Charges} + \left(\dfrac{\text{Preferred Dividend}}{1 - \text{Tax Rate}}\right)}$$

The income tax rate is stated on a decimal basis, *i.e.* 50% = 0.50. For those ratios that use Income Before Interest Charges in the numerator, income taxes includes the taxes shown as operating expenses less income tax credits included in Other Income. The tax credits have been explained in the paragraphs above concerning income taxes. The correct preferred dividend coverage for our example is:

$$\frac{\$500 + \$100}{\$300 + \left(\dfrac{\$50}{1 - .50}\right)} = \frac{\$600}{\$300 + \$100} = 1.50x$$

As a final point, many utilities are entering into long term contracts to purchase electricity from outside sources. As these contracts become more important, credit analysts will have to formulate methods that take into account the fact that these contracts involve obligations for payment that are similar to debt obligations.

Earnings per share (EPS) analysis is based on the average number of shares outstanding during the year. Because utility companies often sell common stock, using year-end shares could be misleading. For example, only a portion of the money received from the sale of shares may have been put to work to produce income during the entire year.

That point is illustrated in the following example, which shows two identical companies, each of which started the year with 800 shares outstanding and ended the year with 1,000 shares. Company A sold new stock at the beginning of the year and had 1,000 shares outstanding for almost the entire period and, therefore, had use of the money from the new shares for almost the full year. Company B sold new shares at the end of the year and had use of the funds for just a few days.

	Company A	Company B
Net income for year	$1,000	$1,000
Year-end shares outstanding	1,000	1,000
EPS based on year-end shares outstanding	$1.00	$1.00
Average shares outstanding	999	801
EPS based on average shares outstanding	$1.00	$1.25

If we were to calculate EPS on the basis of shares outstanding at the end of the year, the investor could conclude incorrectly that the shares of both companies have equal earning power. Is it not likely that Company B, once it puts into use the cash derived from the sale of stock near the end of the year, would show greatly improved earnings per share in the following year?

What happens to earnings? A portion of earnings is retained and the rest is distributed as dividends to stockholders. The dividend payout ratio is the standard measure of how much of the earnings available to common stockholders is paid out in the form of dividends. One comparison we can make is that between the payout ratio and the percentage of earnings derived from AFUDC. Here are two examples:

	Company A	Company B
Reported EPS	$2.00	$2.00
less AFUDC	1.00	0.50
equals EPS - AFUDC	1.00	1.50
Dividends	1.20	1.20
Payout ratio (Div.)/(EPS)	60%	60%
Payout ratio excluding AFUDC from EPS:		
$\left(\dfrac{\text{Div.}}{\text{EPS-AFUDC}} \right)$	120%	80%

Other things being equal, we should be more comfortable with an investment in Company B, because that utility is neither borrowing money nor selling stock to raise the cash for its dividend. All calculations can be based on total dollars, not earnings per share or dividends per share.

$$\text{Dividend payout ratio} = \frac{\text{Common stock dividends}}{\text{Earnings available to common stock}}$$

The payout ratio is one indication of how well the dividend is covered by earnings. Unfortunately the tendency exists to look at the ratio for a single year and to forget that utility earnings have become less stable in recent years because of the timing of rate relief and the sensitivity of earnings to weather conditions. Investors in utilities expect stable or growing dividends. Companies do not raise or lower dividends to maintain a stable payout ratio. A company maintains a stable dividend and lets the payout ratio fluctuate. Most companies have a target payout ratio, which represents an average goal. Remember too that the higher the payout ratio, the less able the company will be to raise the dividend, and the smaller the funds the company will retain to finance future growth.

The Cash Flows Statement

In a period of high cost money, the need to borrow money or to sell stock at inconvenient times in the market cycle could have a serious effect on profitability. On the other hand, if a business can generate cash from operations, that money could be invested in profitable ways. Even in the best of times, electric utilities may require new cash because operations for the year do not generate sufficient funds to finance the purchase of expensive equipment that can serve customers for 30 years. Customers cannot be expected to pay so much for electricity in a single year that the utility can meet its needs for the next three decades.

The cash flows can be analyzed conveniently by rearranging them into a simplified format:

USES OF FUNDS	
Capital expenditures (after subtracting out AFUDC)	$1,000
Purchase of nuclear fuel	100
Allowance for funds used during construction (AFUDC)	100
Total expenditures for plant account	1,200
Refunding	50
Working capital and misc.	50
Total uses of funds	$1,300

SOURCES OF FUNDS

Retained earnings*	$100
Rate deferrals	(5)
Depreciation and amortization	205
Deferred taxes	150
Total internal sources of funds	450
Debt	400
Common stock	300
Preferred stock	150
Total sources of funds	$1,300

* $150 net income for common stock minus $50 dividend.

Internal sources of funds as a percentage of expenditures for plant account =

$$\frac{\$450}{\$1,200} = 37.5\%$$

Internal sources of funds (less AFUDC) as a percentage of expenditures for plant account (less AFUDC) =

$$\frac{\$450 - \$100}{\$1,200 - \$100} = \frac{\$350}{\$1,100} = 31.8\%$$

We want to know how much of the money spent for construction came from internal sources. In the above example, the answer seems to be 37.5%. Part of the earnings, however, came from a non-cash source, the AFUDC. Again, part of the expenditures for plant may not represent cash outlay, but are for AFUDC. Therefore, we could develop a second ratio that excludes AFUDC and that shows that 31.8% of cash expenditures for construction (i.e., what was actually paid to the suppliers and builders) came from internal sources.

Sometimes, we may want to look at the cash flow from operations before it is dispersed. A strong cash flow is a valuable asset to any business if properly deployed. To do so, add up:

Net income for common stock	$ 150
Depreciation and amortization	205
Rate deferrals	(5)
Deferred taxes	150
Cash flow from operations	$ 500

This number tells us how much cash comes in from the day to day business of the company. It excludes non-recurring items, such as profit on sale of property, or writedowns of asset value that involve no cash loss at time of the writedown. We can even calculate cash flow per average share outstanding in the same way as we calculate net income per share. We can compare earnings per share to cash flow per share, and we might prefer to invest in the company that has more cash flow behind each dollar of earnings per share, or behind every dollar of dividends paid.

The above ratios show how much cash is generated from the sale of electricity. Sometimes utilities finance plant expenditures from sources other than their internal savings or from the sale of securities in the current year. For example, funds raised from the sale of securities last year could be used for financing plant construction in the current year. The utility also can sell assets to raise cash. Occasionally those sources are treated as if they were internal. Nevertheless, growing concerns cannot stay in business by living off assets. That leads us to an interesting conclusion. So long as the utility is growing rapidly (needs new plant), the company is not likely to raise sufficient money from internal sources to pay for its new equipment. The company will only be able to generate cash in excess of current needs (cash that can be used to pay debts contracted in the past) when the company's growth slows or stops. At that time, however, the company may need cash for other items. For example, when growth stops, deferred taxes will have to be paid. For that matter, the plant will cease to expand when demand weakens — a time when revenues could decline badly enough to make it difficult for the company to pay debts incurred in the past. Technological changes make obsolete many products and services. Therefore, a prudent management should try to meet its cash needs to the extent possible when that can be done easily and should not put off until tomorrow that which can be paid for today.

That brings up the question of how money should be raised. If an industrial firm builds a factory that will last for 10 years, the company might borrow money for the construction and pay the loan over a 10 year period. Because the firm is unlikely to build a plant each year, the loan will probably be paid from the proceeds of the operation. The loan, in short, will be self-liquidating. Electric utilities, on the other hand, may borrow annually, plow all cash back into plant, and raise funds to repay the loan from sale of additional securities.

Inflation adds to the problem. A utility's cash flow from internal sources is derived from a return on and depreciation of the original cost of assets. Original cost is not adjusted for increases in price levels. Accordingly, the utility can only recover by means of depreciation the actual cost of the asset, not the cost of replacement at current price levels. The utility has to sell additional securities to raise cash with which to replace the asset.

How is that problem different from that of other businesses? Most other businesses do not have so much of their money invested in long-lived fixed assets. Other businesses can raise prices on inventory so that the firms can replace the inventory with a like quantity of more expensive goods. They can also raise prices, if the competition allows, to make sure that they have enough cash to replace fixed assets that now cost more. The utility, of course, cannot raise prices at will. So long as regulation and depreciation are based on original cost of property, the utility has a hard time meeting its needs from internal sources in an inflationary economy.

Other Ratios

In our previous examples, we have examined ratios derived entirely from a single financial statement. Yet, several key ratios use items from several financial statements.

Investors and regulators want to know rates of return — how much profit is made for every dollar invested. When creditors lend the business $100 in return for $10 a year of interest plus repayment of the $100 principal at the end of a given period, they accept a 10% return ($10 a year for every $100 borrowed). When a stockholder puts money into a new business expecting the business to earn $20 for each $100 invested by stockholders, the investor expects a 20% return ($20 a year for every $100 invested). Shareholders also expect to sell their shares for at least $100, so that the $20 a year does not have to be offset against a capital loss. If the business is set up with $100 from creditors, who expect a return of $10 a year, and with $100 from stockholders, who expect a return of $20 a year, the return on the total investment of $200 is:

Debt	$100	x	10%	=	$10	
Equity	100	x	20%	=	20	
	$200				$30	

and:

$$\frac{\$30}{\$200} = 15\%$$

We will discuss several ratios that can be calculated either to present a picture of the utility's profitability or to approximate the return as calculated by the regulatory agency.

Net Operating Income as a Percentage of Net Plant is one of the easiest returns to calculate. Utilities are allowed to earn a given return on the rate base. Commissions differ in their calculations of both income and rate base. The ratio that we are discussing is rarely used by a regulatory agency but it is helpful to investors. It is a calculation of ability to earn a return on net plant from operations alone (and excludes AFUDC, and other nonoperational income). Consider the following example:

SAMPLE UTILITY
INCOME STATEMENT*
($ Millions)

Revenues	$100
Operating expenses	
Fuel	20
Operations and maintenance	20
Depreciation	10
Income taxes	20
Total operating expenses	70
Operating income	30
Other income	
Allowance for funds used during construction	3
Other income and deductions (net)	1
Income before interest charges	34
Interest charges	10
Net income	24
Preferred dividends	3
Earnings on common stock	21
Dividend on common stock	15

*Restated to include both allowances for funds used during construction in one section as part of Other Income.

SAMPLE UTILITY
BALANCE SHEET

Assets

Plant ($400 in service and $100 construction work in progress)	$500
Depreciation	100
Net plant	400
Current assets (all materials and supplies)	50
Deferred charges	5
Total assets	$ 455

Liabilities
Capitalization

Common stock and retained earnings	$125
Preferred stock	50
Long term debt	210
Total capitalization	385
Current liabilities	60
Deferred credits	10
Total liabilities and capital	$455

Rate of return on net plant =

$$\frac{\text{Operating income}}{\text{Net plant}} = \frac{\$30}{\$400} = 7.5\%$$

We can also calculate *Income Before Interest Charges as a Percentage of Net Plant*. Many utilities argue that the AFUDC is good income and should be included in calculating returns. Some regulators include CWIP in the rate base and derive the rate of return by using income before interest charges, rather than by using operating income. For the investor who is interested in determining a rough rate of return on the basis of an approximation of the rate base, the ratio under discussion serves the purpose.

$$\frac{\text{Income before interest charges}}{\text{Net plant}} = \frac{\$34}{\$400} = 8.5\%$$

Return on Rate Base, as used in regulatory proceedings, is often calculated differently from the two previous ratios. Here is one method that can be used, with working capital approximated as materials and supplies plus one-eighth of operating and maintenance expenses.

Rate base calculation (no CWIP in rate base):

Net plant in service =	
Plant in service − Depreciation =	$300.00
Materials and supplies	50.00
One-eighth of operations and maintenance expense	2.50
Rate base =	$352.50

Rate of return on rate base:

$$\frac{\text{Operating income}}{\text{Rate base}} = \frac{\$30}{\$352.50} = 8.51\%$$

Return on Common Equity measures the return on the common stockholders' investment. Return on common equity is a vital component of overall rate of return. A low return on equity usually means that the utility needs (and has a good chance of obtaining) rate relief. On the other hand, a high return on equity might mean difficulty when the company seeks to justify relief. An extraordinarily high return could indicate that the return has no place to go but down and that relief is unlikely before the return has reached a sub-par level.

Return on common equity:

$$\frac{\text{Income available to common stock}}{\text{Common stockholders' equity}} = \frac{\$21}{\$125} = 16.8\%$$

We have based our calculations on the balance sheet at the end of a period. Actually, all the assets may not have been in service for the full year, and therefore may not have contributed to profits. Accordingly, a more meaningful return might be calculated on average plant or on average equity. Rate base may not fit the mold either. Some regulators subtract deferred taxes or plant that was not prudently constructed from the rate base. Regulators use different methods for calculating the working capital component of rate base. Some include part or all of the CWIP in the rate base. When regulators calculate earnings, they make adjustments for unusual items. Some will add all or part of AFUDC to the earnings component. As a result, we should know the formula used or we can simply make approximations for purposes of comparison.

Dividend to Common Equity Ratio is another way of looking at the generosity (and perhaps the safety) of the dividend. The utility tries to maintain a stable or growing dividend. Earnings, from which dividends are paid tend to fluctuate, due to swings in weather and economic conditions, timing of rate relief, and operating problems. Thus, in some years, the dividend payout ratio is high (when earnings are down) or low (when earnings have risen). We know that regulators set an allowed return on the book value of the common equity. Let us say that 12% is the return set by regulators. The utility, we noted above, is earning 16.8% on common equity. That should make us nervous about whether those earnings can be sustained. The company seems to be overearning and could be forced to lower prices. What is it paying out?

Dividend to common equity:

$$\frac{\text{Dividend paid on common stock}}{\text{Common stockholders' equity}} = \frac{\$\,15}{\$\,125} = 12.0\%$$

The utility is paying out a dividend return on its equity equivalent to the return regulators say it should earn. If the regulators lowered the profit to 12.0% on equity, the company would be paying out all its income. That would not be prudent policy. If we had just looked at the dividend payout ratio, we would have calculated:

$$\frac{\text{Dividend on common stock}}{\text{Income available to common stock}} = \frac{\$15}{\$21} = 71.4\%$$

and we would have concluded that the utility was paying out only part of its earnings and that the dividend was perfectly safe. That sort of conclusion could be altered by looking at the dividend as a percentage of common equity. A low dividend to equity ratio might be safer, at times, than a low payout ratio. (Usually, the dividend to common equity ratio is referred to as the dividend to book ratio, and calculations are made on a per share basis. That calculation will be discussed in the next chapter.)

Chapter 29

Market and Per Share Ratios and Ratings

... a stock is worth the present value of its future dividends, with future dividends dependent on future earnings...[9]

John Burr Williams

The financial statements tell us how much the company earns, where the money comes from and where it goes, and how much has been invested in the business. Statements do not tell us the present worth of nor do they indicate how much investors are willing to pay for the flow of cash coming to them from the business. Statements cannot tell us what the company would have to pay for additional funds, nor do they show the amount that could be realized from sale of the business. Managements need that information to make investment decisions, and regulators need the information to determine the utility's cost of capital.

Common Stock

The common stockholder is concerned with stock price, dividend, earnings per share and book value per share.

Price of stock in market	$32.00
Earnings per share (EPS)	4.00
Dividends per share	2.40
Book value per share	30.00

The *price/earnings ratio*, P/E, or multiple for the stock is the price divided by

earnings per share. In the above case:

$$\frac{Price}{Earnings\ per\ share} = \frac{\$32}{\$4} = 8x$$

Generally speaking, the market is willing to pay a higher multiple for each dollar of earnings when the company is extremely solid (risk is lower) or when earnings are growing rapidly. In the case of a rapid-growth company, investors may be willing to pay 16 times earnings on the theory that earnings are increasing so fast that by next year earnings will have doubled. Accordingly, the multiple is actually just eight times earnings for next year. In some instances the investor will pay a higher multiple because net for the current year is unduly depressed and will spring back quickly. Conversely, the investor may pay a low multiple if this year's earnings are unduly high and are expected to fall.

The reciprocal of the P/E ratio is the *E/P* ratio or earnings yield:

$$\frac{\text{Earnings per share}}{\text{Price}} = \frac{\$4}{\$32} = 0.125 = 12.5\%$$

If investors paid $32 for the stock and all earnings were distributed to shareholders, the return on the investment would be 12.5%. Some regulators have confused the earnings yield with the return that the investor expects. The investor buys not only current but also future earnings. Most investors expect earnings to rise in time. Accordingly, current earnings may not provide a return on current price that fully reflects the return expected by investors.

Because most utility stocks are purchased for current income, the *Dividend Yield* is an important element in the investment decision. Although the price-earnings ratio is meaningful, there can be temporary distortions in earnings per share (caused by weather, delays in rate relief, plant breakdowns, etc.). Investors could view the dividend as an indication of normalized earning power. If so, then it might be better to examine the dividend yield in relation to that of other stocks. The dividend yield is:

$$\frac{\text{Dividends per share}}{\text{Price}} = \frac{\$2.40}{\$32.00} = 0.075 = 7.5\%$$

Other things being equal, the investor will accept a lower current dividend yield from an investment in a strong company with good prospects for growth than from an investment in a weaker company with poorer prospects. A lower risk produces a lower return. The prospect of more income in the future will induce investors to accept less income in the present.

The *Total Return* for a stock is the current dividend yield plus growth in value of the shares. Thus, assuming that earnings, dividends and stock price move together over time, a stock with a 7.5% dividend yield and a 5% anticipated growth rate would have an expected total return of 12.5% per year.

Investors often look at the *Book Value* of a stock. (Book value is the total amount of stockholders' equity, as shown on the books of the corporation, divided by the number of outstanding shares of common stock.) In many businesses, book value is only of academic interest, because changes in the value and earning power of assets make it likely that a purchaser of the corporation would pay far more or far less than book value for outstanding shares. In the utility business, rates of return are allowed on book value, and, therefore, book value is a key to the potential earning power of the company. The market/book ratio is:

$$\frac{\text{Price of stock}}{\text{Book value of stock}} = \frac{\$32}{\$30} = 1.067 = 106.7\%$$

The *Market/Book Ratio* indicates to existing shareholders whether new common stock financing will increase or will dilute book value and earning power of their shares. The ratio also indicates to regulators whether return being earned is satisfactory (*i.e.*, high enough to bring the stock at least to book value). In the following example, new stock offerings are made at 50%, 100%, and 150% of book value. The regulator allows the company to earn a 15% return on equity.

| | Before Stock Offering | Situation After $1,000 Is Raised by Sale of Stock at | | |
		50% of Book Value	100% of Book Value	150% of Book Value
Common equity	$1,000	$2,000	$2,000	$2,000
Number of shares	100	300	200	166.7
Book value per share	$10.00	$6.67	$10.00	$12.00
Net income	$150	$300	$300	$300
Earnings per share	$1.50	$1.00	$1.50	$1.80

A low market price/book value ratio means that new financing will be dilutionary. On the other hand, if the ratio is low, the company probably is underearning and potential for improvement exists. The investor must judge whether financing plans will lead to considerable dilution and whether potential for improvement can be realized within a reasonable time.

Sometimes it is easier to calculate ratios from information per share than to go to the statements of the company. The *Return on Book Value* is roughly equivalent to return on equity:

$$\frac{\text{Earnings per share}}{\text{Book value per share}} = \frac{\$4}{\$32} = 0.133 = 13.3\%$$

It is not necessarily identical to return on equity, because the numerator is based on average shares outstanding and the denominator on year end shares, but it is close enough for most purposes.

The *Dividend Payout Ratio* approximates the percentage of earnings available to common stock that is paid out in dividends:

$$\frac{\text{Dividends per share}}{\text{Earnings per share}} = \frac{\$\,2.40}{\$\,4.00} = 0.60 = 60\%$$

Again, the calculation may not produce exactly the same results as using the total dividends paid as a percentage of reported net income, but it is good enough to use.

The *Dividend/Book Ratio* calculates a dividend yield on the book value of the common stock:

$$\frac{\text{Dividend}}{\text{Book Value}} = \frac{\$2.40}{\$30.00} = 0.08 = 8\%$$

Regulators determine return on the book equity of the utility. If the regulator grants a 12% return on equity, and if book value per share is $30, then the utility should earn $3.60 per share (12% of $30), at least in this simplification. Here the dividend is only 8% of book value, which is well below the profit level set by the regulator (and even farther below the $4 or 13.3% return on equity being earned). A high dividend/book ratio may seem generous on the part of the utility, but it makes the dividend vulnerable to reduction if business becomes bad or if regulators decide to lower the allowed return.

The various market ratios are affected by the prospects of individual companies and by alternative investments that are available. A change in prospects for a company or for an entire industry will cause investors to pay higher or lower P/E ratios or to accept lower or higher dividend yields. A change in the returns offered by alternative investments would have the same effect.

The following table illustrates the effect on stock price and ratios of a shift in bond yields from 10% to 13% to 8%, in cases where the alternative is to invest in bonds and investors demand a dividend yield on stocks one percentage point below the interest rate on bonds.

	10% bond yield	*13% bond yield*	*8% bond yield*
Dividend per share	$2.40	2.40	$2.40
Earnings per share	4.00	4.00	4.00
Book value	30.00	30.00	30.00
Stock price	26.67	20.00	34.29
Dividend yield	9.00%	12.00%	7.00 %
P/E ratio	6.67 x	5.00 x	8.57 x
E/P ratio	15.00 %	20.00 %	11.70 %
Market/book ratio	88.90 %	66.70%	114.30 %

The same logic would apply if a utility has steady earnings, and the returns from other investments rise sharply. Assume that investors were accustomed to buying stock in manufacturing firms that could only earn 10% on stockholders' equity and that investors pay a 10% earnings yield (a P/E of 10x) for that level of earnings. Because utility shares supposedly involve lower risk, investors are satisfied when the utility earns 9% on equity, and the stock sells at a 9% earnings yield (a P/E of 11.1x). If the earnings of the manufacturing firm surge upward to 15% on equity, and higher yields are available from alternatives such as bonds, the investor would now expect a 15% earnings yield (a P/E of 6.67x) on the manufacturer's shares. Because of regulation, however, the utility cannot raise its return above 9%. Yet, the investor demands a higher return (14%) on the market value of the utility investment. Consequently, new investors lower the price they are willing to pay for the utility stock, and thus obtain a competitive earnings yield from the shares. In fact, that is what happened to utility stocks in the period from the late 1960s to the early 1980s.

	Pricing of Utility Stock When	
	Manufacturers earn 10% and their shares sell at 10% E/P	*Manufacturers earn 15% and their shares sell at 15% E/P*
Utility Stock		
Earnings per share	$ 0.90	$ 0.90
Book value	$10.00	$10.00
Stock price	$10.00	$ 6.43
Market/book ratio	100.00 %	64.30 %
E/P ratio	9.00 %	14.00 %

Fixed Income

Bonds provide a fixed return (interest) if held to maturity. The *Coupon Yield* is based on the face value of the bond. For example, the 12% series first mortgage bond, due January 1, 2000, pays 12% a year on every $100 of face value. On January 1, 2000, the investor will get back $100 for every $100 face value of bonds issued. Some investors do not choose to hold the bond to maturity and, therefore, sell it at whatever market price is offered. The price offered rises and falls with interest rates. Suppose the market for a bond is as follows:

$$\text{Years to maturity } = \qquad 20$$
$$\text{Coupon } = \qquad 12\%$$
$$\text{Price of bond per}$$
$$\$100 \text{ of face value } = \qquad 90\%$$

If we ignore the payment of a bond at maturity, we calculate *Current Interest Yield* as:

$$\frac{\text{Coupon rate}}{\text{Price of bond}} = \frac{12}{90} = 0.133 = 13.3\%$$

If the acceptable interest rate on the above quality of bond rises to 15%, the price for the bond would have to decline to $80 to give new investors a 15% return.

$$\frac{\text{Coupon}}{\text{Price}} = \frac{12}{80} = 0.15 = 15\%$$

The current yield, however, does not really indicate the total return picture. If investors hold the bond to maturity, they receive not only the coupon every year, but also an extra $10 (in the first case) or $20 (in the second) because they paid less than $100 for the bond. That capital gain is really part of the return expected by investors. The return that includes both coupon and capital gain (or loss) is *Yield to Maturity*. Tables provide accurate yields to maturity. The investor, however, can calculate an approximate yield to maturity.

Where:
  $100 = Face value of bond
  C   = Coupon rate (for each $100 of face value)
  P   = Price of bond
  Y   = Years to maturity

The approximate yield to maturity (A) equals

$$\frac{C + \left(\dfrac{100 - P}{Y} \right)}{\left(\dfrac{100 + P}{2} \right)}$$

In the above example where P = 80:

$$A = \cfrac{12 + \left(\cfrac{100 - 80}{20}\right)}{\left(\cfrac{100 + 80}{2}\right)} = \frac{13}{90} = 0.144 = 14.4\%$$

and in the example where P = 90:

$$A = \cfrac{12 + \left(\cfrac{100 - 90}{20}\right)}{\left(\cfrac{100 + 90}{2}\right)} = \frac{12.5}{95} = 0.132 = 13.2\%$$

Yields calculated by the above formula should be regarded as approximations, and used only when bond tables are not available.

Bonds have quality *Ratings* determined by rating agencies. The largest agencies — Moody's and Standard & Poor's — use letter guides, in declining order of quality:

Moody's	S&P	Comment
Aaa	AAA	Best quality, extremely strong.
Aa	AA	High quality, very strong ability to pay.
A	A	Upper medium grade, strong capacity to pay.
Baa	BBB	Medium grade, adequate strength.
Ba	BB	Speculative, future not assured.
B	B	Speculative, undesirable as an investment.

A plus or minus or a number (the lower the better) after the letter rating is often added to indicate further gradations in quality. Ratings below Baa and BBB are not considered to be of investment quality. Bonds with ratings that begin with the letter C (not shown here) are of companies in or near bankruptcy or are extremely speculative in nature. Many investors are prohibited by law from buying bonds with ratings below certain limits.

A utility may have several kinds of debt with varying degrees of seniority. First mortgage bonds have the greatest seniority and, in theory, must be paid before securities junior to them. Other kinds of debt have lower credit standings and lower credit ratings. Thus, the investor should not be surprised to see the senior debt with a Aa rating and the junior debt of the same utility rated A. For that matter, the ratings for particular issues may differ from rating agency to rating agency. As a rule, ratings do not differ sharply, but it is not unusual for a bond to be rated Aa by one agency and A by another. That is called a split rating.

The market demands a higher yield from riskier bonds. Therefore, bonds with lower ratings generally provide higher yields to maturity than bonds with higher ratings. A drop in rating (the ratings are re-examined and revised periodically) can lead to a drop in bond price (to produce the higher interest rate). Accordingly, investors watch the trend in financial ratios for the companies in which they invest.

Utilities also seek to keep financial ratios at levels that will retain or improve ratings. A lower bond rating might make the bond difficult to sell to certain investors and might force those investors to sell the bonds if the rating fell below desired levels. When investors expect a bond rating to change, they adjust the price that they will pay for the bond (thus requiring a different yield). Accordingly, some bonds provide yields that seem out of line with their present ratings.

Preferred stocks are like bonds in that they pay fixed dividends, but most preferred stocks have no set life. A preferred stock may remain outstanding for the life of the corporation, or it may have some sort of redemption feature that calls for the redemption of the stocks by a certain year. For the standard, non-redeemable preferred stock, investors simply calculate a dividend yield:

$$\frac{\text{Dividend}}{\text{Market Price}}$$

When the preferred has redemption features, investors will have to make calculations similar to those for bonds. Preferred stocks have ratings, too, and investors will want to compare ratings and yields, to make sure that they are getting a higher yield if they are buying a lower quality preferred.

As a final point, the difference in yield between rating groups varies over time. When the market is worried about the state of the economy and the ability of weaker companies to weather the storm, a greater yield differential often exists between low and high quality fixed income securities. At such a time investors see greater risk in low quality securities and demand to be compensated accordingly.

Chapter **30**

Financial Results on the Books
and in the Marketplace

A public utility company is not permitted to enjoy the full fruits of its business successes inasmuch as regulation prohibits a return higher than that which is required to attract capital and provide service at reasonable rates. As a result, it does not have the resources available to absorb the major adversities which it encounters.[10]

Corporation Commission of Oklahoma

In the postwar era, investors in electric utilities rarely did extraordinarily well in the market, although profitability was respectable over time. In less than half the years did utilities provide a total return (dividends plus capital gains) greater than that of industrial stocks[11] just as utilities only occasionally earned a return on equity close to that for industrial corporations. Of course, return should be commensurate with risk, and the investor will accept a lower return for lower risk. At the same time, acceptable return is a relative concept and depends on the returns available elsewhere. When investors can get only 3% interest annually from a bond, they are satisfied to put their money in a utility that can earn 10% on stockholders' equity or in an industrial company that can earn 13% on stockholders' equity. If, on the other hand, investors can collect a 13% interest rate on bonds, they will not be satisfied with a utility investment that earns just 10% on shareholders' money while an industrial firm returns 17% on equity.

Current investors cannot affect the return being earned by the company in which they invest. If competitive returns rise, but the return earned by their company does not, current investors have lost the opportunity to do better elsewhere. New investors, however, can make a choice. New investors will not buy a security unless the expected flow of future income provides an adequate return on the price that they pay. Because future flow of income cannot be changed by the investor to provide an adequate rate of return, the investor instead regulates the price for the security.

Market Performance

Table 30-1 provides information on market activity in the postwar period (1946-1990). Table 30-2 summarizes that same information for five year periods.

In the earliest period (1946-1950), the economy recovered from World War II and fears of renewed depression. Utility holding companies were being broken up, and shares of operating companies were being distributed to security holders. The deliberate policy of the Federal Reserve kept down interest rates. Price controls were being dismantled. The earnings and dividends of industrial firms rose rapidly as did profitability. Gains in the utility industry were more moderate, and return earned on equity was far less than in the industrial sector. At the same time, the return offered by bonds was low and steady. In that period, industrial shares sold at roughly one fifth above book value and utilities sold at close to book value, an indication that industrial companies were probably earning more than cost of capital, while utility earnings were about equal to cost of capital. Utilities sold at consistently higher P/E ratios and provided a slightly lower dividend yield than that of industrials. The total return on an investment in industrial stocks was far greater than that produced by utility stocks or by bonds.

The next period (1951-1955) may have been more representative. The Treasury and the Federal Reserve reached an accord freeing the Federal Reserve System from the responsibility for keeping down interest rates. The rise in long term interest rates, however, was still modest. The profitability of industrial corporations (measured by return on equity) dropped but remained well above that for utilities. Profitability of electric utilities rose. Electric utility stocks maintained higher P/E ratios and provided lower dividend yields than did industrial shares. Both utility and industrial stocks sold above book value. Again the industrials provided a higher total return for investors.

At the beginning of the second half of the Eisenhower Administration, industrial profitability declined further while utility profitability continued to rise. In 1956-1960, utility and industrial shares sold at similar multiples, although utility shares provided slightly higher dividend yields. For the first time since 1936, the dividend yield on electric utility stocks in 1957 was lower on average than the yield for utility bonds.

Interest rates also rose, but not enough to discourage investors who bid the prices for industrial and utility shares up above book value. Electric utility shares also provided a better total return than either industrial stocks or bonds. In fact, the supposedly golden age for utility shares was 1957-1962, during which total return averaged 16.1% a year vs. 8.2% a year for industrials and 4.5% for bonds.

The golden age ended in the 1961-1965 period. Interest rates rose slightly. Return in the utility sector picked up, but not substantially. On the other hand, industrial companies made a dramatic recovery in profitability, despite a poor beginning. Investors obviously had euphoric expectations, because market/book ratios and multiples reached their highest levels, levels which have yet to be equalled since the Great Depression. In the period, electric utility shares sold at higher market/book ratios than industrial stocks. On a total return basis, industrial stocks once again did better than utility stocks and bonds.

By 1966-1970, interest rates began a sharp upturn that was not accompanied by a commensurate rise in return on equity for either the industrial or the utility sector. Oddly enough, despite dull corporate results, the period marked the beginning of the era of performance investing — the go-go years on Wall Street. Utility shares were shoved aside because investors knew that the group could not provide the necessary growth for superior performance. Instead, investors put their money into shares with greater risk. The market/book ratio began to fall for all shares, but even more precipitously for utilities. The P/E ratio for utility stocks declined while that for industrials issues held. As for total return on investment, industrial issues and bonds outperformed utility stocks.

As the 1970s began, the illness of the utility sector became more evident. In 1971-1975, prices for utility stocks fell below book value, as return on utility equity declined while yields on bonds rose further. Industrial companies, on the other hand, were able to raise profitability. With bonds providing a high yield alternative, the market revalued equities. Multiples and market/book ratios fell. Yields rose. Bonds gave investors a higher total return than did industrial stocks, and utilities provided an even lower total return than that for industrial shares.

In 1976-1980, interest rates continued to rise, profitability for utility companies was flat and profitability for industrial companies improved. Because neither group was able to earn a return that rose in line with bond yields, market/ book ratios and multiples slid, and dividend yields rose. Nevertheless, industrials closed above book value in every postwar year. On the other hand, electric utility stocks closed at a price below book value in each year 1973-1980. In terms of total return, industrial stocks again outpaced utility shares and bonds.

In 1981-1985, roles reversed, as utility shares responded to improved profitability, industrial returns declined and interest rates fell from record levels. For the first time since 1972, the price of utility shares rose above book value. During this same period, returns on equity hit postwar highs for utilities, while industrial returns tumbled from the exceptionally high levels of the late 1970s.

The 1986-1990 period was one of lower interest rates, combined with rising industrial and falling utility profitability. The average utility stock did about as well as the average industrial stock, anyway, probably because investors bought utilities for their dividend yields, and the stocks responded to rapidly declining bond yields. Industrial stocks pushed up to record high market/book ratios. Utility stocks rose above book value, but are nowhere near the heady market/book ratios of the early 1960s.

Credit Ratings

Investors in bonds expect to assume an interest rate risk. They want the credit-worthiness of their investment to remain stable or to improve. A higher bond rating indicates more strength. Accordingly, investors will pay more for the

Table 30 - 1
Stock and Bond Yields and Performance
1946-1990

	S&P 400 Industrials					Moody's Electric Utilities					Bonds	
Year	Total Return (%)	Year-end Market/ Book Ratio (%)	Return on Year-end Common Equity (%)	Year-end P/E Ratio (x)	Year-end Dividend Yield (%)	Total Return (%)	Year-end Market/ Book Ratio (%)	Return on Year-end Common Equity (%)	Year-end P/E Ratio (%)	Year-end Dividend Yield (%)	Total Return Long-Term Corporate Bonds (%)	Year-end Yield on Moody's Average Utility Bond (%)
	(1)	(2)	(3)	(4)	(5)	(6)	(7)	(8)	(9)	(10)	(11)	(12)
1946	-8.3	132	11.2	11.8	4.45	9.6	119	8.0	14.9	4.52	1.7	2.77
1947	8.3	122	15.4	7.9	5.48	-17.0	92	7.7	11.9	6.17	-2.3	3.02
1948	5.9	104	16.9	6.1	6.19	8.6	93	7.9	11.8	6.22	4.1	3.06
1949	16.0	109	14.0	7.7	6.87	23.0	107	8.3	13.0	5.50	3.3	2.79
1950	32.9	123	16.5	7.5	7.27	6.5	104	8.8	11.8	6.00	2.1	2.87
1951	18.5	130	13.5	9.6	6.02	16.0	110	7.9	13.9	5.61	-2.7	3.27
1952	16.5	133	12.2	11.0	5.42	17.5	122	8.4	14.4	5.07	3.5	3.19
1953	-2.5	120	12.4	9.7	5.91	10.0	126	8.8	14.2	5.28	3.4	3.37
1954	55.6	169	12.2	13.8	4.24	25.5	148	9.1	16.2	4.50	5.4	3.10
1955	34.8	193	14.3	13.5	4.02	8.4	148	9.7	15.4	4.60	0.5	3.34
1956	7.2	190	13.3	14.3	4.04	3.9	142	9.7	14.6	4.84	-6.8	3.93
1957	-10.5	146	12.0	12.1	4.52	7.7	138	9.4	14.8	4.89	8.7	4.29
1958	41.9	192	9.6	20.0	3.14	36.9	178	9.8	18.3	3.87	-2.2	4.39
1959	12.7	200	10.8	18.6	3.02	3.0	170	9.8	17.2	4.01	-1.0	4.86
1960	-1.6	182	10.1	18.1	3.26	20.9	191	10.8	18.6	3.57	9.1	4.58
1961	26.5	217	9.7	22.5	2.79	33.0	235	10.3	22.9	2.88	4.8	4.62
1962	-9.9	181	10.5	17.2	3.34	0.1	217	10.7	20.4	3.18	8.0	4.41
1963	23.7	208	11.1	18.7	3.05	9.4	221	10.8	20.5	3.25	2.2	4.49
1964	16.3	223	12.1	18.5	2.97	16.3	236	11.1	21.4	3.18	4.8	4.54
1965	13.0	226	12.6	17.9	3.34	2.8	227	11.7	19.4	3.50	-0.5	4.82

Year												
1966	-10.4	187	12.9	14.5	3.05	-4.1	203	12.1	16.8	3.94	0.2	5.65
1967	26.8	220	11.8	18.7	2.97	-3.3	179	12.2	14.7	4.52	-5.0	6.57
1968	10.5	225	12.3	18.3	2.84	10.5	180	11.5	15.6	4.40	2.6	6.85
1969	-7.3	196	11.9	16.6	3.28	-14.2	140	11.4	12.2	5.47	-8.1	8.39
1970	2.6	192	10.3	18.7	3.17	10.3	138	10.8	12.9	5.33	18.4	8.45
1971	15.0	204	10.8	18.9	2.77	2.0	129	10.8	12.0	5.62	11.0	7.92
1972	19.9	226	11.7	19.3	2.48	3.4	119	11.0	10.8	5.87	7.3	7.48
1973	-14.7	174	14.2	12.3	3.35	-21.2	85	10.5	8.1	8.28	1.1	8.17
1974	-26.5	113	14.2	8.0	4.97	-24.4	56	10.4	5.4	11.73	-3.1	10.02
1975	36.8	142	12.1	11.8	3.73	47.3	73	10.3	7.2	8.97	14.6	9.87
1976	22.6	157	14.0	11.2	3.65	28.4	86	10.6	8.1	7.92	18.7	8.61
1977	-8.2	127	14.0	9.1	4.90	11.2	87	11.0	7.9	8.33	3.8	8.65
1978	7.5	120	14.6	8.2	5.16	-3.9	75	10.8	7.0	10.01	0.3	9.67
1979	18.5	123	16.5	7.5	5.27	4.8	69	11.0	6.3	11.24	-2.2	11.68
1980	33.0	143	14.9	9.6	4.24	8.1	65	10.7	6.1	12.26	0.5	14.48
1981	-6.7	118	14.4	8.2	5.11	19.7	70	12.4	5.6	12.52	2.3	15.77
1982	20.2	133	11.1	11.9	4.56	34.9	85	13.1	6.4	10.87	35.5	13.55
1983	22.9	153	12.1	12.6	3.96	14.5	87	14.3	6.1	11.11	9.3	13.48
1984	3.6	150	14.6	10.4	3.99	22.7	94	14.9	6.3	10.44	16.2	12.96
1985	30.1	186	12.1	15.4	3.36	28.1	108	14.4	7.6	9.17	25.4	10.82
1986	18.6	216	11.6	18.6	3.02	29.9	126	14.5	8.7	7.89	16.3	8.96
1987	9.2	213	15.1	14.1	3.05	-9.1	105	12.7	8.2	9.68	1.9	10.99
1988	15.6	230	19.1	12.1	3.03	16.6	115	8.6	13.4	8.63	9.8	10.02
1989	28.9	278	18.2	15.3	2.78	30.6	136	12.4	11.0	7.22	13.3	9.31
1990	-0.9	255	16.1	15.8	3.20	3.2	140	10.7	13.0	7.47	7.4	9.57

Sources

Moody's, Standard & Poors, Merrill Lynch estimates. Total return on long term corporate bonds 1946-1976 from: Roger G. Ibbotson and Rex A. Sinquefield, Stocks, Bonds, Bills and Inflation: The Past (1926-1976) and the Future (1977-2000) (Charlottesville: Financial Analysts Research Foundation, 1977), and Merrill Lynch Corporate Index – All Corporate Bonds for 1977-1990.

Table 30 - 2

Stock and Bond Yields and Performance by Periods
1946-1990

	1946-1950	1951-1955	1956-1960	1961-1965	1966-1970	1971-1975	1976-1980	1981-1985	1986-1990
	(1)	(2)	(3)	(4)	(5)	(6)	(7)	(8)	(9)
Total return/yr. (%)									
Industrials	10.2	23.1	8.6	13.3	3.6	3.4	13.4	13.2	13.9
Utilities	5.3	15.7	13.8	11.7	-0.7	-1.4	9.2	23.8	13.2
Bonds	1.8	2.0	1.4	3.8	1.2	6.1	4.0	17.1	9.2
Market/book ratio (%)									
Industrials	118	149	182	211	204	172	134	148	237
Utilities	103	131	164	227	168	92	76	89	123
Return on equity (%)									
Industrials	14.8	12.9	11.2	11.2	11.8	12.6	14.8	12.9	15.9
Utilities	8.1	8.8	9.9	10.9	11.6	10.6	10.8	13.8	11.8
P/E Ratio (X)									
Industrials	8.2	11.5	16.6	19.0	17.4	14.1	9.1	11.7	15.2
Utilities	12.7	14.8	16.7	20.9	14.4	8.7	7.1	6.4	10.7
Yields (%)									
Industrial dividend	6.1	5.9	3.6	3.1	3.1	3.5	4.6	4.2	3.0
Utility dividend	5.7	5.0	4.2	3.2	4.7	8.7	10.0	10.8	8.2
Utility bond yield	2.9	3.2	4.4	4.6	7.2	8.7	10.6	13.3	9.8
ROE - Bond yield (%)									
Industrials	11.9	9.7	6.8	6.6	4.6	3.9	4.2	-0.4	6.1
Utilities	5.2	5.6	5.5	6.3	4.4	1.9	0.2	0.5	2.0
Div. yield-Bond yield (%)									
Industrials	3.2	2.7	-0.8	-1.5	-4.1	5.2	-6.0	-9.1	-6.8
Utilities	2.8	1.8	-0.2	-1.4	-2.5	0.0	-0.6	-2.5	-1.6

better quality issue. Even if interest rates remain stable, bond investors can show a profit or loss if the bond rating rises or falls.

Table 30-3 shows the rating distribution of a sample of operating electric utilities that are not associated with holding companies. The same companies represented more than 70% of the industry's operating income and long term debt in 1975.[12] Between 1946 and 1950, the percentage of ratings in the two highest quality groups (Aaa and Aa) remained static. In the decade from 1950 to 1960, the sample changed drastically in quality and quantity because of the addition of several companies, and because the quality of the industry improved dramatically in the eyes of the credit experts. Further improvement took place through 1965. Thus, from the end of World War II to the end of 1965, investors were able to depend on a rising trend of credit-worthiness to add value to utility bonds. A modest decline in ratings began in 1965-1970, and a disastrous falloff occurred through 1975. Many seem to believe that the 1973-1975 drop in credit-worthiness (induced by the Yom Kippur War, the oil embargo, a drop in demand for electricity, higher interest rates, and Con Edison's omission of a dividend) produced the low point for the industry. In reality bond ratings continued to decline afterwards, despite a brief upturn in the mid 1980s. Weak utilities with double or triple B ratings find it expensive to sell debt, at times, because many institutions will not buy such low quality securities.

What caused the decline in credit-worthiness? A basic reason is that utilities continued to rely on debt ratios that were inappropriate to the changing circumstances. The companies concentrated on maintaining debt as a given percentage of capital without taking into account that coverages could not be maintained when higher interest rates increased unless the debt ratio were reduced. In addition, plant writeoffs forced by regulators wiped out equity that should have provided a cushion for bondholders during hard times. Thus, when the industry ran into hard times, bond investors suffered along with equity investors. Fortunately, with interest rates down and a modest spending program scheduled for the 1990s, the industry should be able to stabilize or improve its financial standing. Many companies are in the midst of programs to replace high cost debt and preferred stock with lower yielding securities, which should raise interest coverage ratios. Most utilities would prefer to raise their equity ratios, rather than rely on debt as much as in the past, which should help raise credit standings too.

Table 30-3

Debit Ratings and Ratios

Percentage Distribution of Long Term Debt Outstanding by Rating Category
(Year-end, 73 Independent Electric Companies, Unweighted, in %)

	1946 (1)	1950 (2)	1955 (3)	1960 (4)	1965 (5)	1970 (6)	1975 (7)	1980 (8)	1985 (9)	1990 (10)
Moody's Ratings (%)										
Aaa	17.2	13.8	12.1	16.2	19.3	15.5	5.1	1.4	6.8	0.0
Aa	34.5	37.9	47.0	57.4	69.3	62.6	44.0	35.6	34.2	27.4
A	39.7	43.0	33.3	20.6	7.2	18.9	32.5	46.6	32.9	38.4
Baa	6.9	10.3	7.6	7.4	4.2	3.0	18.4	16.4	19.2	30.1
Ba or lower	1.7	0.0	0.0	0.0	0.0	0.0	0.0	0.0	6.9	4.1
	100.0	100.0	100.0	100.0	100.0	100.0	100.0	100.0	100.0	100.0
Standard & Poor's Ratings (%)										
AAA					19.2	14.0	0.0	0.0	0.0	0.0
AA					68.0	65.6	39.1	32.9	35.6	27.4
A					8	17.4	44.2	43.8	32.9	34.2
BBB					4.8	3.0	16.7	21.9	23.3	34.3
BB or lower					0.0	0.0	0.0	1.4	8.2	4.1
					100.0	100.0	100.0	100.0	100.0	100.0
Percentage of Ratings (%)										
Aaa and Aa (Moody's)	51.7	51.7	59.1	73.6	88.6	78.1	49.5	37.0	41.0	27.4
AAA and AA (S&P)	—	—	—	—	87.2	79.6	39.1	32.9	35.6	27.4

Ratios for Industry (all departments)

Debt Ratio:

Long term debt as % of permanent capitalization (excludes short term debt)	46.0	48.9	51.0	52.6	51.7	55.3	52.6	50.2	48.6	49.3
Total debt as % of total capitalization (includes short term debt)	46.2	49.3	52.2	53.4	52.4	56.4	53.7	51.8	49.1	50.4

Pretax interest coverage ratio

Operating income (x)	4.57E	4.79	5.44	5.03	5.15	2.80	2.25	1.94	2.44	2.38
Income before interest charges (x)	4.85E	5.14	5.68	5.17	5.27	3.11	2.66	2.53	3.10	2.50

Notes:
When ratings are not available, sample size is reduced, to 58 in 1946 and 1950, 66 in 1955, 68 in 1960. Income before interest charges includes all allowance for funds used during construction.

Sources:
Moody's, Standard & Poor's, EIA, FPC, EEI.

Chapter **31**

Summary

... the current regulatory climate is sending a very clear signal to utility stockholders, investors and management. That signal is that if you want to protect your economic interest you should liquidate the utility business you are in.[13]

Charles J. Cicchetti

The electric utility's financial structure is based on the heavy use of fixed income securities. The industry also is capital intensive and requires large amounts of fixed assets to produce revenues. As a result, the industry bears a heavy load of fixed costs: interest, preferred dividends, depreciation, and taxes on real property.

Because profitability is controlled and expenditures on long-lived new plant are often huge in relation to funds generated by operations, utilities have not been able to finance the bulk of their capital needs from internal sources. The companies must raise large sums of money in the markets on a regular basis. The need to raise large sums of money at a time of rising capital costs combined with unexpectedly poor demand for power put a crimp on profitability and reduced the coverage of interest charges.

As Table 31-1 shows, in the period from 1965 to 1970, the financial ratios of the electric utilities dropped precipitously. Companies pushed up the debt ratios. More money was tied up in incomplete plant (construction work in progress). The industry became less capable of funding its needs from internal sources. Interest coverage ratios collapsed because interest rates rose by far more than the return earned by the utilities on the money invested. Furthermore, even the reported earnings of the companies fell in quality, as non-cash credits became a larger percentage of earnings. From 1970 on, utilities reduced their use of debt, but most other ratios continued to deteriorate. The return earned on assets rose, but not by an amount sufficient to offset the sharp increase in fixed charges. As a result, profitability for the common shareholders dropped. To make matters worse, the decline in return on stockholders' equity occurred despite the inflation of earnings by non-cash credits. The market's reaction to the deterioration in financial strength and profitability, in the face of the availability of rising returns elsewhere, was predictable. Prices for utility stocks fell as investors, who de-

Table 31-1

Financial Data
Electric Utility Industry
(All Departments)
1965-1990

	1965	1970	1975	1980	1985	1990
Capitalization %						
Long term debt	50.6%	53.0%	50.8%	48.6%	48.1%	48.1%
Short term debt	1.8	3.4	2.9	3.2	1.0	2.3
Preferred and Peference stock	9.3	9.5	12.1	11.7	9.5	7.3
Common equity	38.3	34.1	34.3	36.5	41.4	42.3
	100.0	100.0	100.0	100.0	100.0	100.0
Construction work in progress as						
% of net electric plant	5%	14%	20%	29%	26%	7%
Internal sources of funds as % of						
construction expenditure						
Including AFUDC	55%	30%	42%	39%	70%	78%
Excluding AFUDC	54	26	36	29	61	77
Pretax interest coverage						
—all debt						
Operating Income	5.15x	2.80x	2.25x	1.94x	2.42x	2.38x
Income before interest charges	5.27	3.11	2.66	2.53	3.02	2.50
Rates of return on:						
Average net plant	7.0%	7.4%	8.4%	9.5%	11.2%	9.0
Average common equity	12.5	11.8	11.1	11.4	12.5	10.2
Net income for common stock						
Dividend payout ratio	65%	68%	67%	76%	76%	95%
% of net/common from AFUDC	4	20	35	55	50	13
Average cost of money						
(Moody's)						
New debt	4.7%	8.9%	9.8%	13.1%	11.8%	9.8%
New preferred	—	9.0	10.6	12.3	10.1	9.3
E/P ratio (common)	5.1	8.7	15.2	16.4	14.4	8.1

Note:
  Based on EIA date except for Moody's.

Sources:
  Moody's, FPC, EEI, EIA.

manded higher returns, marked down the stocks until the returns were adequate to attract new investors. By the late 1980s, the reported numbers looked even worse, but that was because of numerous writeoffs, rather than because of dreadful operating results. Investors seemed willing to look beyond the reported results to earnings and cash flows from continuing operations. The fall in interest rates, as well as the seeming stabilization of the industry's finances, caused the market to pay more for the securities than any time since the early 1970s.

During the dramatic declines of the 1960s and 1970s, analysts, academics, and industry executives applied the ruler method of projection. They extrapolated from the trend line and predicted disaster. They awaited a plethora of bankruptcies or even nationalization. Yet, it should have been obvious that the electric industry could not afford to continue to invest in projects that produced a return below the cost of capital. Investors would refuse to buy the securities needed to finance the projects. As shown in Table 31-1, conditions did stabilize.

The industry is paying off short term debt, refinancing high cost securities through the sale of lower cost issues, and cutting down construction projects to reduce the need for outside financing. A handful of companies are in difficulty, having written down major portions of their assets, unable to pay or continue dividends, but most companies are financially sound.

As a result of two decades of financial difficulties, though, utilities have modified their strategies for growth. Most are reluctant to commit funds to large, regulated projects for fear that the capital invested will not receive proper compensation. They, instead, hand the job to non-utility generators, a strategy that seems to reduce the risks to the utility but also diminishes the utility's opportunity to increase rate base and make earnings grow. Utilities are far more careful, now, than they were when everyone was building a nuclear plant, when regulators rarely questioned a decision, and when sales always went up.

Notes

[1]Haskins & Sells, *Public Utilities Manual* (New York: Deloitte Haskins & Sells, 1977), p. 33.

[2]The Averch-Johnson effect was first hypothesized in a 1962 article: Harvey Averch and Leland L. Johnson, "Behavior of the Firm under Regulatory Constraint," *American Economic Review* (December 1962).

[3]"From the financial point of view ... earnings are limited but ... more stable than most industrial companies, bonds ... are widely used in capital structures, and the risk is usually less than for industrial companies because of the essential nature of the service ... and protection against competition." Ralph E. Badger, Harold W. Torgerson, and Harry G. Guthmann, *Investment Principles and Practices* (Englewood Cliffs, N.J.: Prentice Hall, 1961) p. 296.

[4]Badger, Torgerson and Guthmann, *op. cit.*, p. 273.

[5]Ambrose Bierce, *The Devil's Dictionary* (New York: Dover, 1958), p. 26.

[6]Haskins & Sells, *op. cit.*, p. 7.

[7]Benjamin Graham, David L. Dodd, and Sidney Cottle, *Security Analysis* (New York: McGraw-Hill, 1962), p. 1.

[8]Graham, Dodd and Cottle, *op. cit.*, p. 386.

[9]John Burr Williams, *The Theory of Investment Value* (Cambridge: Harvard U. Press, 1938) p. 397.

[10]Corporation Commission of the State of Oklahoma, *Application of Public Service Company of Oklahoma* (Cause No. 27068, Order No. 206560, Jan. 15, 1982), p. 63.

[11]The total returns for utilities are understated to the extent that in the period 1946-1965, many utilities sold new stock to shareholders at a below-market price. Shareholders who did not choose to exercise their rights to purchase the shares could sell those rights, thereby adding to income. In the late 1960s, rights offerings lost popularity. The addition of the value from sale of rights to total return would not change the conclusions of the discussion.

[12]For details, see Leonard S. Hyman and Carmine J. Grigoli, "The Credit Standing of Electric Utilities," *Public Utilities Fortnightly*, March 3, 1977, pp. 24-30.

[13]Charles J. Cicchetti, "Conservation Financing — Its Rate Impact," in *Edison Electric Institute, Proceedings, Sixteenth Financial Conference, October 4-7, 1981* (Washington, D.C.: EEI, 1982), p. 7.

Part Six

The Future of the Electric Utility Industry

Chapter **32**

Introduction

The data indicate that actually generated electricity at current prices, as a way to deliver energy services is already uncompetitive in several energy service markets. Raising the price may just exacerbate the problem. As one of us has suggested. "To say you can solve utilities' problems by raising rates is much like saying we could solve the problems of Chrysler by raising the price of their automobiles." [1]

Roger W. Sant

People tend to project the present into the future. In the late 1950s, and 1960s, everyone knew that the price of electricity would continue to decline as electric utilities continued to find new efficiencies. In the 1970s, this section would have been titled "The Electric Utility Industry: Does it Have a Future?" Too many managements were fighting tooth-and-nail to continue strategies that seemed to make little business sense. Too many regulators either pursued short range political goals or showed little appreciation of the economics of the sector that they regulated. The coerciveness of central station power, the virtues of nuclear energy, and the date of the millennium when the lights would go out were favored subjects for theological-like debates. Meanwhile, customers reduced their consumption of power and the industry sank into a slough of financial despond. Economic and political conditions were unkind to the industry. As a large borrower of funds, the industry was hurt by high interest rates. As an industry that can only raise prices after a delay, it was hurt by inflation. As a major user of oil and gas, it had to spend scarce resources on projects that switched fuels rather than increased productive capability. Because its generating plants dammed running water, spewed out pollutants and produced radioactive waste, and because its transmission lines cut a swath through the landscape, the industry became a target for environmental activists.

During the Reagan administration, the drop in interest rates, de-emphasis of environmental protection activity, and the free market approach to energy policy all reduced the pressure on the hard-pressed electric utilities. But the improvement really came about because the industry was finishing the massive construction projects that had been such a drain on resources. No longer faced with cash outflows and outraged customers, the average electric company could plan for the future rather than fight battles for survival. Some did. Others simply abdicated their role in expansion to non-utility generators. Many channeled their efforts into diversification programs.

Meeting the challenges of the future may require more strategic planning, flexibility and business-like thinking than in the past. Demand could grow faster than anticipated, which would bring up the question of who will build the next power plant, assuming that building a power plant is the right answer. The utilities will have to demonstrate that they have the least cost answers before they act. They will have to deal with new environmental issues better than they dealt with the old ones. Customers want competitively priced electricity, not electricity priced to provide the correct return to the local utility. New power suppliers can help the utility meet its needs, or they can compete directly with the utility by selling directly to the utility's customers. Utilities will have to reprice their services. They may have to disintegrate their assets in the same way as the Bell System, in order to meet competitive rules. Utilities will have to transform themselves into responsive, flexible organizations. And regulators will have to reformulate policies that were relevant when electric utilities really were natural monopolies.

Chapter **33**

Building For the Future

Investment based on genuine long-term expectation is so difficult today as to be scarcely practicable...There is no clear evidence from experience that the investment policy which is socially advantageous coincides with that which is most profitable.[2]

John Maynard Keynes

Spending (in real terms) in the electric utility industry is a function of the need to:

♦ Increase plant to meet the requirements of new customers and the additional requirements of existing customers.
♦ Replace old equipment.
♦ Assure an adequate margin of safety in the level of service.
♦ Modify equipment in order to burn a more available fuel instead of a scarce fuel, or to reduce the emission of pollutants.

In 1990, electric utilities had an adequate reserve margin and heavily depended on coal as a fuel. By 2000, taking into account current construction plans and the industry's 1.8% forecasted growth in peak load, reserve will fall sharply, as can be seen in Table 33-1. Coal will remain the most important fuel. Non-utility generators will account for a small but increasing proportion of capacity and production. If anything, the official predictions for non-utility generation may be too low. The industry has reduced its demand forecast downward again and again since the days of the energy crisis of the 1970s. The sharp increases in the price of electricity and the resulting conservation effort certainly pushed demand down. So did the United States' retreat from heavy industry to a service-oriented economy. But we now face a different situation. The price of electricity may not rise much in real terms, while the decline of American industry may have run its course.

No doubt conservationists will argue, rightly, that Americans can do far more to control consumption of electricity and growth in peak load. In the depressed market for electricity that presently exists in some parts of the country, though, utilities want to encourage — not discourage — demand. Moreover, if they attempt to influence demand through the price mechanism, in the competitive market of

Table 33-1

Energy and Electricity Outlook
1990 - 2000

	1990	2000	Annual Rate of Growth
Energy consumption in USA (quadrillion BTU) (1)	84.4	95.6	1.3
Consumption of energy by electric utilities (quadrillion BTU) (1)	30.1	36.5	2.0
Electric utility production (billion Kwh) (2)	2,889.5	3,435.5	1.7
Summer peak capability (thousand MW)	685.1	774.1	1.2
Summer peak load (thousand MW)	545.5	651.1	1.8
Summer reserve margin (%)	25.5	18.9	--
Over 230 Kv high voltage transmission lines (thousands circuit miles)	147.3	159.9	0.8
Generating capacity by fuel - Summer (%)			
Coal	42.9	39.9	--
Nuclear	14.4	13.6	--
Hydro	10.5	8.8	--
Oil	8.5	8.1	--
Gas	8.2	10.1	--
Dual (oil and gas)	10.2	11.0	--
Misc. utility	2.6	3.9	--
Non-utility (all fuels)	2.7	4.6	--
Total	100.0	100.0	--
Production by fuel (%)			
Coal	53.8	53.5	--
Nuclear	19.8	19.5	--
Hydro	9.5	7.4	--
Oil	3.7	2.6	--
Gas	9.0	9.9	--
Misc. utility	0.4	0.6	--
Non-Utility (all fuels)	3.8	6.5	--
Total	100.0	100.0	--

Notes:
(1)   Total USA, EIA reference case projections.
(2)   Contiguous 48 states for this and all other lines.

Sources:
   Energy Information Administration, Department of Energy, *1991 Annual Energy Outlook* Washington, D.C.: EIA, March 1991), pp.43-44
   North American Electric Reliability Council, *Electricity Supply & Demand 1991-2000* (Princeton: NERC, July 1001), pp.8, el, 44, 121-123.

today they will drive customers to competing suppliers of energy during a period when the electric industry needs the revenue, but they may get the customers back when the energy surplus has shrunk and the customers want to return to a low, controlled price. A free market may not be conducive to rational decision making that involves facilities that last 30 or 40 years. Where demand is growing and electric utilities face the challenge of adding on new facilities without pushing up prices to pay for them, though, conservation and load management programs will be on the utility's agenda. Now that regulators are beginning to allow profits on these programs, the utilities may tackle them with greater enthusiasm. Demand side management has returned to respectability.

If we accept the industry's estimates, we must conclude that capacity will be less and less adequate for the nation's needs through 2000. A large fraction of the projected capacity additions, though, consists of facilities on which no work has begun. Either the utilities will speed up their construction plans, or they will have to give more of the business to nonutility generators. Greater transmission capability would make it easier to move electricity in volume, and would assure greater reliability of service, but little expansion of transmission is planned. Undoubtedly, if demand for electricity rises faster than expected, the utilities will respond by building peaking units and other small power stations that can be put up quickly, and non-utility suppliers will come forth with additional projects. Nuclear power will not play its hoped-for role in the energy market, but it should produce about one-fifth of our electricity. As of 1992, only one nuclear station remained under construction and likely to be completed within a reasonable time period. The nuclear option appears to have been killed off, a victim of cost overruns, technical difficulties, loss of public confidence, lack of political backing, the fall in fuel prices, and slower than expected growth in demand for electricity.[3] Loss of that option could become a problem if fuel prices rise, or foreign nations embargo their energy exports, or if fossil fuel combustion must be reduced in order to prevent damage to the climate. Resurrection of nuclear power will require revival of public confidence, a more certain licensing procedure, and design of a smaller, standardized, safer nuclear plant.

Capacity additions and capital spending may be turning up, after the declines in the late 1980s. Utilities that neglected their facilities because they could not spare money for non-essentials during a period of financial crisis are spending money to correct past neglect. Utilities that avoided generation expenditures for years, because they had overbuilt beyond need, now have to decide how to meet growing demand. Those utilities, moreover, that put off pollution control expenditures for so many years now have to meet the requirements of 1990 legislation, and doing so will cost billions. Even if non-utility generators bear more of the burden of expansion projected in Table 33-1, the utility industry's capital expenditure program will grow (see Table 33-2).

Admittedly, the industry's projections for demand may not fully take into account the potential of load management devices that can reduce demand during

Table 33-2

Estimated Spending and Financing
Investor - Owned Utilities
($ billions)

	Actual		Estimated		
Capital Spending	1989	1990	1991	1992	1993
Generation	$9.9	$8.9	$8.8	$9.4	$10.4
Transmission and distribution	11.2	12.0	12.7	13.6	13.9
Nuclear fuel	1.7	1.5	1.5	1.8	1.7
Miscellaneous	2.2	2.0	2.4	2.3	2.1
Total electric plant	25.0	24.4	25.4	27.1	28.1
Other utility plant	2.6	2.7	2.9	2.9	2.8
Total utility plant	27.6	27.1	28.3	30.0	30.9
Allowance for funds used during construction	(2.4)	(2.0	(1.6)	(1.6)	(1.7)
Cash construction expenditures	25.2	25.1	26.7	28.4	29.2
Internal Sources of Funds					
Retained earnings	$3.0	$1.7	$4.4	$4.5	$5.0
Depreciation and amortization	16.7	16.5	17.2	18.0	19.0
Allowance for funds	(2.4)	(2.0)	(1.6)	(1.6)	(1.7)
Deferred taxes	2.1	1.7	1.9	1.9	1.8
Phase in deferrals	(1.8)	(1.3)	(0.9)	(0.5)	(0.3)
Total internal funds	17.6	16.6	21.0	22.3	23.8
External financing required	$7.6	$8.5	$5.7	$6.1	$5.4
Internal funds as % of cash construction	70	66	79	79	82

Source:
Edison Electric's Institute, *EEI Financial Info*, June 20, 1991 and *Statistical Yearbook 1990*.

peak periods. Most companies are still experimenting in this area and may not emphasize load management until excess capacity is reduced. Demand can also be controlled by means of time-of-use pricing accompanied by computer controls on the premises of the consumer. For instance, the computer could turn on or off certain appliances, based on the price of electricity, and the price would depend on the time of day or the cost of generation at a particular time.[4] That type of system has even greater applicability to industrial processes in which power plays an important role. Ideally, sales promotion and demand side management (such as load management or special pricing) should be integrated into a comprehensive marketing strategy that will encourage profitable and discourage unprofitable demand.[5]

In addition, the industry can improve the operating performance of existing power stations. Doing so should be more cost effective than building new generating units. Proper regulatory incentives to encourage more efficient operations would benefit customers and utility owners.[6]

Fortunately, the industry now tackles expansion in ways that do not require huge, risky projects that have long lead times. New technological options (such as fluidized bed combustion, combined cycle gas turbines or fuel cells) are economical in relatively small sizes, are less polluting, and can be constructed in a few years. Furthermore, non-utility generating firms supply the industry by erecting units that range from hydro projects, to windmills, to cogenerators. It is too early to judge the importance of superconductivity in the industry's plans. Developments in that field could affect transmission, storage, and efficiency of electric motors.

At one time, capital spending was terrific for utilities. The new plant increased efficiency. Cost of new capital was below what the utility could earn on the investment, so spending usually added to profits (at least in the common meaning of the terms). Then the tide changed. New plant turned out to be less efficient and more expensive than expected. On top of those problems, cost of new money was far above the return that the regulators let the utilities earn. Every dollar spent seemed to reduce profitability. Better not spend. Now the tide has turned again. New plant should be smaller and more efficient than the additions of the 1970s and 1980s, and cost of capital seems more in line with allowed returns. That does not indicate a return to the good old days. But at least spending money should not automatically turn into a losing proposition.

Table 33-3

Plant Spending vs Existing Plant

	1989 Electric Plant by Function	1991-1993 Construction Expenditures by Function
Generation	51.8%	35.6%
Transmission and Distribution	33.2	49.9
Nuclear fuels	4.0	6.1
Miscellaneous	11.0	8.4
	100.0	100.0

Note
   Distribution by dollar amount of investment. Investor owned utilities.

Source
   Edison Electric Institute, *EEI Financial Info*, June 20, 1991, pp.2, 4.

Chapter 34

Market, Structure and Regulation

Competition is an indispensable mainstay of a system in which the character of products and their development, the amount and evolving efficiency of production, and the prices and profit margins charged are left to the operation of private enterprise. In our conception ... it is . . . crucial . . . that the customer should be in a position . . . to exert effective discipline over the producer. . . . Otherwise, government would . . . undertake discipline . . . — as it does in the field of public-service industries.[7]

John Maurice Clark

Electric utilities long regarded themselves as the monopoly suppliers of central station power, a narrow view of the market encouraged by the regulatory process. Some competition existed for the end use of that power: oil or gas could be used for heating, as an example. And private generating units could reduce or eliminate the need to purchase electricity from the central station. But that competition seemed trivial. The government regulated electric utilities because they were supposed to be natural monopolies.

Now, the natural monopoly rationale for regulation is under attack. Economies of scale may no longer exist for the generation of electricity, in which case generation could be deregulated, provided that a transmission system exists that could connect competitive generators to customers.[8] Competition exists now in the sense that large customers choose between producing their own electricity or buying it from the local utility. In some instances, customers have even chosen which of neighboring utilities should serve them, basing the choice on price and quality of service.

Perhaps competition has not come faster because of the regulatory process. When regulation depresses the price of central station power below its true economic value, there is no incentive for consumers to self generate or for competitors to bring on new sources that must be priced at current costs in order to show a profit. Thus, where regulators price electricity artificially low, they protect the monopoly status of the electric utility by preventing the development of competitive power resources, until a revolutionary new technology appears that can produce electricity below the regulated price. However, where regulators (or the utility) attempt to price central station power above its economic worth to the consumer, or above what it costs for a customer that self generates, they encourage the development of competitive sources of electricity, thereby endangering the utility's monopoly. Protection from competition has fostered a method of doing business that may have been — in the end — riskier than allowing competitive entry into the market. The protection of regulation, the appearance of monopoly, encouraged utilities to build large, long-lived generating stations that took a decade or more to construct. From an engineering standpoint, such plants seemed to represent the least cost way to service customers. The engineers assumed that the monopoly existed, that risk was low, that the regulators could and would provide the revenue needed to support and pay for the new facility. Yet, if a major change in technology were to occur, enabling non-utilities to offer electricity to some customers from a cheap, unregulated source, raising utility rates to make up for the loss of business that goes to the new source will only drive more consumers to the new source. The low depreciation rates and return earned by the utility are premised on monopoly power through the life of the plant. Technological innovation by a competitor might lead to a situation in which the utility's revenue is insufficient to provide a profit on and recover the cost of its facility. If the utility built smaller, faster-to-construct plants, it could adjust its plans to shorter range considerations and could adjust to what the competition could offer.

A number of utilities are trying to avoid the regulatory and technological risks inherent in large, central stations by offering to purchase power generated by others. Shifting the burden of supply to an outside party does not — in itself — shift risk, unless the outside supplier is better able to do the job than the utility. A commitment to purchase power represents a risk, too. The electricity might not be needed, but it will have to be paid for anyway. Or it might prove to be more expensive than subsequently discovered alternatives. In either case, regulators could disallow the contract expense from what the utility can charge its customers.

The questions of who should build and who should purchase have become intertwined with the question of whether the industry needs competition as a spur to better performance. Some have concluded that competition should be introduced into the electric industry by separating the distribution, transmission and generating functions. Local distribution would remain regulated, because the function continues to be a natural monopoly, although there could be opportunities for competition for customers along the borders between distribution companies. The transmission system is the key to making competition more than a local phenomenon, bringing power from competing generating stations to the purchasers, and permitting distribution systems and large users to tap into power from the cheapest sources. In a competitive market, transmission might have to remain regulated, perhaps as a common carrier, in order to prevent the transmission firms from exercising their monopoly power in a way that strangles the development of competing generating sources. In the competitive scenario, the generating sector (including industrial producers) would be unregulated, because generation has lost economies of scale:

it no longer has the characteristics of the natural monopoly. Low cost producers should get the business. Distribution companies should not be associated with generating entities that they would favor as opposed to picking the low cost source. Therefore, the separation of functions.

The United Kingdom, in fact, chose a competitive model when it privatized its English and Welsh electricity supply industry in 1990. Generation is a competitive business. Transmission is a regulated monopoly. The local electric distribution utility, which is regulated, has two functions: supply and distribution. As a supplier, the utility acts as a wholesaler, buying electricity from the generators, adding a markup, and then selling the electricity to local consumers. (Large local customers can, if they choose, take their supply directly from the generators.) The local utility's second function is distribution. That is, it furnishes the conduits through which the electricity flows, plus substations, meters, and all the other services and apparatus peculiar to the function of distributing electricity at the local level.

Arguments for competition encompass two issues: capital attraction and efficiency. Some proponents of competition really want to encourage the flow of new capital into the generating business. They fear that the electric utilities have been so discouraged by past regulatory actions that they will not invest in new, needed generating capacity. They advocate that new generation should be built in response to requests by utilities. The utility would select the lowest bidder who agrees to build the plant and sell the electricity to the utility. Presumably, the bidders would select prices for output that included their minimum cost of capital requirements, given the level of risk. No firm would build unless the price reflected this *ex ante* assessment of required profit. That would be unlike the present procedure in which the utility builds not knowing what profit level will be set by the regulator on an *ex post* basis, once the facility is completed. Regulators would approve the bidding procedure, and accept the price without questioning the return built into it, because the return is what the market (as indicated in the bidding procedure) requires. The competition is between bidders. To the extent the bidders are more efficient than the local utility, customers might benefit. If the winning bidder suffers cost overruns or runs into operating problems, it suffers the consequences, not the customer of the electric company, because the latter is getting the electricity at the set price, whether the winning bidder makes its expected profit or not. A number of states have ordered utilities to seek bids from outside suppliers of electricity as an alternative to building their own power stations. Some states have made the process more competitive by allowing energy conservation programs to bid against electricity generation.

If competition is limited to the auction at which the winner of a generating contract is chosen, does that produce an efficient, competitive market for electricity? Some consumers might do better if they could find their own electric supplier, cutting out the local distributor (except as a conduit) or generator. (That, of course, is what is happening in Great Britain.) Competition (and freedom from rate of return regulation) only for new supply discourages investment in conservation or cost cutting for existing regulated generation. Limiting new suppliers by means of rigid contracts might prevent the development of a fluid market in which many generators move in and out (and customers choose to take or not take electricity) depending on short term price fluctuations. Certainly, if the utility signs a long term contract with a supplier, the utility's flexibility has been lessened in dealing with new, more competitive power sources.

For the customer or the distributor to get the cheapest power available, perhaps there could be a market for electricity analogous to the stock market. Prices in the marketplace — registered on customers' computers — would depend on supply and demand, affected by plant availability, outages, weather, and fuel costs. Customers would pay for some combination of capacity or access to the system, perhaps, on a steady basis, and then make decisions on current usage depending on short term market prices. When prices rose or fell, the consumer would adjust demand when, for instance, the price exceeded the electricity's value to the customer. Price would clear the market through the interplay of supply and demand. This system would reduce the need for a high reserve margin, because during shortages price would rise until customers cut down on usage, which they presumably would do if they had to pay for what they were getting. Furthermore, firms would have an incentive to build power plants when the market looked profitable, because they could collect a price that reflected the current value of what they were selling. Customers would have reason to reduce usage when price went too high. To continue the stock market analogy, it would be possible to create a futures market for electricity, with those who expect to require the electricity to buy future delivery, and those who plan to supply it taking the money to help finance the construction of the means of supply. (Full fledged trading is more likely to begin in Great Britain than in the United States or Canada.)

Several variants of a competitive system have been proposed. Skeptics cite numerous problems. The transmission network was not designed to handle the anticipated power flows. Access to the transmission network must be assured. The bid and contract procedure could lead to lawsuits from losing bidders and disputes reminiscent of some of the Defense Department contract fiascos. And, what is the nature of the utility's obligation to serve customers in its territory if the utility does not control the source of power, and if the customers need take the utility's service only when it is advantageous to them, but the utility is obligated to serve the customer under adverse circumstances? The prospect of the utility acting as supplier of last resort, with only the most unprofitable accounts wedded to it, is an unpleasant but probable one that would be forced on it by authorities that want both competition and service for those who cannot afford to pay the going rate. (The economist's answer, that the utility should charge the right price, and the government should give the poor customer the funds to buy the electricity, has never been acceptable to politicians in this country, because it would mean exacting a visible tax from voters instead of exacting a hidden tax through cross subsidy of one customer by another.) The utility could play the role of redistributor of wealth when it had a monopoly, when one service could cross subsidize another. It will not be able to play the role once competition forces down the prices on the highly profitable sales, leaving no means of cross subsidy.

The desire for reform is based on the belief that the regulatory system has not worked: it has produced an industry unmindful of costs, because all costs could be passed on to captive customers. Once regulators refused to pass on all costs, the industry retreated from investment for fear of another round of hindsigted refusals to pay. Industry executives, though, still assert that America's electric industry is exceptionally reliable and economical despite its travails, that the regulatory system should be modified not junked, that incentives to make regulated companies more efficient would work, and that risk of construction could be reduced through continuous regulatory oversight and approval.

The Public Utility Regulatory Policies Act of 1978 (PURPA) reintroduced independent power generation, but produced bizarre results, too. Independent power producers that met PURPA requirements could sell to the local utility at the utility's avoided cost, as defined by local regulators. Some contracts were written in a way to force the utility to reduce its own low cost production in order to buy the PURPA power. The added costs were passed on to its customers, of course. Utilities could participate in but not control PURPA projects. Because of the nature of the contracts, many PURPA producers were able to earn profits far higher than what would have been allowed the local utility on a regulated basis. PURPA was a success in that it created a new group of electricity suppliers, rejuvenated interest in cogeneration, and convinced many that independent producers could be integrated into the existing network. But it may not lower costs to customers unless PURPA generators have to compete to supply the utility. The utility should not be forced to buy from all comers just because they have power to sell. Fortunately, the utilities and regulatory agencies have become more experienced about selecting suppliers, have developed bidding and negotiating processes to weed out uncompetitive and unreliable entrants. And they limit supply to what they need, rather than buy anything offered. PURPA's limit on utility ownership had laudable motives: to bring new entrants to the market and to prevent self dealing between a utility and its PURPA subsidiary. It also limited the participation of the most experienced power producers in the alternative power production business, and may have inadvertently created a combination of a hothouse and a cottage industry: one consisting of small firms that require a rigid and high price to survive. Electricity is electricity no matter the ownership of the generator. Why is PURPA electricity worth more than utility electricity? If higher prices are needed to bring forth new sources of electricity, why are they payable only to non-utilities?

Much of the debate about competition and deregulation has a Rube Goldberg-like quality to it. Academics, government officials and regulators want to determine in advance the optimal format of the new system, and in the process they seem determined to erect a complicated structure that will deal with all questions in advance of implementation. In reality, the market will evolve and provide *ad hoc* solutions while the debate drones on. Radical measures that involve wholesale disintegration of utilities or complete repricing of the tariffs might be avoided because of the financial, political and social dislocations that would follow.[9] Mortgage bond indentures alone make it difficult to split utilities into generation, transmission and distribution segments without careful and time-consuming preparation. Piecemeal implementation might be necessary. Consumers buying electricity at a low, regulated price would not want to give up that benefit. High cost producers of electricity would not want to risk losing no longer captive customers to more competitive utilities. Competition and deregulation are more likely to come on a gradual, incremental basis. The easiest route would be to follow the British Telecom model: retain the integrated utility, but declare certain sectors of the business competitive and unregulated, and make certain that customers of the unregulated sector really have choices. If the utility wanted to keep the unregulated customers, it would have to run an efficient operation, and it could not overcharge the other customers because they would be protected by the regulator. (At present, many industrial customers are acting as if they were unregulated customers and the utilities are acting as if they could lose those customers if they do not provide economic service. Perhaps that is the beginning of competition and deregulation.) Severe regulatory problems might induce some utilities to take their chances in a competitive market, on the theory that they could be no worse off than under regulation. Wholesale power contracts, electricity from small producers, and sales to large industrial customers might be deregulated to some extent. Certainly those buying unregulated power should have the opportunity to shop around for the best contracts.

Unbundling of prices might be the most important step to take in preparing utilities, competitive electricity suppliers, and consumers for a more competitive market. Now, most consumers pay one price for a bundle of services that includes generation, transmission, distribution and the functions that assure reliability. The total of all receipts has to cover the total of all costs, and it does not matter if the utility has miscalculated costs of individual components of service, as long as the total comes out right. Once customers start to demand components of the bundle of services — rather than the complete package — the utility must have each component priced correctly. Otherwise, the customer will buy from the utility those services that are priced below cost, and not those services that are priced above cost. All of this means, too, that competition will make it difficult for a utility to use one service to cross subsidize another, because customers will not take the high priced service that furnishes the subsidy to the low priced service. The same principles apply to pricing services by groups of customers. If the utility charges industrial customers too much, in order to make up for the fact that residential customers pay too little, then the utility risks losing the industrial customers, and would have to charge the residential customers more to make up the loss of revenue. The customers left on the system would have to cover the costs of the plant investment that has been idled ("stranded plant") by the loss of the industrial customers. Although many view this scenario as hypothetical, it already has taken place in the natural gas and telephone industries.[10]

The obligation to serve is another leftover from the old days that is bound to cause trouble in a competitive world. The utility has to serve the customer, when asked, but the customer has no obligation to stay with the utility long enough to pay for the facilities dedicated to serving that customer. The customer could take utility service when the utility's price is lower than that of alternatives, switch to alternatives when they are cheaper (knowing that the utility is always there to provide service if moving to the alternative turns out to be a bad idea), and then switch back to the utility when its service is cheaper. During the period when the customer is taking the alternative service, the utility is actually providing a service for which it is not getting paid: a backup service that can be relied on whenever the cheaper service becomes less cheap or less reliable. One might ask: why is this situation different from any supplier to industry? Do not customers switch suppliers? Is that not what the free market is all about? The answer lies in the obligation to serve. Suppliers to industry have no obligation to provide supply, especially not at a price determined by a third party (the regulator). They calculate their chances of making a decent profit before they invest, and they may demand a long term purchase contract from the buyer before they put up a factory to supply that buyer. The utility, on the other hand, is required to serve the customer at a price that may not take into account the risk that the customer will go away, leaving the utility with stranded investment. That issue was not a problem at a time when the utility produced the cheapest power around, and when demand for electricity grew at a fast pace. If the big customer actually found a better deal, the utility could easily find other customers who wanted the output of the electric plant. Nowadays, the big customer may have an alternative to the local utility, and there might not be enough growth in demand by other customers to sop up the excess capacity. The utility faces a mature market plus competition. To succeed under such circumstances, it must free itself from obligations that were appropriate only when it had a secure monopoly. Utilities will have to move toward a system of commercial contracts with large customers, now that utilities need more protection from those customers than *vice versa*.

It appears that the industry is evolving into a group of integrated utilities surrounded and served by many non-utility producers that are partially owned by the integrated utilities. Depending on the regulatory process and developments in the market place, some integrated utilities may move some of their assets into the unregulated arena. Piecemeal evolution of the industry may disturb economic purists who object to the inefficiencies produced by mixing regulated and unregulated elements, but it has an advantage: small mistakes are easier to correct than massive ones.

Regulators have tried to modify the system in order to encourage efficiency by granting higher returns to more efficient companies, or by letting the utility keep part of the profit over the allowed return as long as that extra profit comes about through better operating procedures rather than through rate relief. They are attempting to modify the system in other ways too. Regulators insist that the utility find the least cost method of doing business, rather than following past procedures. And, realizing the value of conservation and load management, regulators have begun to let utilities earn profits on such programs. Some regulators have gone even farther, decoupling profit growth from sales growth, so the utility has no disincentives that would discourage it from pushing conservation efforts. The next step will be to provide an incentive to utilities that find purchasing power is cheaper that generating it. That incentive would come in the form of a profit on the wholesaling function. Regulators are just beginning to learn that they can influence behavior by means of a carrot as well as a stick.

If the utility avoids investment in large, regulated projects, perhaps management attention and company funds can be directed toward diversified activities, best defined as any venture outside the regulated, central station power business. Electric companies have diversified in three ways: portfolio investment, energy related, and unrelated. A number of companies have invested in portfolios of leases and tax-advantaged securities, often planning to liquidate the portfolio when the funds are needed in the utility business. Energy related activities have included fuel production and transportation, conservation activities, engineering, and unregulated electricity production. Unrelated activities, so far, have encompassed everything from banking and insurance through subliminal anti-shoplifting operations to orange groves, most of which have been spectacularly unsuccessful. If one regards the total market for energy, or the end uses to which energy is put, as the market served by the utility, perhaps the utility could better serve the customer by providing a service other than central station power. If that is the case, the utility should have an opportunity to do so. Regulators often assert that diversification could add to the risk of the business and therefore raise cost of capital to the utility. Yet, inability to be flexible in meeting the needs of the customer could increase the risk of investing in the utility. Being locked into a one service, one technology business in an ever-changing world is perilous. At the same time, moving into unfamiliar, unrelated businesses just to expand has already proved perilous. Most utilities have decided to dump unrelated ventures, and instead to refocus on energy-related businesses.

If the market for electricity becomes more competitive, if utilities find a way to reap the benefits of better management, if regulation becomes looser, then well run utilities would see an advantage in taking over and running the laggards. Firms might acquire companies with strategic but unexploited assets. Regulators could step in to force shotgun marriages, too, in order to rescue troubled firms. Utilities might buy and sell assets that are of more value to another company. The complications of regulation, though, could hinder rational asset distribution as well as mergers and acquisitions in the real world. Furthermore, mergers are not always economically rational. They may produce no benefits to customers or shareholders of the acquiring firm, although they may build empires for managements.

Modifications in the Public Utility Holding Company Act may remove enough restrictions on ownership of non-utility generators to cause a major expansion of that industry and to make it easier for utility affiliates to compete in the market. At the same time, the Federal government is working assiduously to diminish utility control over their own transmission lines, in order to make it easier for non-utility generators to gain access to markets. America seems to be moving gradually toward electric deregulation, incrementally rather than in a dramatic, all-or-nothing fashion. Most people seem to want to avoid the logical questions of whether integration of all utility functions in one company still makes sense, or what happens when ultimate customers bypass the local utility in the search for the most competitive energy source, or when will the industry develop unbundled tariff offerings. Those will be the issues of the 1990s, and wishing will not make them go away.

Chapter 35

Conclusion

"Jack could turn on the electric light sometimes, just by snapping his fingers," Flossie said.[11]

William Kennedy

It must seem that easy to the customer. Flick the switch. The lights go on. It certainly has not seemed that easy to the people in the electric utility industry, at least not since 1965. Were the problems due to a string of unrelated difficulties that took place, by sheer coincidence, during the same period of time?

One could argue that the ending of economies of scale marked a turning point in the history of the industry.[12] That is true, but the difficulties that followed might have been avoided had the industry been able (and willing) to set its prices in a manner that reflected the new cost structure.

Perhaps the industry's difficulties, then, are rooted in one problem: inability to properly price the product. If the price for electricity approximated its incremental cost, power demand would have been lower (making much of the construction program unnecessary) and the industry would have had less trouble financing what it had to build. Less resistance to environmental improvement might have existed if the costs could have been easily passed on to customers. Fuel costs, and the use of oil as a fuel, might have been kept down if the utility could have priced in a way to cover the cost of fuel conversion. At the same time, incremental pricing would have encouraged the development of competition for the utility, possibly in ways that would have reduced oil consumption even more.

Thomas P. Hughes, the historian of science and technology, warned that problem solvers must distinguish between the technical and the technological. The technical aspects of the problem involve the "tools, machines, structures, and other devices" while the technological encompasses "technical . . . , economic, political, scientific, sociological, psychological, and ideological . . . "[13] There is no doubt that many utility executives and government regulators doggedly attacked (and are still attacking) problems as if they have simple technical fixes, when the questions and answers involve both technical issues and the societal and economic environment in which they exist. The electric utilities and regulators that examine issues in a technological fashion may not come up with the ideal technical fix but rather with a workable solution.

Although regulators have become increasingly responsive to the need for prices to reflect the cost of doing business, they are not ready to set prices in a way that would simulate the results of a free market. Some makeshift pricing procedures that try to set rates for high use or for peak load periods closer to marginal costs should have some positive results. If regulators are unwilling to use price to dampen demand, they might instead endorse or force load management or energy conservation, because those measures are usually more cost effective than building power plants to meet unfettered demand. That compromise may produce more rational results — economically speaking — than if prices were simply kept down. Without control of demand, the result might be more demand for power placed on an industry that would be hard pressed to finance additional construction.

Utilities are back in the business of building needed facilities, but they have entered the new construction period with caution: avoiding the big projects that caused so many problems in the past, letting non-utility generators take on much of the load.

The age of unrelated diversification seems to have come and gone, leaving behind a trail of bruised egos, dismissed executives, and huge losses. Managements have taken heed of the folk song's advice: watch the doughnut, not the hole. Unregulated ventures now center on energy and electricity.

The industry, though, will undergo more change than through diversification. The market for electricity is becoming more competitive. Utilities cannot run in the old, regulated manner because the consumers will not tolerate that. Inefficient companies will suffer, losing business and even their independence. But, at the same time, the transition to more competition and less regulation could come gradually. The efficient, flexible, market-driven company will come out ahead. So will the customers and power suppliers that understand how to take advantage of the more open environment. Competition, though, does not mean more profits for all. It does mean less certainty for an industry that used to project its future with a ruler.

Notes

[1]Roger W. Sant, *Eight Great Energy Myths: The Least Cost Energy Strategy, 1978-2000* (Pittsburgh: Carnegie-Mellon University Press, 1981), p. 36.

[2]John Maynard Keynes, *The General Theory of Employment Interest and Money* (New York: Harcourt, Brace & World, no date), p. 157.

[3]U.S. Congress Office of Technology Assessment, *Nuclear Power in an Age of Uncertainty* (Washington, D.C.: U.S. Government Printing Office, 1984).

[4]Fred C. Schweppe, Richard D. Tabors, and James Kirtley, *Homeostatic Control: The Utility Customer Marketplace for Electric Power*, MIT Energy Laboratory Report, MIT-EL 81-033, September 1981.

[5]Ahmad Faruqui, "Marketing Electricity — A Military Approach," *Long Range Planning*, Vol. 20, No. 4, pp. 67-77, 1987.

[6]Wallace A. Stringfield, James V. Barker, Jr., and Harinder Singh, "Power Plant Productivity," presented at the Association of Rural Electric Generation Cooperatives, 31st Annual Conference, June 9-11, 1980, Des Moines, Iowa. —, "Power Plant Productivity and State Regulation," presented at NARUC Biennial Regulatory Information Conference, September 3-5, 1980, Columbus, Ohio.

[7]John Maurice Clark, *Competition as a Dynamic Process* (Washington, D.C.: The Brookings

Institution, 1961), p. 9.

[8]Some comments on deregulation include:

William W. Berry, "Let's End the Monopoly," presented at the Edison Electric Institute Fall Financial Conference, October 6, 1981, Palm Beach, Florida.

Edison Electric Institute, *Deregulation of Electric Utilities; A Survey of Major Concepts and Issues* (Washington, D.C.: EEI, July 1981).

—, *A Survey of Deregulation Experience in Selected Industries* (Washington, D.C.: EEI, February 1982).

—, *Alternative Models of Electric Power Deregulation* (Washington, D.C.: EEI, May 1982).

Bennett W. Golub, Richard D. Tabors, Roger E. Bohn and Fred C. Schweppe, "Deregulating the Electric Utility Industry: Discussion and a Proposed Approach," MIT Energy Laboratory Working Paper, MIT-EL 81-043 WP, July 1981, revised August 1981.

Ernst Habicht, Jr., "Restructuring the Role of Electric Utilities: Cogeneration, Conservation, Construction and Competition," presented at Merrill Lynch Economics Seminar on Electric Utility Industry, April 28, 1981, New York City.

Leonard S. Hyman, "Should Electric Utilities be Regulated?", *Public Utilities Fortnightly*, August 14, 1980.

Leonard S. Hyman and Ernst R. Habicht, Jr., "State Electric Utility Regulation: Financial Issues, Influences and Trends," *Annual Energy Review*, Vol. 11, 1986, pp. 163-183.

Pennsylvania Governor's Energy Council, *Report to Lieutenant Governor William W. Scranton III from the Pennsylvania Electric Utility Efficiency Task Force*, (Harrisburg: Pennsylvania Governor's Energy Council, March 29, 1983).

Roger W. Sant, "Cutting Energy Cost," *Environment*, May 1980.

Richard E. Schuler and Benjamin F. Hobbs, "Spatial Competition — Applications in the Generation of Electricity," presented at 1981 Annual Meeting of the Southern Regional Science Association, April 15, 1981, Washington, D.C.

U.S. Congress Office of Technology Assessment, *Electric Power Wheeling and Dealing: Technological Considerations for Increasing Competition*, (Washington, D.C.: Government Printing Office, 1989).

[9]Bennett W. Golub and Leonard S. Hyman, "The Financial Difficulties and Consequences of Deregulation Through Divestiture," *Public Utilities Fortnightly*, February 17, 1983.

[10]Leonard S. Hyman, Richard C. Toole and Rosemary M. Avellis, *The New Telecommunications Industry: Evolution and Organization* (Arlington, Va.: Public Utilities Reports, 1987).

[11]William Kennedy, *Legs*, (New York: Coward, McCann & Geoghegan, 1975), p. 311.

[12]Richard F. Hirsh, *op. cit.*, takes this view.

[13]Thomas P. Hughes, "Technological History and Technical Problems," in Chauncey Starr and Philip C. Ritterbush, eds., *Science, Technology and the Human Prospect* (New York: Pergamon Press, 1980) p. 182.

Appendix: Canada

Canada has one of the largest electric utility industries in the world, despite its small population. Canada has one of the most electricity-intensive economies in the world, too, perhaps because of its abundance of inexpensive hydroelectric resources. Production per capita is at an astounding level, far higher than any of the other large electricity producing countries (see Table A-1).

Canada's industries consume over 40% of the country's electricity. Until recently, they produced a large percentage of electric output, too (Table A-2).

Hydroelectric stations produce about 60% of Canada's electricity. The country has undeveloped hydro sites now, and should be able to add hydro over the coming decade. Newfoundland, Quebec, Manitoba and British Columbia depend most on hydroelectricity. Alberta, Saskatchewan, Prince Edward Island and Nova Scotia emphasize coal. Most of the nuclear capacity is in Ontario. Exports to the U.S.A. should expand in the 1990s. Reserve margins should decline in the same period. Non-utility generation is making an appearance, too, in a small way.

The provinces regulate prices, approve capital expenditures and consider environmental matters. Regulatory agencies set prices for investor-owned utilities based on rate of return regulation similar to the American model. The National Energy Board of Canada authorizes exports. In doing so, the Board must determine that the export power is not needed in Canada, that the revenue from the export recovers the proper share of costs in Canada, that the price may not be lower than what Canadians would pay for the same power, and that the price must not be less than the lowest cost alternative to the purchaser.

Crown corporations (provincially or territorially controlled government agencies) dominate the electric utility industry (Table A-4).

In terms of size, Ontario Hydro is the largest system, followed by Hydro-Quebec, and British Columbia Hydro is a distant third. Those three entities account for over two-thirds of assets, revenues and generation.

The status of ownership varies from province to province:

Newfoundland — Newfoundland and Labrador Hydro is a provincially owned crown corporation that has enormous hydro generation resources, distributes electricity directly to customers in rural areas, and sells to investor-owned Newfoundland Light & Power most of the electricity that firm distributes to its customers in the more populated areas.

Prince Edward Island — Investor-owned Maritime Electric serves the island province, with most power coming by submarine cable from New Brunswick.

Nova Scotia — Nova Scotia Power, owned by the province, serves the entire population. (Partial privatization proposed for 1992.)

New Brunswick — Provincially owned New Brunswick Electric Power Commission generates electricity, serves the bulk of the customers directly, and the balance through municipal systems.

Quebec — Hydro-Quebec, owned by the province, controls vast hydroelectric resources, and generates and distributes throughout the province.

Ontario — Ontario Hydro, provincially owned, generates electricity, sells it mainly through municipally owned distribution systems, and also sells directly to large industrial firms and to customers in rural areas. In addition, small regional utilities generate and distribute electricity in the province.

Manitoba — Manitoba Hydro-Electric Board, another provincial crown corporation, produces and sells throughout Manitoba except for the territory of municipally owned Winnipeg Hydro.

Saskatchewan — The Saskatchewan Power Corporation, property of the province, generates and sells electricity throughout the province.

Alberta — In 1989, an investor-owned company, TransAlta Utilities, generated 72% of the province's electricity. Another investor-owned firm, Canadian Utilities, provided 19%, while 1% was furnished by city owned Edmonton Power. Industry generated another 9%. The companies operate an integrated network.

British Columbia — Provincial crown corporation British Columbia Hydro & Power Authority generates and sells most of the province's electricity. West Kootenay Power is an investor-owned utility, serving part of the province.

Table A-1

International Comparisons
Ten Largest Electricity Producers (1987)

Country	Generation (Billion kwh)	Capacity (Million kw)	Hours of Production per kw of capacity	Kwh per capita	Electricity Intensity
	(1)	(2)	(3)	(4)	(5)
U.S.A.	2,686	744	3,610	11,204	0.7
U.S.S.R.	1,665	332	5,015	5,792	0.7E
Japan	699	177	3,949	5,733	0.5
Germany	530	109	4,862	6,950	0.5
China	497	92	5,402	465	1.8E
Canada	496	101	4,911	17,486	1.2
France	416	97	4,289	5,870	0.6
U.K.	356	64	5,563	5,477	0.6
India	300	58	5,172	271	1.3E
Brazil	217	47	4,617	1,549	0.8E

Notes

Column 5: Kwh per $ GNP (1985$).

Sources

Ministry of Energy, Mines and Resources (Canada),
Electric Power in Canada 1989 (Ottawa: Energy, Mines and Resources Canada, 1991), pp. 8-10, 14.
World Almanac 1990.

Table A-2

**Canadian
Utility and Industrial
Capacity and Production
1930 - 1990**

	Capacity		Generation	
	% Utility	% Industry	% Utility	% Industry
	(1)	(2)	(3)	(4)
1930	83	17	93	7
1940	84	16	91	9
1950	83	17	88	12
1960	80	20	78	22
1970	88	12	84	16
1980	92	8	89	11
1990	--	--	91	9

<u>Sources</u>
Statistics Canada, *Electric Power Statistics*, May 1991.
Energy, Mines and Resources Canada, *Electric Power in Canada 1989.*

Table A-3

Canadian
Production, Sales and Capacity

		Estimated		Annual %
	1989	1990	2000	Growth 1989 - 2000
Generating Capacity (MW)				
Hydro	58,523	58,513	72,228	1.9
Coal	19,248	18,413	22,201	1.3
Nuclear	12,603	12,886	15,517	1.9
Oil	7,413	7,460	8,223	0.9
Gas	3,523	4,443	5,067	3.4
Other	905	544	1,072	1.6
	102,215	102,259	124,308	1.8
Generation (MWH thousands)				
Hydro	287,649	309,709	390,477	2.8
Coal	85,580	85,437	108,305	2.2
Nuclear	75,350	82,097	113,635	3.8
Oil	16,413	20,489	13,954	-1.5
Gas	14,334	10,131	13,897	-0.5
Other	2,832	2,823	19,349	19.1
	482,158	510,686	659,617	2.9
Peak Demand (MW)	81,466	82,180	105,266	2.4
Hydro as % of generation	59.7	60.6	59.2	--
Electricity exports to U.S. as % of generation	3.8	5.5	7.1	--
Reserve Margin %	25.5	24.4	18.1	--

Source

Electric Power in Canada 1989

Table A-4

Electricity Industry in Canada (1989)

	Capacity	Production
Crown Corporations	82.8%	82.2%
Four largest investor-owned utilities	5.8	7.3
Municipally owned utilities	1.6	0.8
Industrial establishments	6.0	8.0
Small utilities	3.8	1.7
Total	100.0	100.0

Source
Electric Power in Canada 1989.

Appendix: Chronology
1800 - 1990

Year	Technological	Institutional USA and Canada
1800	* First electric battery — A. Volta (Italy).	
1801	* Principles of arc light — H. Davy (UK).	
1808	* First effective arc lamp — H. Davy (UK).	
1816		* Gas Light Co. of Baltimore founded by R. Peale — first energy utility in USA, predecessor of Baltimore G & E.
1820	* Relationship of electricity and magnetism confirmed — H.C. Oersted (Den.)	* Congress gives City of Washington authority to regulate some prices.
1821	* First electric motor — M. Faraday (UK).	
1826	* Ohm's Law — G.S. Ohm (Ger.).	
1831	* Principles of electromagnetism, induction, generation and transmission — M. Faraday (UK).	
1832	* First dynamo — H. Pixii (France). * Faraday publishes on induction (UK). * J. Henry publishes on induction (USA).	
1837	* First industrial electric motors — T. Davenport (USA).	

Year	Technological	Institutional USA and Canada
1839	* First fuel cell — W. Grove (UK).	* Rhode Island sets up regulatory commission.
1860	* Lead storage battery — G. Plante (France).	
1865	* Mathematical theory of electromagnetic fields — J.C. Maxwell (UK).	
1870	* First effective dynamo — Z.T. Gramme (Bel.)	
1873		* Outdoor Arc Lighting, Winnipeg.
1876	* Improved arc light, Jablochoff candle, P. Jablochoff (France).	* Arc lights at Philadelphia exposition.
1877		* *Munn v. Illinois* — U.S. Supreme Court upholds regulation.
1878	* Efficient arc lamp and open coil dynamo — C.F. Brush (USA).	* Edison Electric Light Co. (USA) and American Electric and Illuminating of Montreal founded.
1879	* T.A. Edison (USA) and J. Swan (UK) independently invent practical incandescent lamp.	* First commercial power station opens in San Francisco, uses Brush generator and arc lights. * British Columbia Electric Railway.
1880		* First isolated power system, from Edison, for S.S. Columbia.
1881	* Electric streetcar — E.W. V. Siemens (Ger.).	
1882		* Edison's Pearl Street Station.

Year	Technological	Institutional USA and Canada
1883	* Transformer invented — L. Gaulard (Fr.) and J. Gibbs (UK).	First electric lighting plant in Canada, Cornwall, Ont. * First electric tramway in USA, Richmond, Va. — F. Sprague design.
1884	* Steam turbine invented — C. Parsons (UK).	* Edison takes control of Edison Light Co. * Streetlights, Montreal and Toronto.
1886	* W. Stanley develops transformer and AC electric system (USA).	* Westinghouse Electric formed.
1888	* N. Tesla invents induction motor and polyphase AC system (USA). * O. Shellenberger invents induction motor, first AC meter to measure consumption (USA).	
1889		* Edison General Electric formed. * National Association of Regulatory Commissioners founded as association of railway commissioners.
1890		* First execution in electric chair. * The North American Co. formed. * United Electric Securities organized by Thomson-Houston.
1891	* Westinghouse transmits hydro AC at 3.3 kv for 13 miles, Oregon. * C. Brown transmits at 3.0 kv for 110 miles (Ger.).	

Year	Technological	Institutional USA and Canada
1892	* T. Willson develops electric furness process to produce calcium carbide (Canada).	* General Electric (GE) formed by merger of Thomson-Houston and Edison General Electric. * C.Steinmetz, theoretician of AC and mathematician joins GE, beginning corporate industrial research in USA.
1893	* Westinghouse displays AC system at Chicago World's Fair. * Folsom Powerhouse in California transmits at 11.0 kv 3 phase AC, 22 miles to Sacramento.	* AC chosen for Niagara Power.
1895		* Niagara station completed.
1896	Niagara line, 11.0 kv, 3 phase AC, 20 miles.	* Niagara transmission line (Niagara Falls to Buffalo) opened.
1897	* J. Thompson discovers electron (UK).	* C. Yerkes proposes state regulation for streetcars and long franchises.
1898		* *Smith v. Ames.* Supreme Court decrees just compensation on fair value. * S. Insull proposes state regulation of utilities.
1900	* Highest voltage transmission line 60 kv.	
1901	* Westinghouse offers 3.5 MW turbine. * 2.0 MW turbine, largest installed in USA.	
1902	* 5.0 MW turbine for Fisk St. Station, Chicago.	

Year	Technological	Institutional USA and Canada
1903		* World's first all turbine station, Chicago. * Shawinigan Water & Power installs world's largest generator (5000W) and world's largest and highest voltage line — 136 km and 50kv (to Montreal).
1905		* Work begins on Great Southern Grid, which, by 1914, transmits in N.C., S.C., Ga., and Tenn. * Pacific G&E incorporated. * Electric Bond and Share founded. * Ontario Hydro founded.
1906		* Associated G&E incorporated.
1907	* Electric vacuum cleaner — J.Spangler (USA). * Electric washing machine — A. Fisher (USA).	* State utility regulation in Mass., N.Y., and Wis.
1910	* Neon lamps. * Tungsten wire filament.	* S. Insull electrifies rural communities.
1911	* Air conditioning — W. Carrier (USA).	* Calgary Power incorporated.
1912	* Largest generator 35 MW, highest transmission voltage 150 kv.	*Insull starts holding company.
1913	* Gas filled incandescent lamps. * First air pollution control device — cinder catcher — T. Murray (USA). * Electric refrigerator — A. Goss (USA).	

Year	Technological	Institutional USA and Canada
1914		* Illinois forms regulatory agency.
1916		* Federal government begins construction of Muscle Shoals, Ala., dam to supply electricity to munitions complex. Origin of TVA.
1919	* Atomic fission — E. Rutherford (Can.).	
1920	* First U.S. station to only burn pulverized coal.	* Federal Power Commission (FPC).
1922	* 175 MW largest generating station.	* Associated Gas and Electric Incorporated. * Connecticut Valley Power Exchange (CONVEX) starts, pioneering interconnection between utilities.
1923	* Television components — V. Zworykin (USA).	* Bluefield decision calls for reproduction cost rate base.
1924		* Cities Service Power & Light.
1926		* A.B. Collins creates Reddy Kilowatt.
1927		* First regional power pool, Pennsylvania-New Jersey Interconnection. * *Rhode Island PUC v. Attleboro* case — selling electricity interstate cannot be regulated by state.
1928	* Construction of Boulder Dam begins.	* Federal Trade Commission begins investigation of holding companies.

Year	Technological	Institutional USA and Canada
1929	* GE produces 208 MW generating unit, largest in service through 1953.	* Commonwealth & Southern and United Corp. organized. * Stock market crashes.
1930	*Transmission at 240 kv.	
1932	* Sodium light.	* Middle West Utilities, National Electric Power, Seaboard P.S. collapse — end of Insull empire.
1933		* Tennessee Valley Authority (TVA) established.
1934	* Nuclear chain reaction described — L. Szilard (UK).	
1935		* Public Utility Holding Co. Act. * Federal Power Act. * Securities and Exchange Commission. * Bonneville Power Administration. * First night baseball game in major leagues (Cincinnati, Ohio).
1936	* Highest steam temperature reaches 900 degrees Fahrenheit vs. 600 degrees Fahrenheit in early 1920s. * 287 kv line runs 266 miles to Boulder (Hoover) Dam. * Boulder Dam completed.	* Rural Electrification Act.
1938	* Man-made fission of uranium — O. Hahn and F. Strassman (Ger.).	* Supreme Court affirms Holding Co. Act of 1935 in *Electric Bond & Share v. SEC*.

Year	Technological	Institutional USA and Canada
1940	* Steam pressure in generation reaches 2400 pounds per square inch (psi) vs. 1100 psi in early 1920s.	
1942	* Sustained nuclear reaction — E. Fermi (USA).	
1943		* SEC orders divestments of Engineers P.S. subsidiaries, begins breakup of holding companies.
1944		* Hydro-Quebec formed. * *F.P.C. v. Hope Natural Gas* decision establishes new rules for regulation.
1945	* Atomic bomb.	
1946		* Atomic Energy Act, establishes Atomic Energy Commission (AEC).
1947	* Transistor invented. * Mercury vapor lamp. * Highest steam temperature in generation reaches 1000 degrees Fahrenheit.	
1953	* First practical nuclear reactor — for submarines. * First 345 kv transmission line — American Electric Power.	* First nuclear power station ordered — Shippingport, Pa. * Atoms for Peace program announced by Eisenhower.
1954		* Atomic Energy Act of 1954 allows private ownership of nuclear reactors.
1955	* Nuclear submarine Nautilus commissioned by U.S. Navy. * Construction of Shippingport begins.	

Year	Technological	Institutional USA and Canada
1956		* AEC issues first permits for commercial nuclear plants. * GE begins "Live Better Electrically" campaign.
1957	* Generator steam reaches 1150 degrees Fahrenheit and pressure 4500 psi at Philo station, first supercritical unit in USA. * Shippingport goes operational.	* Price Anderson Act promotes nuclear development. * Washington Public Power Supply System formed.
1959		* TVA Revenue Act restricts TVA boundaries.
1961	* SL-1 Excursion accident at Idaho AEC reactor kills three. * Largest generating unit in Canada, 300 MW.	
1962		* Rachel Carson's *Silent Spring* published, beginning environmental movement.
1963		* Clean Air Act. * Columbia River Treaty ratified, opens way for international hydro developments.
1964	* 500 kv lines, Virginia and Tennessee.	* FPC conducts National Power Survey.
1965	* First 765 kv transmission line (Canada).	* Northeast Blackout.
1966	* Accident at Fermi nuclear plant (Michigan).	* Endangered Species Act. * Hydro development on Nelson River, Manitoba begins.
1967	* First commercial CANDU nuclear reactor (Canada).	* P-J-M power interruption.

Year	Technological	Institutional USA and Canada
1968		* National Electric Reliability Council formed.
1969		* National Environmental Policy Act of 1969.
1970		* National Power Survey by FPC. * Environmental Protection Agency (EPA) formed. * Water and Environmental Quality Act. * Clean Air Act of 1970. * Earth Day — April 22.
1972		* Electric Power Research Institute (EPRI). * Clean Water Act of 1972.
1973		* Arab oil embargo begins, price of oil quadruples. * Endangered Species Act of 1973. * Natural gas production peaks.
1974	* Number of nuclear plants on order or under construction reached peak.	* First drop in sales since 1946. * AEC split up into Energy Research and Development Administration (ERDA) and Nuclear Regulatory Commission (NRC). * Consolidated Edison omits dividend. * Churchill Falls hydro plant completed (Canada).
1975	* Brown's Ferry nuclear accident.	* Thirteen nuclear projects canceled.

Year	Technological	Institutional USA and Canada
1977		* New York City blackout. * Department of Energy (DOE) formed. * Carter energy plan.
1978		* Public Utilities Regulatory Policies Act (PURPA) passed, ends utility monopoly over generation. * Natural Gas Policy Act partially deregulates wellhead prices. * Power Plant and Industrial Fuel Use Act limits use of natural gas in electric generation (repealed 1987). * U.S. Supreme Court affirms primacy of FERC ratesetting in Narragansett decision.
1979	* Three Mile Island nuclear accident.	* Hydro-Quebec's James Bay project begins operation (Canada). * Oil prices jump $11 due to Iranian Revolution.
1980	* First U.S. windfarm (N.H.).	* Pacific Northwest Electric Power Planning and Conservation Act establishes regional regulation and planning.
1981		* PURPA ruled unconstitutional by Federal judge — Mississippi (decision overturned 1982).

Year	Technological	Institutional USA and Canada
1982	* Shippingport retired from service. * Record drop of 19 plants from list of nuclear plants in operations, under construction, or ordered.	* Nuclear Waste Policy Act directs DOE to build geological repository for waste. * U.S. Supreme Court upholds legality of PURPA in *FERC v. Mississippi* (456 US 742).
1983	* First denial of operating license by NRC (Byron, #1, Illinois).	* Washington Public Power Supply System defaults on $2.25 billion of bonds due to inability to complete five nuclear reactors. * P.S. of Indiana cancels Marble Hill nuclear plant, cuts dividend. * Cincinnati G & E suspends Zimmer as nuclear project, announces conversion of Zimmer to coal. * Production of electricity from non-utility sources hits lowest level since 1950.
1986	* Chernobyl nuclear accident (USSR).	
1988	* NASA scientist J. Hansen tells Congress that greenhouse effect already taking place.	* Public Service of New Hampshire files for bankruptcy due to nuclear project — first utility bankruptcy in more than 50 years. * FERC approves merger of Pacific P & L and Utah P & L with conditions that require transmission access for other utilities — precursor of program to open transmission networks.

Year	Technological	Institutional USA and Canada
1989	* Shippingport becomes first nuclear plant in world to be decommissioned to "greenfield" condition.	* Long Island Lighting sells Shoreham nuclear plant to state: first completed and commissioned nuclear plant to be abandoned without commercial operation.
1990		* Clean Air Act amendments mandate additional pollution controls. * Non-utility generation reaches record level.

Appendix: Selected Bibliography

This bibliography is designed to give the reader standard sources of information, with emphasis on those that are easily found, relatively recent, and understandable. In addition, there is a huge body of speeches and technical papers that circulates within the industry in a samizdat manner. And, of course, there are many articles in learned journals and an abundance of extremely technical books. The bibliographic references are grouped by general topic. The readings are grouped by one category, although some ought to be in several categories. The footnotes within the text cite numerous additional sources.

Statistics and Reference

The standard sources are publications of the Energy Information Agency, Edison Electric Institute, the various financial services, *Electrical World*, *Public Utilities Fortnightly* and *Electric Light & Power*.

Deloitte Haskins & Sells, *Public Utilities Manual* (No place of publication: Deloitte Haskins & Sells, 1980).

Edison Electric Institute, *Statistical Year Book of the Electric Utility Industry* (Washington, D.C.: Edison Electric Institute, various years).

Edison Electric Institute, *Year-End Electric Power Survey* (Washington, D.C.: Edison Electric Institute, various years).

Edison Electric Institute, *1990 Electric Power Equipment Report* (Washington, D.C.: Edison Electric Institute, 1991).

Edison Electric Institute, *EEI Pocketbook of Electric Utility Industry Statistics* (Washington, D.C.: Edison Electric Institute, various years).

Edison Electric Institute, *Financial Review* (Washington, D.C.: Edison Electric Institute, various years).

Electric Light & Power (various issues).

Electrical World (various issues).

Electricity Branch, Energy Sector, Ministry of Energy, Mines and Resources Canada, *Electric Power in Canada* (Ottawa: Ministry of Supply and Services, various years).

Haskins & Sells, *Public Utilities Manual* (New York: Deloitte Haskins & Sells, 1977).

Moody's Public Utilities Manual (New York: Moody's Investors Service, various dates).

Pacific Gas and Electric, *Resource: An Encyclopedia of Utility Industry Terms* (San Francisco: Pacific G&E, 1984).

Public Utilities Fortnightly (various issues).

Statistics Canada, *Electric Power Statistics*, (Ottawa: Statistics Canada, various dates).

U.S. Department of Energy, Energy Information Administration, *Statistics of Privately Owned Electric Utilities in the United States* (Washington, D.C.: U.S. Government Printing Office, various years).

U.S. Department of Energy, *Electric Power Monthly* (various issues).

U.S. Department of Energy, *Monthly Energy Review* (various issues).

U.S. Department of Energy, *Annual Energy Review* (various years).

U.S. Department of Energy, *Annual Energy Outlook* (various years).

U.S. Department of Energy, *Annual Outlook for U.S. Electric Power* (various years).

U.S. Department of Labor, Bureau of Labor Statistics, *Monthly Labor Review* (various issues).

U.S. Federal Power Commission, *Statistics of Privately Owned Electric Utilities in the United States* (Washington, D.C.: U.S. Government Printing Office, various years).

Regulation and Economics

Numerous texts on regulation have been written. Probably almost everything that has been or will be said was covered by Bonbright. Kahn's work deals with all aspects of regulation, not exclusively with utilities. Public Utilities Fortnightly is an excellent source for keeping up with current issues. Welch's book provides a clear exposition of regulatory law and texts of cases as well. EEI studies cover the issues well, too.

Adelaar, Richard H., and Leonard S. Hyman, "The Comparable Earnings Approach as a Useful Tool in Utility Regulation," *Public Utilities Fortnightly*. Vol. 87, No. 5, March 4, 1971.

Anderson, Douglas D., *Regulatory Politics and Electric Utilities* (Boston: Auburn House, 1981).

Arthur Andersen & Co., *Return Allowed in Public Utility Rate Cases* (Vol. I 1915-1954 and Vol. II 1955-1961). No date or place of publication.

Bain, Joe S., *Industrial Organization* (New York: John Wiley & Sons, 1959).

Balk, Walter L., and Jay M. Shafritz, eds., *Public Utility Productivity: Management and Measurement* (Albany: The New York State Department of Public Service, 1975).

Bonbright, James C., *Principles of Public Utility Rates* (New York: Columbia University Press, 1961).

Bonbright, James C., Albert L. Danielsen and David R. Kamerschen, *Principles of Public Utility Rates* (Arlington, Va.: Public Utilities Reports, 1988).

Cicchetti, Charles J.,"Conservation Financing — Its Rate Impact," in Edison Electric Institute Proceedings, *Sixteenth Financial Conference, October 4-7, 1981* (Washington, D.C.: EEI, 1982).

Clark, J. Maurice, *Studies in the Economics of Overhead Costs* (Chicago: The University of Chicago Press, 1962 impression).

Clark, J. Maurice, *Competition as a Dynamic Process* (Washington, D.C.: The Brookings Institution, 1961).

Corey, Gordon R., *"Some Observations on Bulk Power Markets in the United States," Public Utilities Fortnightly*, Sept. 14, 1989: "Additional Observations on Bulk Power Markets in the United States," *Public Utilities Fortnightly*, Sept. 28, 1989: "Transmission Service Pricing Can Make All the Difference," *Public Utilities Fortnightly*, Oct. 1, 1991.

Crew, Michael A., ed., *Issues in Public-Utility Pricing and Regulation* (Lexington: D. C. Heath, 1980).

Crew, Michael A., ed., *Deregulation and Diversification of Utilities* (Boston: Kluwer Academic Publishers, 1989).

Edison Electric Institute, *Economic Growth in the Future* (New York: McGraw-Hill, 1976).

Edison Electric Institute, *Deregulation of Electric Utilities: A Survey of Major Concepts and Issues* (Washington, D.C.: EEI, July 1981).

Edison Electric Institute, *A Survey of Deregulation Experience in Selected Industries* (Washington, D.C.: EEI, February 1982).

Edison Electric Institute, *Alternative Models of Electric Power Deregulation* (Washington, D.C.: EEI, May 1982).

Glassman, Gerald J., "Discounted Cash Flow Versus the Capital Asset Pricing Model (Is g Better Than b?)," *Public Utilities Fortnightly*, September 14, 1978.

Gordon, Richard L., *Reforming the Regulation of Electric Utilities* (Lexington: D. C. Heath, 1982).

Hyman, Leonard S., and Ernst R. Habicht, Jr., "State Electric Utility Regulation: Financial Issues, Influences and Trends," *Annual Energy Review*, Vol. II, 1986, pp. 163-183.

Kahn, Alfred E., *The Economics of Regulation* (New York: John Wiley & Sons, 1970-1971).

Metcalf, Lee, and Vic Reinemer, *Overcharge* (New York: David McKay, 1967).

Morin, Roger A., *Utilities' Cost of Capital* (Arlington, Va.: Public Utilities Reports, 1984).

Pennsylvania Governor's Energy Council, *Report to Lieutenant Governor William W. Scranton, III, from the Pennsylvania Utility Efficiency Task Force*, (Harrisburg: Pennsylvania Governor's Energy Council, March 29, 1983).

Phillips, Charles F., Jr., *The Regulation of Public Utilities: Theory and Practice* (Arlington, Va.: Public Utilities Reports, 1984).

Primeaux, Walter J., Jr., "A Reexamination of the Monopoly Market Structure for

Electric Utilities," in A. Phillips, ed., *Promoting Competition in Regulated Markets* (Washington, D.C.: Brookings Institution, 1975).

Resources for the Future, *Price Elasticities of Demand for Energy — Evaluating the Estimates* (Palo Alto: Electric Power Research Institute, September 1982).

Rodgers, Paul, J. Edward Smith, Jr., and Russell J. Profozich, *Current Issues in Electric Utility Rate Setting* (Washington, D.C.: National Association of Regulatory Utility Commissioners, 1976).

Saltzman, Sidney, and Richard E. Schuler, eds., *The Future of Electrical Energy: A Regional Perspective of an Industry in Transition* (New York: Praeger, 1986).

Sant, Roger W., *Eight Great Energy Myths: The Least Cost Energy Strategy, 1978-2000* (Pittsburgh: Carnegie-Mellon University Press, 1981).

Schurr, Sam H., and Bruce C. Netschert, *Energy in the American Economy, 1850-1975* (Baltimore: Johns Hopkins Press, 1960).

Stalon, Charles D., "Deregulation of the Electric Generating Industry: Some Unsystematic Observations," *Proceedings: Edison Electric Institute Sixteenth Financial Conference October 4-7, 1981* (Washington, D.C.: Edison Electric Institute, 1982).

Turvey, Ralph, *Optimal Pricing and Investment in Electric Supply* (London: George Allen and Unwin, 1968).

Vandell, Robert F., and James K. Malernee, "The Capital Asset Pricing Model and Utility Equity Returns," *Public Utilities Fortnightly*, July 6, 1978.

Welch, Francis X., *Cases and Text on Public Utilities Regulation* (Washington, D.C.: Public Utilities Reports, 1968).

Westly, Steven, ed., *Energy Efficiency and the Utilities: New Directions* (San Francisco: California Public Utilities Commission, 1980).

Wilcox, Clair, *Public Policies Toward Business* (Homewood, Ill.: Richard D. Irwin, 1960).

Finance

Although it was not written for the purpose, Dewing's text provides extraordinary insight into the regulation, finance and development of the electric utility industry. The classic text on security analysis is still Graham and Dodd.

Dewing, Arthur Stone, *The Financial Policy of Corporations* (New York: The Ronald Press, 1953).

Graham, Benjamin, David J. Dodd, Sidney Cottle, with Charles Tatham, *Security Analysis* (New York: McGraw-Hill, 1962).

Hyman, Leonard S., "Utility Stocks in 1967-72: A Tale of Woe," *Public Utilities Fortnightly*, Vol. 93, No. 5, Feb. 28, 1974.

Hyman, Leonard S., "Market to Book Ratio: Statistical Confirmation or Aberration?", *Public Utilities Fortnightly*, Dec. 19, 1979.

Hyman, Leonard S., and Carmine J. Grigoli, "The Credit Standing of Electric Utilities," *Public Utilities Fortnightly*, Vol. 99, No. 5, March 3, 1977, pp. 24-30.

Ibbotson, Roger G., and Rex A. Sinquefield, *Stocks, Bonds, Bills and Inflation: The Past (1926-1976) and the Future (1977-2000)* (Charlottesville: Financial Analysts Research Foundation, 1977).

Merrett, A.J., and Allen Sykes, *The Finance and Analysis of Capital Projects* (London: Longman, 1983).

O'Brien, Betsy, and Andrew Reynolds, *Impacts of Financial Constraints on the Electric Utility Industry* (Washington, D.C.: U.S. Government Printing Office, 1982).

Sykes, Allen, "The Project Overview — The Key to the Successful Accomplishment of Giant Projects," in Allen Sykes and A.J. Merrett, eds., *The Successful Accomplishment of Giant Projects* (London: Willis Faber, 1978).

Young, Harold H., *Forty Years of Public Utility Finance* (Charlottesville: The University of Virginia, 1965).

History and Structure

For an industry that passed its centennial, one would have expected more solid new material on how it got the way it is. Even some of the oft-cited classics seem to have some amazing blind spots. The EPRI Journal's special issue and Hughes' book probably put together the story as well as any sources.

Conot, Robert, *A Streak of Luck* (New York: Seaview Books, 1979).

Dillon, Mary Earhart, *Wendell Willkie* (Philadelphia and New York: J.B. Lippincott, 1952).

Electrical World, June 1, 1974. Special Issue: The Electric Century.

EPRI Journal, March 1979. Special Issue: Creating the Electric Age.

Electric Power Research Institute, *Proceedings: 1989 Utility Strategic Issues Forum — What Does the Future Hold for the Electric Business?* (Palo Alto: Electric Power Research Institute, 1990).

Friedel, Robert, and Paul Israel with Bernard Finn, *Edison's Electric Light: Biography of an Invention* (New Brunswick: Rutgers University Press, 1986).

Hughes, Thomas P., *Networks of Power: Electrification in Western Society, 1880-1930* (Baltimore: The Johns Hopkins Press, 1983).

Joskow, Paul L., and Richard Schmalensee, *Markets for Power: An Analysis of Electric Utility Deregulation* (Cambridge: The MIT Press, 1983).

Josephson, Matthew, *Edison* (New York: McGraw-Hill, 1959).

McDonald, Forest, *Insull* (Chicago: The University of Chicago Press, 1962).

Morris, David, *Be Your Own Power Company* (Emmaus, Pa.: Rodale Press, 1983).

Plummer, James, Terry Ferrar and William Hughes, eds., *Electric Power Strategic Issues* (Arlington, Va. and Palo Alto, Cal.: Public Utilities Reports and QED

Research, 1983).

Ripley, William Z., "From Main Street to Wall Street," in Louise Desaulniers, ed., *Looking Back at Tomorrow* (Boston: The Atlantic Monthly, 1978), p. 125.

Rodgers, William, *Brown-Out* (New York: Stein and Day, 1972).

Schlesinger, Arthur M., Jr., *The Age of Roosevelt: The Crisis of the Old Order* (Boston: Houghton Mifflin, 1957).

Sporn, Philip, *Energy — Its Production, Conversion, and Use in the Service of Man* (New York: Columbia Graduate School of Business, 1963).

Sporn, Philip, *The Social Organization of Electric Power Supply in Modern Societies* (Cambridge: MIT Press, 1971).

Starr, Chauncey, and Philip C. Ritterbush, eds., *Science, Technology and the Human Prospect* (New York: Pergamon Press, 1980).

Stoler, Peter, *Decline and Fail: The Ailing Nuclear Power Industry* (New York: Dodd, Mead, 1985).

Tomain, Joseph P., *Nuclear Power Transformation* (Bloomington: Indiana Univ. Press, 1987).

Wyatt, Alan, *Electric Power: Challenges and Choices* (Toronto: The Book Press, 1986).

Operations and Environment

Environmental literature tends to get argumentative and operational literature technical. The EEI and the North American Electric Reliability Council (NERC) produce numerous publications about operations and planning. The EPRI Journal provides easily read studies, and Science and Forum are good sources of information on energy and environmental issues. Marcus and Bryant may have produced the easiest books to read. The Annual Review of Energy covers numerous issues from regulation and pricing to environment.

Abelson, Philip H., ed., *Energy: Use, Conservation and Supply* (Washington, D.C.: American Association for the Advancement of Science, 1974).

Abelson, Philip H., ed., *Energy II: Use, Conservation and Supply* (Washington, D.C.: AAAS, 1978).

Annual Review of Energy (various issues).

Brown, Harold J., editor, *Decentralizing Electricity Production* (New Haven: Yale University Press, 1983).

Bryant, David, *Electricity* (Sevenoaks, Kent: Hodder and Stoughton, 1987).

Commoner, Barry, *The Poverty of Power: Energy and the Economic Crisis* (New York: Alfred A. Knopf, 1976).

Electric Utility Task Force on the Environment, *The Electric Utility Industry and the Environment, A Report to the Citizens Advisory Committee on Recreation and Natural Beauty by the Electric Utility Task Force on Environment* (no place or date of publication, Library of Congress Card No. 68-57661).

Environment (various issues).

EPRI Journal (various issues).

Forum for Applied Research and Public Policy (various issues).

Hirsh, Richard F., *Technology and Transformation in the American Electric Utility Industry* (Cambridge: Cambridge U. Press, 1989).

Institute for Technology and Strategic Research, George Washington Univ., *Electricity in 2024: Can We Reconcile Demand and Environment?* (Washington, D.C.: George Washington U., 1990).

Kahan, Archie M., *Acid Rain: Reign of Controversy* (Golden, Colo.: Fulcrum, 1986).

Marcus, Abraham, and Rebecca B. Marcus, *Power Unlimited!* (Englewood Cliffs: Prentice-Hall, 1959).

Moss, Thomas H., and David L. Sills, eds., *The Three Mile Island Nuclear Accident: Lessons and Implications* (New York: N.Y. Academy of Sciences, 1981).

North American Electric Reliability Council, *Reliability Assessment* (Princeton: North American Reliability Council, various years).

North American Electric Reliability Council, *Electricity Supply & Demand* (Princeton: NERC, various years).

Sant, Roger W., "Cutting Energy Cost," *Environment,* May 1980.

Schindler, D. W., "Effects of Acid Rain on Freshwater Ecosystems," *Science,* 8 January 1988, Vol. 239. pp. 149-157.

Schumacher, E. F., *Small Is Beautiful: Economics As If People Mattered* (New York: Harper & Row Perennial Library, 1975).

Science (various issues).

Swanson, Christina, and Patrick Reddy, "A Risky Business," *Environment,* July/ August 1979, p. 28.

U.S. Congress Office of Technology Assessment, *Nuclear Power in an Age of Uncertainty* (Washington, D.C.: U.S. Government Printing Office, 1984).

U.S. Congress Office of Technology Assessment, *Electric Power Wheeling and Dealing: Technological Considerations for Increasing Competition* (Washington, D.C.: Government Printing Office, 1989).

U.S. Department of Energy, *Interim Report: National Energy Strategy* (Washington, D.C.: Department of Energy, April 1990).

Vaughan, William A., *Canadian Hydropower: Potential Resources and Implications for U.S. Industrial Competitiveness* (Washington, D.C.: Electricity Consumers Resource Council, 1987).

SUBJECT INDEX